INVESTMENT

5th edition

Jane Cowdell

institute of financial services

CIB Publishing
c/o The Chartered Institute of Bankers
Emmanuel House
4-9 Burgate Lane
Canterbury
Kent
CT1 2XJ
United Kingdom

Telephone: 01227 762600

CIB Publishing publications are published by The Chartered Institute of Bankers, a non-profit making registered educational charity.

Typeset by Kevin O'Connor

Printed by Selwood Printing, Burgess Hill

© Jane Cowdell 2000

ISBN 0-85297-553-8

CONTENTS

Contents

Contents

Contents

INTRODUCTION

The Concept of the Course

This workbook has been written for students studying for banking and finance qualifications and also for practitioners in financial services who are looking for a practical refresher.

Each unit is divided into sections and contains:

- Learning objectives;

- Clear, concise topic-by-topic coverage;

- Examples and learning activities to reinforce learning, confirm understanding and stimulate thought;

- Often, past examination questions to try for practice;

- Self-assessment questions to test your knowledge, understanding and skills.

Learning Activities

Learning activities are provided throughout. These come in a variety of forms. For example, they:

- Test your ability to recall information, your ability to analyse material, or assess whether you have appreciated the full significance of a piece of information.

- Require discussion with colleagues, friends or fellow students.

- Require you to do some research.

  Virtually all require you to record something in writing and you should keep your notes/answers for later reference.

Syllabus

The key sections of the Investment syllabus are:

- Cash and Interest-bearing Investment

- Public Company Securities

- Other Kinds of Investment

- London Stock Exchange – Procedures and Settlement

- Investment Theory and Analysis
- Practical Investment Considerations
- Investment by Trustees.

Your Contribution

Although this workbook is designed to stand alone, as with most topics, certain aspects of this subject are constantly changing. Therefore it is very important that you keep up-to-date with these key areas.

We anticipate that you will study this course for one academic year, reading through and studying approximately two units every three weeks. However, note that because topics vary in size and knowledge tends not to fall into uniform chunks, some units are unavoidably longer than others.

The masculine pronoun 'he' has been used in this workbook to encompass both genders and to avoid the awkwardness of the constant repetition of 'he and/or she'.

Study Guide

Below we offer advice and ideas on studying, revising and approaching examinations.

Studying

As with any examination, there is no substitute for preparation based on an organized and disciplined study plan. You should devise an approach that will enable you to complete this workbook and still leave time for revision of this and any other subject you are taking at the same time. Many candidates find that about six weeks is the right period of time to leave for revision, enough time to get through the revision material, but not so long that it is no longer fresh in your mind by the time you reach the examination.

This means that you should plan how to get to the last chapter by, say, the end of March for a May sitting or the end of August for an October sitting. This includes not only reading the text, but also making notes, working through the study plan supplied.

We offer the following as a starting point for approaching your study.

- Plan time each week to study a part of this workbook. Make sure that it is 'quality' study time: let everyone know that you are studying and that you should not be disturbed. If you are at home, unplug your telephone or switch the answerphone on; if you are in the office, put your telephone on 'divert'.

- Set a clearly defined objective for each study period. You may simply wish to read through a unit for the first time or perhaps you may want to make some notes on a unit you have already read a couple of times.

- Review your study plan. Devise a study checklist and/or timetable so that you can schedule and monitor your progress. Do not panic if you fall behind, but do think how you will make up for lost time.

- Look for relevant examples of what you have covered in the 'real' world. If you work for a financial organization, this should provide them. If you do not think about your experiences as an individual bank or building society customer or perhaps about your employer's position as a corporate customer of a bank. Keep an eye on the quality press for reports about banks and building societies and their activities.

Revising

The period which you have earmarked for revision is a very important. Now it is even more important that you plan time each week for study and that you set clear objectives for each revision session. So ...

- Make use of a timetable.

- Use time sensibly. How much revision time do you have? Remember that you still need to eat, sleep and fit in some leisure time!

- How will you allocate the available time between subjects? What are your weaker subjects? You will need to focus on some topics more than others. You will also need to plan your revision around your learning style. By now, you should know whether, for example, early morning, early evening or late evening is best.

- Take regular breaks. Most people find they can absorb more if they attempt to revise for long uninterrupted periods of time. Award yourself a five-minute break every hour or so. Go for a stroll or make a cup of coffee, but do not turn the television on!

- Believe in yourself. Are you cultivating the right attitude of mind? There is absolutely no reason why you should not pass the exam if you adopt the correct approach. Be confident, you have passed exams before so you can pass this one.

The examination

Passing examinations is half about having the required knowledge, understanding and skills, and half about doing yourself justice in the examination. You must have the right technique.

The day of the exam

- Have something to eat but do not eat too much; you may feel sleepy if your system is digesting a large meal.

- Do not forget pens, pencils, rulers, erasers – for this subject, calculators – and anything else you will need.

- Avoid discussion about the exam with other candidates outside the exam hall.

Tackling the examination paper

First, make sure that you satisfy the examiner's requirements.

- Read the instructions on the front of the exam paper carefully. Check that the exam format has not changed. It is surprising how often examiners' reports remark on the number of students who attempt too few – or too many – questions, or who attempt the wrong number of questions from different parts of the paper. Make sure that you are planning to answer the right number of questions.

- Read all the questions on the exam paper before you start writing. Look at the weighting of marks to each part of the question. If part (a) offers only four marks and you cannot answer the 16 marks part (b), then do not choose the question.

- Do not produce irrelevant answers. Make sure you answer the question set, and not the question you would have preferred to have been set.

- Produce an answer in the correct format. The examiner will state the format in which the question should be answered, for example in a report or memorandum. If a question asks for a diagram or an example, give one. If a question does not specifically asks for a diagram or example, but it seems appropriate, give one.

- Second, observe the following simple rules to ensure that your script is acceptable to the examiner.

- Present a tidy paper. You are a professional and it should always show in the presentation of your work. Make sure that you write legibly, label diagrams clearly and lay out your work professionally. Assistant examiners each have dozens of papers to mark; a badly written scrawl is unlikely to receive the same attention as a neat and well laid out paper.

- State the obvious. Many candidates look for complexity that is not required and consequently overlook the obvious. Make basic statements first. Plan your answer and ask yourself whether you have answered the main parts of the question.

- Use examples. This will help to demonstrate to the examiner that you keep up-to-date with the subject. There are lots of useful examples scattered through this workbook and you can read about others if you dip into the quality press or take notice of what is happening in your working environment.

- Finally, make sure that you give yourself the opportunity to do yourself justice.

- Select questions carefully. Read through the paper once, then quickly jot down any key points against each question in a second read through. Reject those questions against which you have jotted down very little. Select those where you could latch on to 'what the question is about' – but remember to check carefully that you have got the right end of the stick before putting pen to paper.

- Plan your attack carefully. Consider the order in which you are going to tackle questions. It is a good idea to start with your best question to boost your morale and get some easy marks 'in the bag'.

- Read the question carefully and plan your answer. Read through the question again very carefully when you come to answer it.

- Gain the easy marks. Include the obvious if it answers the question and do not spend unnecessary time producing the perfect answer. As we suggested above, there is nothing wrong with stating the obvious.

- Avoid getting bogged down in small parts of questions. If you find a part of a question difficult, get on with the rest of the question. If you are having problems with something the chances are that everyone else is too.

- Do not leave the exam early. If you finish early, use your spare time to check and recheck your script.

- Do not worry if you feel you have performed badly in the exam. It is likely that the other candidates will have found the exam difficult too. As soon as you get up and leave the exam hall, forget the exam and think about the next – or, if it is the last one, celebrate!

Do not discuss an exam with other candidates. This is particularly the case if you still have other exams to sit. Put it out of your mind until the day of the results. Forget about exams and relax.

1

OVERVIEW

Objectives

After studying this unit, you should be able to:

- define investment;

- understand the motives for saving and investing;

- understand the differences between saving, speculation, investment and gambling;

- understand the terms 'direct investment' and 'indirect investment';

- define real and financial assets;

- list and briefly describe the types of financial asset held by investors;

- understand the relevance of saving and investment.

1   Introduction

Financial institutions receive daily requests for guidance from a wide range of potential savers and investors. These include:

- Those who receive a relatively large sum of money by way of redundancy or early retirement pension;

- Those who inherit large sums of money and other assets;

- Those who win large sums of money from the National Lottery or Premium Savings Bonds;

- Smaller investors who have purchased shares issued by former public corporations as part of the government's privatization programme or from an Employee Share Option scheme;

- People who wish to set aside regular or occasional sums of money to build up funds for future purchases, which may be long term, e.g. saving for a house, or short term, e.g. saving for a holiday.

There is a wide choice of financial institutions that offer products and services to savers and investors. A.D. Bain divides these into three categories:

● Banks, building societies and National Savings, which generally provide capital guaranteed savings and investment accounts offering ready access to funds and a rate of interest;

● Life assurance and pension funds, the former providing savings and financial protection in the event of early death, the latter doing the same in the event of lengthy survival. These institutions are differentiated from the first group in that early surrender or lapse of investments may result in suffering a capital loss or having funds 'locked in';

● Unit trusts, investment trusts and stocks and shares. The capital value of these assets can change on daily basis. Their value can rise or fall.

Traditionally, each set of financial institutions had a highly defined role in the provision of personal savings and investment products and services. This was partly due to their respective specializations and expertise, but also due to government controls, often implemented as part of monetary policy. These demarcations have broken down since 1980, with institutions making inroads into the markets of their competitors. Most of the retail and mortgage banks and all of the large building societies now provide a full range of services, often with specialist subsidiary and associated companies.

For these reasons, many customers now approach a single financial institution to meet a whole array of financial needs instead of having to go to different organizations for each need.

Some financial products and services are regulated by the Financial Services Act 1986. Generally, these are products that can involve capital risk or whose performance is subject to market conditions. Although anyone can give factual information to customers on these products, investment advice relating to whether a customer should or should not invest in them requires the adviser to be licensed under the Act.

2 Motives for Saving and Investing

The famous economist John Maynard Keynes, writing in 1936, identified three reasons for saving:

● Precautionary – saving for a rainy day;

● Transactionary – saving to buy something in the future;

● Speculative – moving out of money and into non-money assets in anticipation of a financial return.

More recently, the monetarist Milton Friedman proposed his portfolio theory as to why people hold different financial assets. This suggests that people will satisfy their cash demands before considering any other assets. They will then fulfil their needs for highly liquid accounts (those that can be quickly converted to cash, such as current and deposit accounts), then less liquid but potentially higher return assets.

The motive for saving or investing has an effect on responses to changes in market conditions. For example, in a period of high inflation:

● Those saving for a specific future purchase will probably spend now and withdraw savings, if necessary borrowing the difference between price and savings balance, in fear that the price of the purchase will increase in the future;

● Those saving for a rainy day will save more as they perceive that the value of their savings is no longer adequate in real terms for the purpose intended.

3 Factors Affecting Customer Choice

When saving and investing, customers are driven by various stimuli. These vary according to personal need and preference, as well as factors such as averseness to risk.

The following factors usually drive customer demand for funding products offered by financial institutions:

● Rate of interest

● Potential for capital growth

● Risk of capital loss

● Convenience

> liquidity requirements (the perceived need to be able to convert the asset back into cash)

> simplicity – the ease with which the product or service can be understood by the customer

> tax efficiency – some products are tax free such as TESSAs, PEPs (which have now been withdrawn but are still held by investors) and NSCs and ISAs, others deduct tax at source (bank and building society accounts) and others pay gross interest (offshore funds).

4 Risk, Time and Return

Requirements of different investors

Different investors have different risk and time preferences. A person with only £500 to invest will not wish to take much risk, and will probably require the money to be readily available to meet any sudden bills. This investor will have entirely different requirements to an investor with an existing portfolio of about £200,000 who has just won £5,000 on the National Lottery. This latter investor will have a much greater willingness to accept a high-risk, long-term investment in the hope of a higher return.

The link between risk, time and return

Generally speaking, the greater the risk and time involved, the greater the potential return if all goes well. (Risk and return are covered fully in Unit 9.)

5   Difference between Saving, Speculation, Investment and Gambling

Saving – short term: safety/low risk

Saving is putting money aside so that it is readily available for any sudden financial emergency. The saver has a low risk and short time preference. Examples of savings vehicles are bank deposits, building society accounts, and accounts with National Savings. These funds are often called 'cash investments'. The best 'home' for savings is the account that gives the best after-tax return for the particular investor, coupled with low risk and ready accessibility. The return is usually purely in the form of interest, with the capital remaining at its face value.

Speculation involves a short timescale with a potentially high reward by way of capital gain. An example of the difference between investment and speculation can be seen in the British Telecom new issue of 1984. Some people bought the shares with a view to making a quick profit by selling within a few days. Such speculators in this case were well rewarded because the share price more than doubled over two weeks. Others who bought the shares as a long-term investment retained them and resisted the temptation to make a quick profit. (They have been rewarded by good growth of both dividends and capital value.) If it appears likely that demand for the shares will exceed the number of shares available with a new issue, the shares will start trading at a higher price than when they were issued.

Another form of speculation is purchasing very low-priced equities that are called 'penny shares'. The Personal Investment Authority (PIA) defines penny shares as: "shares with a bid-offer spread of 10% or more of the offer price". The bid price is the price at which the market maker (see Unit 2, Section 8) will buy the shares from the shareholder. The offer price in the price the market maker will sell the shares at to a purchaser. Thus the bid price is the lower of the two prices quoted for a share. They are in companies that could quite possibly fail but where there is just a chance of a dramatic change of fortune. If a share is priced at 20p and the investor puts £500 into these shares he will receive 2,500 shares (£500 ÷ 20p). If one month later the shares rise to 22p each and he sells them he will receive 2,500 x 22p = £550 (ignoring dealing costs). Thus he has made a profit of £50. If the shares rise by 2p in the period of one month the profit is equal to an annual interest rate of 120%. If he had, however, invested £500 in shares costing 200p each he would have received 250 shares. If the price had risen over the period of one month to 202p (i.e. the same rise of 2p a share) he would have received only £505 (ignoring dealing costs). This profit would have been equal to an annual interest rate of just 12%. Other forms of speculative investments are warrants, options and traded options (also called derivatives).

Investment – longer term: low to high risk/reward

Investment has a higher risk and longer timescale than saving, and the return can come in the form of income, or capital gain, or a mixture of the two. When you come to consider portfolio planning in Units 16 and 17, you will see that nobody should invest until he has adequate savings to meet any unforeseen financial emergency. One form of investment is equities (ordinary shares) because in the long-term, say five years or more, the capital value of equities and their dividends should grow as the economy grows.

Gambling – extremely high risk: little chance of reward

Gambling involves a very high risk with a very short timescale. It is usually an 'all or nothing' situation when you either lose all of your stake or may make a large gain. Gambling winnings are free of income and capital gains tax.

6　Direct and Indirect Investment, Real and Financial Assets

Financial assets are those represented by a piece of paper, whereas real assets can be seen, touched and enjoyed personally. The following table gives examples that will enable you to understand the differences.

Table 1.1: Financial assets and real assets

Financial assets	Real assets
Pension plans	Property (owner occupied)
Life insurance policies	Property (not owner occupied)
Unit trusts	Chattels (e.g. paintings, antiques, jewellery, fine wines)
Investment trusts	
Equities	
Loan stocks (including gilts, local authority loan stocks and company loan stock)	
National Savings investments	
Stocks and shares	
Cash investments (e.g. bank and building society accounts)	
Property bonds	
Individual Savings Plans (ISAs)	

Table 1.2: Direct investment and indirect investment

Direct investment	Indirect investment
Equities	Unit trusts
Loan stocks (as described above)	Investment trusts
Stocks and shares	Insurance policies (qualifying and non-qualifying)
National Savings investments	Pension plans
Property	Property bonds
Chattels	Friendly society bonds

Note: ISAs could be classed as direct or indirect investments, depending on the rules of the particular plan under consideration.

Summary of differences between the above types of investment

Direct investments are ones that the individual investor personally selects, and ones that are registered in his name. Indirect investments are a pool of investments managed on behalf of a number of investors by professional managers. For example, an investor could buy a property in the hope of acquiring rental income and a capital gain on subsequent sale. All decisions are taken by the investor. One indirect investment alternative is a property bond that is an investment in a diversified portfolio of commercial property, professionally managed by an institution on behalf of a number of investors.

An example of an indirect investment is a unit trust. The managers select and manage Stock Exchange investments. Investors buy units in the trust and the units have a value based on the value of the underlying stocks and shares. The unit trust managers do not select investments that meet a specific investor's needs, but select them for the type of trust specified in the trust deed, e.g. aimed at income, capital growth or investing in a certain overseas market or geographical area.

Note: full details of all the above mentioned indirect and direct investments are covered later in the workbook.

7 Difference between Equities, Loans, Property and Chattels

Equities (commonly known as ordinary shares)

A shareholder is a part-owner of a limited company but he has no personal liability for the company's debts provided the shares are fully paid. The cash return on equities, known as a dividend, depends on the profits of the company and on the policy of the directors. Full details of equities and other forms of company securities are given in Unit 8.

Loan stocks

The holder of a loan stock has lent money to the government, local authority, public body or limited company that has issued the stock. He has no right to say how the money he has lent is used. In return he receives a fixed rate of interest. Some government stocks, commonly called gilts, have a class that pay interest linked top the Retail Price Index (RPI). Most loan stocks carry a date when they will be redeemed; i.e. the investor will receive back the nominal value. Some stocks carry two dates, which means that they will be redeemed at the borrower's option at some point between the two dates. There are also some undated gilts and local authority stocks that will never be repaid, unless the coupon (i.e. rate of interest shown in the title of the stock) is above the general level of interest rates. Full details of British government securities are given in Unit 7 and full details of all other loan stocks are given in Unit 8.

Property

Apart from an owner-occupied house, property is purchased with the intention of gaining a rental income and a capital gain on any subsequent sale. The basic difference between owning property, as opposed to owning equities or loans, is that property is a tangible asset that the owner can manage on a day-to-day basis. As we shall see in Unit 8, ordinary shareholders in practice have very little control over day-to-day operations of their company.

Chattels

Examples of chattels are stamp collections, jewellery, antiques, fine wine or objets d'art. No income is generated, but the owner usually hopes to make a capital gain on ultimate disposal. (A more detailed examination of both property and chattels can be found in Unit 9.) Chattels are also purchased to give pleasure as well as capital appreciation.

8   The Principal Types of Asset held by UK Residents

The principal types of financial investments held by UK residents and their suitability for short-term or long-term savings are as follows.

Cash investments

These are bank accounts, building society accounts, National Savings Bank accounts, National Savings Products, ISAs, money market and finance house deposits. All of these are short-term investments because the capital invested always remains the same and the sum, or any part of it invested, can be withdrawn either immediately or at short notice.

National Savings investments

These include items such as National Savings Certificates and Pensioners Guaranteed Income Bonds. These can always be encashed (sold) without loss of capital, but they really should be held for their full term, for example, five years in the case of National Savings Certificates.

Life insurance policies

These take various forms ranging from policies that pay out only if the investor dies before a certain date to ones that pay out, at a set date or earlier death, a minimum sum plus profits (i.e. a share of the profits that the insurance company has made and allocated to the individual policies). This is a long-term investment, the minimum time for this type of policy being 10 years.

Pension plans

These are a form of long-term saving whereby the investor saves a certain amount each month or per annum from the time his employment commences until he retires. Some pensions are non-contributory, i.e. the employer makes the payments into the pension scheme, not the employee. In either case the pension belongs to the investor.

Unit trusts and investment trusts

With these an investor can either save on a monthly basis or invest a lump sum. The money invested is added to money invested by others in these trusts and is used by the managers to purchase stocks and shares. This is an indirect form of investment, with professional managers employed by the trusts to look after the money invested. Because the underlying investments are stocks and shares, this type of investment should be undertaken only as a long-term investment.

Individual Savings Plans (ISAs)

The maximum amount that can be invested in an ISA is £5,000 per annum. The investments held in an ISA are cash, stocks and shares, unit and investment trusts, life insurance and national savings.

Investments held in an ISA must be listed on a recognized Stock Exchange, and the investments can consist of gilts, company loan stocks, unit trusts, investment trusts and OEICs. Overseas investments are allowed if they comply with these rules.

ISAs come in two forms – mini and maxi.

A **Mini ISA** allows the investor to choose the best fund manager/bank or building society for each element of the fund.

A **Maxi ISA** has all the investments purchased from the same management company. All classes of investments are available via a Maxi ISA. There is no restriction on how the money is invested in a maxi ISA, e.g. all the £5,000 can go into shares or cash etc., unlike a mini ISA.

This is a long-term investment for the same reasons as equities are a long-term investment. If the investor is allowed to select his own shares or corporate bonds, the ISA will be classed as a direct investment, but if the managers select the shares or corporate bonds or if the investor holds unit or investment trusts, then the ISA will be an indirect investment.

Equities and loan stocks

These are direct investments, where the investor himself decides which equities or loan stocks to purchase. This is a long-term investment, the reason being that prices of these investments fluctuate in the short term and you can never be sure that you will get back as much as you invested. In the long term, though, prices have shown an upward trend.

Summary

Now that you have studied this unit, you should be able to:

● define investment;

● briefly explain the relationship between risk, time and return;

● distinguish between saving, speculation, investment and gambling;

● explain the differences between direct and indirect investment and categorize investments into direct or indirect;

● explain the difference between real and financial assets and categorize investments into real or financial;

● describe the main types of financial asset held by UK residents and explain whether they are more suitable for long- or short-term investment.

2

THE LONDON STOCK EXCHANGE

Objectives

After studying this unit, you should be able to:

- understand the role of the London Stock Exchange as a primary market;
- understand the role of the London Stock Exchange as a secondary market;
- describe the different types of capital raised on the London Stock Exchange;
- ● describe the other functions of the London Stock Exchange;
- define what is meant by 'personal investors' and 'institutional investors';
- understand the principles of corporate governance;
- describe recent trends in share ownership;
- understand the functions of the members of the London Stock Exchange.

1 Background to the London Stock Exchange and its Developments

The Stock Exchange was originally established as a market in which stocks and shares could be bought and sold, in much the same way that markets exist for commodities such as wheat, tea, wool and metals.

The market developed in the second half of the seventeenth century, dealing mainly in the shares of trading companies, government sponsored lottery tickets and loans contracted by Charles II and James II. Government loans formed the nucleus of the National Debt, officially recognized by William III in 1688.

2 Functions of the Stock Exchange – Overview

The Stock Exchange has the following broad functions, all of which will be described in detail in this unit.

● It enables capital to be raised by the government and by companies. This is achieved by the government issuing loan stock more commonly known as gilts and by companies issuing various classes of securities. The latter can be shares, representing equity (part ownership) investments in companies, or loan capital such as company loan stocks, representing the stake of long-term creditors in those businesses.

● It provides a secondary market through which existing securities can be bought and sold by shareholders and loan stock holders.

● It advertises security prices, enabling investors to follow the progress of quoted stocks and shares.

● It protects investors against fraud. The Main Market, formally called the 'Official List' is a guarantee that securities meet stringent entry requirements, and that the company is reputable at the time of listing. Permission to deal is not given unless the FSA is satisfied that this is so. Once the shares are admitted to the Main Market, if there is any doubt about the probity of the company the FSA will suspend dealing.

● It serves as a barometer of the health of the economy. Movements in the market can provide important indicators of the prospects of quoted, industry group companies, e.g. retailers, and of the country as a whole.

3 The Stock Exchange as a Primary Market and a Secondary Market

A primary market is one that raises new capital for companies or for the government. A secondary market is one that deals in stocks and shares that have already been issued.

If you consider the British Telecom (now known as BT) issue, the original subscribers for the shares were participants in the primary market, whereas subsequent sales by these subscribers took place on the secondary market.

There is a close connection between the two markets. Without an effective secondary market the primary market would fail, because investors subscribe to new issues only if they are hopeful of being able to sell at a profit at some time in the future.

4 The Stock Exchange as a Primary Market

The Stock Exchange is a vital cog in the primary market. This is where new money is raised, and thus it is an important function of the Exchange. (The mechanics of this market are covered in Unit 3.)

There are several distinct facets of the primary market:

● New issue market in British government securities and in ordinary shares;

○ Privatizations;

○ Demutalizations;

● Rights issues;

○ New fixed-interest capital.

New issue market in British government securities

The largest market by far is the new issue market in British government securities, more commonly called 'gilts' (or gilt-edged securities). Usually government expenditure exceeds government income, and the government has to borrow to meet the difference. This gap is known as Public Sector Net Cash Requirement (PSNCR).

The primary market has been very successful and sales of new gilts have helped to fund the PSNCR. New gilts can always be sold by the government, but only at the current market rates of interest. Finance can be raised very quickly by this method, but at a price. Other considerations apart from PSNCR affect the decisions to issue new gilts, but detailed examination of money supply and interest rate policy is beyond this syllabus.

Privatization

Privatization is another example of the use of the primary market to raise new funds for the government. The last Conservative government started the policy of selling state-owned assets, and the method used is to transform these organizations into public limited companies. Shares in these companies are then issued, and quotation on the Stock Exchange is gained usually by an offer for sale.

The first British Telecom (now BT) issue in 1984 was in fact a watershed for privatization, because failure would have embarrassed the government and jeopardized future privatizations. Since that issue, vast sums have been raised by privatization.

Although the majority of privatization issues are taken up by the institutional investors, the government is keen to see wider share ownership, i.e. more individuals owning shares directly. In order to encourage this wider share ownership various incentives have been given on privatization issues. The main incentives have been:

○ Priority application for private investors, particularly if they are customers of the concern, e.g. the water companies and electricity companies privatizations;

○ Bill vouchers to be used against future bills from the company, e.g. British Telecom, British Gas and electricity companies;

○ Free shares if the investor holds the shares for a preset number of years, e.g. BAA, British Telecom;

○ Instalment payments whereby the investor pays only a small amount initially and the balance is paid over one or two periods several months later, e.g. the electricity companies, British Telecom;

- Cheap dealing services, or share shops, which have agreed to provide low rates of commission on sales of the privatized shares.

Incentives have also been used by a few, non-privatized, companies when they have their shares listed. For example Thompson Travel Group created a 'founders Club' for investors in their new issue. This Club provides discounts on Thompson Travel Group holidays to founder members.

Demutualizations

Building societies and many life insurance companies were set up on a mutual basis. This meant that the owners of the organization were its members. The financial services industry has seen major changes because a considerable number of 'mutuals' have gained a listing on the Stock Exchange. Organizations such as the Halifax and Norwich Union are two examples of large-value demutualizations. Other mutuals have lost that status because they have been taken over by quoted companies.

The members of the demutualized companies receive monetary compensation or shares as an incentive to vote for demutualization.

Rights issue

Turning to the private sector, the most successful activity on the primary market has been the rights issue. Rights issues involve already quoted companies selling new shares to existing shareholders. Undoubtedly, the fact that the companies have a track record and are selling to existing shareholders has helped these issues to succeed. There are, however, occasions when rights issues do fail, because the shareholders were uncertain of the likely success of the venture for which the money was being raised.

New fixed-interest capital

In 1997 £2,417.8m and in 1998 £1,044.9m was raised through issues of convertibles, debentures, other loan stocks and preference shares. Although these are large sums of money, more money was raised via issues of ordinary shares.

Even when interest rates were relatively low in 1998, companies tended to raise new equity capital, rather than new loan capital which carries more obligations to the issuing company than equities. In 1997 £6,939.8m and in 1998 £4,115.1m was raised by new issues of equity (ordinary shares). (See Unit 8 for more details of these classes of stocks and shares.)

How successful is the primary market?

We have already said that the primary market is successful as regards new issues of gilts, equities for well-established companies and rights issues. There was another area in which the Stock Exchange was conspicuous by its absence, and that was in the raising of new equity capital for new companies. In the 1970s North Sea oil exploration was financed by bank loans, rather than by new issues of shares, because none of the companies involved had a track record.

However, in 1980 the Stock Exchange created a new market, the Unlisted Securities Market (USM), in an attempt to help new companies raise equity finance. However, the USM faced problems and the majority of the companies found that the USM failed to match up to its early promise. In 1995 there was an announcement that the Unlisted Securities Market would close in the following year. This has been replaced by the Alternative Investment Market, or AIM, which will be considered fully in Unit 3.

Money Raised By New Issues

The table below shows the importance of the Primary Market function to industry and the Government.

Table 2.1: Money raised by new issues of shares, rights issues and British Government securities (gilts) 1993 – 1998.

	Money raised from new issues of equity, loan stock and other issues by listed UK companies £m	Money raised from rights issues £m	Money raised by the issue of British Government securities £m
1993	49134.8	11377.6	57230.2
1994	57523.7	7103.7	32640.0
1995	37573.0	5059.1	29720.0
1996	55192.5	4746.6	43813.8
1997	58291.1	2195.8	31911.4
1998	66751.1	1211.1	12768.6

Source: Fact File 1998 and Fact File 1999, London Stock Exchange

5   The Secondary Market

The need for a secondary market

It is on the secondary market that investors who hold existing shares, gilts or loan stocks can sell them to other investors. Without an efficient secondary market the primary market would fail. People who invest in new issues or new gilts need to know that they in turn could sell them to someone else if the need were ever to arise. This market is successful in that gilts or quoted shares can always be sold at the current price and that the market makers are honest.

The progress of the secondary market can be assessed from the two main indices, the FTSE Actuaries Share Indices, and the FTSE 100 Indices, and other indices covered in Unit 17.

Sales on the secondary market

A shareholder or the owner of a quoted stock or share can normally sell his holding very quickly on the Stock Exchange. The problem is that he will have to sell at the prevailing market price. Current prices can always be ascertained from a stockbroker or on-line broker. In addition prices can be obtained from Ceefax and Teletext, but there is approximately a 20 minute delay in these prices being updated. If an investor is forced to sell at an unfavourable time, he may well end up by making a loss.

6   Other Functions of the Secondary Market

Share price movements

The Stock Exchange acts as a 'barometer' of the health of the economy. If the market as a whole expects economic prospects to improve, share prices will rise, and vice versa. In 1987 the FT indices rose to record levels until Monday 19 October when the world stock markets crashed, triggered by worries over the US economy. This was known as 'Black Monday' and heralded the first major fall in UK equity prices since 1972-74.

However, the UK stock market is still very volatile and large upward and downward movements in share prices have been seen since then. Factors such as the Federal Reserve announcing interest rate rises in the USA, or an expectation of slowing economic growth in the USA, can have an adverse, if short-term, effect on UK share prices.

Such large falls are caused because investors feel that there could be an adverse effect on the strength of the UK economy.

An individual company's share price movements should, in theory, reflect the prospects of that company. This is not always the case in practice because a company's share price is often influenced by general market sentiment. At other times an individual company's share price may fall when record profits have been announced. This paradox is explained by the fact that the market had anticipated even higher profits and was disappointed by the outcome.

Factors affecting price movements

Share prices are set by the market forces of supply and demand.

Supply is affected by the amount of new issues being made at a particular time.

It is further affected by the amount of shares or gilts being sold by investors. At times of panic, such as 1974-75, many investors decided to sell their shares. As a result the *Financial Times* Ordinary Index reached its lowest level for many years, falling from over 500 in the early 1970s to 146 at its lowest point in January 1975. Even after the October 1987 crash, the FT Ordinary Index still stood at 1,527.3 on 21 October 1987, and on 8 October 1999 it had further risen to 3,765.4.

Demand is influenced by how investors view the prospects of the economy and interest rates. Such demand is not always rational, and prices tend to rise to a peak and then fall back.

Factors that tend to influence supply and demand for shares in general are:

- Political prospects;
- Balance of payment statistics;
- Economic statistics such as money supply figures. (If money supply figures are 'good' it could mean that there is scope for a fall in interest rates.) Other statistics include the inflation rate, exchange rate, and level of industrial production;
- The amount of money invested by institutions;
- Government actions such as tax changes, controls over companies, dividend controls, credit restrictions, wage freezes;
- Changes in consumer spending levels or patterns.

Factors that tend to affect supply and demand for a particular share are:

- Changes in dividends, profits or net assets values;
- Announcement by the company of expected good or poor trading figures;
- Adverse or favourable press comment;
- A takeover bid;
- The introduction of a new product;
- New management;
- Large purchases or sales by institutions;
- Development of a new product or discovery of a new area, e.g. oil or gas fields.

Program trading

This is a computer-based system where the computer is programmed to buy or sell if the stock or share reaches a certain price or fluctuates by a certain percentage. The October 1987 crash was partially blamed on the US fund managers who use program trading very heavily on Wall Street. Because share prices fell so rapidly the computers were triggering sales, thus worsening the situation. The USA 'pulled the plug' on the computers – but not before the effects were felt throughout the world.

Some US markets have now employed 'uptick and downtick' rules which restrict trading if prices move up or down by a certain percentage in a given period. These are called 'circuit breakers' in the UK. Opinion on whether these serve any useful purpose is divided. Some argue that circuit breakers can remove the volatility caused by rapid and sudden changes in market sentiment, whereas others regard them as a means of delaying the inevitable, as the forces of supply and demand will eventually bring about changes whatever artificial constraints are used.

Derivatives

A derivative is an instrument whose price is affected by (or 'derived' from) an underlying market. When these derivatives seem to be 'cheap' compared with the stock market, shares are sold and the derivatives are bought.

The three main types of derivative linked to the Stock Exchange are:

- Options contracts – these provide the investor with an option, but not an obligation, to buy or sell an underlying asset by a specified date. Options have a short life span, of up to 9 months. They cannot be traded on the Stock Market, but the underlying asset is quoted on the Stock Market. (See Unit 8 for further details.)

- Warrants, where the investor has the right but not the obligation to buy shares at a set price by a specified date. Warrants have a life of several years from issue. Warrants can be traded on the Stock Market. (See Unit 8 for further details.)

- Futures contracts – these are contracts to buy or sell a specified volume of a commodity or security at a specified price on a specified date.

7 The Various Types of Investor on the Stock Exchange

The private investor and the institutional investor

As we shall see, the bulk of stocks and shares by value are still owned by the institutional investors, which consist of pension funds, insurance companies, unit trusts and investment trusts.

In 1998 (the latest available figures), the institutions and overseas investors owned 75% by value of the UK Stock Market. The remainder of the shares were owned by private investors, accounting for 25% of the value of the UK Stock Market.

Although private investors only own 25% of the shares by value, there are around 11 million private investors, about 25% of the population. (Fact File 1998, London Stock Exchange.)

This contrasts with 1957 when 66% of shares were owned by private investors, 18% by the major institutions, with the remainder of 16% owned by the smaller institutions and overseas investors, as shown above.

Reasons for the change from private individuals to institutional investors

Redistribution of wealth

Prior to World War II a relatively small number of wealthy individuals owned a large proportion of the country's wealth, while the ordinary working person had just about enough pay to survive on. After World War II a Labour government was elected which had as one of its major policies the redistribution of wealth. It achieved this objective by putting a heavy tax burden on the wealthy through high levels of income tax, capital gains tax and death duties (now called Inheritance Tax). This resulted in large tax bills that the wealthy could pay only by selling some of their assets – the most easily saleable being stocks and shares.

At the same time the ordinary working man began to have more money than he actually needed just to survive and he wanted to find a home for his savings. He looked first towards the areas he knew and understood, life insurance and pension funds. Then, as he became more financially aware, he began to look at other institutional investments as a way of making his money work. He began to invest in unit and investment trusts.

Growth of the institutional investors

Insurance companies
Even before World War II the ordinary working man was familiar with life insurance through the weekly payment of small sums that would provide, on death, enough to pay the funeral expenses. As living standards began to improve after the war, other insurance policies became more popular. These policies were investment vehicles rather than providers of 'death cover'. People were able to invest in life policies that paid out a guaranteed amount if the individual lived until a certain age, or died prior to that date. The government made this form of saving even more attractive by allowing tax relief on the premiums paid on life policies. This tax relief was abolished for new policies taken out after March 1984, and this has had the effect of making certain types of life insurance less attractive to investors. As a result, life insurance companies have had a fall-off in the amount of money invested with them since March 1984 and this has caused them to rethink their marketing strategies. Many of the major life insurance companies launched unit trusts in order to try to attract funds back.

Pension funds
Many companies and nationalized companies provide pensions for their employees. Over the last 40 years or so pension funds have grown into one of the most important of the institutions. The growth in pension funds has been phenomenal, the value of their assets have more than doubled since 1983. Many smaller companies use commercial pension fund managers rather than 'in-house' managers, simply because they do not have the resources to manage a pension fund effectively.

The UK pension funds have freedom to invest in UK stocks and shares, overseas stocks and shares, index-linked investment, cash and property. However, the largest area of investment is UK equities.

Pensions are a tax-efficient way of saving for old age. Contributions are tax deductible, and the pension fund itself pays no direct tax. However tax credits on dividends cannot be reclaimed. On receipt of a pension, the pensioner is liable to tax at his marginal rate of income tax on his regular pension payments.

Unit trusts and investment trusts
These organizations provide professional management, simplified paperwork and a diversified portfolio of stocks and shares. The majority of private investors lack the time and expertise to manage direct holdings of stocks and shares, but many wish to have Stock Exchange

investments in their portfolios. These organizations provide a simple way to achieve this aim.

As a result of the growth of the institutional investor, virtually all people in employment have an interest in the stock market, although they may not realize this. If they hold pension plans or life insurance, the amount they receive will depend on the success of the institution's investment policy on the stock market. Thus at one remove 'the man in the street' is affected by stock market conditions.

Nationalization
The postwar Labour government nationalized, i.e. brought into public ownership, many companies. The major companies nationalized were the Bank of England and the gas, electricity, coal, railway, steel and air/aviation companies. To pay for this nationalization the government issued £3,500 million of British government securities (gilts). Most of these companies were owned by private investors, who received the money, but did not reinvest directly into the stock market in large numbers. However, subsequent privatizations have returned many of these companies to private ownership and provided the Government of the day with cash which was used to reduce the Public Sector Borrowing Requirement (now called the Public Sector Net Cash Requirement) at the time.

Corporate governance
In 1992 the Cadbury Report on Corporate Governance was published. Sir Adrian Cadbury was responsible for chairing the committee on 'The Financial Aspects of Corporate Governance'. Paragraph 2.5 of the Cadbury Report defines corporate governance as: 'the system by which companies are directed and controlled'. The report covered a wide range of issues and produced a 'Code of Best Practice' which, it was recommended, should be adopted by all listed companies in the UK. This Code has now been updated by the Combined Code on Corporate Governance, June 1998.

The issue of corporate governance has grown due to a number of reasons:

● The effects of the recession on listed companies and the discovery that financial reporting and controls were not always adequate (as was seen in relation to Queens Moat House Hotels);

● The standards of financial reporting and accountability (as seen by the problems with BCCI and Robert Maxwell);

● The controversy over directors' pay.

Although the Combined Code covers the areas that companies should be addressing, such as regularity of board meetings, the appointment of non-executive directors, full disclosure of executive directors' total emoluments, and reporting and control procedures, especially in relation to establishing an audit committee, it is not legally binding at present. This is where the role of the shareholder comes into play. The institutions are the major shareholders in virtually all UK quoted companies, thus it is to these shareholders that the task of 'encouraging' companies to adopt the Combined Code falls. Shareholders will find improved standards of information if the Combined Code is adopted, thus it is in their interests to encourage adoption of the Combined Code.

The Stock Exchange requires all listed companies to adopt the Combined Code.

The effects of the change to institutional ownership of shares

The private individual now has an indirect interest in the stock market. The value of his life policy, pension plan or unit or investment trusts will depend in the long run on the performance of the stock market. There are now far more people affected by stock market conditions than ever before because of their indirect investments in the stock market.

Ownership is divorced from control. A shareholder in theory is part-owner of a company, but in the past institutions tended to favour a 'hands-off' approach, except when takeovers were involved. However, institutions now intervene to prevent abuses, e.g. the institutions tend to scrutinize very carefully any 'golden handshakes' paid to directors who have been fired for incompetence.

The 'weight of money' theory says that much of the vast cash flow of the institutions will be invested in the stock market, thus keeping prices from falling. However, the institutions are not bound to invest in UK equities merely because they are cash rich, and they will invest in this way only if they are confident that prospects are good.

However, against this is the well known 'herd instinct' whereby all the institutions tend to act in the same way (i.e. all buy or all sell a particular company's shares). This herd instinct could account for the volatility of share prices.

The conclusion seems to be that there is a 'floor price' below which shares will not fall, but there will be violent fluctuations above this minimum level. When market prospects seem good, the cash from institutions will tend to be invested in UK shares, thus raising share prices.

The fall and rise of the private investor

In 1975 the FT ordinary index had fallen to 146 from 500 in 1972. The private investor sold his shares and left the market. However, the private investor has been tempted back. Fact File 1999 showed that in 1998 private investors owned 25% of listed shares by value.

Share ownership is generally only one or two shares for many investors. The aim is to encourage deeper share ownership, i.e. people having a number of different shares instead of one or two.

Many of the changes since 1979 can be directly attributed to government initiatives:

● Privatization of businesses previously state owned;

● Favourable tax treatment for employee share option schemes (ESOPs);

- More favourable tax treatment for private investors, e.g. abolition of investment income surcharge, indexation allowances for capital gains, reduction of income tax levels;

- Introduction of Personal Equity Plans (PEPs) (now phased out) and latterly Individual Savings Accounts (ISAs);

- Reduction in stamp duty from 2% to 0.5%;

- Exchange control was abolished leading to freedom to invest overseas;

- The property market has made people wealthy on paper, and as elderly parents die, or people trade down for retirement, it has released large sums of money for individual investment;

- There has been a gradual increase in the income of individuals who have started to invest, albeit modestly, in shares. This was encouraged particularly by the privatization issues that offered payment in instalments and other perks such as bill vouchers for British Telecom (BT) and British Gas (BG);

- There has been an increase in the amount of financial information available in the popular press and on television, so people are finding it easier to understand the stock market;

- Banks and other financial institutions have become more involved in buying and selling shares. Some banks have computer-based dealing screens in the branch, making dealing quicker and cheaper;

- In addition, the demutualization of building societies and insurance companies has resulted in more private share ownership.

There are several factors that could reverse the trend in share ownership and reduce the amount of shares directly held by individuals:

- A rise in commission rates has been seen due to the increased costs of broking firms, however this has been offset by the cheap dealing services available by telephone and on-line brokers such as Yorkshare and E*Trade;

- A fall in the number of broking firms that are willing to deal with the small, private investor, because the firms do not consider the business to be profitable;

- During the mid-1990s there was a gradual improvement in the economy, interest rates and inflation fell rapidly and are now (January 2000) relatively low;

- The growth of personal pension plans due to the attractive tax treatment of premiums may make investors turn to a longer-term, indirect investment rather than shares.

8　　The Functions of Members of the Stock Exchange

Introduction

Stock Exchange firms conduct their business from screen-based systems at various locations and the Stock Exchange floor is no longer used for the trading of stocks and shares. A variety of types of member firms exist and these are described below.

Broker/dealers

Technically, all Stock Exchange firms are broker/dealers, i.e. a combination of the old functions of broker and jobber, but not all firms wish to act in this dual capacity.

Market makers

Market makers fulfil the traditional wholesaler role.

Market makers will fill securities orders from their 'book', which is a common term used to describe stocks or shares owned by the market makers themselves. These organizations will take positions in stocks by increasing their 'book' in shares that are expected to rise in price, and reducing their book in shares that are expected to fall. The profitability, or otherwise, of a market maker will depend on correct anticipation of market movements.

A market maker is committed to making a buying or selling price on demand, but technically he need quote prices on SEAQ only in equities in small amounts of shares, and deal in up to the minimum quote size (see Unit 5). Some firms will choose to be market makers in a small number of equities, rather than being obliged to quote prices in every quoted share on the market.

Usually a market maker will deal 'net'. This means that an investor who deals directly with the market maker will simply pay the market maker's selling price (offer price), or receive the market maker's buying price (bid price) without any commission being charged.

The function of a market maker is to provide liquidity, so that investors can always deal either way at the current market price. Inter-dealer brokers (IDBs) act as intermediaries between market makers, thus aiding liquidity.

Agency broker

The agency broker is more commonly called a stockbroker. He will act as an intermediary between the investor and the market maker, will give advice and will charge a fee for this service. Some stockbrokers, however, have moved away from giving advice and have instead chosen to act as 'execution-only' brokers, i.e. purely taking orders and carrying out deals but not providing advice.

Because there are no fixed rates of commission, these 'execution-only' brokers have chosen to charge very low fees – well below those charged by ordinary agency brokers. These execution-only brokers provide a cheap dealing service for the private investor who knows exactly what he wants.

You may wonder why any investor would wish to use an intermediary (even an execution-only broker) who charges commission, when he could deal directly with the market maker on a 'net' basis.

There are four reasons:

- The fund managers want the best City brokers to survive because they need the brokers' research and ideas, especially for smaller companies;

- There are no conflicts of interest when an agency broker is used because the function of this member of the Stock Exchange is to act in his client's (i.e. the investor's) best interests. Hence the broker will shop around for the best deal;

- The private investor loses access to the research facilities of the broker if he deals directly with the market maker;

- Market makers will deal only with very large orders given directly by the client. Effectively, the client will be one of the institutions because they are the major buyers and sellers of stocks and shares.

The gilts market

Market makers in the gilts market (GEMMs)

The gilt market functions through direct dealings between the Bank of England and a gilt-edged market maker (GEMM).

The function of a GEMM is to make, on demand and in any trading conditions, continuous and effective two-way prices at which he stands committed to deal. Only organizations that have given an undertaking to the Bank of England to act in this way will be designated as GEMMs. Their profits will in the main be derived from gains between their selling and buying prices. The market maker who makes most money will be the one who best anticipates the market movements.

Operation of the gilts market

The Bank of England will ask the GEMMs to make competitive tenders for new issues of the gilts, and the Bank will respond to each bid entirely at its discretion. The Bank will prevent any single purchaser from acquiring more than 25% of a particular new issue of a gilt. Successful bidders will be issued with the stock at the actual price they offer. In addition, the Bank will also be able to deal with the GEMMs in the secondary market if it wishes. Do not fall into the trap of believing that only GEMMs can bid. Applications for new issues can be made by anyone, but the minimum application is £1,000.

GEMMs will inevitably go 'over bought' or 'over sold' in a particular stock at some time or other. Such positions can be unwound by selling an 'over bought' stock to another GEMM, or buying an 'oversold' stock from another GEMM. There would be problems in direct deals between GEMMs, because they will be in fierce competition with each other. The Bank of England's solution to this dilemma is to bring into being an organization called an inter-dealer broker (IDB). Any GEMM who wishes to deal with another GEMM will do so through an IDB. (It is estimated that 90% of gilts business goes through IDBs.)

Gilt-edged auctions for new issues of gilts were introduced in May 1987. There is no minimum price at an auction and successful bidders pay what they actually bid. Most bids come via GEMMs. As a concession to private investors they can apply at the 'non-competitive bid price' (the average price paid by all successful competitive bidders). Institutions can also trade on a 'when-issued' basis. This is done after the auction has been announced (the announcement is 17 calendar days before the auction). 'When-issued' means the institutions instruct the GEMMs that they will purchase at x price 'when issued', i.e. when the gilt begins trading.

Many new issues of gilts are made in partly paid form. For example, 61/4% Treasury 2010 was issued via the means of an auction, with £50 per £100 nominal stock payable on application (closing date being 10 a.m. on 26 January 1994), and the balance of £50 per £100 nominal payable on 14 March 1994. If the non-competitive sale price is less than £100 per £100 nominal, the excess is refunded by cheque. If the non-competitive sale price is above £100 per £100, nominal applicants have to pay the excess on receipt of a letter from the Bank of England (thus, it is effectively added to the first instalment).

Allotment letters are issued after the closing date when the first instalment is received and any excess or refund is paid.

Summary

Now that you have studied this unit, you should be able to:

describe the difference between the primary and secondary markets;

● explain how money is raised on the primary markets by companies and the Government;

explain how successful the primary market has been at raising funds;

● describe the functions of the secondary market;

● describe the factors that move share prices;

describe the main types of investor on the Stock Exchange;

explain the relevance of corporate governance;

explain the reasons for the change in share ownership;

explain the effects of the change in share ownership;

describe the functions of:

➤ broker/dealers
➤ market makers
➤ inter-dealer brokers
➤ agency brokers;

describe how the gilts market operates.

3

THE NEW ISSUE MARKET

Objectives

After studying this unit, you should be able to:

- explain what a new issue is;

- understand why companies seek a listing and the requirements for obtaining a listing on the Stock Exchange and the Alternative Investment Market;

- describe the procedure prior to issue;

- understand the role and functions of an issuing house;

- describe the principles of underwriting;

- understand the role and functions of a company broker;

- explain how a listing can be withdrawn;

- list and describe each of the methods of obtaining a listing;

- understand new issue strategy;

- define bulls, bears and stags, and understand the effects of the activities of each of these investors on the market.

1 New Issues

A new issue is an issue of shares by:

- A quoted company to the public to enable it to raise capital; or

- An unquoted company by an offer for sale, offer for subscription, placing or introduction, on the Main Market or the Alternative Investment Market (AIM).

The two markets

A company can obtain a quotation on one of the two markets operated by the Stock Exchange. The market it chooses will depend on various factors such as company size and track record. The largest companies will gain a full listing on the Main Market; smaller companies will obtain a listing on the AIM.

The Main Market (previously called the Official List)

The requirements for a full listing are laid down in the *Admission of Securities to Listing*, more commonly called the 'Yellow Book'. A company will have to produce listing particulars, have a total market capitalization of at least £700,000 but normally over £10 million for market liquidity and cost reasons, and make at least 25% of its issued ordinary share capital available to the public.

The Alternative Investment Market (AIM)

The Alternative Investment Market (AIM) commenced trading in June 1995. The Alternative Investment Market is designed to provide companies with an opportunity to raize capital, a trading facility for their shares and a way of placing a market value on their shares.

The type of company likely to be traded on the AIM includes young and fast-growing businesses, management buy-outs and buy-ins, family-owned companies, former Business Expansion Scheme companies and companies where shares have been traded under Rule 4.2. (Source: *A Guide for Advisors and Brokers*, London Stock Exchange.)

The rules for joining the AIM are fewer and simpler than for a full listing.

Member companies must appoint and retain a nominated adviser to guide them on rules and procedures. They must also appoint and retain a nominated broker to make a market in the company's shares. These two nominated roles can be carried out by the same firm.

To join the AIM the company must produce a prospectus containing detailed financial information on the company. This must be sufficient and suitable for an informed assessment to be made of the company's financial health.

As a member of the AIM, the company must keep investors fully informed. It must publish audited accounts each year along with information on dividends, changes in shareholders and directors. Any 'price sensitive' information must also be published.

Companies that are members of the AIM can represent a higher risk to investors than those quoted on the Main Market. The AIM is therefore more suited to the experienced professional investor.

Shares quoted on the AIM are traded on SEATS PLUS – the Stock Exchange Automated Trading Services PLUS, that provides facilities for both market makers and order-driven trading. This helps to provide liquidity (i.e. the ability to buy and sell shares easily).

Reasons given by companies to want a stock market listing

- The existing shareholders wish to sell some of their shares in order to receive a cash sum. While still retaining control, they can enjoy the results of their work in building the business up to its current size.

- The company wishes to raise new finance by way of an equity issue either to fund new developments or to repay existing loans.

- The company hopes that the prestige of a quotation will provide useful publicity for its products.

- The company wants its shares to become freely marketable so that at some time in the future it can use its shares as consideration for a takeover.

- The company may find it easier to raise debt finance because of greater confidence being generated by its quotation.

- Improved marketability of the company's shares can aid the establishment of an employee share option scheme as an additional incentive to employees to perform well.

- A ready market can be gained for disposal of shares for inheritance tax purposes.

2 Stock Exchange Listing Requirements

For a full listing

The Stock Exchange lays down its listing requirements in the 'Yellow Book' (*Admission of Securities to Listing*). All companies must comply with these conditions before their securities can be quoted on the Stock Exchange. In addition, the Financial Services Act 1986 sets out the procedures for companies seeking admission to the Main Market and the Alternative Investment Market (AIM).

Listing particulars

Listing particulars contain the published information made available to prospective investors prior to a new issue. While the format of the listing particulars will vary depending on the business of the company, there are certain requirements that must be included. The listing particulars are extremely detailed and easily run to 40 or more pages. Summaries of the main points of existing particulars, together with comments on their significance, are shown below.

- A statement that a copy of the listing particulars and other specified documents have been delivered to the Registrar of Companies, and that application has been made for the securities to be admitted to the Main Market.

- The name of the issuing house must be included. This is of great interest to a prospective investor, because certain issuing houses have built up their reputations over the years in dealing with new issues of certain types of company. Thus the issuing house's good name is at risk if the issue should fail.

- Details of the capital structure of the company and the price of the shares being issued.

- Names and addresses of directors, company secretary, bankers, solicitors, auditors and sponsors. As with the issuing house, these firms and people are putting their reputation on the line and the prospective investors will be looking for names with a good reputation.

- The history of, description of, and analysis of the company. The growth should be shown as steady and new developments must be shown to be well researched.

- Details of directors' functions, their other relevant business interests and activities. Further details such as the age of the directors are usually given. If a company's board consists of directors all approaching retirement age, this shows a lack of forward planning and would cast doubts on the company's future prospects once these directors retire. The listing particulars must also disclose details of any shares reserved for employees, directors and existing shareholders who already hold 3% of the shares.

- Working capital is always stated to be adequate after taking into account net proceeds of the issue. This statement is made in a document called a 'letter of comfort'.

- Prospects, profits and dividends, including earnings and dividends per share over the last three years, five years' balance sheets, and interim figures covering the last six months if the last published accounts are for a year ended more than nine months ago.

- Accountant's report. This analyses the balance sheets and trends in the company over the past three years. Again the name of the accountants will carry great weight for the prospective investor, and it should be one of the top five firms in order to generate investor confidence.

- Statutory and general information covering share capital history, memorandum and articles of association, material contracts, subsidiary companies, directors' interests, other substantial shareholdings in the company, directors' service agreements, and an indication (as far as it is known) of people who exercise or could exercise control over the company, with the proportion of voting capital held.

Prospectus

For a listing on the Main Market or AIM the above details are contained in a prospectus. An abbreviated form of the listing particulars is often published in the press and this is also known as a 'prospectus'. A 'pathfinder prospectus' contains the information about the company, but does not state the price at which the shares are to be issued. The price can be set just before launch date in the light of prevailing market conditions.

Other stock exchange requirements for a listing on the Main Market

Apart from the very full details included in the listing particulars, the following points must also be complied with.

- The total market capitalization must be at least £700,000, and the market capitalization of any single security must be at least £200,000. At least 25% of the issued ordinary share capital must be made available to the public. The company must be a public limited company.

- The application for listing must be supported by a sponsor and normally two firms of market makers who are prepared to deal in the securities. Sponsors will normally be corporate brokers, merchant banks, solicitors, accountants and venture capitalists. The listing particulars must be published in at least two leading newspapers.

- Copies of the numerous documents must be submitted to the Stock Exchange Quotations Department for formal approval, and the listing particulars must not be published before this approval has been granted.

The sponsor (who also often acts as the issuing house) carries out most of the work and thus has a large measure of responsibility for the application procedure.

Once this process has been completed and the Quotation Department agrees to grant a listing, the company must join in the 'Continuing Obligations'. It does not matter whether it is the Government, a local authority or a company seeking a listing, they all must join in the 'Continuing Obligations'.

Continuing obligations

The continuing obligations cover matters that the company must adhere to in order to retain its listing.

- Prompt notification to the Quotation Department of information necessary for investors to appraise the company's position. This is particularly important where the information could be 'price sensitive', i.e. cause a movement in the share price. Information about profits, dividends, rights issues or issues of any new types of securities must be given to the Quotation Department immediately after the meeting sanctioning such items.

- Issue of proxy forms with provision for two-way voting (i.e. for or against the resolution).

- Submission of circulars and announcements to shareholders.

- Issue of interim reports, which are required half-yearly and must be published within four months of the period end. The interim report is unaudited.

- Prompt registration of transfers of stocks and shares and issue of certificates.

- Prior approval of members to any issues of equity capital (or similar) for cash other than to existing equity shareholders.

Requirements for the Alternative Investment Market

For a listing on the AIM the requirements are somewhat less stringent.

- Only 10% of the issued ordinary share capital need be available to the general public.

- The company signs the 'General Undertaking' that obliges the company to maintain an adequate, continuing level of disclosure of its affairs. This ensures that an informed market in the shares is maintained.

3   Procedure Prior to Issue

This is the same for both full and AIM listings.

- The company approaches an issuing house in order to gain its support and expertise.

- The issuing house and the directors agree the terms of reference of the accountant's report, known as the long form report. The accountants chosen by the issuing house will normally be one of the top five firms, and the purpose of the long form report is to give a professional view on the affairs of the company, to protect both the public and the issuing house.

- The long form report is confidential to the directors and issuing house, and takes around three months to prepare. From the long form report the listing particulars are compiled.

The issuing house will have to be satisfied from the report that the company is suitable for flotation on the Stock Exchange, and the report will help to decide the offer price of the new shares.

For companies seeking an AIM listing a long form report is not required, provided 10% of the shares are already in the public's hands prior to the listing.

During the three months or so during which the long form report is being compiled, advice is taken on whether the company's legal structure is suitable for the market, corporation tax, and personal tax purposes of the present shareholders.

- If the issuing house decides it is necessary, a new chairman will be appointed who has the necessary reputation and expertise to gain investor confidence.

- If the long form report is satisfactory, listing particulars can be prepared. Advance copies of the listing particulars will be filed with the Stock Exchange Quotations Department for approval.

- The issue price is provisionally agreed. This will be within one week of the issue date.

- The final price is agreed a day or two before issue date.

The amount of money to be raised will depend on the following factors:

- The company's expansion plans;

- The state of the company's balance sheet and projected earnings;

- How much of the company's capital is to be made available under the issue.

The whole process takes around six months to complete.

4   The Role of the Issuing House

An issuing house can be a merchant bank, a stockbroker or other financial institution.

An issuing house is an organization that specializes in the arrangement of new issues. Issuing houses are staffed by financial experts who guide the company through the necessary procedures to obtain a listing. Because the issuing house has a reputation to maintain, it will look very closely at the company it has been asked to assist. It may require certain changes to be made so that the company will be attractive to the investors, e.g. the issuing house may require the appointment of a new chairman who is well known to the financial institutions.

The timing of the new issue is vital, as is the pricing, and method of issue. The issuing house will advise on these, using its knowledge of the prevailing conditions to time the issue correctly at an attractive price, and to use the most appropriate method of issue.

The issuing house acts in one of two roles regarding the issue, as agent or as principal.

● As agent it will distribute the listing particulars and allot shares on application. In return it earns a commission.

● As principal it will purchase the whole of the issue from the company and then offer it for sale to the public or to its own clients (selective marketing).

When the issuing house acts as principal it does not charge a commission for its services; it makes its profit by selling the shares at a higher price than it paid. From the company's point of view this means that it knows exactly how much cash it will receive because the whole issue has been taken up. The danger to the issuing house in this operation is that if the shares do not find buyers it will be left holding shares that it has already paid for and cannot sell.

5 Underwriting

The danger that the company (or issuing house if acting as a principal) runs is that the whole of the share issue may not be taken up. This means that less money is received than is expected, and can seriously affect the future plans of the company. To prevent this occurrence the issue can be underwritten.

Underwriters are organizations who agree to subscribe for any shares not taken up at the time of issue. It is usually the issuing house that underwrites the whole issue, and it will then arrange with sub-underwriters for a proportion of the issue to be taken. Sub-underwriters are usually banks, broker/dealers, unit trusts, investment trusts, insurance companies and pension funds.

In return for underwriting an issue the underwriter receives a commission related to the value of the issue. For a good-class equity issue this will be around 2% of the value of the issue. When the underwriter agrees to pass on some of the liability for underwriting the issue to sub-underwriters, the underwriter will pay the sub-underwriter a commission out of its own commission. If the underwriter's commission were 2%, then around 1.5% would be paid by it to the sub-underwriters.

The majority of issues are fully subscribed, in which case the underwriters and sub-underwriters will just take their commission. However, in the event of the issue being undersubscribed, the underwriters and sub-underwriters will have to buy the shares themselves. In order to recoup their losses, they may sell the shares on the market over a period of time, or they may hold them for a lengthy period until the market has picked up. The choice of action will depend on many factors, but the main one will be the reason for the failure of the issue. If the failure was caused by short-term market sentiment affecting the market in general rather than the company in particular, then the share price should improve quickly and a sale should soon be possible at a reasonable price. If the failure was caused by adverse news about the company or its market sector, the course of action would be rather more difficult to decide.

6 The Functions of a Company Broker

Every quoted company must have a formal link-up with a broker. If the formal link is severed, the company must find another broker very quickly or it will lose its Stock Exchange listing.

When a company first comes to the market the company broker will advise on the methods of obtaining a listing (see Section 12), and it will ensure that all legal formalities are complied with.

Once a company is officially listed, the obligations of a company broker are to ensure that formal announcements of results, acquisitions and disposals are made in accordance with the rules of the Stock Exchange.

Further optional functions are:

- Public relations/research – this is the publication of brokers' circulars containing well-informed research notes that should enhance the company's image;

- Market making – not all company brokers wish to fulfil this function;

- Corporate finance – advice on rights issues or any other methods of raising finance.

Occasionally a company broker will sever its links with its company.

7 Advantages and Disadvantages of Obtaining a Listing

These apply equally to a full listing and an AIM listing.

Advantages

- The company gains prestige from being quoted. The rigorous inspections carried out before a listing is granted engender confidence in the company from both prospective investors and prospective customers.

- If further finance is required at a later date, it is easier to obtain by way of a further issue of shares called a rights issue. Rights issues are covered in Unit 4. Alternatively, new long-term loan capital could be issued on the stock market.

- If the company intends to grow by acquiring other companies, the offer of its own marketable securities as a part, or all, of the consideration can be attractive to the other company's shareholders.

- Shares can be traded and valued easily, thus allowing the original shareholders a means of unlocking their capital and valuing their wealth.

- The introduction of outside shareholders, coupled with the potential threat of a hostile takeover, will provide the directors with an incentive to perform.

Disadvantages

- The Stock Exchange requires a much higher level of disclosure of information than the Companies Act 1985 and 1989. Any adverse factors are quickly brought to the attention of investors and are quickly reflected in the share price.

- Because the financial press will be reporting on any facts appertaining to the company that may be relevant to the public, the company must ensure that all it says or does is without reproach. A casual aside may well be repeated and misunderstood out of context, thus damaging the company's image, and probably its share price as well.

- Shareholders will wish to see their dividends increasing, especially as the company expands. This can result in a dividend policy that may not necessarily be in the best interests of the company, but may be the only way the directors can maintain their seats on the board.

- With an unquoted company the shares and hence control are in the hands of just a few directors, but once the company is listed there will be many outside shareholders totally unconnected with the company. This dilution of control means that directors do not have a completely free hand to run the company as they wish, because they are responsible to the shareholders.

- Because the directors are elected by the shareholders they need to balance the interests of the company with the interests of the shareholders. This can, of course, result in a less than perfect situation where opportunities must be forgone in the interests of one or other party.

- It is a long, complicated and expensive process to obtain a listing.

8 Withdrawal of Listing

The Council of the Stock Exchange can withdraw a listing either for a temporary period (called 'suspended') or permanently (called 'cancelled'). The company can itself also request that its listing be suspended or cancelled.

A listing may be cancelled if only a small number of securities remain in public hands, for example, following a takeover. It will also be cancelled if the company goes into liquidation.

A listing can be suspended for anything from a few hours to a few months. This occurs in order to protect investors who are not in full possession of all the relevant information about the company. This may be due to financial difficulties, fraud, takeover or merger with the company concerned. A suspension is often seen if there is takeover activity in the shares and the Stock Exchange feels that a false market is being created in the shares due to the takeover activity. In such a case a suspension will be for a short period of time to take the heat out of the situation. If the suspension has continued for a very long period (over a year), the listing may be cancelled.

9 Methods of Obtaining a Listing

There are four methods of obtaining a listing: an offer for subscription, offer for sale, selective marketing (or placing) and introduction.

Offer for subscription

An offer for subscription can be either fixed price or by tender and occurs where the issuing authority offers the shares directly to the public without using an intermediary.

This method can be used by the Government for issuing gilts, or by a company. Most companies use the intermediary method, but some investment trusts have issued their shares directly to the public using this method.

Offer for sale

With the offer for sale the issuing house purchases the securities from the original shareholders, and re-sells them at a slightly higher price to the general public. This is the most frequently used method of obtaining a listing for shares. The resale can be either fixed price or by tender.

Full details of the contract between the issuing house and the company are published in the listing particulars.

It is not uncommon for this type of issue to occur when a reorganization of the share capital is undertaken. Often the issue does not raise any new capital for the company, but is used to allow the existing shareholders (usually the directors) to reduce their financial commitment to the company and realize some of the wealth they have tied up in the company.

Any company coming to market with an offer for sale of £15 million or more must advertise its full prospectus in two national newspapers.

Placing

A City organization, known as a 'sponsor', buys the whole issue and then agrees terms for sale of 50-95% (depending on the value of the issue) to its own clients. Technically these shares are 'placed' with the clients of the sponsor. The percentage of the issue that can be placed depends on the value of the issue.

The remaining unplaced shares must be sold to a second broker, known as an intermediary. The terms of this sale will have been agreed before the issue comes to market and the price will have been prearranged.

For all practical purposes the private investor has little chance of obtaining shares offered by a placing unless he is a client of the sponsor or intermediary.

All placings must be advertised by means of at least one advertisement in one national newspaper. For a medium and large offer the advertisement must include the full listing particulars or AIM particulars, a mini-prospectus, an offer notice and an application form. For a small offer the advertisement merely needs to advertise the availability of listing or AIM particulars.

Introduction

This method is available only to companies that already have a good spread of shareholders. It is not uncommon for AIM companies to graduate to a full listing by this means, because they often have a reasonable number of shareholders (100 or more). The other type of company commonly to gain a listing via an introduction is one that is already quoted on an overseas stock exchange.

With an introduction no new capital is raised. The existing shares are merely granted a listing. The advantage is with the shareholders who benefit from the increased marketability of their shares that comes with a listing.

The Stock Exchange does encourage the company to make some of its shares available on the market for any interested parties, but this is not compulsory.

Tender issues (applies to both offer for sale and offer for subscription)

Offers for sale or subscription are usually on a fixed-price basis but some issues are offered for tender. With a tender the public is invited to make an offer at or above a minimum stipulated price for the shares. It is usual for a minimum tender price to be fixed; below that offers will not be accepted.

Some gilts have been sold by means of a tender issue, and some company issues also use this method.

If a tender issue is expected to be successful, investors will tender at higher than the minimum tender price. If the offer is oversubscribed the issuing authority will take the highest bids first and work downwards until all the shares are allotted. The lowest accepted price is called the striking price. Investors who offer above the striking price will receive their shares in full, plus a refund of the difference between their offered price and the striking price. Investors who tendered at lower than the striking price will receive a refund because their bids will not have been accepted.

Example of calculation of the striking price

A company offers 3,000,000 shares for sale by tender at a minimum price of 175p. The issue is oversubscribed and offers are received as detailed below:

400,000	184p
600,000	183p
700,000	182p
800,000	181p
500,000	180p 3,000,000 shares applied for
700,000	179p
600,000	177p
800,000	175p

In this case the striking price would be 180p.

In reality there will never be tenders for exactly the number of shares offered. When the offer is oversubscribed, those who tendered at above the striking price receive their shares in full, and the remaining tenders at striking price are balloted. A variation on this is to ballot all the tenders at or above striking price to allot the shares. The details of the method to be used will be laid down in the listing particulars. In some cases the listing particulars have specified that if the price tendered is above the 'striking price' then the shares are sold to the individual or institution at the price it has tendered. This factor needs to be borne in mind by investors who are subscribing via a tender issue. The best advice in all cases is not to tender a price higher than you are prepared to pay for the shares as a long-term investment.

Summary of common points between all four methods

- If the new issue is undersubscribed the shares will commence trading at a lower price than that paid by the initial shareholder. If undersubscription occurs the 'successful' shareholder will make an immediate capital loss when trading starts.

- If the new issue is oversubscribed the shares are usually allotted by ballot. The successful shareholder receives his shares, the unsuccessful ones receive a refund of the money they submitted.

- If the new issue is oversubscribed the shares will open at a premium to the price paid. This is due to the effects of supply and demand. Institutional investors who do not receive all the shares they require will have to buy them on the Stock Market, thus driving up prices because demand exceeds supply.

● Provided the company (or issuing house, depending on method of issue used) has had the issue underwritten, it will receive the full amount of cash expected regardless of the success or failure of the issue.

10   Investor Strategy with New Issues

The strategy adopted by the prospective investor depends entirely on the method of issue used.

Offer for subscription

A deadline is set, and after that no applications will be accepted. The investor should wait for as long as possible before deciding whether or not to invest and how many shares to purchase. He must read the financial press for their comments on the issue, and obtain a broker's opinion on the prospects of both the company and the degree of success that the issue is likely to achieve.

If the investor then decides that the issue is likely to be oversubscribed, he needs to decide which course of action to adopt. He could:

● Apply for more shares than he wanted on the basis that the applications will be scaled down; or

● Apply for an odd number of shares, e.g. 5,200 instead of 5,000. If the issue is oversubscribed and a ballot is used to allocate the shares, the odd number may place him in a higher balloting bracket and increase his chances of obtaining shares. (The reason for this is that there are fewer applications for a large number of shares, thus the chances of successful inclusion in the ballot are higher.)

The danger with both these methods occurs if the issue is not fully subscribed. If this happens then the investor will be allotted all the shares he applied for, and this may mean a cost that is in excess of the investor's financial capability to pay. It will also mean that the shares will commence trading at a lower price than he paid. Thus the shareholder will incur an immediate capital loss if he sells the shares at this time.

Offer for sale

Even though the issuing house is acting as principal for the issue, rather than as an agent, the strategy to adopt is the same as for an offer for subscription.

Placing

The private investor has little opportunity unless he is a client of the sponsor or of the intermediary. The best hope for a private investor is to try to acquire the shares in the 'after market'.

Introduction

With this method of issue a document containing information similar to that in the listing particulars is circulated in the Extel Statistical Service. If the investor wishes to purchase these shares he must contact his broker immediately, because only a few shares may be made available.

The Stock Exchange does not lay down rules regarding the percentage of shares to be made available to the general public, but it does exert pressure on the issuing house to satisfy demand from market makers. This 'satisfaction of demand' will last only a short while, so time is of the essence.

Tender issues (both offer for sale and offer for subscription)

The same detailed look at the company is needed for this method of issue as for all others, but with the additional feature that the investor must decide on the price he will tender for the shares.

If the investor tenders a price higher than he actually wishes to pay it is quite probable that he will obtain the shares. However, if the striking price is set at a higher level than he would have wished, because the offer is heavily oversubscribed and other investors have used the same strategy, then he must pay the full amount regardless.

If the issue is undersubscribed the investor will pay the minimum tender price (which will become the striking price). However, the shares will commence trading at a lower price than he paid and he will incur an immediate capital loss if he sells the shares at that time.

The safest strategy is to tender the price he is willing to pay for the shares as a medium-term (5 to 10 years) investment. If the offer is heavily oversubscribed and the striking price is set above the level he has tendered, then he will receive no shares. If the striking price is below the price tendered, then he will be allotted the shares plus a refund of the difference between the price tendered and the striking price. The timing of the tender is the same as for an offer for sale or subscription, i.e. he should wait until the last possible moment before putting in his tender.

Note: the investor must initially check to see whether the price tendered will be the price paid, or whether one striking price will apply to all successful applicants.

11 Factors Affecting the Decision to Invest in New Issues

The investor must bear in mind that it is illegal to make multiple applications for a new issue of shares. The Stock Exchange in the past tended to overlook this practice, but the 1986 British Telecom issue resulted in legal action against some investors who made multiple applications. In all cases detailed study of the financial press is necessary to judge the mood of the market regarding the issue.

A broker's opinion should be sought on the issue, especially if the financial press seems uncertain as to the outcome. The broker can also provide advice based on the listing particulars that are rather long and are too involved for most investors to study with any degree of comprehension. In addition, the investor must watch the timing of his application, looking at the points covered in Section 11.

12   Stags

Along with bulls and bears, stags are one of the 'animals' of the Stock Exchange.

'Stags' are investors who apply for new issues of shares with the intention of selling them as soon as, or shortly after, dealings commence. Effectively, they are speculators whose intention is to make a quick profit on the shares. If they are successful (which means they have been allotted shares that commence trading at a price higher than they paid), they do not have to pay out any money. The reason for this is that new issues are dealt with on the Stock Exchange for 'cash', i.e. the investor receives the sale proceeds the day after the sale is made. The investor's cheque, which accompanies his application for the shares, usually takes several days to clear, and it is thus usual for the cheque to be cleared after the sale proceeds have been received.

Stagging of new issues is a mixed blessing. It does ensure that an issue is fully subscribed because stags go only for issues that look successful. The other advantage is that it does make shares available on the market for unsuccessful applicants (or those who 'missed the boat' with their timings).

The problem, however, is with fixed-price issues that are heavily stagged. The oversubscription causes a tremendous amount of paperwork in allotting the shares, and it does prevent the genuine investor from obtaining shares at the outset.

In the past, stags used the 'multiple application' method with popular issues. However, the legal action taken over multiple applications has curbed this. The other remedies to decrease the work involved on a stagged issue are:

- A requirement that the application be accompanied by a banker's draft. This deters the stag because he must pay for the draft when it is issued, and it may be a couple of weeks before he is allotted any shares;

- A requirement that the cheques sent with the application be cleared prior to the allotment being made. Again this involves the stag in laying out money before he can sell the shares;

- The use of the tender method of issue, whereby the striking price is set when all the shares have been allotted. This means that for a successful issue the company gains more capital, and the stag has less opportunity for selling the shares quickly at a profit, because the opening price will tend to be around the striking price.

Summary

Now that you have read this unit, you should be able to:

- understand the reasons for a company wanting to gain a listing;

- explain the advantages and disadvantages of having a listing;

- list the contents of the listing particulars;

- explain the contents of Continuing Obligations;

- distinguish between the requirements for a full listing;

- describe the procedure a company must go through prior to obtaining a listing, and explain the length of time involved;

- describe the role of the issuing house;

- explain the importance of, and responsibility of, underwriters;

- explain the functions of the company broker;

- identify the costs of obtaining a listing;

- explain why a listing may be withdrawn or cancelled;

- describe the four methods of obtaining a listing;

- describe how a tender issue operates;

- describe the strategy an investor should use in relation to the four different methods of obtaining a listing;

- explain the factors an investor should bear in mind when deciding whether to subscribe for a new issue;

- explain the role of stags in new issues.

4

CAPITALIZATION ISSUES, RIGHTS ISSUES AND ALLOTMENT LETTERS

Objectives

After studying this unit, you should be able to:

- describe a capitalization issue and the effect it has on a company's balance sheet;
- explain the effect of a capitalization on the share price;
- explain why a company makes a capitalization issue;
- differentiate between a share split, a share consolidation and a scrip issue;
- describe the features of a renounceable certificate;
- explain what is meant by a rights issue;
- explain the reasons for a company to make a rights issue;
- describe the advantages and disadvantages of a rights issue to the company;
- understand the timetable for a rights issue;
- list and explain the courses of action a shareholder can take in relation to a rights issue;
- describe a deep-discounted rights issue;
- in relation to a rights issue, be able to calculate:
  - ➤ the ex rights price
  - ➤ nil paid price
  - ➤ value of the rights and explain what each of these means;
- describe a vendor placing;
- describe an open offer;
- describe the functions of an allotment letter;
- describe the choices an investor has in relation to an allotment letter.

1   Introduction

In Unit 3 we discussed new issues of shares for companies that did not already have a Stock Exchange quotation. In this unit we examine capitalization and rights issues, which are new issues of shares for companies already quoted on the Stock Exchange. (While private companies can make both of these types of issue, considerations are outside the scope of the syllabus; suffice it to say that the basic principles are in any case very similar.) In both capitalization and rights issues the new shares are first offered to the existing shareholders on a pro rata basis. At the end of the unit you will study renounceable certificates and allotment letters that form part of the administrative procedures for these issues.

2   Capitalization Issues

The various alternative names for this type of issue

Other names for capitalization issues are 'bonus issues' or 'scrip issues'. All three names mean exactly the same, although the technically correct term is 'capitalization issue'.

What is a capitalization issue?

A capitalization issue is made by a company, not to raise new capital but to increase the number of shares in issue. This operation is usually carried out where the price of a single share is extremely high and the company feels that its shares are less attractive to investors because of the high unit price. A capitalization issue will cause the price per share to fall (see example below).

A capitalization issue is simply a bookkeeping exercise where a proportion of a company's reserves in the balance sheet are transferred to share capital. Reserves can consist of share premium account, reserves from the revaluation of fixed assets or from retained profits (sometimes shown as the profit and loss balance in the balance sheet). If a company has a share premium account this will be used first, ahead of other reserves.

Example

A company's balance sheet prior to a capitalization issue could be:

	£000		£000
600,000 ordinary shares of £1 each	600	Net assets	1,200
Share premium account	60		
Reserves	540		
	1,200		1,200

The company may decide to make a one-for-one capitalization issue, which means that every shareholder will receive one new fully paid share for every one he owns, and no money will be paid to the company for the 'privilege'.

After completion of the capitalization issue, the company's balance sheet will appear as follows (assuming no other factors apply):

	£000		£000
1,200,000 ordinary shares of £1 each	1,200	Net assets	1,200
	1,200		1,200

The balance sheet above is deliberately simplified to highlight the effect, or to be more accurate the non-effect, of a bonus issue. As can be seen, the balance sheet is neither stronger nor weaker than before, since the net assets remain unchanged. All that has happened is that there has been a change in the way shareholders' funds are shown, and such changes are merely cosmetic. Share capital, reserves and retained profits are regarded as a single item by lending bankers and other creditors.

Effect on the share price

Other things being equal, the price of the shares after the capitalization (known as the 'ex cap' price) will fall in direct proportion to the increase in share capital. In our example, if the quoted share price immediately before the capitalization issue had been 300p, the ex cap price would have been expected to fall to 150p, because there are twice the number of shares, but only the same asset backing and earning capacity.

This explanation began with the words 'other things being equal', but of course they rarely are equal. Factors that will prevent the ex cap price from changing by exactly the amount that would be expected are that:

● The lower price per share makes the shares more marketable. There is no logical reason for it, but private investors particularly find a lower priced share more attractive than one with a higher price. If the new shares are more attractive, then under the basic law of supply and demand their price must rise.

Nobody can explain why the lower price makes the shares more marketable, but one explanation could be that an investment of £12,000 (ignoring costs) in the pre-capitalization shares would purchase 4,000 shares, while the same amount invested in the shares ex cap would result in acquisition of 8,000 shares, which makes the investor feel he has more for his money. If the company operates an employee share option scheme, whereby relatively small amounts are saved over a five-year period, then a highly priced share may be less attractive to the employee.

Generally speaking, capitalization issues can be made only when a company has been successful in the past. Shares could have been issued at a premium only if buyers were confident of success. Revenue reserves can be acquired only from undistributed profits, and revaluations of fixed assets at least mean that the company's property has risen in value. In addition to all this, a capitalization issue is often accompanied by a good profits forecast.

Thus an aura of success generally surrounds a capitalization issue, and this, together with increased marketability, usually ensures that the ensuing ex cap price is above the one that would be expected from a simple mathematical calculation.

Why does a company make a capitalization issue?

There are no obvious tangible benefits to a company from a capitalization issue, but possible intangible benefits are:

● A capitalization issue can be a useful public relations exercise, bringing the past successes and future forecasts to the attention of shareholders and others.

● The issued share capital shown in the balance sheet can come more into line with net asset value.

● The rate of dividend per share can remain unchanged, but actual dividends can be increased. In our example the original 600,000 shares were doubled to 1,200,000 shares. Before the capitalization issue a dividend of 5p net per share would have resulted in a total payment to shareholders of £30,000, whereas after the issue a dividend of 5p per share would have resulted in a total payment of £60,000.

● When negotiating with consumers or other interested parties there can be problems if the other party is aware that the dividend rate has doubled. However, these problems are likely to be less if the dividend rate remains constant but the number of shares has increased.

Difference between a capitalization issue, share split and a share consolidation

Share split

A share split occurs when the company's total nominal capital remains unchanged, but when the nominal value per share is reduced. Let us recall our simplified pre-capitalization balance sheet, which was:

	£000		£000
600,000 ordinary shares of £1 each	600	Net assets	1,200
Share premium	60		
Reserves	540		
	1,200		1,200

Quoted price per share 300p

Using the appropriate resolution, the directors could authorize a 1 for 1 share split. This would reduce the nominal value per share from £1 to 50p. In this case the balance sheet immediately after the split would be:

	£000		£000
1,200,000 ordinary shares of 50p each	600	Net assets	1,200
Share premium	60		
Reserves	540		
	1,200		1,200

With a share split the share price would be expected to fall in line with the reduction in the nominal value. The expected share price would fall to 150p, however increased marketability and market forces in general would also affect the price of the new shares.

Share consolidation

A share consolidation is the exact reverse of a split, so that in the example above a share consolidation could involve the nominal value per share being increased to £2. In such a case, the ordinary share capital in the balance sheet would remain at £600,000 but would be represented by 300,000 shares of £2 nominal each.

With a share consolidation, the price would be expected to rise in line with the share consolidation. In this case it would be expected to double to 600p, subject to market forces.

Table 4.1: Summary of effect of a capitalization issue, share split and share consolidation

	Nominal Value	Number of shares issued	Share price after issue	Number of shares held after issue	Value of holding after issue
Position prior to issue	£1	600,000	300p	1,000	£3,000
Capitalization issue	Unchanged at £1	1,200,000	150p	2,000	£3,000
Share split	Reduced to 50p	1,200,000	150p	2,000	£3,000
Share consolidation	Increased to £2	300,000	600p	500	£3,000

Renounceable certificates

When a company makes a capitalization issue it sends every shareholder a new renounceable certificate for the number of shares to which he is entitled. If the shareholder wishes to retain the shares, he need do nothing at all. On the back of the renounceable certificate is stated an 'expiry date', and if the shareholder takes no action by this date the certificate becomes a conventional registered share certificate.

On the other hand, if the form on the reverse of the certificate is signed by the shareholder before the expiry date (the process of signing is called 'renunciation'), the shares represented by the capitalization issue can be transferred into the name of a third party without the need for a signed stock transfer form.

3   Rights Issues

What is a rights issue?

A rights issue is an issue of new shares to existing shareholders in proportion to the number of shares already held by each shareholder. The price at which the new shares are issued is below the current market price of the shares to encourage the shareholders to take up the issue. The new shares rank pari passu (equally) with all other shares of the same category once the issue is completed.

Apart from the need to be below the current market price, the actual price at which the new shares are issued depends on the size of funds needed by the company, the status of the company and market conditions in general.

The shareholder will receive a renounceable letter detailing information, number of shares provisionally allotted and due date for payment. This renounceable letter is also called a provisional allotment letter.

The reasons for a company to make a rights issue

The purpose of a rights issue will differ from company to company, but there are three main reasons why a company may *need* to make a rights issue, and one reason why a company may *wish* to make a rights issue.

The main reasons for making a rights issue are:

● When a company wishes to expand it may well request extra cash from its shareholders by way of a rights issue to finance that expansion;

● Extra fixed assets may be acquired and current assets will no doubt increase. However, while additional credit may finance some of these extra demands, an increased capital base by way of a rights issue may also be required. Another method of expansion is by means of takeovers, which will need additional equity finance;

● A company may need to strengthen its balance sheet by obtaining extra share capital.

When a company has too high a ratio of interest-bearing loan capital compared with its shareholders' funds, it is said to be highly geared. Highly geared companies can suffer if there is a squeeze on profits, because the interest on the borrowing is a debt that is payable whether or not profits are made;

● One final reason a company may wish to make a rights issue, as opposed to needing to make one, is simple opportunism. In some cases rights issues have been used to finance takeovers.

When share prices are relatively high shareholders are generally quite happy to subscribe for further shares by way of a rights issue. Some companies then put the money so raised on deposit in the money markets, while searching for a suitable business to take over.

Advantages of a rights issue to a company

Subject to the Articles of Association, a rights issue may be made at the discretion of the directors, whereas under the 1985 Companies Act and the Rules of the Stock Exchange, all issues of shares for cash, apart from rights issues, must be approved by shareholders in a general meeting.

The administrative costs are less than for a new issue of shares because there is no need to publish listing particulars provided the rights issue will increase the class of capital to which it relates (usually ordinary capital) by less than 10%. However, even where the publication of listing particulars is waived, information must still be published in the form of a brochure available to the public.

Shareholders who take up their rights will retain the same percentage of the company's share capital, and hence will retain the same voting powers.

Disadvantages of a rights issue for a company

Most rights issues are underwritten, because there is no legal obligation on the part of shareholders to subscribe (although the shares must first be offered to existing shareholders). However, should the issue be left with the underwriters, this is in effect a vote of no confidence in the directors by shareholders and the Stock Market in general.

The timetable for a rights issue

Each company will lay out a timetable for the rights issue in the information provided to the shareholder. The shareholder needs to take note of this so that he does not omit to take any necessary action with regards to the rights issue. The following information shows how the timetable operates:

Expected timetable for the rights issue (all dates are in the same year)	
Latest time for receipt of proxies	9 am on Saturday 1 June
Extraordinary general meeting	9 am on Monday 3 June
Provisional allotment letter despatched	Monday 3 June
Dealings in new shares commence, nil paid	Tuesday 4 June
Latest time for splitting, nil paid	3 pm on Thursday 20 June
Latest time for acceptance and payment in full	3 pm on Monday 24 June
Dealings in new shares commence, fully paid	Tuesday 25 June
Latest time for splitting, fully paid	3 pm on Friday 12 July
Latest time for registration of renunciation	3 pm on Tuesday 16 July
Definitive certificates for new shares despatched	Tuesday 30 July

With this issue, as with many rights issues, the company first requires a resolution to be passed. Voting can be done in person or by arranging for someone else to vote on your behalf (a proxy). The first two dates of 1 and 3 June relate to the extraordinary general meeting. Once the resolution is passed provisional allotment letters will be sent to shareholders on 3 June. The rest of the timetable gives the cut-off dates and times for each of the stages subsequent to the rights issue being completed. The whole process will be completed on 30 July when the new share certificates are sent out to the shareholders.

4 Choices of the Shareholder When a Rights Issue is Made

The shareholders can subscribe for the new shares (this is sometimes called taking up the rights). If the shareholder has sufficient cash resources to buy the new shares, and if he feels the company will use the money so raised in a profitable way, he should take up the rights.

If the shareholder feels the new shares are worth having, but he lacks the cash to pay for them, he can sell sufficient of the rights to enable him to take up the balance. The detailed calculations appear in Section 6.

The subscriber can sell the rights. The new shares are cheaper than the current market price, and both new and old shares will rank pari passu (on equal footing) when the formalities have been completed. Thus the new nil paid shares have a value for which a third party would be willing to pay. If the shareholder is not happy about the rights issue or requires some extra cash he should sell the rights. Usually the rights are sold via a broker who will charge commission.

An alternative to selling the rights is to do nothing at all. Under the terms of all UK quoted company rights issues, if the amount payable for the new shares has not been received by a stipulated deadline the company will sell the new shares in the market. This may be advantageous if the shareholding and hence the rights in respect of it are very small. The shareholder will then receive the sale proceeds of the new shares, less the rights price (the amount due to the company for the new shares) and any expenses, except where the proceeds do not exceed £3, in which case the proceeds may be kept for the company's benefit.

Before pursuing this course of action the shareholder must check the terms of the issue, because in a minority of cases the rights simply lapse, i.e. the rights become worthless to the shareholder, if no action is taken by the stated deadline. This applies quite commonly to shares of overseas companies. Although most UK shareholders will not hold such shares, those who do need to be aware of the dangers.

In deciding on his course of action the shareholder should simply ask himself two questions:

- Do I wish to invest more money in the company?
- If so, have I the cash to meet the necessary subscription?

If the answer to the first question is 'yes', then he will consider the second. If he has enough cash, then he will take up the rights. If he has insufficient cash he can sell enough of the rights to purchase the remainder. If the answer to the first question is 'no', then he will either sell the rights or let them lapse.

5 Deep-discounted Rights Issues

These differ from ordinary rights issues in, which the issue is not underwritten because new shares are priced substantially below the current share price. This is done virtually to ensure that the issue is taken up in full. Stock Exchange rules state that the subscription price of a deep discounted rights issue is 20% or more below the current market price.

A deep-discounted rights issue also reduces the price per share considerably, which makes the shares more marketable. This is similar to the effect of a capitalization issue, but with the added bonus that the company raises new capital at the same time.

Problems do arise for the individual shareholder with a deep-discounted issue if he wishes to sell enough of the rights to purchase the remainder at no cost (an operation called 'tail swallowing'). Because shares are sold there is a potential CGT liability. With a conventional rights issue this is less likely to happen, but with a deep-discounted issue this is a common problem.

6 Rights Issue Calculations

Introduction
Ultimately the ex rights price (the price of the shares after the rights issue has been completed)

will be decided by market forces in just the same way as is the ex cap price in a bonus issue. Rights issues are often accompanied by a forecast of the rate of dividend on the enlarged capital. Nevertheless, it is possible to calculate the theoretical ex rights price, together with other relevant calculations that will be explained below.

The ex rights price

This is the price that all shares, both old and new, will be expected to reach once the rights issue has been completed and the new shares are fully paid.

Let us look at a typical example. Suppose a company decides to make a rights issue of one new share for every three held, and the amount payable to the company for each new share is 80p (subscription price). Let us suppose that the price of the shares immediately prior to the rights issue is 100p. The ex rights price is calculated as follows:

3 old shares prior to the rights issue are worth	300p
+ 1 new share for which 80p is payable	80p
4 shares ranking pari passu after the issue are worth	380p
Therefore 1 share after the rights issue should be worth	95p

Thus the ex rights price is 95p.

This is the price that the shares will be expected to trade at on the stock market when the issue is complete. Ex rights means that the purchaser of these shares will have no right to the new shares (ex meaning 'without').

Price of the new shares in nil paid form

Because the new shares are expected to be worth the ex rights price of 95p, and because a payment of 80p must at some time be made to the company, the price of the new shares in nil paid form, i.e. nothing yet paid to the company, can be expected to be 15p (95p – 80p).

The formula for calculating the price of new shares in nil paid form is ex rights price minus subscription price. This price is the amount a third party would theoretically be willing to pay for each new share in nil paid form.

Value of the rights

This is the difference between the price of the shares prior to the rights issue commencing and the expected ex rights price. In our example the value of the rights would be 5p (100p – 95p).

This value of the rights is the amount (excluding deductions for costs) that a shareholder would expect to receive if he sold the rights attaching to a single share.

Note that the ratio of the value of the rights to the price of the new shares in nil paid form is in the same proportions as the terms of the issue (1:3 in this example). This is a useful check on arithmetical accuracy.

To calculate the number of new shares to be sold to enable a shareholder to finance the purchase of the balance of the new shares to which he is due, start with the formula:

$$\text{no. of nil paid shares sold} = \frac{\text{subscription price x no. of new shares allotted}}{\text{ex rights price}}$$

In our example, a shareholder who owned 3,000 shares immediately prior to the rights issue would have the right to subscribe to 1,000 new shares at 80p per share (i.e. one new share for every three old shares held). Using the formula we see:

$$\frac{\text{subscription price x no. of new shares allotted}}{\text{ex rights price}} = \frac{80 \times 1,000}{95}$$

$$= \underline{842.1}$$

As you can sell only full shares, the number taken up is rounded down to 157 shares (1,000 – 843).

Check: 157 new shares with a payment of 80p per share	=	£125.60 to pay.
Cash received from sale of 843 new shares at 15p each	=	£126.45.

Notes:

1   Always round down the number of new shares to be retained, because you cannot sell a fraction of a share. If you round up the number, then there will be a small extra amount to be paid.

2   If the sale of the nil paid shares raises more than 5% of the current market value of the investment, there is a potential capital gains tax liability.

Summary of rights issue calculations

Let us now sum up the position of our shareholder who owned 3,000 shares prior to the commencement of the one for three rights issue already described.

● When the shareholder has decided to take up the rights:

➢   prior to the issue the value of his holding was £3,000 (3,000 x 100p);

➢   after the issue has been completed he will own 4,000 shares expected to be worth £3,800 (4,000 x 95p), and the amount paid for the new shares to the company will be £800 (1,000 x 80p).

The net result is that our shareholder has paid £800 and the value of his shareholding is expected to increase by the same amount.

● When the shareholder has decided to sell his rights:

➤ prior to the commencement of the rights issue his shareholding was worth £3,000;

➤ after the issue has been completed his 3,000 shares should be worth £2,850. However, the expected loss in value of £150 has been compensated for by the sale proceeds of £150.

● The sale proceeds can be calculated in one of two ways:

3,000 x value of rights, i.e. 5p   = £150

or

1,000 new shares sold in nil paid form for 15p each = £150

● When he sells sufficient new shares to enable him to purchase the balance:

➤ prior to the rights issue his holding was worth £3,000;

➤ after completion of the formalities he now owns 3,157 shares expected to be worth £2,999.15 (3,157 x 95p).

Note: the 85p difference is caused by the rounding down shown above.

It will be seen that a net 85p will be left in the shareholder's hands, representing the difference between the amount of the sale proceeds and the amount due to the company on the subscription for the new shares and allowing for the fraction of a share that is rounded down.

● We can see from the calculations that the shareholder in a rights issue does not receive something for nothing. This reinforces the fact that the amount of the discount is immaterial, and that the investor's decision depends on the answers to the two questions:

➤ Do I wish to invest more money in this company?

➤ If so do I have the cash to meet the necessary subscription?

7   Vendor Placings as an Alternative to a Rights Issue

As we already know, one reason for a rights issue is to help to finance takeovers or acquisitions. An alternative method of raising finance for this purpose is a vendor placing.

For example, if Company A wanted to purchase a subsidiary from Company B for, say, £100 million in cash, a vendor placing would work as follows. A issues new shares to B, and simultaneously A's merchant bank buys these new shares from B for £100 million. The merchant bank will then place the shares with its own clients; usually institutional clients. A common refinement is to introduce a 'claw back' provision whereby the shareholders in A have the right to acquire the shares from the merchant bank on the same terms as are offered to the placees, and in priority to the placees.

Vendor placings cannot be made without the approval of the shareholders.

A variation on a vendor placing is a vendor rights issue. This is where the shares issued are purchased by a single buyer (usually an issuing house). The shares are then offered to the shareholders of the issuing company as in a rights issue. This avoids the dilution that takes place with a vendor placing.

8   Comparison of Capitalization and Rights Issues

We can now summarize the similarities and differences in the following table.

Table 4.2: Capitalization issue	Rights issue
1 A mere bookkeeping exercise that does not raise any cash.	A means of raising cash for the company.
2 The new shares are issued free to existing shareholders on a pro rata basis.	The new shares are issued at a price below the current market price to existing shareholders on a pro rata basis.
3 The ex cap price will fall in proportion to the amount of new shares issued, in theory. In practice the ex cap price will be determined by market forces.	In theory the ex rights price will fall in proportion to the new shares issued, but fall will be offset by the amount of cash payable to the company on the new shares. In practice the ex rights price will be determined by market forces.
4 The administration is by renounceable certificate.	Administration is by way of allotment letter.
5 The shareholder need not make any decisions.	The shareholder must decide whether to: (a) take up the rights; (b) sell sufficient new shares to finance purchase of the balance; (c) sell the rights; (d) do nothing.

9   Open Offer

An open offer is an invitation to existing shareholders to purchase shares in proportion to their holdings. It is often made in conjunction with a placing (see Unit 3, Section 9) which is made with the city institutions rather than to the private shareholders of the company. The open offer is usually made to the existing private investors who 'would find their stakes in the company watered down by this, so the company will usually make an open offer at the same time'. (Source: *Investors Chronicle*, 25 February 2000, page 82.)

The offer price is nearly always at a discount to the current share price, however there are some offers where the price is at a premium. A premium price can occur when the company is in urgent need of capital due to financial difficulties and needs a refinancing or capital re-organization to survive.

The shareholder will receive an assignable or transferable application form with an open offer, which has the facility to be split. He must pay for the shares straight away.

An open offer is basically similar to a rights issue. The main differences for our purposes are as follows:

● With a rights issue the shareholder receives a renounceable letter and with an open offer receives an assignable or transferable application form;

● With a rights issue there is a period of time, usually around 21 days, when the rights can be sold 'nil paid'. With an open offer the investor has to pay the full amount by the acceptance date - there is no concept of 'nil paid' with an open offer;

● Investors can sell the shares acquired via an open offer only once the new shares are issued;

● With a rights issue if the investor does nothing, the rights will be sold and the proceeds remitted to him (unless these are less than £3). With an open offer, if the investor does nothing he will receive no cash from the sale of the shares not taken up thus diluting his equity stake in the company.

Companies may prefer to use an open offer to raise funds because they receive their money more quickly than in a rights issue. It can also be cheaper to the company to underwrite an open offer than a rights issue because of the timing of the cash received from investors.

10   Allotment Letters and Letters of Acceptance

The functions of these documents

Letters of allotment or letters of acceptance are used in connection with a new issue by way of an offer for sale or an offer for subscription. With a rights issue a provisional allotment letter is issued. There is no practical difference between any of these documents and we can consider the terms to be synonymous.

When a new issue or a rights issue is made the published details, whether contained in listing particulars or in a prospectus, will state how and in what instalments the subscription is to be paid.

Having sent a cheque for the initial amount required on application, the successful investor will receive an allotment letter. This is a legal document that:

- Acts as a receipt for money paid to the company for shares;
- Gives details of the remaining instalments (if any) required;
- Can be exchanged for a share certificate when fully paid, on the terms set out in the allotment letter itself;
- Acts as a document of title to the shares prior to the issue of the definitive certificate. To transfer ownership, the holder signs renunciation form X. He then hands the allotment letter to the purchaser, who completes forms Y and Z. (Note some allotment letters have only a form Y.)

Specimen provisional allotment letter

See Fig. 4.1.

Figure 4.1: British Aerospace allotment letter

CAPITALISATION ISSUES, RIGHTS ISSUES AND ALLOTMENT LETTERS

SPLIT FROM No.	REFERENCE No.	ALLOTMENT No.
	04364667	00812502

THIS DOCUMENT IS OF VALUE AND IS NEGOTIABLE. IF YOU ARE IN ANY DOUBT AS TO THE ACTION YOU SHOULD TAKE, PLEASE SEEK PERSONAL FINANCIAL ADVICE FROM YOUR STOCKBROKER, SOLICITOR, ACCOUNTANT OR OTHER PROFESSIONAL ADVISER AUTHORISED UNDER THE FINANCIAL SERVICES ACT 1986 IMMEDIATELY.
IF YOU HAVE DISPOSED OF ALL YOUR ORDINARY SHARES AND/OR PREFERENCE SHARES (OTHER THAN EX-RIGHTS) PLEASE HAND THIS DOCUMENT TO THE PERSON THROUGH WHOM YOU MADE THE DISPOSAL FOR ONWARD TRANSMISSION TO THE TRANSFEREE.

Application has been made to the Council of the London Stock Exchange for the new Ordinary Shares which have been provisionally allotted, nil paid, to be admitted to the Official List. It is expected that such listing will become effective on 8th October, 1991. In the event that such listing does not become effective on or before 10.30 a.m. on 8th October, 1991 or such later time and date, (not being later than 10.00 a.m. on 15th October, 1991) as Kleinwort Benson Limited and the Company may agree, this document will not be of any value and will have no effect. The Listing Particulars relating to the Company (copies of which have been delivered for registration to the Registrar of Companies as required by Section 149 of the Financial Services Act 1986, are contained in the Circular from the Company dated 11th September, 1991 (the "Circular"). The definitions in the Circular apply in this provisional allotment letter.
The new Ordinary Shares and the provisional allotment letters have not been registered under the United States Securities Act of 1933, as amended (the "Securities Act") or under the securities laws of any state of the United States or of any province or territory of Canada and, accordingly, the new Ordinary Shares, this provisional allotment letter and the rights with respect to new Ordinary Shares arising hereunder may not be offered or sold, directly or indirectly, in the United States or Canada except pursuant to an exemption from, or in a transaction not subject to, the registration requirements under the Securities Act and in accordance with any applicable securities laws of any state of the United States or, in the case of an offer or sale in Canada, in accordance with any applicable securities laws of any province or territory of Canada.

BRITISH AEROSPACE Public Limited Company

Registered in England: No. 1470151   Registered Office: 11 Strand, London WC2N 5JT
RIGHTS ISSUE OF 117,398,242 NEW ORDINARY SHARES OF 50p EACH AT 380p PER SHARE PAYABLE IN FULL ON ACCEPTANCE NOT LATER THAN 3.00 pm ON 28th OCTOBER, 1991

THIS ENTIRE DOCUMENT MUST BE PRESENTED WHEN PAYMENT IS MADE

PROVISIONAL ALLOTMENT LETTER

```
0084696
UNITED REFORMED
CHURCH EAST MIDLANDS PROVINCE INC
57 CHATSWORTH ROAD
WORKSOP
NOTTINGHAMSHIRE    S81 0LD
```

At the office of the Registrar,
Lloyds Bank Plc, Registrar's Department,
Goring-by-Sea, Worthing, West Sussex BN12 6DA
Telephone: Worthing (0903) 502541

Latest time for:
Acceptance and payment in full
(See paragraph 2 below) — 3.00 p.m. on 28th October, 1991
Registration of renunciation — 3.00 p.m. on 21st November, 1991
Despatch of certificates — 12th December, 1991

At the office of the Registrar,
Lloyds Bank Plc, Registrar's Department,
Issue Section, P.O. Box 1000, 2nd Floor,
Bolsa House, 80 Cheapside, London EC2V 6EE
Telephone: London (071) 248 9822

Latest time for:
Splitting – Nil paid — 3.00 p.m. on 24th October, 1991
Acceptance and payment in full
(See paragraph 2 below) — 3.00 p.m. on 28th October, 1991
Splitting – Fully paid — 3.00 p.m. on 19th November, 1991

(1) Holdings of Ordinary and Preference Shares at close of business on 27th September, 1991	(2) Number of new Ordinary Shares provisionally allotted to you	(3) Amount payable on acceptance in full at 380p per share
	766	**£2910.80**

ORDINARY
PREFERENCE   **16000**

DEAR SIR OR MADAM: 7th October, 1991

1. Subject to and in accordance with the provisions of the Circular and this provisional allotment letter you have been provisionally allotted, subject to the Memorandum and Articles of Association of the Company, the number of new Ordinary Shares set out in column 2 above, at a price of 380p per new Ordinary Share. New Ordinary Shares have been allotted to holders of Ordinary Shares (other than certain overseas holders of Ordinary Shares) on the basis of 2 new Ordinary Shares for every 5 Ordinary Shares and to the holders of the Preference Shares (other than certain overseas holders of Preference Shares) on the basis of 1 new Ordinary Share for every 20.87508 Preference Shares held, in each case at the close of business on 27th September, 1991. Entitlements to new Ordinary Shares have been rounded down to the nearest whole number. New Ordinary Shares representing fractional entitlements have not been allotted to shareholders but will be aggregated and sold in the market for the benefit of the Company.

2. If you wish to take up the new Ordinary Shares provisionally allotted to you, YOU MUST COMPLETE THE NATIONALITY DECLARATION SET OUT IN BOX A ON PAGE 2 and send this **entire provisional allotment letter** accompanied by a remittance for the full amount payable on acceptance shown in column 3 above to Lloyds Bank Plc, Registrar's Department, Goring-by-Sea, Worthing, West Sussex BN12 6DA, so as to arrive **by not later than 3.00 p.m. on 28th October, 1991.** Provisional allotment letters may also be lodged for acceptance by that time, by hand, at Lloyds Bank Plc, Registrar's Department, Issue Section, P.O. Box 1000, 2nd Floor, Bolsa House, 80 Cheapside, London EC2V 6EE. This provisional allotment letter will then be returned to the person lodging it, duly receipted. Payment will constitute acceptance of the provisional allotment. Cheques should be made payable to Lloyds Bank Plc and crossed "Not negotiable — A/c British Aerospace". All payments must be made by cheque or banker's draft in pounds sterling drawn on a bank in the United Kingdom which is either a member of the Clearing Houses Association or which has arranged for cheques and banker's drafts to be cleared through the facilities provided for the members of that Association. No interest will accrue on payments made before the due date. The Company reserves the right, but shall not be obliged, to accept (i) provisional allotment letters and accompanying remittances which are received through the post not later than 10.00 a.m. on 28th October, 1991, the cover bearing a legible postmark with a date no later than 26th October, 1991 and (ii) acceptances in respect of which remittances are received prior to 3.00 p.m. on 28th October, 1991 from an authorised person (as defined in the Financial Services Act 1986) specifying the new Ordinary Shares concerned and undertaking to lodge the relevant provisional allotment letter duly completed in due course.

3. **Procedure in respect of rights not taken up:** In certain circumstances, as outlined above, acceptances received after 3.00 p.m. on 28th October, 1991 may be treated as valid. Subject thereto, if payment in full is not received by 3.00 p.m. on 28th October, 1991, the provisional allotment will be deemed to have been declined and will be cancelled. Any new Ordinary Shares not taken up will be sold in the market by not later than 3.00 p.m. on 31st October, 1991 if they can be sold at a price at least equal to the subscription price and expenses of sale. Any net proceeds after deduction of the subscription price and the sale expenses will be distributed pro rata, by cheque, to the provisional allottees originally entitled thereto, except that individual amounts of less than £3.00 will be retained for the benefit of the Company.

4. Further instructions as to how to deal with this provisional allotment letter are set out on pages 2 and 3 and should be studied carefully. These instructions are an integral part of this provisional allotment letter.

5. The new Ordinary Shares will, when issued and fully paid, rank pari passu in all respects with the Ordinary Shares now in issue, save that they will not rank for the proposed interim dividend in respect of the year ending 31st December, 1991 nor entitle holders to participate in the Interim Scrip Dividend Scheme.

6. Entire provisional allotment letters with the stamp of Lloyds Bank Plc duly impressed on page 1 or, in the case of renunciations, on pages 1 and 2 thereof, may, **provided that the nationality declaration set out in Box A on page 2 and, if applicable, the nationality declaration set out in Box B on page 4 have been duly executed**, be exchanged for share certificates from 22nd November to 10th December, 1991. In such cases, the share certificates will be despatched by 12th December, 1991. After 21st November, 1991, and pending the issue of share certificates, transfers will be certified by the Company's Registrar, Lloyds Bank Plc, Registrar's Department, Goring-by-Sea, Worthing, West Sussex BN12 6DA, against surrender of provisional allotment letters, stamped as aforesaid on pages 1 and 2. After 12th December, 1991, provisional allotment letters will cease to be valid for any purposes whatsoever and Lloyds Bank Plc will, subject to receipt of a duly signed nationality declaration, forward by ordinary post any share certificates remaining in its hands to the registered holder (or in the case of joint holders, to the first-named holder) at his registered address. All share certificates, other documents and cheques will be despatched through the post at the risk of the person(s) entitled thereto.

7. By taking up the rights represented hereby, you represent and warrant that no such rights are being taken up, directly or indirectly, by or for the account or benefit of a person in the United States, except rights being taken up by or for the account or benefit of qualifying U.S. institutional shareholders each of which has executed and delivered an investment letter (the form of which may be obtained from Lloyds Bank Plc, Registrar's Department) which, in the case of rights being taken up by a nominee for the account or benefit of a qualifying U.S. institutional shareholder, is delivered herewith or, in the case of a qualifying U.S. institutional shareholder with a registered address in the United States, was delivered directly to Lloyds Bank Plc prior to 2nd October, 1991.

By Order of the Board,
S.D. Windridge, Secretary.

Lodged for payment by:	**Received the amount payable on acceptance**	ACCOUNT NUMBER	ALLOTMENT NUMBER
		04364667	00812502
			766
			£2910.80
	Stamp for Lloyds Bank Plc and date		British Aerospace Public Limited Company
			Rights Issue of 117,398,242 new Ordinary Shares

Figure 4.1 cont.: British Aerospace allotment letter

PAGE 2

CONSOLIDATION PROCEDURE
Consolidation Listing Forms on pages 2 and 4

This procedure should be followed when it is desired to register the new Ordinary Shares comprised in several provisional allotment letters in the name of one holder (or joint holders).

The procedure is as follows:—

1. The Form of Renunciation (Form X on page 4) must have been completed on each provisional allotment letter.

2. The provisional allotment letters should be sorted into allotment number order by reference to the allotment number at the top of page 1.

3. The nationality declaration (Box A on page 2), the Registration Application Form (Form Y on page 4) including the nationality declaration contained in Box B on page 4 and the Duplicate Registration Application Form (Form Z on page 2) on the first provisional allotment letter (the "Principal Letter") should be completed.

4. Details of each provisional allotment letter (including the Principal Letter) should be inserted in allotment number order in both Consolidation Listing Forms on pages 2 and 4 in the Principal Letter.

5. The allotment number of the Principal Letter should be inserted in the space provided on pages 2 and 4 in each of the remaining provisional allotment letters.

6. All the provisional allotment letters should then be lodged for registration in one batch with the Principal Letter on top and the others in allotment number order.

7. If the spaces in the Consolidation Listing Form in the Principal Letter are not sufficient, the particulars may be listed on separate sheets (in duplicate) and attached to the Principal Letter.

FORM Z   DUPLICATE REGISTRATION APPLICATION FORM

In cases of renunciation, the person(s) completing the Registration Application Form (Form Y on page 4) must also complete the details below. Attention is drawn to note 8 on page 3 of this document regarding Stamp Duty Reserve Tax payable on the acquisition of the right to the new Ordinary Shares represented by this document

PLEASE USE BLOCK CAPITALS

(1) Given name(s) .... (in full)
Address (in full) ....
Surname ....
Mr., Mrs., Miss or Title ....

(2) Given name(s) .... (in full)
Address (in full) ....
Surname ....
Mr., Mrs., Miss or Title ....

(3) Given name(s) .... (in full)
Address (in full) ....
Surname ....
Mr., Mrs., Miss or Title ....

(4) Given name(s) .... (in full)
Address (in full) ....
Surname ....
Mr., Mrs., Miss or Title ....

FOR CONSOLIDATION PURPOSES	
LISTING FORM Duplicate	
ALLOTMENT NUMBER	NUMBER OF SHARES
TOTAL NUMBER OF LETTERS	TOTAL NUMBER OF SHARES
ALLOTMENT NUMBER OF PRINCIPAL LETTER	

BOX A   NATIONALITY DECLARATION – ALL JOINT HOLDERS MUST SIGN

To be completed by all **ORIGINAL ALLOTTEES** who wish to be registered as the holder(s) of the new Ordinary Shares represented by this document. Other persons who wish to be so registered should sign Box B.

I/We hereby declare that all new Ordinary Shares comprised in this provisional allotment letter and to be registered in my/our name(s)—

*(a) will not be Foreign-held Shares as defined on page 2; or
*(b) will be Foreign-held Shares as defined on page 2.
*delete as appropriate

Dated 1991

Signature(s) of ....

allottee(s) or ....

renouncee(s) ....

DEFINITIONS

"Foreign-held Share" means any Share (other than a Qualifying Share) of which any Owner is a Foreigner, Foreign Corporation or Corporation under Foreign Control.

"Foreigner" means any individual who is not a British citizen, a British Dependent Territories citizen or a British Overseas citizen by virtue of the British Nationality Act 1981

"Foreign Corporation" means:
(i) any corporation other than a corporation which is incorporated under the laws of any part of and which has its principal place of business and central management and control in the United Kingdom; or
(ii) a government or government department or government agency or body other than of the United Kingdom or any part thereof; or
(iii) any municipal, local, statutory or other authority or any undertaking or body established in any country other than the United Kingdom

"Corporation under Foreign Control" means any corporation (other than a Foreign Corporation):
(i) of which one third or more of the directors (or persons occupying the position of directors by whatever name called) are Foreigners or Foreign Corporations or are accustomed to act in accordance with the suggestions, instructions or directions of Foreigners or Foreign Corporations, or
(ii) of which shares carrying more than thirty per cent of the votes which are ordinarily eligible to be cast on a poll at General Meetings of the corporation are for the time being held by Foreigners or Foreign Corporations

"Owner", in relation to any Share, means:
(i) any person who holds, whether alone or jointly with any other person, any Share, or
(ii) any person on whose behalf any Share is, directly or indirectly, held, or with or to whom any holder of any Share has agreed or committed himself or become obliged (whether or not in a manner which is legally binding) to exercise or to refrain from exercising voting rights attaching thereto in accordance with that person's suggestions, instructions or directions

"Qualifying Share" means any share in the capital of the Company which is at the material time held by, or by a nominee or custodian trustee for, the trustees of:
(i) any retirement benefits scheme for the employees of a business or undertaking carried on (wholly or mainly) in the United Kingdom otherwise than by a Foreigner or Foreign Corporation which is, or is treated by the Commissioners of Inland Revenue as, an exempt approved scheme for the purposes of the Finance Act 1970, or
(ii) any charity which is registered under the provisions of the Charities Act 1960, or
(iii) any exempt charity within the meaning of that Act
other than (in any such case) a retirement benefits scheme, charity or exempt charity of which the majority of the trustees are Foreigners, Foreign Corporations or Corporations under Foreign Control

"Share" means any share in the capital of the Company (not being a share for the time being held by the trustees of any profit sharing scheme established by the Company and approved pursuant to the Finance Act 1978) which carries the right to vote on a poll at General Meetings of the Company, whether ordinarily or only in specified circumstances.

"United Kingdom" means Great Britain, Northern Ireland, the Channel Islands and the Isle of Man.

NOT TO BE WRITTEN ON

For use from 22nd November to 10th December, 1991.

Lodged for certificate by:
Name ....
Address ....

Note: To be completed only if the certificate is to be sent to a third party.

The title of the renouncee will not be recognised unless the Stamp of Lloyds Bank Plc appears in this space.

Figure 4.1 cont.: British Aerospace allotment letter

THIS PAGE MUST NOT BE DETACHED
INSTRUCTIONS

These instructions are an integral part of this provisional allotment letter
IF YOU ARE THE PERSON(S) NAMED ON PAGE 1

1. ACCEPTANCE AND PAYMENT (Latest time, 3.00 p.m. on 28th October, 1991)

If you wish to accept all the new Ordinary Shares provisionally allotted to you, you **must complete the nationality declaration and sign box A** and lodge this **entire provisional allotment letter with Lloyds Bank Plc, Registrar's Department, Goring-by-Sea, Worthing, West Sussex BN12 6DA, so as to be received not later than 3.00 p.m. on 28th October, 1991,** together with a remittance for the amount shown in column 3 on page 1 of this document. **Provisional allotment letters may alternatively be lodged for acceptance by that time, by hand, at Lloyds Bank Plc, Registrar's Department, Issue Section, P.O. Box 1000, 2nd Floor, Bolsa House, 80 Cheapside, London EC2V 6EE.** Cheques should be made payable to Lloyds Bank Plc and crossed "Not negotiable — A/c British Aerospace". All payments must be made by cheque or banker's draft in pounds sterling drawn on a bank in the United Kingdom which is either a member of the Clearing Houses Association or which has arranged for cheques and banker's drafts to be cleared through the facilities provided for the members of that Association.

Having made such declaration and payment, you need do nothing further if you wish to retain the new Ordinary Shares provisionally allotted to you. Share certificates will be despatched as indicated in paragraph 6 on page 1. If payment is received together with this entire provisional allotment letter at the places and dates referred to above but the nationality declaration has not been signed, the Company may at its discretion regard you as having accepted all the new Ordinary Shares provisionally allotted to you, subject to Article 40 of the Company's Articles of Association, and you will be asked to complete, sign and return a fresh nationality declaration returned to you with this provisional allotment letter. You will not be registered as the holder of any new Ordinary Share until a nationality declaration has been duly signed and completed.

2. RENUNCIATION (Latest time, 3.00 p.m. on 21st November, 1991)

If you wish to dispose of all the new Ordinary Shares comprised in this provisional allotment letter to one person, or to persons who will be joint holders, you must sign the Form of Renunciation (Form X on page 4) and send the entire provisional allotment letter to the person(s) to be registered or to the broker or other agent who has acted for you in the transaction to be dealt with in accordance with the instructions set out below.

3. SPLITTING (Latest time — nil paid, 3.00 p.m. on 24th October, 1991; fully paid, 3.00 p.m. on 19th November, 1991)

If you wish to have only some of the new Ordinary Shares comprised in this provisional allotment letter registered in your name(s) and to dispose of the remainder, or if you wish to dispose of all of the new Ordinary Shares but not all to the same person, you must have this provisional allotment letter split. For this purpose you must sign the Form of Renunciation (Form X on page 4) and forward this provisional allotment letter to L̶ ̶ds Bank Plc, Registrar's Department, Issue Section, P.O. Box 1000, 2nd Floor, Bolsa House, 80 Cheapside, London EC2V 6EE, to be received **not** la̶. ̶ than 3.00 p.m. on 24th October, 1991 if nil paid, or 3.00 p.m. on 19th November, 1991 if fully paid. The number of split provisional allotment letters ("Split Letters") required and the number of new Ordinary Shares to be comprised in each should be stated when this provisional allotment letter is sent for splitting and the aggregate of the new Ordinary Shares stated therein must equal the number of new Ordinary Shares stated in column 2 on page 1 of this document. On receipt of the Split Letters, you should keep the one representing any new Ordinary Shares which you wish to retain (paragraph 1 above applies) and send the other(s) to the person(s) to be registered or to the broker or other agent who has acted for you in the transaction, to be dealt with in accordance with the instructions set out below.

4. OVERSEAS SHAREHOLDERS — the attention of overseas shareholders is drawn to paragraphs 5 and 9 of Part V of the Circular. It is the responsibility of all such shareholders to obtain the requisite governmental or other consents or to observe any other formalities necessary to enable them to take up their rights. **Acceptance of the new Ordinary Shares comprised herein by any person shall be deemed a declaration by such shareholder as to the matters set forth in paragraph 9(a) of Part V of the Circular, in each case, as if the declarations as to such matters were set forth herein in full. In addition, the new Ordinary Shares comprised herein may not be taken up by shareholders in any jurisdiction in which any legal requirement would thereby be contravened.**

IF YOU ARE THE PERSON(S) IN WHOSE FAVOUR
THIS PROVISIONAL ALLOTMENT LETTER HAS BEEN RENOUNCED

5. ACCEPTANCE AND PAYMENT (Latest time, 3.00 p.m. on 28th October, 1991)

If this provisional allotment letter has been renounced before the payment due on 28th October, 1991 has been made, you must lodge the entire **provisional allotment letter, accompanied by a remittance for the amount due on acceptance, with Lloyds Bank Plc, Registrar's Department, Goring-by-Sea, Worthing, West Sussex BN12 6DA, so as to be received not later than 3.00 p.m. on 28th October, 1991. Provisional allotment letters may also be lodged for acceptance by that time, by hand, at Lloyds Bank Plc, Registrar's Department, Issue Section, P.O. Box 1000, Bolsa House, 80 Cheapside, London EC2V 6EE.** Cheques should be made out in accordance with the instructions set out in paragraph 1 above.

6. REGISTRATION (Latest time, 3.00 p.m. on 21st November, 1991)

If you wish to be registered as the holder of the new Ordinary Shares comprised in this provisional allotment letter, you must complete Form Y ̶ ̶luding the nationality declaration contained in Box B on page 4 and Form Z on page 2, and lodge the entire provisional allotment letter with L. ̶Js Bank Plc, Registrar's Department, Goring-by-Sea, Worthing, West Sussex BN12 6DA, so as to be received not later than 3.00 p.m. on 21st November, 1991.

Lloyds Bank Plc will record the renunciation and return pages 1 and 2 which, subject to receipt of the nationality declaration, may in due course be exchanged for a share certificate. **The title of the renouncee will not be recognised unless the stamp of Lloyds Bank Plc appears in the space provided on page 2.**

Unless these instructions have been complied with by 3.00 p.m. on 21st November, 1991, the new Ordinary Shares comprised in this provisional allotment letter, if paid for, will, subject to receipt of a duly signed nationality declaration, be registered in the name(s) shown on page 1, and thereafter will only be transferable by transfer in the usual common form, subject to stamp duty or stamp duty reserve tax.

7. SHARE CERTIFICATES

Share certificates will be despatched as indicated in paragraph 6 on page 1.

8. STAMP DUTY RESERVE TAX/STAMP DUTY

An agreement by you (whether as original allottee(s) or as subsequent transferee(s)) to sell some or all of the rights represented by this provisional allotment letter or a Split Letter (whether nil paid or fully paid) on or before the latest time for registration of renunciation will not be liable to stamp duty but the purchaser(s) will normally be liable to stamp duty reserve tax at the rate of 50p for every £100 or part of £100 of the actual consideration paid. If you are such a purchaser you need take no action if stamp duty reserve tax has been included in the contract note issued by the bank, stockbroker or other financial intermediary through whom you purchased the provisional allotment letter or Split Letter. In any other case, you should contact the Inland Revenue and pay the stamp duty reserve tax.

An agreement by you (whether as original allottee(s) or as subsequent transferee(s)) to sell the rights to the new Ordinary Shares represented by this provisional allotment letter after the latest time for registration of renunciation will be subject to *ad valorem* stamp duty (or, if an unconditional agreement to transfer the new Ordinary Shares represented in this provisional allotment letter is not completed by a duly stamped transfer within two months, stamp duty reserve tax) in each case payable by the purchaser(s) at the rate of 50p for every £100 or part of £100 of the actual consideration paid.

No stamp duty or stamp duty reserve tax will be payable on the registration of the original holder(s) of this provisional allotment letter of his/their renouncees.

9. OVERSEAS PERSONS The attention of overseas persons is drawn to paragraphs 5 and 9 of Part V of the Circular. It is the responsibility of all such persons to obtain the requisite governmental or other consents or to observe any other formalities necessary to enable them to take up new Ordinary Shares. **Application for registration of the new Ordinary Shares comprised herein by any person shall be deemed a declaration by such persons as to the matters set forth in paragraph 9(a) of Part V of the Circular, in each case, as if the declarations as to such matters were set forth herein in full. In addition, the new Ordinary Shares comprised herein may not be taken up by person in any jurisdiction in which any legal requirement would thereby be contravened.**

NOTE—Surrender of this provisional allotment letter purporting to have been signed in accordance with these instructions shall be conclusive evidence in favour of the Company and Lloyds Bank Plc of the title of the person(s) surrendering it to deal with the same and to receive Split Letters and/or share certificates. Provisional allotment letters, Split Letters, share certificates and remittances will be sent though the post at the risk of the person(s) entitled to them.

Figure 4.1 cont.: British Aerospace allotment letter

PAGE 4
ALLOTMENT
❋❋765❋❋

REFERENCE
04364667

ALLOTMENT No.
00512502

BRITISH AEROSPACE PUBLIC LIMITED COMPANY

RIGHTS ISSUE OF 117,398,242 NEW ORDINARY SHARES OF 50p EACH AT 380p PER SHARE

FORM X   # FORM OF RENUNCIATION

(Not available after 3.00 p.m. on 21st November, 1991.)

To be completed if the original allottee(s) desire(s) to renounce all the new Ordinary Shares comprised herein up to 3.00 p.m. on 21st November, 1991, or to obtain Split Letters, nil paid, up to 3.00 p.m. on 24th October, 1991, and Split Letters, fully paid, up to 3.00 p.m. on 19th November, 1991.

To the Directors of

BRITISH AEROSPACE PUBLIC LIMITED COMPANY

    I/We renounce my/our right to any new Ordinary Shares comprised in this provisional allotment letter in favour of the person(s) named in the Registration Application Form (Form Y) in relation to or including such new Ordinary Shares.

    I/We represent that none of the rights to the new Ordinary Shares which are being renounced hereby are owned by or for the account or benefit of a person in the United States.

> All joint holders must sign
> A corporation must execute under its common seal, which should be affixed in accordance with its Articles of Association or other regulations. Alternatively, a company to which section 36A of the Companies Act 1985 applies may execute this letter by a director and the company secretary or by two directors of the company signing the letter and inserting the name of the company above their signatures. Each of the officers signing the letter should state the office which he holds under his signature

Signature(s)
of
person(s)
named on
page 1

....

....

....

Dated .... , 1991

In the case of Split Letters, this Form will be endorsed "Original Duly Renounced".

FORM Y   ## REGISTRATION APPLICATION FORM

    THIS FORM SHOULD ONLY BE COMPLETED WHERE THERE HAS BEEN A RENUNCIATION. The entire provisional allotment letter must be lodged with Lloyds Bank Plc, Registrar's Department, Goring-by-Sea, Worthing, West Sussex BN12 6DA, so as to be received NOT LATER THAN 3.00 p.m. on 21st November, 1991, providing payment has been made by 3.00 p.m. on 28th October, 1991. Box A and Form Z on page 2 must also be completed. Your attention is drawn to Note 8 on page 3 of this document regarding stamp duty reserve tax, which may be payable on the acquisition of the right to the new Ordinary Shares represented by this document. The Company reserves the right to refuse to register any renunciation in the name of any person with an address in the United States or Canada.

PLEASE USE BLOCK CAPITALS

(1) Given name(s) ....
(in full)
Address (in full) ....
....

Surname ....
Mr., Mrs., Miss or Title ....

(2) Given name(s) ....
(in full)
Address (in full) ....
....

Surname ....
Mr., Mrs., Miss or Title ....

(3) Given name(s) ....
(in full)
Address (in full) ....
....

Surname ....
Mr., Mrs., Miss or Title ....

(4) Given name(s) ....
(in full)
Address (in full) ....
....

Surname ....
Mr., Mrs., Miss or Title ....

BOX B   **NATIONALITY DECLARATION – ALL JOINT HOLDERS MUST SIGN**

To be completed by all **RENOUNCEES** who wish to be registered as the holder(s) of the new Ordinary Shares represented by this document.

I/We hereby declare that all new Ordinary Shares comprised in this provisional allotment letter and to be registered in my/our name(s)—

*(a) will not be Foreign-held Shares as defined on page 2; or

*(b) will be Foreign-held Shares as defined on page 2.

*delete as appropriate

Dated .... ,1991

Signature(s) of ....

allottee(s) or ....

renouncee(s) ....

Registration is requested in the above name(s) of the new Ordinary Shares specified in this provisional allotment letter and in the several provisional allotment letters (if any) detailed in the Consolidation Listing Form totalling

☐   new Ordinary Shares.

* Insert the number of new Ordinary Shares to be registered which must be the number of new Ordinary Shares comprised in this provisional allotment letter, or, if the Consolidation Listing Form is used, the total entered in that Form

Control No. 085703

Stamp or name and address of Agent (if any) lodging this Form

FOR CONSOLIDATION PURPOSES

LISTING FORM
For instructions see page 2

ALLOTMENT NUMBER	NUMBER OF SHARES
TOTAL NUMBER OF LETTERS	TOTAL NUMBER OF SHARES

ALLOTMENT NUMBER OF PRINCIPAL LETTER

Printed by Burrups Ltd, St Ives plc London and Tokyo B60806/SH

As previously stated, letters of acceptance and allotment letters are for all intents and purposes the same. The specimen British Aerospace provisional allotment letter was in connection with a new issue by way of a rights issue.

Further points on allotment letters

Oversubscription

Sometimes the terms of the issue, as shown in the listing particulars or prospectus, ask for an initial payment on application, and a second payment on allotment. In such cases, the successful allottee must immediately return the allotment letter to the relevant authority, together with payment of the sum due on allotment.

When an issue is oversubscribed, and the allottee receives less stock than he requested, any surplus proceeds will be applied towards the allotment monies.

When the terms of the issue prescribe a long time lag between the payment on application and the next due payment, any surplus proceeds are returned to the allottee.

Splitting

This occurs when an allottee wishes to:

- Sell only part of his allotment, possibly with a view to using the proceeds to pay for the balance of a rights issue;

- Give away his allotment to two or more people, thus requiring the original to be split into two or more allotment letters.

Consolidation

It can happen that a purchaser acquires a number of allotment letters that he would prefer to consolidate into a single document.

The purchaser will complete the consolidation listing form on one allotment letter and send all the allotment letters to the issuing authority to be replaced by one new allotment letter.

Choices to be made by the allottee who receives a letter of acceptance or allotment letter

Whether the issue concerned is a new issue or a rights issue the administrative procedures whereby the ultimate buyer obtains the relevant certificate are the same.

The person to whom the allotment letter is sent, the allottee, has the following choices, as have already been described, for a rights issue:

- Retention – take up the shares represented by the allotment letter, and pay any calls due. The fully paid allotment letter will be replaced by a share certificate;

- Renunciation in whole or part, sell sufficient to finance the purchase of the balance, or sell all the shares represented by the allotment letter. In either case the allottee will sign form X, the form of renunciation, and send the allotment letter to his broker (preferably by registered post because it is effectively bearer in nature because it is signed in blank);

● Consolidation – the exchange of several allotment letters for a single one;

● Splitting, where the allottee wishes to sell or give some of the shares to two or more people, he will sign form X and send the allotment letter to the issuing authority with details of the desired split.

Lost allotment letters

If an investor loses an allotment letter, he must apply to the organization handling the issue to ask for a duplicate.

Before a duplicate can be issued, the investor will have to complete a letter of indemnity that basically promises to reimburse the issuing organization for any loss it may incur from issuing the duplicate document.

The letter of indemnity will require counter-signature from a bank or insurance company, and it will countersign only if the investor is creditworthy for the value of the underlying securities. Banks will ask the investor to sign an authority, known as a counter-indemnity, to authorize the debiting of the customer's account if the bank has to pay up under the letter of indemnity. Banks and insurance companies make a charge for joining in letters of indemnity.

11   Worked Example of Allotment Letter Calculations and Procedures

Mr A has made an application for £5,000 (nominal) in a new public offer for sale of a 15% debenture stock. The issue price of this stock is 98.5%: payment is 10% on application, 15% on allotment, and the balance in four months' time. The issue is oversubscribed and he receives an allotment of £2,000 (nominal) of stock. He wishes to transfer this allotment equally to his wife and his daughter (aged 30).

Indicate the procedure necessary from the time of completing the application form to the issue of the individual certificates in the names of Mrs A and of Miss A.

Suggested answer

● Mr A will have sent a cheque for £500 (10% of nominal amount applied for).

● He receives an allotment letter for £2,000 nominal which will indicate that the amounts due on application and allotment have been paid. The total due after application and allotment is 25% of the nominal amount of stock (2,000 x 25% = £500). The excess £300 submitted with the application will be used to pay the allotment monies.

● Mr A will require the allotment letter to be split. He therefore signs the form of renunciation (form X) and completes the detail of the required split. The allotment letter is then sent to the issuing house indicated thereon.

The issuing house will return two 25% paid allotment letters for £1,000 nominal each, and the form of renunciation will be stamped 'original duly renounced'.

● Mr A will give the new allotment letters to his wife and daughter who will each complete their names on the respective registration application forms, form Y and form Z (if there is a form Z).

The wife and daughter will pay the balance due on the stipulated date. This amount is computed for each allotment letter as follows:

➤ Full issue price 98.5% of £1,000   = £985

➤ Less: 25% of nominal already paid   = £250

➤ Balance due in four months' time   = £735

➤ There will be no brokers' commissions to pay.

Once the allotment letters are fully paid, the certificates will be sent in accordance with the procedures laid down in the allotment letter.

Summary

Now that you have studied this unit, you should be able to:

● describe a capitalization issue and the effect it has on a company's balance sheet;

explain the effect of a capitalization on the share price;

explain why a company makes a capitalization issue;

differentiate between a share split, share consolidation and a scrip issue;

describe the features of a renounceable certificate;

explain what is meant by a rights issue;

explain the reasons for a company to make a rights issue;

describe the advantages and disadvantages of a rights issue to the company;

understand the timetable for a rights issue;

list and explain the courses of action a shareholder can take in relation to a rights issue;

describe a deep-discounted rights issue;

in relation to a rights issue, be able to calculate:

➤ the ex rights price

➤ nil paid price

➢ value of the rights and explain what each of these means;

● describe a vendor placing;

● describe an open offer;

● describe the functions of an allotment letter;

● describe the choices an investor has in relation to an allotment letter.

5

THE STOCK EXCHANGE DEALING PROCESS

Objectives

After studying this unit, you should be able to:

- understand rolling settlement;
- describe CREST;
- describe how registered securities are transferred;
- explain how lost share certificates are dealt with;
- explain the Stock Exchange dealing costs;
- understand the purpose of contract notes;
- understand what bulls and bears are and the effects of their actions on the market;
- understand the dealing process;
- understand SEAQ;
- describe how SETS operates;
- explain Normal Market Size.

1   Rolling Settlement

On 18 July 1994 the Stock Exchange introduced rolling settlement. With rolling settlement a stock exchange transaction becomes due for settlement a set number of working days after the deal was made.

Rolling settlement for equities

Initially settlement for purchases or sales of equities (ordinary shares) was made 10 working days after the deal made (T+10). It was reduced to five days (T+5) in 1995 and will move to 3 days (T+3) in February 2001, then 2 days (T+2) in the future. This will bring the UK into line with European Stock Exchanges that settle between two and seven days after the deal is done.

Settlement for deals can be done by CHAPS transfer, cheque, or debit card.

Rolling settlement for company loan stocks

Company loan stocks have been on rolling settlement for a number of years and settlement is five working days $(T+5)$.

Cash settlement

Not all deals are settled on a rolling settlement basis. Certain deals are done on cash settlement when payment is due on the next working day after the deal has been arranged. In practice payment is due as and when stated on the contract note and periods of up to seven days from the date of the deal to the cash settlement date can be seen.

Cash settlement normally applies to transactions in the following securities:

- British Government stocks (gilts);
- Commonwealth and foreign government securities;
- UK corporation and county stocks;
- New issues in allotment letter or renounceable certificate form;
- Bearer bonds;
- Foreign currency securities;
- Unit trusts.

2   CREST and Stock and Share Certificates

Description and purpose of stock and share certificates

All owners of registered stocks and shares are legally entitled to share certificates showing the details recorded by the company registrar in the register of owners. There is no obligation to use CREST. However, the trend is towards dematerialization of stock and share certificates, where holdings exist only in electronic (uncertificated) form in CREST. The details that can be expected to appear on the certificate are:

- Name of the company or issuing authority;
- The type of stock or share;
- The holder's name (with or without the address);
- The number of shares or amount of stock represented by the certificate;
- Certificate number.

A certificate is merely a record of an entry in the register of shareholders, but the shareholder should take care not to lose it because missing share certificates can cause problems when ownership is to be transferred.

CREST is a book-entry transfer system with electronic messages passing between CREST and company registrars relating to changes in ownership of UK stocks and shares against payment. No certificates are issued for stocks and shares held on the CREST.

The CREST system gives the shareholder one of three options to:

● to hold share certificates in their own name. CREST provides facilities for investors holding certificates to sell their shares or for buyers to receive certificates if they wish to;

● to hold shares through a nominee account operated by a bank or stockbroker, which is likely to be held electronically in CREST, but does not have to be;

● to become a 'sponsored member' of CREST, meaning that shares are held electronically in the name of the individual investor, but the operation of the electronic interface with CREST is carried out by a bank or stockbroker appointed by the investor.

Note: CREST is the name of the system, the letters are not an acronym (i.e. an abbreviation of words to make a single word).

Lost share certificates (for non-CREST holdings)

When a shareholder loses a certificate, he can apply to the company registrar for a duplicate certificate. However, before such a document can be issued, the registrar will require an indemnity to which a bank, insurance company or stockbroker is a party.

The bank, insurance company or broker will agree to compensate the company registrar for any loss he may incur by issuing a duplicate certificate. This indemnity will therefore involve these financial bodies in a contingent liability, because in theory a claim, based on the original certificate, could arise at any time for the value of the shares represented by that document. Thus there is usually a charge levied for issuing indemnities, and the investor is asked to sign a counter indemnity agreeing to reimburse the financial institution for any claims it is required to meet. Most banks delete all reference to indemnities for lost share certificates 10 years after issue.

When the investor wishes to sell the securities, and only then discovers that his certificate is lost, he can save time by forwarding the indemnity to the selling broker along with a signed stock transfer form. There is no need to wait for the duplicate certificate in this case.

The moral of this story is to keep share certificates in safe custody at a bank, or in a nominee name, or hold in uncertificated form in CREST. By choosing one of these options there is less likelihood of losing the certificate.

Balance certificates

It is perfectly in order to sell only part of a share holding. In such cases the seller will surrender the original certificate and receive a new certificate for the unsold balance in due course. The stock transfer form signed by the seller will specify the number of shares he actually wishes to sell. If the shares are on the CREST system then an entry relating to the balance will be made.

3   Transfer of Registered Shares

Registered shares explained

A registered share is a share where the company concerned keeps a record of shareholders. This record, or register, is maintained by the company registrar, who records all changes of ownership. However, before he will record a change of ownership, the company registrar will require the share certificate and a stock transfer form (if held in certificated form) signed by the seller. Once these documents have been received, the company registrar will issue a new certificate to the buyer, having cancelled the old one.

Simple transfer of shares between two parties

It is not legally necessary for quoted shares to be sold on the Stock Exchange. A privately negotiated deal can be arranged, and in such cases the company registrar will change the registration details on receipt of the old certificate and signed standard stock transfer form.

4   Stock Exchange Dealing Costs

Broker's commission

The rates of commission are quoted as a percentage of the consideration, which is the number of shares multiplied by the dealing price per share or the amount of stock multiplied by the dealing price of the stock.

Broker's commission is, technically, negotiable, but brokers have their own set of commissions for private clients. In the exam you will be given the commission rates to use. Commission is charged on the consideration (i.e. the number of shares multiplied by the price). Examples of the calculation of commission and other costs are shown below.

If the deal is done via an agent, e.g. a bank, then the broker's commission will be divisible with the agent. This fact will be shown on the contract note.

If the investor is purchasing gilts or other fixed-interest stocks, the consideration has added to it, or subtracted from it, accrued interest. The broker's commission is calculated on the combined figures.

PTM levy

This is a levy to fund the Panel for Takeovers and Mergers. It applies to all deals (except gilts) of over £10,000 consideration, on either purchase or sale.

● Gilts are exempt from the PTM levy.

● On all other deals it is a flat rate of 25p on deals over £10,000 consideration.

Stamp duty

Stamp duty (also called transfer stamp duty) is levied on all purchases of equities at the rate of 0.5% of the consideration on shares. The minimum amount to be paid is 50p. Stamp duty on CREST holdings is rounded up to the nearest 50p and rises in 50p steps.

For shares held in certificated form (i.e. outside of CREST), the rate is also 0.5%, but the minimum is £5, rising in £5 stages .

Examples of the effect of dealing costs

(a) On Monday 10 January 2000 an investor purchases 5,000 shares in Alpha plc at 125p. Broker's commission is 1.65% on the first £7,000, and 1.2% on the next £3,000. The total payable would be, assuming the shares are held in CREST:

Consideration (5,000 x 125p)	6,250.00
Broker's commission (£6,250 @ 1.65%)	103.12
* Stamp duty (£6,250 @ 0.5%)	31.50
PTM levy	Nil
Total payable	6,384.62

The settlement day will be 17 January 2000 (T+5 **working** days after the deal was done).

* Stamp duty £6,250 @ 0.5% = £31.25 – this is rounded up to the nearest 50p, thus is £31.50.

(b) On the following day, 11 January 2000, the investor sees that the share price of Alpha plc has risen to 150p. He decides to sell the 5,000 shares he purchased the previous day. Explain how the settlement procedure will operate and the net profit he will make.

Consideration (5,000 x 150p)		7,500.00
Less: broker's commission		
£7,000 at 1.65%	115.50	
£ 500 at 1.2%	6.00	
PTM levy	Nil	121.50
Total receivable		7,378.50

NB: Stamp duty is charged only on purchases.

The settlement day will be 18 January 2000 (T+5 **working** days after the deal was done).

Even though the investor has bought and sold the same shares on consecutive days, he will have to send his cheque for £6,384.63 for settlement on 17 January, and will receive a cheque for £7,378.50 on 18 January.

His net profit is £993.88 (£7,378.50 – £6,384.62).

5 Contract Notes

A contract note is issued by a broker to a client as evidence of a deal that has been made on his behalf. The contract note includes the following details:

- Name and address of the broker;
- Whether the transaction is a purchase (bought) or a sale (sold);
- The full details of the security dealt in;
- The price, consideration and all charges, so as to show a total payment due to or from the broker;
- The bargain number;
- The date of the bargain and the time the bargain was effected;
- Settlement date;
- Client's name and address;
- The SEDOL code;
- Whether the deal was Certificated or Uncertificated;
- With a CREST deal, the CREST account number will be shown;
- Whether the broker/dealer acted as an agency broker or as a principal;
- The letters 'IF', indicating that the deal was done 'intra firm'; in other words the broker/dealer in effect acted as a principal and acquired the shares from the market making arm of the same organization.

The precise layout of the contract note will vary from broker to broker.

Points for the investor to bear in mind on receipt of the contract note

The most important step is for the investor to check the details to ensure that they represent the instructions that he actually gave the broker. In practice the few discrepancies that do occur can be sorted out with a minimum of fuss, provided the broker is notified immediately.

There may well be a difference between the price at which the shares were dealt in by the broker and the price at which the shares were quoted in the *Financial Times* of that day. The price shown in the *Financial Times* is the middle price of the shares the previous day at the close of business.

The contract note gives the time the deal was done in order that in the event of a dispute over the price the Stock Exchange can check the price ruling at the time stated on the contract note. All deals and all prices are recorded constantly for monitoring purposes.

The price will be different from the mid-price, even if the deal were done at the exact close of business because of the market maker's 'turn', that is the difference between the price at which he will buy (bid) and the price at which he will sell (offer). The bid price is always lower than the offer price, because the market maker would wish to profit on the deal. Thus if the shares were purchased the price would be above the mid-price, and if they were sold the price would be below mid-price.

A 'turn' of 2p would be quite common on a large NMS (Normal Market Size) share. For shares in which there are relatively few dealings the market maker's turn could be wider. The term 'narrow market' describes the situation where there are few transactions in a particular share.

Contract notes should always be retained. Purchases and disposals of securities must always be declared on the tax return for the year, and the necessary details will be shown on the contract note.

Ownership of the relevant securities vests in the purchaser from the moment the broker, acting as the purchaser's agent, makes a deal with the market maker. The 'bought' contract note is evidence of the date of ownership, and this can be important if there are any rights issues or bonus issues made around the time of the deal. The contract note also shows whether the purchaser is entitled to the next dividend or interest payment. The purchaser is so entitled unless the contract note specifically states 'ex div'. In cases where the contract note shows the transaction to be 'ex div', the next dividend will be the property of the seller of the shares.

The various abbreviations used with stock/share prices

These abbreviations are found on contract notes, in the *Financial Times* and the Stock Exchange Daily Official List (SEDOL).

- 'x' is an abbreviation for 'ex', meaning 'without'.

- xd or ex div = ex dividend.

  This means that the seller will retain the next dividend (or interest payment in the case of fixed-interest stocks).

  With shares the company will specify a date just before the due date of the dividends. All deals between that date and the date the next dividend is due will be ex div.

  xd applies to both stocks and shares.

- xr = ex rights. When a rights issue is made, the original shares are marked xr, to show that any rights made remain with the seller.

  If someone sold the shares 'xr' it would mean that he (the seller) would subsequently receive and be entitled to the provisional allotment letter for the rights. The ex rights price is the price at which all the shares are expected to settle once the rights issue has been completed.

  xr applies only to shares.

- xc = ex capitalization.

  When a capitalization issue is made, the original shares are marked 'xc'. The capitalization issue will be received by the seller of the shares, not the buyer, and the price of the sale will be the expected ex capitalization price.

  xc applies only to shares.

- xa = ex all.
  Sometimes a capitalization issue, rights issue and a dividend payment are made simultaneously. Ex all means that all capitalization shares, all rights and the next dividend are vested in the seller.

  xa applies only to shares.

- cd or cum div = cum dividend.
  This abbreviation is not found against a stock or share price, but if the stock or share is not xd then it will be cd. Cum dividend means that the purchaser will receive the next dividend or interest payment due.

  xd, xr, xc and xa are all abbreviations found in the *Financial Times*. However, xa does not appear in SEDOL and xd is shown simply as 'x' in SEDOL (Stock Exchange Daily Official List).

6   Bulls and Bears

Bulls

A bull is a general term for someone who expects share prices to rise. He will buy shares in the hope of selling them for a higher price within a few days. When a bull buys shares in anticipation of a short-term price rise which does not occur he is called a 'stale bull'.

With the advent of rolling settlement a bull will have to pay for the shares prior to receiving the sale proceeds. He may be able to come to some agreement with his broker to net the proceeds and pay interest or a fee for this service, but this is entirely up to the broker.

Bears

A bear is the opposite of a bull because he sells shares he does not own, hoping to buy the shares very quickly at a lower price. If the bear has correctly anticipated the price movement he will settle in the same way as described for a bull, except he will receive the cheque first and pay the purchase costs later. When the bear already owns the shares and sells because he expects their price to fall, he is called a 'covered bear'. The theoretical potential loss for an uncovered bear is unlimited, since the price of the shares could rise to infinity.

Bulls and bears will be seriously affected by the move to rolling settlement. Previously they were heavy account dealers, taking their profits (or losses) on settlement day. Rolling settlement will probably see a reduction in bull and bear activity, although some stockbrokers may offer a service for good clients along the old account lines – but at a fee.

Bull and bear markets

The terms 'bull' and 'bear' are also used to describe the mood of the stock market in general. If share prices in general are rising, the market is said to be 'bullish', and when prices in general are falling, the market is said to be 'bearish'. When there is a sudden turn in market sentiment, and prices that had been falling suddenly rise, uncovered bears are said to be 'squeezed'.

7   An Outline of the Dealing Process

Agency brokers (Stockbrokers) as intermediaries

An agency broker performs the function of the more commonly known 'stockbroker'. He acts as an agent between the investor and the market maker. Although the correct term for a stockbroker is an 'agency broker', there is a tendency still to use the term 'stockbroker'.

The investor and agency broker (stockbroker)

It is now possible for an investor to approach a market maker direct. However, the majority of small, private investors will still use the traditional intermediary system because market makers will deal only with high value, i.e. institutional investors. Information required by the broker in all cases will be:

- Whether to buy or sell;

- Full details of the security;

- The amount of stock or number of shares to be dealt in;

- Whether the deal is at 'best' (i.e. the best price that can be obtained at the time) or whether there is a limit on the price of the security above which a purchase must not be effected and below which a sale must not be carried out.

- Once the deal is agreed the investor becomes the owner of the shares.

- The broker will send out a contract note with full details of the deal. This acts as evidence of ownership, pending receipt of the certificate or CREST statement. Details of the transaction are input into SEAQ.

● On settlement the investor pays the broker.

Points that may require clarification when dealing in stocks and shares

Because the Stock Exchange works on the basis of dictum meum pactum or 'my word is my bond', it is essential that all instructions to the broker are clear and precise.

Two major complications can arise: first, the need to distinguish between 'buy' and 'invest'. The problem regarding 'buy' or 'invest' occurs when the security being purchased is denominated in stock units.

Take 9% Treasury 2008 with a price of £119.52 as an example. For this stock the price of every nominal £100 is £119.52. Thus the instruction 'buy £4,000 9% Treasury 2008' would involve a basic cost, excluding charges, of £4,780.80, whereas 'invest £4,000 in 9% Treasury 2008' would mean the purchaser was to pay a basic £4,000 excluding charges. (See Unit 7 for calculations relating to British Government securities)

Secondly, the need to ascertain whether a buy and sell order are contingent upon each other.

Sometimes an investor may simultaneously instruct a broker to buy one security and sell another. If both orders are 'at best', there is no problem, but when one or both orders has a limit, then complications can arise. Should the order with a limit prove incapable of being transacted, ought the other order to be executed? If the unexecuted order is a 'sell', then the client may have been looking to the sale proceeds to finance the purchase. If the unexecuted order is a 'buy', the client may not wish to go liquid (i.e. hold cash).

Thus clear instructions as to whether the execution of one order is contingent on another must be given at the time the client instructs the broker.

8 SEAQ and SEAQ International

SEAQ is the Stock Exchange Automated Quotation system. It is a continuously updated system that distributes market makers' bid and offer prices to the market. Market makers must maintain their prices during the Mandatory Quote Period (MQP), which is 09.00 to 16.30, Monday to Friday.

The main functions of SEAQ are:

● To convey prices and other information to dealers via terminals to enable brokers to obtain quickly the 'best prices' available for their clients;

● To provide an 'audit trail' to check suspicious price movements, e.g. because of insider dealings. This is why all equity contract notes must show the time as well as the date of dealing.

SEAQ International

SEAQ International provides market price information for the leading international stocks. It provides a firm dealing price in a large number of securities from many countries.

Spread and touch

Shares have two prices – the bid price (the price at which the market maker will buy shares) and the offer price (the price at which the market maker will sell shares). The difference between these two prices is called the spread.

Different market makers will quote different bid and offer prices for the same shares. The touch is the closest price between the different prices quoted by the different market makers. For example: the following bid/offer prices are quoted on SEAQ for Alpha plc:

> 198-203
>
> 197-201
>
> 199-204

The touch on these shares is 199-201 (i.e. the highest bid price and the lowest offer price. An investor who wished to sell shares in Alpha would go to the market maker offering the bid price of 199p, and an investor who wished to buy Alpha shares would go to the market maker quoting 201p.

The wider the touch, the less liquid the shares. The average touch is around 1.1%, but for shares in smaller companies which are infrequently traded the touch will be much wider.

9   SETS – Also Called The Order Book

The order book is based on an order-matching system in which firms display their bid (buying) and offer (selling) orders to the market on an electronic order book. When bid and offer prices match, orders are automatically executed against one another on screen. The book is open from 09.00 to 16.30, Monday to Friday. It provides fully automated electronic trading for FTSE 100 securities, stocks in the Eurotop 300 index and securities with traded options on LIFFE.

There are four types of order:

- **limit** – which specifies the size and price at which an investor wishes to deal. If matches can be found, the order is immediately executed, in whole or part. If not, it remains on the order book until a suitable match comes along within the expiry date or it is deleted;

- **at best** – buy or sell orders are entered on the system, and are executed immediately at the best price available in the system;

- **fill or kill** – these are either executed immediately in full or rejected. They may include a limit price;

● **execute and eliminate** – similar to 'at best' but with a specified limit price, so that it is matched immediately down to the specified price. Any unexecuted part of the order will be rejected.

Dealing in non-SETS securities

For non-SETS securities, market makers are obliged to display their prices to the market throughout the trading day for all of their registered stocks. They must also display their bid and offer prices and the maximum transaction size to which these prices relate.

Market makers compete to offer the best quote – and make their income by buying and selling stocks at a profit. The competing quote system is supported by the SEAQ service.

Market makers' bid and offer prices and sizes are shown, and these are used to create the SEAQ 'yellow strip'. The yellow strip identifies at any moment in the trading day, from an investor's point of view, the best bid and offer price for every SEAQ security, and the identities of up to four market makers quoting this price. Other market makers' names and quotes can also be viewed.

10   SEATS PLUS

SEATS PLUS is the Stock Exchange Alternative Trading System. SEATS PLUS mainly supports the trading of AIM stocks. SEATS PLUS is a combination of competing quotes and/or firm offers. These quotes are often from one market maker, or two or more in the case of AIM shares. The SEATS PLUS system aims to make it easier to trade in smaller company shares, including shares quoted on AIM.

11   Normal Market Size

Normal Market Size (NMS) is a figure calculated for each stock and based on a percentage of the stock's average daily customer turnover in the preceding year. The percentage is intended to represent the normal institutional bargain in a stock or share.

The NMS values range from 100 shares to 200,000 shares and the values are recalculated and amended every quarter.

Securities with an NMS of fewer than 2,000 shares are the less liquid securities. On the SEAQ (Stock Exchange Automated Quotation System) screen the NMS of a share is shown in thousands (thus if the NMS is 50, the normal market size of that share is 50,000). All shares with an NMS of 2,000 or more have the price of the trades shown immediately up to a maximum trade of 3 x NMS. Trades in excess of this size (called the Maximum On-line Publication Level (MPL)) will be reported 90 minutes afterwards. Trades in the less liquid securities will not be published on SEAQ, except where such trades are either agency crosses (i.e. one market maker selling to another market maker), or when the company is involved in a takeover bid. In such cases these trades will be published immediately.

NMS and Marketability:

To indicate marketability of the share. For example if Alpha plc has an NMS of 100,000 and a share price of around 350p, this means that the market considers a normal transaction in Alpha's shares to be worth £350,000. However Delta has an NMS of 500 and a share price of around 80p, thus a normal value transaction would be just £400. To the investor this indicates that the Delta deal involving more than 500 shares would show a bigger bid-offer spread, thus the shares are less marketable if the deal is in excess of 500 shares.

To increase marketability of shares, because the London Stock Exchange requires at least two market makers to display firm quotations on SEAQ for stocks with an NMS below 1,000 shares. Previously these smaller companies would not necessarily have had two market makers, thus marketability would have been poorer. (Poor marketability does not mean that shares cannot be bought or sold, but that the difference between buying and selling price is larger.)

To increase the number of deals done automatically, i.e. to utilize SETS.

Summary

Now that you have studied this unit, you should be able to:

- explain how rolling settlement operates;
- explain the effect of CREST upon share certificates;
- explain what happens when a share certificate is lost;
- list all types of securities that are dealt with on a cash settlement basis;
- understand the costs involved in dealing on the Stock Exchange and be able to calculate the costs of buying and selling;
- list the items that appear on a contract note;
- describe the purposes of a contract note;
- explain the meaning of 'x', 'xd', 'xr', 'xc', 'xa' and 'cd';
- describe how ownership of registered shares can be transferred;
- describe the purpose of a share certificate;
- describe bulls and bears, and bull and bear markets;
- outline the dealing process for buying or selling shares;
- explain the workings of SEAQ, SETS and SEATS PLUS;
- describe the classification of shares and normal market size.

6

PERSONAL TAXATION

Objectives

After studying this unit, you should be able to:

- understand the principles of income tax, capital gains tax, inheritance tax and National Insurance;

- calculate tax liabilities in respect of the above, given a description of an individual's or family's circumstances.

1 Introduction

Taxation is a very complex subject on which whole books have been written.

In this unit we look at three taxes:

- Income tax

- Capital gains tax (CGT)

- Inheritance tax (IhT).

    plus National Insurance that specifically affects individuals.

National Insurance is not specifically classed as a tax, but is levied on certain earned income. Many investors who are liable to National Insurance have little understanding of the impact of this on their disposable income or on the pension they will receive upon retirement.

Income, capital gains and inheritance taxes that affect the investment strategy of private individuals are examined in this unit so as to give an overview of tax in general. This unit will form a useful background to help in understanding the detailed yield calculations in the gilts unit, Unit 7. Likewise, an understanding of the general taxation scene will be essential when considering portfolio planning.

Briefly, income tax applies, as would be expected, to income, whereas capital gains tax applies when assets are bought and subsequently sold at a profit. CGT applies when an asset has actually been sold at a profit or otherwise disposed of, although as we shall see, there are many exemptions and allowances. An IhT liability can arise in two major situations

– when a person dies leaving a large estate, or on lifetime transfers that occur when assets are passed between individuals who are not husband and wife.

If an individual holds shares, income tax could apply in the case of dividends, capital gains tax could apply to any profit on a subsequent sale, whereas IhT could apply after the death of the holder when the shares were transferred to a beneficiary under the will, or if the shares were given to a party other than the spouse during the life of the donor.

Tax is calculated on a period called the 'tax year' which runs from 6 April to 5 April the following year.

2   Income Tax

Persons liable and income assessable to income tax

As stated above, the tax year begins on 6 April each year. With a few exceptions, all income received by an individual is assessable to income tax including the following:

- Pensions. It does not matter whether the pension is received from an ex-employer, or whether it is a state pension or regular payments from a private pension plan. All are taxable. A common error in examinations is for students to say that a person aged over 65 is a pensioner and therefore pays no tax. This is not true. A pension is taxable income and once this amount, together with any other income such as interest, exceeds the tax-free allowances figure then income tax will be payable;

- Salaries, wages, bonuses and commission;

- Interest from any source, dividends and the 'income' element of an annuity;

- Benefits in kind are, generally speaking, taxable only where the recipient earns £8,500 or more per annum or is a director of the company giving the benefits. These benefits include rent-free accommodation occupied by some employees, and company cars (calculated on car value and engine capacity);

- Tips;

- Lump-sum redundancy payments, but only on the amounts in excess of £30,000. The first £30,000 is tax free;

- Rents received and other income from land and property;

- Profits from business and professions;

- Certain Social Security benefits are taxable (knowledge of these is outside the scope of the syllabus).

Income that is not taxable

The main exceptions that constitute non-taxable income are:

- Interest on National Savings Certificates, Children's Bonus Bonds and TESSAs;

- The first £70 of interest received on a National Savings Bank Ordinary Account. Any additional interest over the £70 is taxable;

- Interest on contractual savings under any SAYE scheme;

- Dividends received under Personal Equity Plans (PEPs) and Individual Savings Accounts (ISAs).

3   The Meaning of the Term 'Allowance'

Not every penny of income is taxable. Everyone is entitled to an 'allowance', which is a monetary amount below which no tax is payable. The allowance to which you are entitled depends on whether you are married, divorced, single or widowed, or whether you are a one-parent family. Pensioners, or to be more precise, single people aged 65 or over and married couples where at least one partner is of that age, are also entitled to a special 'age allowance'. There is an allowance available to a person registered as blind, called the blind person's allowance. A widow receives a widow's bereavement allowance for the tax year in which her husband dies, and for the following tax year provided she does not remarry before the start of that year. However the allowance is not available to those newly widowed on or after 6 April 2000. (For full details of allowances see below.)

Rates of tax allowance

The allowances given relate to the tax year 1999-2000. The rates to be used in the examination are given on the paper itself, thus the rates do not need to be memorized.

	Personal allowances £	Married couple's allowances £
Basic personal allowance	4,335	1,970
Age allowance 65-74*	5,720	5,125
75 and over*	5,980	5,195
Widow's bereavement allowance	1,970	
Blind person's allowance	1,380	

*   If income is in excess of £16,800, the age allowance is reduced by £1 for every £2 of additional income.

Other allowances are available to offset against income tax. These relate to mortgage interest, pension contributions, and any sum expended wholly, exclusively and necessarily in the performance of duties. This final allowance is wide ranging and includes items such as subscriptions to professional bodies and safety clothing necessary for the performance of duties.

Personal allowances

- Basic personal allowance
- Married couple's allowance
- Single parent's allowance
- Widow's bereavement allowance
- Age allowance
- Blind person's allowance
- Mortgage interest
- Pension contributions
- Professional and union subscriptions.

Basic personal allowance

This is available to everyone. The moment a child is born he or she is entitled to a basic personal allowance of £4,335 to offset against any income he or she receives. The basic personal allowance is given to single people and to husbands and wives separately. The unused basic personal allowance or any unused part cannot be transferred to another person. Persons over the age of 65 receive a higher allowance.

Married couple's allowance

This is available to every married couple living together for all or part of the tax year. A husband is treated as living with his wife unless they are separated under a court order or a deed of separation. Persons over the age of 65 receive a higher allowance, as shown above. However, this allowance is being abolished on 6 April 2000, except for couples where one person is aged 65 or over on 5 April 2000.

Upon marriage, the married couple's allowance is payable for one-twelfth of each tax month (or part tax month) of marriage. (A tax month runs from the 6th to the 5th of the following month.)

The married couple's allowance is automatically given to the husband, but if his income is insufficient to utilize fully the married couple's allowance, the unused allowance, or part of the allowance, can be transferred to the wife. In order to transfer the allowance, the husband must give written notice to the Inland Revenue.

Note: it is only the married couple's allowance that is transferable, not the basic personal allowance.

Single parent's allowance

This allowance is paid to any single parent with one or more qualifying children resident with them. Only one allowance of £1,970 is paid, irrespective of the number of children qualifying.

A 'qualifying child' is one who is under the age of 16 in the current tax year or is over the age of 16 and receiving full-time education for a minimum two-year period. The allowance ceases when the child reaches the age of 18. This allowance is being abolished on 6 April 2000 and will be replaced with a new allowance called the Children's Tax Credit.

Widow's bereavement allowance

This allowance is paid only to widows who were living with their husbands at the time of the husband's death.

The allowance is paid of right for the tax year in which the death occurs, and for the following tax year provided that the widow has not remarried.

A widow with a qualifying child will receive both the widow's bereavement allowance and the single parent's allowance for the requisite period.

Note: the married and widow's bereavement allowances are restricted to 10% in 1999-2000 and being abolished on 6 April 2000.

Age allowance

There are two bands of age allowance: 65-74 and over 75. The age allowance is not available in full to every person in those age bands, but is scaled down if the income before deducting allowances exceeds £16,800. The scaling down is done by reducing the allowance by £1 for every £2 of additional income. The formula is:

$$\text{Age allowance} \quad - \quad \frac{\text{Total income (before allowances) of £16,800}}{2}$$

If the resultant figure is below the basic personal allowance, the basic personal allowance is given in place of the age allowance.

Note: the scaling down calculation is done only if income exceeds £16,800. In the case of a married couple where the age allowance is reduced below the basic personal allowance, the married couple's allowance is scaled down by the excess.

Blind person's allowance

This is available to anyone registered blind, and it can be transferred between husband and wife. The allowance is £1,380 and is given in addition to any other allowances.

Mortgage interest

The interest on the first £30,000 of a mortgage is subject to tax relief at 10%. For most borrowers this relief is deducted by the lender, and the relief is known as MIRAS – Mortgage Interest Relief At Source. If the lender is not in the MIRAS scheme, interest is paid gross and 10% tax relief will be given through the tax code, but only at 10%. Note: MIRAS is being abolished on 6 April 2000.

To qualify for tax relief the mortgage must be used to purchase the main residence.

The interest on the first £30,000 of a mortgage receives tax relief at 10% but the position with married couples needs to be clarified.

If the mortgage is in one name only, the tax relief will go automatically to that person.

When the mortgage is held jointly in the husband's and wife's name, the tax relief is shared equally between them. Each will be granted relief on interest up to £15,000 of the mortgage. However, the couple can make an election to have all the relief granted to one spouse, or split in any other proportion they may desire, e.g. 25% to the wife, 75% to the husband.

In the case of a MIRAS-eligible mortgage there is little point in opting for the interest to go to one spouse, because the Inland Revenue does not 'claw back' the relief granted if one spouse happens to be a non-taxpayer. However, if the mortgage is outside the MIRAS scheme, and one spouse does not have any, or enough, taxable income to take full advantage of the tax relief, then the election will be worthwhile.

If each individual owns a house and has a mortgage in his/her individual name on the house, he/she can still have relief on only one property.

If the couple are eligible for the higher age allowance, then the gross mortgage relief is calculated (even if the mortgage is under the MIRAS scheme). This interest is then offset against all other income to establish whether or not the higher age allowance can be claimed. Thus if the mortgage is in joint names, the election for the relief to be given to one spouse could be beneficial, because it would reduce the income and thus may reduce the effect of the '£1 for every £2 of every additional income over £16,800'.

Pension contributions

Contributions to pension plans are eligible for tax relief at the investor's highest rate of income tax. Most pension contributions are made to an occupational scheme, and the maximum percentage of salary that is allowable for tax relief is 15%. If an individual has a personal pension plan, the percentage of his salary he can pay into the plan is set by his age as follows:

Age	Personal Pension plan: maximum %
Up to 35	17.5
36 to 45	20
46 to 50	25
51 to 55	30
56 to 60	35
61 and above	40

Notes 1.   The percentages for personal pension plans are given on the examination paper.

2.   Pensions are covered in Unit 14.

Independent taxation

When calculating tax payable for a married couple, each person is treated entirely separately. The married man's allowance is given automatically to the husband, but can be transferred to the wife if he has insufficient income to utilize the allowance.

Income Tax Bands for 1999-2000

Once an individual's taxable income has been calculated by deducting the relevant allowances from their gross income, they pay tax as follows:

Taxable income	Rate of tax (%)
Up to £1,500	10 (lower rate)
£1,501 to £28,000	23 (basic rate)
On the remainder	40

The 10% band is called lower rate tax, the 23% rate is called basic rate tax, and the 40% rate higher rate tax.

Note: Where basic rate tax is referred to within the text, the basic rate is the 23% rate.

4   The Income Tax Position of Dividends and Interest

Tax position of dividends

Dividends are paid net of 10% tax, and all recipients must declare such dividends on their income tax return. The company that pays the dividend has already deducted 10% tax at source, thus having already borne tax the dividend has a tax credit of 10%. In order to calculate the tax implications we must first of all 'gross up' the net dividend. This means that the amount of the dividend is multiplied by 100 and divided by 100 less 10%. Thus the dividend is grossed up by 100/90.

Other things being equal, there will in effect be no change to the net dividend a company will pay out to its shareholders, only to the attached tax credit and consequently the gross value of the dividend. Basic rate taxpayers will not be affected by the change to the taxation of dividends because when they receive their net dividend they will be deemed to have met their tax liability in full. The income tax due on the dividend at the new rate of 10% will already have been deducted at source.

However, non-taxpayers and tax-exempt investors such as pension funds, charities and PEP investors will all suffer a fall in income as a result of the new tax regime.

Non-taxpayers and most institutional investors cannot reclaim the 10% tax credit. However special rules apply to shares held in a PEP or an ISA, which will have the tax credit paid into the account up to 5 April 2004. Registered charities will receive a reducing proportion of the tax credit up to 5 April 2004.

Higher-rate taxpayers will have to pay a total of 32.5% tax on the gross dividend, which will satisfy the 40% tax liability.

'Gross' means before tax, and if I receive a dividend of £90 net of basic tax, it is the equivalent of £100 of taxable income, assuming I am a basic-rate taxpayer. In this case, ignoring the timing implications, £100 gross would be worth only £90 after deduction of basic-rate tax, therefore £90 net of basic tax is the equivalent of £100 gross.

Numerical example of taxation as applied to dividends

Suppose a shareholder received a dividend cheque for £168.75. What are the tax implications?

First of all we gross up the £168.75 to obtain a gross equivalent of £187.50, i.e.

$$\frac{168.75 \times 100}{(100 - 10)} \quad = \quad £187.50$$

We shall then study the effect which will depend on the tax position of the shareholder.

If the shareholder is a non-taxpayer

	£
Gross equivalent	187.50
Less amount of tax deducted at source (10%),	
i.e. tax credit	18.75
Net paid by company	£168.75

The Inland Revenue will NOT refund £18.75 to the non-taxpayer. Thus the dividend is worth £168.75 to the non-taxpayer.

If the shareholder is a 10% taxpayer

The gross equivalent of the dividend is £187.50. The shareholder has no further liability to income tax, but cannot reclaim the tax deducted at source. Thus the dividend is worth £168.75 to the 10% taxpayer.

If the shareholder is a basic-rate taxpayer

As far as the Inland Revenue is concerned the 10% tax credit satisfies the basic rate taxpayer's liability to any further tax on the dividend. Thus the dividend is worth £168.75 to the 23% taxpayer.

If the shareholder pays tax at the top rate of 40%

	£
Gross equivalent	187.50
Less amount deducted at source	18.75
Net paid by company	£168.75

In this case there is a further tax liability of £42.19 calculated thus:

	£
Gross equivalent	187.50
Tax due at 32.5%	60.94
Less tax already paid by company	18.75
Tax due to Inland Revenue	£42.19

Another way of looking at this is to say that he must pay a further 22.5% (32.5% - 10%) on the gross amount. Thus the dividend is worth £126.56 to the 40% taxpayer.

Tax position of interest

If interest is paid by a company on a loan stock, by a bank or building society, or on a British Government security, the position is that 20% tax is deducted at source. The tax deducted at 20% satisfies a 20% and basic-rate taxpayers' liability to tax. Thus, interest and dividends are treated differently for tax purposes.

Interest paid on British Government securities can be paid gross. Interest paid on National Savings Bank accounts is automatically paid gross (i.e. without the deduction of tax). In such a case the non-taxpayer will simply declare the interest, but have no further liability for tax. The 20% and 23% taxpayers will have to pay tax at 20% and the 40% taxpayer will have to pay tax at 40% on the gross interest.

If interest is paid by a bank or building society, it is paid with 20% tax deducted. However non-taxpayers can have the interest paid gross upon signing a declaration that they are non-taxpayers. Thus dividends and interest are treated differently for income tax purposes.

Numerical example of taxation as applied to bank, building society or loan stock interest

Taking the amount of interest paid as being £150 from any of the above holdings, the tax implications are as follows:

If the investor is a non-taxpayer

Gross equivalent	187.50
Less tax deducted at source (20%)	37.50
Net interest paid	£150.00

The Inland Revenue will refund the tax deducted of £37.50 to the non-taxpayer. Thus the interest is worth £187.50 after the tax refund.

If the investor is a 20% taxpayer

Gross equivalent	187.50
Less tax deducted at source	_37.50_
Net interest paid	**£150.00**

This satisfies the 20% taxpayer's tax liability, thus the interest is worth £150 after tax.

If the investor is a basic-rate taxpayer

As far as the Inland Revenue is concerned, the 20% tax deducted at source satisfies the investor's tax liability. Thus the interest is worth £150.

If the investor is a 40% taxpayer

Gross equivalent	187.50
Less tax deducted at source	_37.50_
Net interest paid	150.00
Additional tax liability at 20%	_37.50_
Interest after tax	**£112.50**

The 40% taxpayer is liable to a further 20% (40% − 20%) tax on the gross equivalent interest, i.e. £37.50. He therefore receives £112.50 after his tax liability has been met.

Summary of tax position re dividends and interest

	INTEREST	DIVIDENDS
Rate of tax deducted	20%	10%
Satisfies basic rate liability?	Yes	Yes
Reclaimable by non-taxpayer?	Yes	No
Higher rate of tax charged	20% (40-20)	32.5% (but the 10% tax deducted is offset against this amount)
Net interest/dividend grossing up	<u>100</u> **80**	<u>100</u> **90**

Note: changes are being made to the taxation of Interest, but final details are not available at the time of writing (December 1999)

5   National Insurance

The impact on investment decisions of National Insurance contributions must be assessed. In effect, this means that the calculations of an investor's marginal rate of income tax will now have to include the effect of National Insurance contributions where they are applicable.

Who pays National Insurance contributions?

Class 1 contributions

You must pay National Insurance (Class 1 contributions) if you are:

- Employed in Great Britain or Northern Ireland;

- Aged between 16 and 60 (women), or 16 and 65 (men);

- Earning above the lower earnings limit, which is £66 per week (£3,432 per annum).

The earnings ceiling for National Insurance is £500 per week – £26,000 per annum. The amount paid then depends upon whether your pension is contracted in to SERPS (State Earnings Related Pension Scheme) or contracted out of SERPS. Employees who are contracted out of SERPS will be making payments into an occupational (employer's 'approved') pension scheme that is contracted out of SERPS. An employee who is contracted out will receive the basic state pension on retirement, but not the additional pension from the state, i.e. the SERPS pension.

The 1999-2000 Class 1 contribution rates are:

Employee Weekly earnings	On the first £66	On the remainder	
		Contracted out	Not contracted out
Up to £65.99	Nil	Nil	Nil
£66 to £500	2%	8.4%	10%
Over £500	Nil	Nil	Nil

Note: if earnings are £66 per week or more, then all the earnings are subject to National Insurance, not just the excess over £66. All rates necessary for tax calculations in the examination will be given on the question paper. None of the above rates needs to be memorized.

Class 2 contributions

Most self-employed people will pay Class 2 contributions, some will also have to pay Class 4. Class 2 contributions are paid at a flat rate of £6.55 per week, however much you earn. However, self-employed people earning less than £3,770 p.a. may be granted the 'Small Earnings Exception', thus having no liability to Class 2 contributions. Class 2 contributions are not payable by people aged under 16 or over 60 (women) or 65 (men). Most basic state benefits are available to Class 2 contributors, the major exception being unemployment benefit.

Class 3 contributions

These contributions are entirely voluntary and help to provide for the basic state pension or widow's benefit if:

- There is no liability to Class 1 or Class 2 contributions; or

- The self-employed person has the 'Small Earnings Exception' from Class 2 contributions granted; or

- The individual does not have a good enough contribution record to qualify for benefit, e.g. a married woman who has taken several years out of employment to raise a family may not have a good enough contribution record to gain full benefits on returning to work. The rate of the contributions is a flat rate of £6.45 per week.

Class 4 contributions

Self-employed people whose profits or gains are between £7,530 (lower profits limit) and £26,000 (upper profits limit) are assessed at 6% of profits and gains between those limits. The maximum amount paid in Class 4 contributions can be deducted from profits before working out the income tax due. Thus, such a deduction reduces the amount of income liable to tax, reducing the amount of income tax payable. This is the ONLY class of National Insurance Contributions that can be offset against income tax.

To summarize, the four classes of National Insurance are paid by:

- Class 1   Employer and employee

- Class 2   Self-employed (at a basic flat rate)

- Class 3   Voluntary contribution

- Class 4   Self-employed on profits or gains.

6   Examples of Income Tax and National Insurance Calculations

The allowances and tax rates used are given above.

(a)   A married man aged 50 whose wife does not work earns £42,000 gross during 1999-2000 and makes pension contributions to a contracted-out pension scheme of £2,000. The amount of income tax and National Insurance he would pay would be:

	£	£
(i) Gross income		42,000
Less: basic personal allowance	4,335	
Pension contributions	2,000	6,335
Taxable income		£35,665
Tax payable:		£
On first £1,500 at 10% =		150.00
On next £26,500 at 23% =		6,095.00
On remaining £7,665 at 40% =		3,066.00
Tax payable		9,311.00
Less married couple's allowance (£1,970 at 10%)		197.00
Income tax payable		£9,114.00

(ii) National Insurance

£3,432*	at 2%	68.64
£22,568**	at 8.4%	1,895.71
£26,000		£1,964.35

* Calculated. £66 x 52 = £3,432

** Calculated (£500 – £66) x 52 = £22,568

Thus he pays a total of £11,078.35 income tax and National Insurance.

(b) John Smith is a widower aged 69, and has a gross income of £12,960.

Tax position		£
Gross income		12,960.00
Less: age allowance (65-74)		5,720.00
Taxable income		£7,240.00
Tax payable:	£1,500 at 10% =	150.00
	£5,740 at 23% =	1,320.20
	Tax payable	£1,470.20

No liability to National Insurance because he is over 65.

(c) Martin Jones is aged 77, married and has a gross income of £17,200. His wife does not have any income in her own right.

Tax position
Because his gross income exceeds £16,800, the age allowance will have to be scaled down thus:

$$£5,980 \quad - \quad \frac{£17,200 - £16,800}{2} \quad = \quad £5,980 - £200$$

Reduced age allowance   = £5,780

Because £5,780 is above the basic personal allowance, the age allowance is reduced by £200 to £5,780. The married couple's age allowance is unchanged at £5,195.

	£	£
Gross income		17,000
Less: reduced age allowance		5,780
Taxable income		£11,220
Tax payable:	1,500 at 10% =	150.00
	9,720 at 23% =	2,235.60
	Tax payable =	2,385.60
Less married couple's age allowance (£5,195 at 10%)	519.50	
		£1,866.10

(d) Judy Pearson is a single, aged 38 and earns £45,000 p.a. She makes contributions to a personal pension plan of £10,000 p.a.

Tax position
Maximum eligible pension contributions into her personal pension plan are 20% of £45,000 = £9,000 (20% is for age 36-45). Thus £1,000 of the pension payments are not eligible for tax relief. Personal pensions are not part of SERPS, thus she will pay the contracted-out rate of National Insurance.

	£	£
Gross income	45,000	
Less: basic personal allowance	4,335	
Pension contributions	9,000	13,335
Taxable income		£31,665
Tax payable:		
10% on £1,500 =		150.00
23% on £26,500 =		6,095.00
40% on £3,665 =		1,466.00
Income tax payable		£7,711.00

National Insurance payable

	£
£3,432 at 2%	68.64
£22,568 at 8.4%	1,895.71
£26,000	£1,964.35

Thus she pays a total of £9,675.35 income tax and National Insurance.

(e) Peter Henderson is aged 23, married, with a gross unearned income of £3,000 p.a. as a student. His wife Susan is aged 24 and earns £9,500 p.a. gross. She pays pension contributions of 5% of her salary into a SERPS scheme.

Peter's tax position	£
Gross income	3,000
Less: basic personal allowance	4,335
Taxable income	Nil

Married couple's allowance automatically goes to the husband, but he cannot utilize this allowance. Peter is a non-taxpayer. (There is no refund of unused allowances.)

Peter is not liable to National Insurance because his income is unearned.

Susan's tax position	£	£
Gross income		9,500
Less: basic personal allowance	4,335	
Pension contributions	475	4,810
		4,690
Tax payable		
£1,500 at 10% =		150.00
£3,190 at 23% =		733.70
		£883.70
National Insurance		£
£3,432 at 2%		68.64
£6,068 at 10%		£606.80
£9,500		£675.44

However, as a couple they have not organized their affairs in the most tax efficient manner. Because Peter is a non-taxpayer, he is wasting the benefit of the transferable married couple's allowance. They should apply jointly to the Inland Revenue for this to be transferred to Susan. The effect on Susan's tax position would be:

	£	£
Gross income		9,500
Less: basic personal allowance	4,335	
Pension contribution	<u>475</u>	<u>4,810</u>
		<u>4,690</u>
Tax payable: £1,500 at 10% =		150.00
£3,190 at 23% =		<u>733.70</u>
		883.70

Less married couple's allowance transferred to Susan:

£1,970 at 10%		<u>197.00</u>
Taxable income		<u>£686.70</u>

Note: the National Insurance position is unchanged. There is a total saving of income tax of £197.00 (£883.70-£686.70).

Peter will still be a non-taxpayer because his gross income remains below the basic personal allowance.

7　Capital Gains Tax (CGT)

Introduction

Capital gains tax is levied when assets are purchased and subsequently sold at a profit. All 'disposals' or sales of assets subject to CGT are to be declared on the tax return so that the Inland Revenue can calculate the total taxable capital gains for the tax year. If a disposal of an asset is made not by sale but by disposing of it in some other way, e.g. by way of gift, by total destruction or, in the case of shares in a company declared insolvent, the loss is treated as a disposal. If, at the end of the tax year, there are net capital losses, these can be carried forward to a future year and offset against future gains. There is an annual exemption of £7,100 (1999-2000) per person which means that an investor with total chargeable gains of £7,100 or less in 1999-2000 will not pay CGT. Any chargeable gains in excess of £7,100 are taxable at the investor's marginal rate of income tax, although it is still called capital gains tax. The chargeable gains in excess of the £7,100 allowance are added to the taxable income to establish the investor's marginal rate of tax. Any unused part of the £7,100 exemption cannot be carried forward. Husbands and wives each have their own CGT allowance. Any unused allowance is not transferable between husband and wife.

Any purchases or sales of assets (basically stocks and shares for our purposes) must be recorded on the investor's tax return. Most tax experts suggest that the Inland Revenue may not take the indexation allowance into consideration unless the investor draws their attention to it. Ideally the investor should submit the details of the indexation allowance calculation on his tax return, but at the very least he should specifically request the Inland Revenue to take the allowance into account.

8 Investors Who are Subject to CGT and Assets that may Incur CGT on Disposal

In the terms of the Inland Revenue a 'chargeable person' is either UK resident or ordinarily resident for the year in which the relevant disposal occurs, and has disposed of a 'chargeable asset' during the tax year. Any form of property in the widest sense is a chargeable asset, even if the property is situated outside the UK.

Any losses incurred on disposal of chargeable assets are termed an 'allowable loss'. Allowable losses are set off against chargeable gains to establish the net taxable gain. However, not every asset will incur a chargeable gain or establish an allowable loss on disposal.

9 Assets that are Outside the Scope of CGT

The main exceptions that are outside the scope of CGT are gains or losses in connection with:

- British coins, including post-1836 gold sovereigns;

- British Government securities (more commonly called gilts), stocks issued by public corporations and local authorities;

- Chattels where the sale proceeds of an individual item are below £6,000;

- Company fixed-interest loans or debentures (but not convertible loan stocks);

- Foreign currency or sterling that was acquired for family or personal expenditure;

- Gambling winnings, including prises from premium bonds;

- Life insurance policy proceeds in the hands of the policyholder or his beneficiary;

- Medals and decorations for valour so long as they have been sold by the original recipient or by the recipient of these medals by way of a legacy;

- National Savings certificates, yearly plan, premium bonds, SAYE schemes, personal equity plans (PEPs) and Individual Savings Accounts (ISAs);

- Sale of a dwelling house that was the vendor's only or principal residence prior to such disposal;

- Sale of a property occupied rent-free by a dependent relative as his or her main residence, provided the property was so occupied before 6 April 1988;

- Wasting assets, i.e. items that have a predictable life of less than 50 years e.g. motor cars.

10 Bodies that are Exempt from CGT

These are:
- Registered charities
- Pension funds
- Friendly societies
- Non-residents.

11 Indexation Allowance on Capital Gains

The indexation allowance was first introduced by the Finance Act 1985 and amended by the Finance Acts 1988, 1994 and 1998. It takes into account the fact that many capital gains are created or increased by inflation. All gains are subject to indexation relief on the value at 31 March 1982 or cost if acquired after this date.

The Finance Act 1994 altered the manner by which the indexation allowance can reduce the taxable capital gain in real terms, but cannot be used to turn a monetary gain into an indexed capital loss nor to increase a monetary capital loss by application of the indexation allowance. This ruling came into force for disposals made on or after 30 November 1993.

Effect of the indexation allowances and taper relief on capital gains

Indexation allowance enabled gains to be identified on a 'real gain' basis, i.e. removing the effect of inflation. The Finance Act 1998 froze the indexation allowance as at 5 April 1998 when the RPI was 162.6. Taper relief was introduced, which alters the way capital gains are calculated.

Taper relief

Taper relief reduces gains on a sliding sale according to the COMPLETE number of years, up to a maximum of 10, that an asset has been held from purchase or 6 April 1998. For assets held prior to 6 April 1998, indexation relief is applied to the cost up to that date and taper relief applied to that indexed cost according to the number of years held subject to a maximum of 10 years.

For assets subject to CGT and purchased after 6 April 1998, taper relief does not apply until Year 3 of ownership.

For assets purchased prior to 17 March 1998 an extra year is added, e.g. an asset purchased in February 1998 and sold in June 2002 receives 5 years taper relief (4 complete years plus the extra year because it was purchased prior to 17 March 1998).

Taper relief and gains on sale of assets

Number of whole years in qualifying holding period	Percentage reduction available %	Percentage of gain chargeable
1	0	100
2	0	100
3	5	95
4	10	90
5	15	85
6	20	80
7	25	75
8	30	70
9	35	65
10 or more	40 maximum	60 maximum

12   How to Calculate the CGT Payable on Disposal of Shares

Calculation of indexation factor

Calculate the indexation factor using the formula

$$\frac{RD - RI}{RI}$$ worked to 3 decimal places

RD is the Retail Price Index (RPI) in the month the sale took place (disposal) up to April 1998.

RI is the RPI in the month the shares were purchased, or the RPI for March 1982 if the shares were bought before this date.

Apply the indexation factor to the cost of the shares or the March 1982 value if held at that date. The factor is applied by first multiplying it to the cost/March 1982 value, then adding it to the cost/March 1982 value.

If the shares were purchased before March 1982 the indexation factor (calculated on the March 1982 RPI) can be applied to the purchase cost, however this would be of use only if the purchase cost were higher than the March 1982 value.

Calculate the taxable gain as follows – **taper relief not applicable**:

£

Net sale proceeds

Less purchase cost adjusted by indexation allowance _____

Taxable gain ========

Taper relief applicable:

£

Net sale proceeds

Less purchase cost adjusted by indexation allowance _____

Gain before taper relief

Number of years taper relief % _____

Taxable gain ========

The cost of shares includes all dealing costs, and the sale proceeds are the net proceeds after dealing costs. If the resultant figure shows an indexed loss, then the actual taxable gain/loss will be NIL.

Work out the tax
Note: the Inland Revenue can provide a free leaflet giving the market prices of all quoted shares on 31 March 1982. This will enable the investor to establish the amount to which he should apply the indexation allowance for shares bought before March 1982.

Calculation of CGT when more than one purchase of the same shares has been made – the process known as 'share pooling'.

As sometimes happens, investors make a further investment in the same class of a company's shares at a later date. In this case CGT is calculated thus:

(a) Calculate the indexation factor for the period between first and second purchases. Apply the factor to the original (or March 1982) cost. This gives you the starting cost for the next step;

(b) Calculate the indexation factor for the period between sale and starting cost as established above. Apply the factor to the starting cost established in (a) plus the cost of subsequent purchase;

(c) This figure is then added to the cost established in (b) and is then subtracted from the sale proceeds and CGT allowance to establish the taxable gain.

13   Numerical Examples

An investor invested £10,000, including all costs, in the 10p ordinary shares of Z plc in February 1987. In April 1998 he sold them for £25,000. This is his only disposal for CGT purposes in the current tax year.

● The RPI in February 1987 was 100.4.

● The RPI in April 1998 was 162.6.

Calculate his liability to CGT assuming:

(a)   His taxable income was £12,000;

(b)   His taxable income was £28,000;

(c)   His taxable income was £30,000.

Solution

Before calculating the CGT liability it is necessary to calculate his taxable capital gain.

Note: he has not made any other disposals for CGT purposes in the current tax year, thus the £7,100 allowance is offset against the gain.

(i) Indexation factor = $\dfrac{162.6 - 100.4}{100.4}$ = 0.620

(ii) Indexation allowance   = cost x factor

= £10,000 x 0.620

= £6,200

	£	£
(iii) Sale proceeds		25,000
Less: cost	10,000	
Add: indexation allowance	6,200	16,200
Net gain		8,800
Less: CGT allowance		7,100
Taxable gain		£1,700

(a)   Taxable income £12,000 + taxable capital gain £1,700 means the total of £13,700 leaves him in the basic-rate tax band.

CGT payable   =   £1,700 at 23%

=   £391.00

£

(b) Taxable income   28,000

Taxable capital gain   <u>1,700</u>

<u>£29,700</u>

This makes his marginal rate of tax 40%, however tax is not applied to the whole of the gain at 40% but first the unused part of the basic-rate band is utilized as shown below:

CGT payable: £

On first £1,500 (£29,500 – £28,000) at 23% =   345

On balance of £200 at 40%   <u>80</u>

CGT payable   <u>£425</u>

(c) Because his marginal rate of tax is already 40%, the whole of the capital gain is taxed at 40%.

CGT payable   =   £1,700 x 40%

=   <u>£680</u>

An investor made the following purchases of ordinary shares in Delta plc:

July 1982   £15,000 including all costs

February 1985   £11,000 including all costs

In April 1998 he sold the shares for £80,000. He had no other capital gains or losses during the tax year. His marginal rate of income tax is 40%.

Calculate the CGT   68.7

RPI February 1985   93.4

RPI April 1998   162.6

Solution

Indexation factor Jul 82 – Feb 85 = $\dfrac{93.4 - 68.7}{68.7}$ = 0.360

Indexation factor July 97 – Feb 85 = $\dfrac{162.6 - 93.4}{93.4}$ = 0.741

July 82 cost (£15,000 x 0.360) + £15,000 = £5,400 + £15,000

= £20,400

February 85 cost ((£20,400 + £11,000) x 0.741)) + £31,400

= £23,267.40 + £31,400

= £54,667.40

CGT payable	£
Sale proceeds	80,000.00
Less cost	54,667.40
	25,332.60
Less CGT allowance	7,100.00
Taxable gain	18,232.60
CGT payable = £18,232.60 x 40%	7,293.04

14   Inheritance Tax

Introduction

Basically Inheritance Tax (IhT) is a tax on the estate of a deceased person, but the tax is also payable on lifetime gifts when these exceed £231,000.

Rates of IhT

Death rate

- First £231,000   Nil

- £231,001 and above   40%

If a gift is made during the lifetime of the donor and is not a potentially exempt transfer (PET), inheritance tax is payable at half the rate at death, i.e. 20%. A common example of such a gift is a transfer into a discretionary trust.

Lifetime gifts rate

Years before death	% of death rate
Not more than three	100
More than three but not more than four	80
More than four but not more than five	60
More than five but not more than six	40
More than six but not more than seven	20
Over seven years	Nil

Lifetime gifts that are not taxab●
- Any amount transferred between husband and wife provided both are domiciled in the UK, and that the transfer is for the total use, and totally at the disposal of, the spouse

to whom the assets are transferred. If one spouse is a foreign domiciled spouse, transfers are exempt only up to £55,000.

● £3,000 in any tax year. Husband and wife each have a £3,000 tax-free allowance, and any unused balance can be carried forward into the next year only. Thus if neither husband nor wife have made any gifts within the previous tax year their combined allowance would be £12,000 in the following fiscal year.

Wedding gifts of up to £5,000 by each parent, £2,500 by the bride or groom and each grandparent and up to £1,000 by any other person.

Gifts that are from normal taxed income; in other words, any gifts that are paid from your income rather than from your capital.

Small gifts up to a maximum of £250 to any one individual. It is therefore possible to make gifts up to £250 per person to any number of people without incurring IhT.

Transfers to a charity where the gift becomes an asset of the charity.

Transfers of heritage property and other assets of value to the nation or bodies such as the National Trust.

Gifts to qualifying political parties.

Business and Agricultural Property Relief

Business Relief

Business property relief is available on valuing transfers of business property subject to certain conditions relating to the length of ownership and type of business.

● For transfers on and after 10 March 1992, and any recalculation of tax on earlier transfers following death on or after 10 March 1992, the relief is:

➢ A business or interest in a business (including a partnership share)   100%

➢ Transfers out of unquoted shareholdings   100%

➢ Transfers out of a controlling shareholding in a quoted company
(including control through 'related property' holdings)   50%

➢ Land or buildings, machinery or plant used for a business carried on by:
a company of which the donor has control; or a partnership in which the
donor was a partner; or the donor, being settled property in which he had
an interest in possession   50%

The property transferred must normally have been owned by the donor throughout the previous 2 years.

Business property relief is not available when the business consists of dealing in stocks and shares (except market makers on the Stock Exchange and discount houses), dealing in land and buildings or holding investments (including land that is let).

Aricultural Relief

Agricultural property relief is available on the transfer of agricultural property subject to certain conditions. Agricultural property is defined as 'land or pasture, woodland and buildings used for rearing livestock or fish where the occupation of the woodland and buildings is ancillary to that of the agricultural land, and cottages, farm buildings and farmhouses occupied with the agricultural land'. ss115 - 124C Finance Act 1987 s58.

The agricultural property must have been either occupied by the donor for agriculture throughout 2 years ending with the date of transfer or owned by the donor throughout the previous 7 years and occupied for agriculture by him or someone else throughout that period.

Relief is given at the rate of 100% where the donor has the right to vacant possession immediately prior to transfer, or the right to obtain vacant possession within the next 24 months, or where the property is valued broadly at vacant possession value despite the tenancy.

For other tenanted agricultural property the relief is 100% for transfers of property where the letting started on or after 1 September 1995.

Where agricultural property meets the conditions for business property relief, agricultural property relief is given first and business property relief given on the non-agricultural value.

Both business and agricultural property relief is given without the need for a claim to be lodged.

Potentially exempt transfers (PETs)

If a transfer does not fall within the exempt transfers listed above, it does not mean that there is an automatic liability to IhT.

Lifetime gifts that could be subject to IhT are ones that are made during the donor's life. If the donor survives for seven years there will be no liability to IhT. The potential liability arises if the donor dies within seven years of making the gift. Lifetime gifts made within seven years of death are added back to establish the size of the estate on death. If the total exceeds the annual exemption allowance at time of death, the IhT will be payable. However, the transfer may not be subject to 100% of the tax; there is a sliding scale whereby the tax is mitigated if death occurs after three years.

One way of protecting the beneficiary of a lifetime transfer should death occur within the seven-year period is to take out a life policy that pays out only if death occurs before a set date. Provided the policy is written in trust for the beneficiary of the transfer, the proceeds themselves will not attract IhT but should supply the cash to pay any such liability on the PET.

Example of IhT liability and a PET

Mr R made a gift of domestic property worth £300,000 to his son on 20 July 1995. He had already made gifts that absorbed the annual exemption that year. On 3 January 2000 Mr R died. His estate was valued at £325,000 after subtracting all reliefs and exemptions. The total IhT bill is calculated thus.

(a)   On the PET of £300,000

   Mr R died more than four but not more than five years after making the gift. IhT will therefore be charged at 60% of the death rate of 40%

		£
Value of gift	£300,000	
Tax payable on first	£231,000	Nil
On balance of	£69,000 at 24%*	16,560
IhT payable		£16,560

   * calculated 60% of 40% = 24%

(b)   On the estate

   Value at death   £325,000

   IhT on £325,000 at 40% = £130,000

   Note: the £231,000 is offset against the lifetime gift first, and any unused portion carried over to the remainder of the estate. The death rate of 40% applies in full to the value of the estate on death.

15   Taxation of Children's Investment Income and Capital Gains

Every child is entitled to a single person's income tax allowance of £4,335. However, where the money for the investment has been provided by a parent, the investment income and capital gain will be treated as the donor parent's for tax purposes. However, if the income is less than £100 p.a., it is disregarded for the parental tax position. If the income exceeds £100, the whole of the income is taxed at the donor parent's marginal rate of income tax. The main exception is for money invested in the Children's Bonus Bonds (see Unit 15), which do not attract a tax liability for the parent.

On the other hand, where the money for the investment has been provided by someone other than a parent, for instance a grandparent, the income from that investment is treated as the child's for tax purposes. Provided the child's total income in these circumstances is below £4,335, he will not have to pay tax.

16   Tax and the Examination

In the examination you will find the various rates of tax and allowances required to answer the questions given on the paper. These are the rates you must use. However, you will still have to be able to produce the tax computations given in this unit.

17   Conclusion

We have studied income tax, national insurance, CGT and IhT in this unit in general terms. The unique tax aspects of certain investments, such as unit trusts, investment trusts, offshore funds and insurance products will be examined in detail in the relevant chapters covering those investments.

Summary

Now that you have studied this unit, you should be able to:

- describe when income tax, National Insurance, capital gains tax and IhT apply;
- describe a person's liability to income tax and National Insurance;
- list the income that is subject to income tax;
- list the income that is not subject to income tax;
- describe what is meant by 'allowances';
- understand the usage of the various income tax allowances;
- explain the effect of independent taxation;
- calculate income tax and National Insurance liability for different individuals;
- explain the treatment of dividends and interest;
- describe a person's liability to capital gains tax (CGT);
- explain the operation of CGT;
- list the assets that are exempt from CGT;
- understand the usage of the indexation allowance and taper relief;
- calculate the liability to CGT for different individuals;
- describe a person's liability to IhT;
- describe when IhT applies;
- list the lifetime gifts that are exempt from IhT;
- describe PETs;

- calculate the liability to IhT;
- describe the taxation of children.

Suggested further reading on taxation:

To⬤'s Tax Guide 1999-2000; A. Homer and R. Burrows, Tolley Publishing 1999. (This book is updated annually.)

7

GILT-EDGED SECURITIES

Objectives

After studying this unit, you should be able to:

- understand the Government's requirement to borrow and how this is addressed;
- explain the types of gilt and how they are taxed;
- understand how gilts are issued;
- calculate yields;
- match gilt investments with the needs of different investors;
- understand switching;
- understand dealing on the Bank of England Brokerage Service;
- understand the gilt repo market.

1 The Government as a Borrower

The Government has several ways available to raise capital. One major source of funds is the issue of British Government securities, which are more commonly called 'gilt-edged securities' or 'gilts'.

Gilts are quoted on the Stock Exchange and are the safest form of quoted investment because the Government will never default on the interest or capital repayments. There are stocks issued by other bodies that are virtually as safe as gilts, such as corporation loan stocks and public board securities. However, there is still a slightly higher chance of default with these stocks than with ones issued by the Government. These other stocks are classed as near- or quasi-gilts.

The Government uses the funds raised by issuing gilts to help to finance the Public Sector Net Cash Requirement (PSNCR), which was previously called the Public Sector Borrowing Requirement (the PSBR).

The Bank of England uses sales and repurchases of gilts to the banking sector as a means of influencing short-term levels of interest rates for monetary policy purposes. This is done via the gilt repo market (see Section 9).

The gilts issued carry a fixed rate of interest (called a coupon) per nominal £100 stock held and for index-linked gilts both the coupon and nominal value are linked to the RPI.

The price that the Government fixes on a new issue of gilts, or the price that is paid by the investor on the Stock Market, determines the actual rate of interest the investor will receive.

Virtually all stocks carry a date on which they must be redeemed (repaid) by the Government. In such cases it is quite common for the Government to make a new issue of gilts to raise the funds to repay the maturing gilt.

Whatever the reason for issuing gilts, they are of major importance, not only to the Government, but also to the investor. Although there are only around 80 gilts, compared with around 2,400 shares in UK companies quoted on the Stock Exchange, the value of the average deal relating to gilts is more than £3 million, whereas the value of the average deal relating to equities is around £67,650.

2 Categories of Gilts

Gilts are divided into five categories: shorts, mediums, longs, undated and index-linked. When you purchase any gilt you will always see figures in the title, e.g. 5% Treasury 2004. The 5% is called the 'coupon' and it means that an investor will receive £5 interest per annum for every nominal £100 of stock he holds. The 2004 in the title is the date on which the stock will be redeemed (repaid).

Shorts

These are gilts that have less than five years to run until redemption.

Mediums

These stocks have between 5 and 15 years to run to redemption.

Longs

These stocks have more than 15 years to run to redemption, but they will always carry a redemption date. In 1999 the longest-dated of these stocks was 6% Treasury 2028. The date means that the stock will be redeemed by the government in 2028.

Undated

The government is under no obligation ever to redeem undated stocks. However, there is just one undated stock that will eventually be redeemed, and that is 3½% Conversion 1961 aft. The reason for this is that a sinking fund exists whereby each year the government redeems 1% of this stock, either by purchasing it in the open market, or if insufficient stock is available in the market, by a ballot.

Another point about undated gilts is that some of them carry a date followed by the abbreviation 'aft', for example, 3½% Conversion 1961 aft and 3% Treasury 1966 aft. 'Aft' is an abbreviation of 'after' and means that when the stock was issued it would be redeemed in 1961 or 1966 (depending on the stock) or at some time after. The option to redeem lies with the Government and the decision to redeem or not depends on the general level of interest rates and the coupon of the stock. Because the coupons of these stocks are low at 3% and 3½%, the Government is borrowing the money far more cheaply then it could do elsewhere. It is obviously in the Government's interest not to redeem these stocks unless the general level of interest rates falls below 3 or 3½% (an occurrence not seen since before World War II). All undated gilts carry coupons of 4% or less.

Only three gilts pay interest quarterly, all undated. They are 2½% Consolidated (Consols), 2¹/₂% Annuities and 2³/₄% Annuities. One gilt, again undated, always pays interest gross to its holders, 3¹/₂% War Loan.

Note: the two annuity stocks mentioned above are not shown in the **Financial Times**, thus there is a common misconception that there are only six, not eight, undated gilts.

Index-linked

These gilts are unique in two ways. First, the coupon is index-linked to the Retail Price Index (RPI), so that each half-year when the interest is paid, the investor will receive coupon rate plus index linking. For the investor this means that the purchasing power of the interest received will remain constant in real terms, unlike all other fixed-interest stock where inflation erodes the purchasing power of fixed-interest payments. Secondly, the capital is also index-linked. The index linking of the capital is calculated by using the RPI eight months prior to the issue date, and the RPI eight months prior to redemption date. With an index-linked gilt the nominal £100 is index-linked on redemption, so the investor will receive more than £100 actual cash. The index linking of the capital applies only on redemption, but the price of index-linked gilts at any time reflects the element of index linking that is occurring and is likely to occur in the future.

The **Financial Times** shows the RPI eight months prior to the issue date against each of the index-linked gilts.

Convertible gilts

There are several gilts that are convertible into longer-dated gilts. In the **Financial Times** their title is 'Conversion' or 'Conv'.

The stock allows an investor to take a view on future interest rates. He knows when he purchases these gilt exactly what the interest and redemption yields on the stock will be if he does not convert. He also knows the terms of conversion and the details applicable to the stock into which he can convert. This conversion option allows him to take a view on future interest rate movements. Full details of the conversion terms and the gilt into which the conversion can take place should be obtained from a broker.

The conversion takes place at the holder's option. If he feels which the stock into which he can convert is unattractive, he will retain the original and it will be redeemed at the earlier date. The gross redemption yields of convertible gilts are lower than for comparable non-convertible gilts. This takes into account the attraction of the conversion option.

3   Issuing of Gilts

Gilts are issued to fund the Public Sector Net Cash Requirement (PSNCR). When there is a requirement for more money for the PSNCR, gilts are used to fund it. When the PSNCR is negative gilts are purchased by the Government either on the Stock Market or by a reverse auction (see Section 3 for details of an auction). In 1993 the net amount (new issues minus redemptions) raised was £50,965.2 million, compared to just £133.6 million in 1998. This indicates a major fall in the PSNCR.

Offer for sale – fixed price or tender

Gilts have been issued via an offer for sale by tender. With the tender issue there is a minimum price set below which bids will not be accepted. All investors pay the same price for their gilts: the striking price. If the issue is oversubscribed, the striking price will be above the minimum price and bids below the striking price will be rejected. If the issue is under-subscribed, the striking price and the minimum price will be the same. All unsold stock that arises from undersubscription will be sold as tap stock. The issue of gilts is not underwritten, and any gilts not subscribed for are taken up by the Debt Management Office (DMO). These are then sold as tap stocks over a period of time as the market conditions are suitable.

Auction method

Gilts are also sold via an auction. Whereas with the offer for sale by tender investors all pay the striking price, with the auction method the situation is different. There is no minimum price set, and investors bid the price they are willing to pay. Stock is allotted starting with the highest bid and working down until all bids are satisfied, or the stock available has been sold. Each bidder pays the price he bid. With both auction and tender issues, the Government may decide to issue the stock in partly-paid form. The balance will be due at a later date, set by the Government at the time of issue.

A private individual can avoid the difficulty of buying gilts by auction by applying for a 'non-competitive bid'. This means that the price he pays is the average price of all the auction bids made by the institutions. The maximum amount a private investor can subscribe for on a non-competitive bid basis is £500,000.

Tap stocks

Stock can also be created and placed by the Debt Management Office (DMO) in the form of 'tranches'. These stocks are called tap stocks, and they are shown in the **Financial Times** with a black circle by the stock's name. Tap stocks are issued in the secondary market, not the primary markets as is the case with new issues via auctions.

4 Taxation of Gilt-edged Stocks

All interest paid on gilts is subject to income tax in the hands of a private investor, or corporation tax in the case of a limited company investor. Gilts are held on the Bank of England Register and the interest received has lower rate (20%) tax deducted. It is possible to have interest paid gross upon completion of the relevant forms. For non-taxpayers this will save them having to reclaim the tax paid on the interest, although it must still be declared on a tax return.

All gilts are totally free of capital gains tax in the hands of the investor, but the full effect of the taxation of gilt-edged stocks will be seen below where the yield calculations show the effect of taxation on gilts for various classes of investor.

5 Yield Calculations

Yield can be defined as the rate of return from an investment, expressed in percentage terms. The yield calculations are important to investors when deciding on the gilt to purchase. Gilts not only have a variety of maturity dates, but also a wide variety of coupons. The coupon of a gilt is the first figure found in the title of a stock and it is the rate of interest an investor will receive per nominal £100 of stock held. The price of the gilt is the price per nominal £100 of stock. If a gilt is quoted at 75.84 this means that (ignoring all dealing costs) the investor will have to pay £75.84 to purchase £100 nominal. A gilt that is priced below £100 per £100 nominal of stock is said to be 'under par'. If a gilt is priced at 113.73 it means the investor will have to pay £113.73 for £100 nominal of stock. In this case the stock is said to be 'over par' par because the price of £100 is higher than £100 nominal.

Gilts are priced in decimals down to 2 decimal places.

Interest yield (also 'flat' or 'running' yield)

You may see all three of the above terms used, thus you should be familiar with them. The interest yield expresses the annual interest payments produced by a fixed-interest investment, such as a gilt, in percentage terms. The formula used to calculate interest yield is:

$$\frac{\text{Coupon} \times 100}{\text{Market price}}$$

To start with a simple example, if there was a gilt called 10% Exchequer Stock 2010 that had a market price of 50 then the interest yield would be:

$$\frac{10 \times 100}{50} = 20\%$$

In other words, £100 invested in this stock would produce gross interest of £20 per annum.

Because this is a fixed-interest stock the investor will continue to receive £20 per annum until the stock is redeemed in 2010, or until he decided to sell the stock.

The interest yield calculated here of 20% is the gross interest yield, i.e. no reduction is made for the effect of the investor's marginal rate of tax. To arrive at the net interest yield, which is the after-tax return to the investor, his marginal rate of tax must be deducted from the gross interest yield.

Taking the example given of a gross interest yield of 20%, to arrive at the after-tax figure for two different investors, one paying a marginal rate of tax of 23% and the other a marginal rate of 40%, the following formula used is:

$$\text{Gross interest yield} = \frac{(100 - \text{marginal rate of tax})}{100}$$

For the 23% taxpayer this gives:

$$\text{Net interest yield} = 20 \times \frac{(100 - 20)}{100}$$

$$= \frac{20 \times 80}{100}$$

$$= \underline{16\%}$$

(NB: For a basic-rate taxpayer fixed interest is taxed at only 20%)

For the 40% taxpayer this gives:

$$\text{Net interest yield} = 20 \times \frac{(100 - 40)}{100}$$

$$= \frac{20 \times 60}{100}$$

$$= \underline{12\%}$$

So for the 23% taxpayer the actual after-tax interest received is £16.00 per £100 invested, and for the 40% taxpayer £12. Only a non-taxpayer would actually receive £20 per £100 invested per annum – the gross interest yield.

Redemption yields

For all fixed-interest stocks that carry a date upon which they must be redeemed it is possible to calculate a redemption yield. The situation is slightly different for index-linked gilts (see Sections 10 - 19). The redemption yield takes into account any capital gain made (if the stock was standing under par when purchased) or capital loss (if the stock was standing over par when purchased).

The redemption yield assumes that the stock is held until maturity, and calculates the gain on an annual basis. Because gains on gilts are free of capital gains tax, the calculation of redemption yields starts after the interest yield has been calculated.

Gross redemption yield

Going back to the example above of the 10% Exchequer Stock 2010 priced at 50, assuming that it is purchased in 2000, there are 10 years to go to maturity. Thus there is an annual capital gain of $50 \div 10 = 5$ points per annum.

To arrive at the gross redemption yield the formula used is:

Gross interest yield $\pm$ annual capital gain/loss.

So for this stock the gross redemption yield $= 20 + 5 = 25\%$. Obviously this calculation is somewhat inaccurate regarding the capital gain element because the stock is assumed to be purchased and redeemed on the same dates in 2000 and 2010, whereas the dates will almost certainly be different. The other factor ignored is the effect of inflation, which erodes the purchasing power of the capital over the 10-year period. However, the highly involved calculations, using discounted cash flow techniques, are not required in this syllabus, but the fact that calculations as shown are somewhat inaccurate must be appreciated. In the examination the question will usually state 'calculate the approximate redemption yield for this stock', to take account of this fact.

Net redemption yield

This is calculated using the formula:

Net interest yield $\pm$ annual capital gain/loss.

This calculation takes into account the differing tax treatment of income and capital gain, and is used to assess which stock is most suitable for a particular taxpayer.

Going back to our 23% and 40% taxpayers, the net redemption yield is:

23% taxpayer $= 16 + 5 = 21\%$

40% taxpayer $= 12 + 5 = 17\%$

Grossed-up net redemption yield (also called gross equivalent yield)

This calculation is used to compare the grossed-up return on a fixed-interest stock, such as a gilt, with the gross return on a fixed-interest, fixed-capital investment such as a bank money market term deposit. It takes the net redemption yield of the stock and grosses it up at the investor's marginal rate of tax. The resultant figure shows the return the fixed-capital investment would have to give to equal the return on the gilt. The formula is:

$$\text{Net redemption yield} = \frac{100}{(100 - \text{marginal rate of tax})}$$

Again, taking the two taxpayers in the previous example, the figures for grossed-up net redemption yield would be:

$$23\% \text{ taxpayer} = 21x \quad \frac{(100)}{(100-20)}$$

$$= \frac{21 \times 100}{80}$$

$$= \underline{26.25\%}$$

$$40\% \text{ taxpayer} = 17x \quad \frac{(100)}{(100-40)}$$

$$= \frac{17 \times 100}{60}$$

$$= \underline{28.33\%}$$

In this case a 23% taxpayer would need to find a fixed-interest, fixed-capital investment paying in excess of 26.25% gross, whereas the 40% taxpayer would need one paying in excess of 28.33% gross, in order to receive a higher return than the gilt.

Obviously the examples here are hypothetical because no gilt with a coupon of 10% would be priced as low as 50, but they serve to give a simple introduction to the method of calculation.

6   Example of Gilt Calculations

From the following information:

● name of stock – 9% Conversion 2011

● market price – 128.20

● nominal stock – £1,560.06

● market cost – £2,000 (ignoring all dealing costs).

Calculate

(a) How the market cost of £2,000 gives a nominal holding of £1,560.06;

(b) The gross interest yield;

(c) The net interest yield assuming the investor pays tax at 23%;

(d) The gross redemption yield (assuming it is now 2000);

(e) The net redemption yield for a 23% tax payer (assuming it is 2000);

(f) The gross amount of interest received per annum;

(g) The grossed-up net redemption yield for a 23% taxpayer.

(h)   What is the purpose of the grossed up net redemption yield calculation?

Answer

(a) Nominal $\qquad$ = $\dfrac{\text{Market cost} \times 100}{\text{Market price}}$

$\qquad$ = $\dfrac{2,000 \times 100}{128.20}$

$\qquad$ = £1,560.06

(b) Gross interest yield $\qquad$ = $\dfrac{\text{Coupon} \times 100}{\text{Price}}$

$\qquad$ = $\dfrac{9. \times 100}{128.20}$

$\qquad$ = 7.02%

(Note: always work to two decimal places.)

(c) Net interest yield $\quad$ = $\quad$ gross interest yield x $\dfrac{(100 - \text{marginal rate of tax})}{100}$

$\qquad$ = $7.02 \times \dfrac{(100 - 20)}{100}$

$\qquad$ = $\dfrac{7.02 \times 80}{100}$

$\qquad$ = 5.62%

(d) Gross redemption yield = gross interest yield ± annual capital gain/loss.

$\qquad$ Annual capital gain/loss $\quad$ = $\dfrac{(\text{par} - \text{price})}{\text{number of years to maturity}}$

$\qquad$ = $\dfrac{(100 - 128.20)}{(2011 - 2000)}$

$\qquad$ = $\dfrac{-28.20}{11}$

$\qquad$ = -2.56 (capital loss)

$\qquad$ Therefore gross redemption yield = 7.02 – 2.56

$\qquad$ = 4.46%

(e) Net redemption yield = net interest yield ± annual capital gain/loss.

$\qquad$ = 5.62 – 2.56

$\qquad$ = 3.06%

(f) The gross amount of interest received p.a.

$$= \frac{\text{coupon x nominal}}{100}$$

$$= \frac{9 \times 1,560.06}{100}$$

$$= \underline{\pounds140.41}$$

(g) Grossed-up net redemption yield

$$= \text{net redemption yield x } \frac{100}{(100 - \text{marginal rate of tax})}$$

$$= \frac{3.06 \times 100}{(100 - 20)}$$

$$= \frac{3.06 \times 100}{80}$$

$$= \underline{3.83\%}$$

(h) The purpose of the grossed-up net redemption yield calculation is to find the required gross return from a fixed-interest, fixed-capital investment such as a money market deposit that will give an equivalent return for a particular taxpayer. It takes into account the differing tax treatment of income and capital gains on gilts.

7   Gilt Prices in the *Financial Times*

The **Financial Times** lists the prices, yields and other details of gilts under 'UK Gilts Prices' in the 'Companies and Markets' section of the paper and are listed as:

- Shorts (lives up to five years)
- Mediums (five to 15 years)
- Longs (over 15 years)
- Undated
- Index-linked.

For the first four categories the information printed is the same. However, for the index-linked gilt it is not possible to print exact yields because the rate of inflation between now and redemption is unknown. To give investors an approximate guide as to the yield of index-linked gilts, the **Financial Times** assumes two different rates of inflation, one being 5%, the other 3%. They also print next to the title of the gilt the RPI base month for indexing, i.e. eight months prior to issue.

Calculations based on the *Financial Times* yields

Dated gilts

Monday's edition of the **Financial Times** provides slightly different information about these stocks. It gives the dates upon which the interest is due and the date the stock last went ex dividend. To see how the information differs between the Monday and the Tuesday to Saturday information, we show below the details appertaining to the same stock on the two different dates.

Monday edition

	Notes	Price £	Wk % +/-	Amount £m	Interest due	Last xd	City Line
Treas		118.23	0.5	3,450	Mr25	16.9	1336
8pc 2009					Se25		

Tuesday – Saturday edition

	Notes	Yield Int	Red	Price £	+ or -	52 Week High	Low
Treas 8pc 2009		6.75	5.54	118.57	+.14	132.91	114.73

The first example shows that the price of 8% Treasury 2009 was £118.23 per £100 nominal stock. The price of the stock has risen by 0.5% over the week (calculated on a Friday-to-Friday basis). There was £3,450 million nominal of the stock issued. The interest dates are 25 March and 25 September and the last time the stock went ex-div was 16 September. The City Line is the phone number to call to obtain up-to-date information about the stock.

The second example shows that the highest price the stock reached during the past 52 weeks was £132.91 and the lowest £114.73 per nominal £100 of stock. The current price is £118.57 per nominal £100 stock and the stock price rose 0.14 from the previous day's close of business.

If you then calculate the gross interest and redemption yields using the formulae given in Section 6, you will find that the interest yield you calculate is virtually identical to that in the **Financial Times**, but the redemption yield differs from the one quoted in the **Financial Times**.

Using the Tuesday to Saturday edition information:

$$\text{Gross interest yield} \quad = \quad \frac{8 \times 100}{118.57}$$

$$= \quad \underline{6.75\%}$$

(Assuming it is 2000)

$$\text{Annual capital loss} \quad = \quad \frac{(100 - 118.57)}{(2009 - 2000)}$$

$$= \quad \frac{18.57}{9} = 2.06$$

$$\text{Gross redemption yield} \quad = \quad 6.75 - 2.06$$

$$= \quad \underline{4.69\%}$$

The gross interest yields in the **Financial Times** are easy to reconcile, because the price of gilts is quoted clean, i.e. accrued earned interest is accounted for by means of a separate transaction. Thus the formula shown will agree.

With the gross redemption yield there is a difference. If you take the **Financial Times** gross interest yield of 6.75% and deduct the annual capital loss calculated by the method shown above, the result is $6.75 - 2.06 = 4.69\%$, whereas the **Financial Times** figure is 5.54%. The **Financial Times** capital gain/loss is calculated by adding/subtracting the gross redemption yield from the gross interest yield. Thus in the above example the capital loss $= 5.54 - 6.75 = -1.21$. This differs from the one calculated above because of two factors. The first is that the **Financial Times** uses the actual date the stock will be redeemed so, instead of the arbitrary nine years, the time is exact. The second is that the effect of inflation, which erodes the purchasing power of the capital, is allowed for in calculations that are very complicated. The purchasing power of £100 nominal received in nine years' time is not the same as £100 received today. However, the detailed calculations are outside this syllabus.

Index-linked gilts

In the **Financial Times** the details of index-linked gilts are as follows:

Monday edition						
Notes	Price £	Wk % +/-	Amount £m	Interest due	Last xd	City Line
4⅛% (135.1)	179.35	+1.0	2,150	Ja 16	13.7	1134
I.L. Treas '30				Jy 22		

Tuesday – Saturday edition

Notes	Yield		Price	+ or -	52 Week	
	(1)	*(2)*	£		High	Low
4¹/₈% (135.1)	1.76	1.81	168.9	+2.49	193.23	168.42
I.L Treas '30						

The information shows that 4¹/₈% Treasury Stock 2030 is priced at £179.35 per nominal £100 of stock. The '+ or -' column indicates that the price has risen by 2.49. The first yield column shown as (1) shows the prospective real redemption rate on a projected inflation rate of 5% and column (2) on a projected inflation rate of 3%. The figure in brackets after the name of the stock under 'Notes' (135.1) is the RPI base month for indexing, i.e. eight months prior to issue.

In order to compare the gross yield figures to conventional gilt yields, you simply add the figure given for the gross prospective real return to the rate of inflation assumed. Thus for the 4¹/₈% Treasury 2030, an equivalent conventional gilt would need to give a return of (5 + 1.76) 6.76% assuming inflation stays constant over the period at 5%, and a rate of (3 + 1.81) 4.81% if inflation is constant at 3%.

To produce the inflation-adjusted coupon, you multiply the coupon by the current RPI and divide by the RPI given by the date of the stock. In the above example, assuming the current RPI is 168.9, the inflation adjusted coupon is:

$$\frac{4.125 \times 168.9}{135.1}$$

$$= \underline{5.16\%}$$

To calculate the current redemption value, the same calculation is done, using the £100 nominal value.

$$\text{Current redemption value} = \frac{100 \times 168.9}{135.1}$$

$$= \underline{£125.02}$$

This would be the current redemption value of the stock, assuming it was redeemed in eight months' time.

The nearer the stock gets to maturity, the closer the price will move towards the redemption value. The current price is £168.90, thus the gilt is over par because it is above its redemption value.

It is possible to estimate a redemption value of the gilt assuming different rates of inflation. If inflation were assumed to run at 3% p.a. until the stock were redeemed, and assuming that it is now 2000, the Treasury stock will be redeemed in 30 years' time.

To calculate the redemption value in 30 years' time, you multiply the current redemption value of £125.02 by $(1.03)^{30}$.

Note if your calculator cannot multiply to the power of 30, simply multiply £125.02 x 1.03, and repeat the process 30 more times.

Redemption value at 3% inflation $\quad$ = £125.02 x $(1.03)^{30}$

$\qquad\qquad\qquad\qquad\qquad\qquad$ = £303.46

(The longer method starts off:

125.02 x 1.03 = 128.7706

128.7706 x 1.03 = 132.633718

132.633718 x 1.03 = 136.61272954

and so on.)

The only danger an investor runs with an index-linked gilt is when inflation rises rapidly in the eight months prior to redemption. The base month and redemption month RPIs are both the RPI figures for eight months prior to issue/redemption. A rapid rise in the RPI in the eight months before redemption will not be reflected in the proceeds paid at maturity.

8 Ex div and cum div

Gilt prices are said to be either ex div (or xd) or cum div (or cd), 'div' being the abbreviation for dividend. Stocks are quoted ex div about five weeks before interest is due to be paid. The government pays interest only to the holders of stock on its books at the date they are closed. Once the books are closed the stock is shown in the **Financial Times** with 'xd' immediately after the price. The interest is paid on an ex div stock to the seller of the stock. If the stock is not shown in the **Financial Times** as 'xd' then it is always cum div, in which case the purchaser will receive the next dividend due.

Interest on gilts is payable half-yearly, with the exception of three undated gilts, $2^{1}/_{2}$% Consols, $2^{1}/_{2}$% Annuities and $2^{3}/_{4}$% Annuities, where the interest is paid quarterly on 5 January, April, July and October for all these stocks. The two annuity stocks are infrequently traded on the market, and thus are not readily available for purchase. (The reason these two stocks are infrequently traded is that the holders are in the main institutions who do not buy and sell these stocks very often because they fill an important niche in their portfolios.)

9 Gilt-edged Switching

This is an operation that is generally carried out by institutional investors to maximize returns on their gilt portfolios. Although a 0.06 or 0.03 price movement is virtually of no interest to the small private investor, to the institutional investor with multi-million pound gilt portfolios, such movements are of vital importance. There are three forms of gilt-edged switching: anomaly, policy and taxation switching.

Anomaly switching

Institutional investors deal in huge amounts of stocks at a time, the result of which can mean that the price of two comparable gilts can get out of line with each other. If only one of the gilts is dealt in, that gilt's price will appear high compared to the other one if that gilt has been purchased, and low if it has been sold. These price movements would be picked up by other institutional investors through their use of computers or graphs to plot movements. Some institutions plot graphs of all gross redemption yields of gilts compared with the number of years to redemption, and any price movement obviously affects the gross redemption yield. Once a stock has got out of line another institution will take the opposite action and bring the gilt back into line. Normally the gilt yield curve slopes gently to the right, and any stocks that are out of line are easily spotted.

Figure 7.1: The yield curve of an anomaly stock

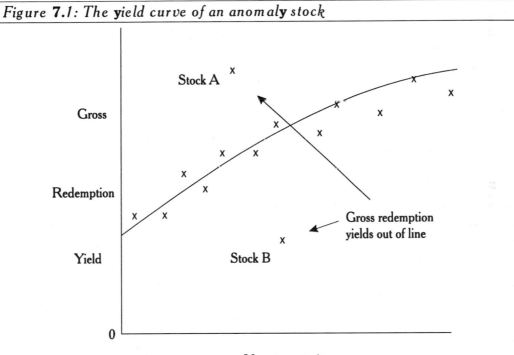

In Fig. 7.1 the x's represent the gross redemption yields of comparable gilts. Stocks 'A' and 'B' are out of line with the others and are thus 'anomaly' stocks. Stock 'A' has a higher than average gross redemption yield and the investors who plotted this graph would purchase this stock because the price is 'artificially' low in relation to the average, thus pushing up the gross redemption yield. On the other hand, Stock B's gross redemption yield is below average, and the holders of such stock would sell it and benefit from the 'artificially' high price that exists.

As a result of those actions the price of Stock A will rise and Stock B fall as the law of supply and demand works to readjust the prices and yields back into line.

Policy switching

When an investor takes a view on the way that the general levels of interest rates are going to move, he may take action within his portfolio to switch the gilts to match his view. If the investor expects the current levels of interest rates to fall in the future, he could sell his short-dated gilts and purchase long or undated gilts. This would enable him to lock into the current high yields available on the long and undated gilts. If investors do purchase long and undated gilts, their gross interest and hence gross redemption yields will fall because the price of these gilts will rise. In contrast the price of the shorts (and medium-dated if the same action is taken) will fall and the gross redemption yields of these stocks will rise.

When the investor feels that future interest rates are going to rise he may shorten the date of his portfolio. Short-dated gilts are virtually unaffected by market forces, they will always approach par (£100) as redemption draws near (i.e. they have a 'pull to maturity'). If investors as a whole do switch from longs to shorts, the price of long-dated stocks will fall, and their yields will rise. The investor who has shortened the life of his portfolio by selling his longer-dated and undated stocks will be unaffected by the interest rate rise because he holds shorts, and once he feels that interest rates have risen as far as they will go, he could sell his shorts and reinvest in longs or undated.

If an investor feels that inflation will rise, he can still take effective action within the gilt market by switching his holdings into index-linked gilts. This will give him an annual interest payment revalued in line with the Retail Price Index and on redemption his capital will be revalued in line with the Retail Price Index also. This action will protect the purchasing power of both his interest and capital.

Yield curves and the effect of policy switching

It is possible to plot yield curves relating to both rising and falling interest rates and their effect on the gross redemption yields of gilts over the number of years to maturity. The 'normal' yield curve, where there is an uncertain financial environment but no specific expectation of a change in interest rates, will show higher yields on longs than on shorts. This reflects the greater risk involved in long-term lending of any sort as opposed to short-term lending.

According to the expectations theory, the changes in shape of a yield curve will reflect the market's expectations of future movements in interest rates (see Fig. 7.2 (a) and (b)). However, other theories contradict this. According to the segmentation theory, future interest-rate expectations have no effect on the shape of the yield curve, because the major investors are locked into their own segment of the market and will not switch whatever the likely forecast of interest rates. Banks, building societies and general insurance companies invest mainly in the short end of the market, whereas life assurance and pension funds invest mainly at the long end. The truth must lie somewhere between these two extremes, but it is a fact that yield curves are studied by some as a means of predicting interest rate moves.

The yield curves are not actual examples, and in the examination you would not be expected to plot accurate yield curves, but be able to show thorough understanding of the effect that an expected change in interest rates could have on the gross redemption yields of gilts in relation to the number of years to redemption. Thus a small freehand drawing indicating these trends would be adequate.

*Figure **7.2** (a): **Yield curve and the expectation of rising interest rates***

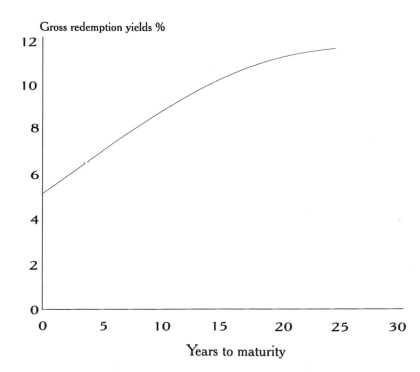

Figure **7.2 (b)**: *Yield curve and the expectation of falling interest rates*

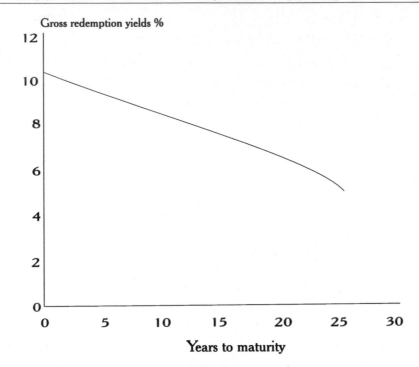

Taxation switching

Two gilts may have similar redemption yields, but one may be a high-yielding gilt with little if any capital gain, whereas the other may be low-yielding with a large capital gain element. However, a taxpayer would firstly calculate the net redemption yields of the stocks to ascertain the most appropriate one for his needs. Because the highest rate of tax is now just 40%, low-coupon gilts do not necessarily give the best return to a high (i.e. 40%) taxpayer.

Taxation switching is of little interest to the institutional investor who is not concerned with the interest yield element of the stock, but with the gross redemption yield. Whether the gross redemption yield consists of high-interest yield and low capital gain or vice versa is usually irrelevant. The private investor is more concerned with taxation switching.

10   Dealings on the Bank of England Brokerage Service

Gilts that are already in issue can be purchased in one of two ways, either via a stockbroker or via the Bank of England Brokerage Service. New issues of gilts can be purchased from the Debt Management Office (DMO) or via an Auction (see Section 3).

Advantages of dealing on the Bank of England Brokerage Service

● This is a simple process using clear forms that are available at any main Post Office, from the Bank of England itself or from the Bank of England's web site.

● All interest is can be paid gross provided the box on the purchase application form has been ticked, but it must still be shown on the investor's tax return.

● The costs of purchasing and selling stock on this register are low.

Cost of purchase or sale transactions

Purchase

Cost of Stock	Rates of Commission
Up to £5,000	0.7% subject to a minimum charge of £12.50
Over £5,000	£35 plus 0.375% of the amount in excess of £5,000

Sale

Cost of Stock	Rates of Commission
Up to £5,000	*there is NO minimum charge on sales*
Over £5,000	£35 plus 0.375% of the amount in excess of £5,000

These are the only charges to be paid on sales or purchases of gilts.

Disadvantages of dealing on the Bank of England Brokerage Service

● It is not possible to know the price of the stock prior to sale or purchase, because the price ruling is the one when the Bank of England's Registrar's Department receives the buy or sell form.

● Even with first-class post there is a minimum of one day's delay between the order being posted and acted upon by the Registrar's Department.

● It is not possible to deal via telephone or to place a 'limit' as it is with a stockbroker. All deals must be conducted by post.

● The maximum amount that can be invested in a single stock in any one day is £25,000. This will not affect small investors, but for anyone investing well in excess of £25,000 in one stock it would be quicker and cheaper to use a broker.

● There is no limit to the amount of stock that can be sold in any one day, provided the stock was registered on the Bank of England Register.

● The Registrar's Department is not able to give any advice regarding suitability of an investment, whereas a stockbroker will give detailed advice.

As a conclusion, the Bank of England Brokerage Service is suitable for small investors, especially non-taxpayers. However, for investors with larger amounts to invest, it could be cheaper to use a stockbroker, because dealing costs are usually on a greater downward sliding scale than the Bank of England rates the larger the deal with the broker.

Gilt Repo Market

The Gilt Repo Market was opened on 2 January 1996. A gilt 'repo' is a sale and repurchase agreement under which party A sells gilts to party B with a legally binding agreement to purchase equivalent gilts from part B at an agreed price at a specified future date. The market effectively allows stock (gilts) to be lent. The main participants in the repo market are clearing banks, building societies, major European banks, discount houses, gilt-edged market makers (GEMMs) and international security houses.

The Bank of England specifies that gilts are 'strippable'. Note that not all gilts are 'strippable'.

Gilt strips were introduced in December 1997. Stripping is the process of separating a fixed-rate interest-bearing gilt into its individual interest (coupon) and redemption payments. These can be held separately and traded in their own right as non-interest bearing or zero coupon bonds.

Example: a gilt with exactly 6 years to redemption could be divided into 12 strips.

One strip would be for the repayment of the principal in 6 years time. This would be called a zero coupon strip because no interest is payable on the maturity of the gilt. The holder would receive a payment for the strip's nominal value. Zero strips would trade at a discount to the nominal value in the period prior to maturity. The zero strip would not be subject to capital gains tax because gilts are exempt from CGT.

The remaining 11 strips would relate to each of the half-yearly interest payments due in the next 6 years. The interest received would be treated as any other interest payment – subject to tax at the investor's marginal rate of income tax.

Summary

Now that you have studied this unit, you should be able to:

- describe why the Government borrows money by issuing gilts;
- list the categories of gilts;
- describe how gilts are issued;
- describe how gilts are taxed;

● calculate the following yields:

  ➤ gross interest

  ➤ net flat

  ➤ gross redemption

  ➤ net redemption

  ➤ gross-up net redemption;

● explain how gilt prices in the **Financial Times** are calculated;

● describe the difference between the gilt information given in the **Financial Times** on Monday and that given during the rest of the week;

● explain what is meant by ex div and cum div;

● understand the three types of gilt-edged switching – anomaly, policy and taxation – and describe when each will be carried out;

● describe the advantages and disadvantages of dealing on the Bank of England Brokerage Service;

● Understand the Gilt Repo Market.

8

COMPANY, OTHER SECURITIES AND DERIVATIVES

Objectives

After studying this unit, you should be able to:

- understand the different types of stocks and shares issued by companies and describe the main features of each;

- explain how assets of a company are treated on liquidation;

- describe the constitutional rights of shareholders, particularly in respect of meetings and voting;

- understand how companies and local authorities raise debt and describe the instruments used;

- describe the main features of permanent interest-bearing shares issued by building societies;

- understand the nature of derivatives;

- understand how warrants and traded options work and describe their main features;

- understand yields, yield gaps and the relationship of these concepts to risk.

1   Introduction

This unit sets out to examine some of the various types of investment other than gilts that are available as direct investments to the private investor.

2   Ordinary Shares (Equities)

By law, the only class of capital a company must have is ordinary shares. These are more commonly called 'equities'. Some companies' ordinary shares are issued as ordinary or deferred stock – but there is no difference for our purposes. (One major company that has deferred stock instead of shares is P&O.)

Is a shareholder personally liable for company debts?

A shareholder is a member, or part owner, of a limited company. Legally, a shareholder is a separate legal entity from his company and owners of fully paid shares do not have any legal responsibility for the company's debts. Obviously shareholders may undertake such liability if they sign a guarantee, but mere ownership of fully paid shares in itself cannot make the shareholder personally liable.

With partly paid shares the position is different, because in the event of liquidation the shareholder could be liable for the amount of uncalled capital on his shares. For example, if the issue price of a company's shares were 50p, and the shares were only 20p paid, in liquidation the shareholders could be personally liable to pay over the 'uncalled' 30p per share to the liquidator. This payment would be required only if the company's funds were insufficient to meet its external liabilities.

Finally, a holder of partly paid shares could still find himself personally liable for the debts of his company even if he had sold the shares prior to liquidation. A liquidator will call upon the registered owners of partly paid shares at the time of the liquidation, if he needs the uncalled capital. If it proves impossible to obtain the money from this source, the liquidator has the right to claim from any previous owner of the partly paid shares who had sold the shares within 12 months of liquidation. This liability on the part of partly paid shareholders explains why banks are reluctant to take a full legal mortgage of such shares as security. Legal mortgagees of shares are the registered shareholders, and as such could become liable in the event of liquidation.

Most quoted shares are fully paid, apart from a few that have only just been issued and on which the various calls are not yet due.

Distribution of a company's assets in liquidation

If a company goes into liquidation its assets are all sold and the resultant pool of cash is distributed by the liquidator to the various parties so entitled. The order of repayment is:

- Secured creditors to the extent of money realized from their security;
- Liquidator's expenses;
- Preferential creditors;
- Creditors who hold a floating charge;
- Unsecured creditors;
- Subordinated loan stockholders;
- Preference shareholders;
- Ordinary shareholders.

Ordinary shareholders are entitled to receive any surplus only after payment of all external liabilities. When there are insufficient funds to pay off all the external liabilities, the ordinary shareholder has no personal liability, provided his shares are fully paid.

Types of ordinary share

So far we have considered ordinary shares (equities) as a single entity. However, within this single class of shareholder there can be various subdivisions.

Preferred ordinary shares

Such shares may carry restricted rights to dividends, and in liquidation shareholders of preferred ordinary shares may not be entitled to as much of any surplus as would be the ordinary shareholders. However, they are repaid before other ordinary shareholders.

Redeemable ordinary shares

Companies can issue ordinary shares that carry a set date for redemption. The shares will be redeemed either by the proceeds of a new issue of shares or by making transfers from profits into a specific capital redemption reserve. Where non-voting preferred shares or redeemable ordinary shares exist, there must also be some conventional ordinary shares that do not suffer from the restrictions.

Deferred ordinary shares

These shares are essentially founders' shares. Sometimes the original owners of the share capital of a company that is about to obtain a Stock Exchange quotation will try and encourage the new issue by agreeing to waive all dividends on their own shares until the rest of the shares have received a minimum stated dividend (say 10%).

Note that in all cases the precise rights of the holders of various classes of ordinary shares will be set out in the company's articles of association.

Dividend payments

Dividends can be looked upon as cash payments to shareholders out of the profits of a company. Usually there are two dividends per year, an interim dividend and a final dividend.

Interim dividends may be declared by the directors and are usually paid at the start of the second half of a company's accounting year. Final dividends are proposed by the directors and are paid after the company's annual general meeting (AGM). Shareholders at the AGM have the power to reduce or prevent payment of any final dividend, but they may not vote to increase the dividend that has been proposed.

Dividends can be paid only from available profits, thus the maximum dividend that the directors could propose is limited by the profits available. However, retained profits and revenue reserves from previous years can be used to maintain a dividend if the current year has seen low profits.

The rights of ordinary shareholders

Ordinary shareholders are the owners of a company, but day-to-day control is in the hands of the directors. You will no doubt recall from Unit 2 that in the case of quoted companies 'ownership is divorced from control'. A moment's thought will soon make it clear why day-to-day control must be in the hands of directors. Imagine, in the case of a UK clearing bank, the chaos that would ensue if every loan application from a prospective borrower had to have the approval of the shareholders!

However, the Companies Acts 1985 and 1989 and the Stock Exchange have laid down clear rules to protect the shareholders from being exploited by not being involved in day-to-day affairs.

The main rights of ordinary shareholders are as follows:

- To receive notices of all meetings of the company and to attend, speak and vote at such meetings;

- To appoint a proxy to attend and vote at a meeting on their behalf;

- To share in the profits of a company on a pro rata basis. Thus every single ordinary share will receive the same dividend unless the shares are preferred or deferred shares. Profits can be shared both by paying a dividend and by retaining them for future use by the company;

- To receive bonus issues on a pro rata basis;

- To be given the opportunity to subscribe for rights and convertible issues on a pro rata basis. (If this were not so it would be easy for new shares to be issued to certain shareholders only, thus giving them effective control of the company.) This is called the 'pre-emptive right'. However, in certain circumstances there are exceptions to this 'pre-emptive right'. Provided the shareholders pass a special resolution to disapply pre-emptive rights, new issues of shares can be made without first being offered to existing shareholders;

- To sell their shares or transfer them without restriction. The Stock Exchange insists on free transferability, although the articles of association of some private companies may restrict the transfer of shares;

- To vote to remove directors and to appoint new ones in their place. With quoted companies this sometimes happens when the company is the 'victim' of a successful takeover bid when the new controlling shareholders prefer to appoint their own directors. The removal and appointment of new directors has also been seen when a company has had a poor trading record, and the shareholders feel that new leadership is required.

  ➤ In general, voting at most meetings of shareholders is by show of hands where each member has one vote irrespective of how many shares he owns. However, on important matters a poll will be held, and indeed a poll can be demanded by five or more members or by members representing one tenth of the voting capital. In a poll, the usual procedure is to allow one vote for each share.

➤ For a vote to be valid, there must be a quorum, i.e. a set minimum number of shareholders present at the meeting. The Companies Act 1985 set the minimum at two for a quoted company, but the company can specify a higher minimum in its articles of association.

➤ When a shareholder cannot attend a meeting in person he can appoint someone else, known as a proxy, to act on his behalf. A proxy need not be a shareholder, he cannot vote except on a poll, and he can speak only to demand, or join in the demand for, a poll.

➤ Where a corporate body, usually an institution or a limited company, owns shares in another company, the corporate shareholder can either appoint a proxy to attend the meetings, or it can appoint a 'representative'. Under the Companies Act 1985, a representative has all the rights of a shareholder;

● To receive the annual report and accounts (including the auditor's report) at least 21 days before the annual general meeting;

● To receive 14 days' notice of an extraordinary general meeting;

● Under the Companies Act 1985 an auditor who resigns must state whether or not there are circumstances that should be reported to the shareholders. If necessary, a resigning auditor could demand that an extraordinary general meeting be held so that shareholders may be informed of such circumstances;

● The Stock Exchange insists that quoted companies provide information over and above that required by the Companies Act. This extra information consists of:

➤ An explanation by the directors of failure to meet any published forecast;

➤ An interim unaudited set of accounts covering the first six months of the company's financial year that must be sent to shareholders;

➤ Where the audited accounts are qualified by the auditors because they do not conform to Financial Reporting Standards (FRS), the directors must explain why this has arisen.

Company meetings and resolutions

A company must hold an annual general meeting at the end of each financial year. The maximum time period allowed between AGMs is 15 months. A company can hold meetings at other times, as and when it is necessary for the shareholders to vote on various matters. Such a meeting is called an extraordinary general meeting.

AGM (Annual General Meeting)

The items dealt with at the AGM are usually items that would be classed as ordinary business as defined by the company's articles of association. Such items are the:

- Consideration of the director's report and accounts;
- Declaration of the final dividend;
- Election (but not the removal) of directors;
- Appointment (but not the removal) of the auditors, and the fixing of the auditor's fee.

Twenty-one days' notice of the AGM must be given to shareholders.

EGMs (Extraordinary General Meetings)

These can be called at any time to deal with business that is classed as 'special business'. Items that would be classed as ordinary business can be dealt with at the AGM, but often these items arise, and have to be dealt with, more quickly than once a year. Such ordinary business can be dealt with at an EGM.

Fourteen days' notice of an EGM must be given to shareholders.

Resolutions

There are three types of resolution: ordinary, special and extraordinary.

Ordinary resolutions deal with normal business matters such as declaring a dividend, increasing share capital, or the election of directors. An ordinary resolution requires 51% of votes cast in favour for it to be passed.

Special resolutions cover such items as changing the name of the company, changing the objects clause or reducing the share capital. A special resolution requires 75% of votes cast in favour for it to be passed.

Extraordinary resolutions deal with major items, for example winding up the company. An extraordinary resolution requires 75% of votes cast in favour for it to be passed.

3 Companies Buying Back their own Shares

Section 166, Companies Act 1985 gave companies the right to purchase their own shares provided the articles of association allow it to do so. The company must always have some irredeemable ordinary shares remaining in issue.

In theory if a company buys back its own shares when their market price is below net asset value, the supply of ordinary shares is reduced with the remaining shares having a greater earning capacity and net asset backing per share. (Net asset value is the theoretical surplus available to ordinary shareholders in a possible liquidation, divided by the number of shares. The resultant figure is the theoretical amount per share that a shareholder would receive in liquidation.)

There are tax benefits provided the correct procedures are followed. Any rise in the share price of the remaining shares will incur CGT to shareholders only on disposal, as opposed to the normal income tax liability when dividends are declared. The company can purchase its shares either on-market or off-market.

- **On-*market purchase:*** An ordinary resolution must first be passed at an AGM or EGM. This resolution will specify the maximum number of shares to be purchased and the maximum and minimum price to be paid. The company will then instruct its brokers to purchase the shares on the London Stock Exchange.

- **Off *market purchase:*** A special resolution must first be passed at an AGM or EGM. The owners of the shares to be purchased cannot vote on this matter. The company will then buy the shares.

4 Nominal Values of Ordinary Shares

Under UK law, shares in UK companies must have a nominal value. The nominal value of most company shares is 25p, and all shares quoted in the *Financial Times* have a nominal value of 25p unless otherwise stated.

Nominal value is of very little significance to a shareholder, because what matters to him is the market price of the shares. Even in liquidation, nominal value is immaterial, because any surplus will simply be divided up between the ordinary shareholders on a pro rata basis.

The only time nominal value does matter is if the dividend is declared as a percentage of a share's nominal value. A holder of a share with a 25p nominal value would receive a net dividend of 2.5p per share if a 10% dividend had been declared. Obviously the total dividend a company pays is influenced by available profits and the policy of the directors. Nominal value plays no part in influencing the total dividend that can be paid out.

Some overseas countries have recognized the irrelevance of nominal value, and issue shares of no par value, for example in the USA shares are issued with no par value. In this case dividends are declared as so much (e.g. 2.5p) per share.

5 Concessions

Concessions arise when a company allows its shareholders to use the company's products on preferential terms. There are advantages to the company in that:

- The share price could rise because the shares are more attractive;

- The concessions may help to increase turnover and profits and may provide useful publicity.

Shareholders benefit because there is no tax on these 'perks' and the concessions are not normally affected at times of dividend restraint.

Institutional shareholders are not overly keen on concessions because they often cannot use them. Some companies do allow their concessions to be transferred to someone other than the named shareholder, and in this way institutions can use the concessions by giving them to their directors or staff. However this has no impact upon the performance of the shares.

Company concessions usually come in the form of discounts on the company's products or services, thus if the concessions are used, the company has increased sales.

Shareholder concessions should not be the sole criteria for selection of shares, but it is worth finding out about them, if only to make sure you do not narrowly miss the minimum qualifying holding.

6 The Difference between Stocks and Shares

Although stock is a colloquial term for equities, it is more accurately defined as paper debt issued by the Government or companies in consolidated form, tradable in any amount. Shares can be bought and sold only in whole units.

Gilts

Gilts and corporation stocks are generally priced at so much per nominal £100 of stock. Thus if 3½% War Loan is quoted at 72.96, it means that £100 nominal can be purchased for £72.96. (Incidentally, gilts are transferable in units of one penny, so investors are not restricted to buying round £100s of nominal value.)

Company loan stocks

Company fixed-interest loan stocks are generally priced in the same way as gilts, but they are usually transferable in units of 25p, 50p, or £1. When they are transferable in units of less than £1, the units are usually specified on the certificate. Thus a company loan stock certificate may show £100 on the nominal value, but that it is transferable in units of 50p. If the price in the *Financial Times* appears as 80, then that certificate represents stock worth £80.

Ordinary or deferred stocks of limited companies

When a company issues ordinary stock as opposed to ordinary shares, the certificate will once again show the units in that stock can be transferred.

In the case of ordinary stock, the price quoted in the *Financial Times* is that of a single stock unit as opposed to that of £100 nominal of the stock. Thus a certificate of ordinary stock that shows £100 nominal represented by 400 units of 25p each, would be worth £320 if it were quoted as 80 in the *Financial Times*. In this example '80' represents the price in pence of a single ordinary stock unit.

7 Preference Shares
The difference between preference shares and ordinary shares in liquidation

All companies that are quoted on the Stock Exchange must have ordinary shares, but they need not have preference shares. Where preference shares exist, they are classed as part of the share capital, but usually rank before ordinary shares in liquidation. The precise position would depend on the company's articles of association, but generally speaking any surplus after repayment of all external liabilities will be split as follows:

● To the preference shareholder up to the nominal value of such shares (thus in liquidation the nominal value of preference shares can be important, whereas for ordinary shares nominal value is immaterial);

● Any residue after satisfaction of preference share claims is then vested in the ordinary shareholders.

Preference dividends

Dividends on preference shares are said to be fixed, in that the maximum possible dividend is limited to an amount that is shown in the title of the share. A preference share entitled '7% Preference Share' will pay the registered holder a maximum dividend of 7% net of basic rate. The tax implications for the shareholder are the same as for ordinary shares, and the position has already been set out in detail in Unit 6.

Although there is a maximum dividend payable on preference shares, this is not guaranteed. Preference dividends can be paid only from available profits and at the discretion of the directors. Thus even when profits are available to cover it, the preference dividend may not be paid. However, no dividend can be paid on other, lower ranking capital while the preference dividend is in arrears. This precedence as to dividend and as to capital rights in liquidation shows why the term 'preference' is used to describe this class of capital.

Types of preference share

Cumulative preference shares

Most preference shares are cumulative, and indeed a preference share will be cumulative unless it is expressly stated to be non-cumulative. The right to any unpaid dividend continues indefinitely, in that no dividend can ever be paid on lower ranking capital, such as ordinary shares, until the preference shareholders have received their full arrears of dividend. There is no time limit with cumulative preference shares and for some unsuccessful companies there are many years of overdue preference dividend to be paid before the ordinary shareholders can receive any dividend payment at all.

For non-cumulative preference shares, once the dividend is not paid for a particular period it is lost forever. In the following year the preference shareholder would be entitled to one year's dividend only, and the ordinary shareholders could receive a dividend only provided that the current year's preference dividend had been paid in full.

Participating preference shares

These shares carry the right to an 'extra' dividend when the available profits exceed a stated amount. Although the terms of the issue of such shares differ widely, there is generally an upper maximum dividend per share.

Redeemable preference shares

As the title implies, these shares are redeemable, but only subject to certain conditions. Although there may be a set date for redemption, or redemption may be at the company's discretion, it may take place only if there are sufficient available profits or if the necessary cash can be raised from the proceeds of a new issue.

Thus there is no guaranteed capital gain from the purchase of a redeemable preference share at less than its nominal value. The position is by no means the same as occurs from the purchase of a dated gilt at a price below par.

Convertible preference shares

Convertible preference shares are preference shares that carry the right to be exchanged into ordinary shares on the terms set out in the issue. As with all preference shares, the rate of dividend is as stated in the title, and that dividend is paid net of basic rate tax.

Zero-dividend preference shares

These preference shares are issued by investment trusts as one of the types of share issued by a split-level investment trust. (See Unit 13 for details of investment trusts.) The zero-dividend shares (commonly called 'capital shares') set a redemption date and do not pay any dividend during their life. When the trust is wound up, the zero dividend preference shareholders receive the remaining capital after all other claims have been paid.

Voting by preference shareholders

The precise voting rights will be set out in the articles of association, but generally speaking preference shareholders have the right to vote only if their dividend is in arrears, or if there are any other matters that directly affect them. Whenever a company wishes to vary the rights of any particular class of share, such as a preference share, it must call a separate class meeting. Only holders of the relevant class of share will be eligible to vote at that class meeting.

Are preference shares an attractive investment?

From the point of view of the private investor, the answer is usually 'no'. In liquidation there are all the disadvantages of ranking as a shareholder, and thus being entitled to capital repayment only when all outside creditors have been paid off.

As regards income, there is no obligation on the directors to pay the preference dividend, and yet in times of vast profit increases, only the ordinary shareholders or, to a limited amount, holders of participating preference shares will receive the benefit of increasing dividends. All capital gains on preference shares will count for CGT purposes, whereas gilts and other fixed-income stocks are free of all CGT. The interest on a loan stock is a debt that is legally payable, and, in the case of a gilt, is guaranteed by the Government. The right to a preference dividend is not an enforceable one, and the preference share is only as secure as the company.

Despite these drawbacks, preference shares in sound companies are attractive to institutional investors. Preference dividends, like ordinary dividends, are 'franked investment income', which means that there are tax benefits to institutional, as opposed to private, investors. Because of the tax benefits, preference shares are suitable for institutions but unsuitable for private investors.

8 Company Loan Stocks and Debentures

The difference between a loan stock and a debenture

Quoted loan stocks and debentures usually carry a fixed coupon and have a redemption date. Technically speaking, there is no difference between the two stocks because a debenture is strictly a 'written acknowledgement of debt'. However, debentures are commonly so-called because there is some security available to the stockholders to enforce their rights against the company. Loan stock is normally so-called because it is unsecured. In practice, this generalization is too sweeping, and the precise position can be determined only by examining the terms of each individual issue.

Sinking funds

A company may decide to set a sum aside from profits each year in order to facilitate redemption of a loan stock. Such arrangements are known as sinking funds.

Non-cumulative sinking fund

A non-cumulative sinking fund arises when funds are set aside each year to purchase other investments (for instance gilts with redemption dates around the same time as the loan stock). When the loan stock is due to be redeemed, there are adequate funds available for redemption.

Cumulative sinking fund

With a cumulative sinking fund, a set sum is generally put aside to cover repayment of loan interest and redemption of part of the capital. As time goes by, the fixed sum will redeem more and more capital, because the interest will diminish in line with the diminishing principal.

Suppose a company issues £10,000,000 of loan stock with a 10% coupon, repayable in 10 years, and suppose there is a cumulative sinking fund of £1,500,000 per annum. In the first year, £1,000,000 will be required to meet the interest and £500,000 will go towards capital redemption. In the second year £950,000 will be required to cover interest and £550,000 will be available towards loan repayment.

Sometimes the company purchases its own loan stock on the open market, whereas in other cases a proportion of the loan stock may be redeemed at par each year. When part is redeemed at par, the decision as to which loan stockholder is to be repaid will be made by ballot. When the market price is under par, the 'lucky' stockholders will benefit, whereas when the market price is over par the stockholder whose stock is redeemed will lose out.

The precise terms of a cumulative sinking fund must be carefully studied, but companies will prefer open market purchase when stock is currently priced under par, and will prefer redemption at par when the market price exceeds nominal value.

Sinking funds make a loan stock more attractive because they provide an assurance that positive steps are being taken to ensure the obligations of the company will be honoured.

The functions of trustees (in connection with company loan stocks)

Quoted companies that issue debentures or loan stocks appoint a trustee to look after the interests of the loan stockholders. The trustee is usually a bank or insurance company and must be independent of the company. A trust deed governing the terms of the issue will be drawn up.

The trustee will ensure that the terms of the trust deed are complied with. Matters covered by the trust deed will be:

- Rate of interest and dates of payment;

- Redemption date;

- Details of any sinking fund arrangement;

- Details of security for the loan. This may be a fixed charge over a specific asset. In this case the company cannot deal with it in any way without the trustees' consent. Alternatively, the charge may be a floating charge covering all assets. With a floating charge the company may deal with the assets without restriction in the ordinary course of business. A combination of a fixed charge over the land, buildings and book debts with a floating charge over other assets could be taken;

- Details of the rights of the trustee if the company is in default of the terms of the issue.

    The security can be realized by the trustees only on behalf of the loan stockholders. An individual loan stockholder cannot do this.

The advantages of appointing a trustee are that:

- It would be difficult for the company to make arrangements with each individual loan stockholder regarding the creation of security;

- A trustee is better placed to act in the interests of the loan stockholders. The trustee has professional expertise;

- When decisive action is called for, the various loan stockholders probably would not be able to agree among themselves.

Comparison of ordinary shares and company loan stocks from the point of view of an investor

Ordinary shares	Company loan stocks
1 Ordinary shareholders are members of the company. They own the company and can vote at meetings. The value of a vote is more apparent than real, because a private individual will probably own insufficient shares to exert a decisive vote. Day-to-day control is in the hands of the directors.	Holders of loan stocks are creditors who cannot normally vote at meetings. However, the terms of the issue will sometimes allow loan stockholders a vote if the payment of interest or capital is in arrears. Loan stocks are normally held by institutions not private investors.
2 Ordinary shares are never secured.	Loans can be secured (debentures always are) or unsecured, depending on the terms of issue.
3 Ordinary shares are not normally redeemed except by special court order. They are automatically redeemed only if they were issued as redeemable ordinary shares.	Loan stocks normally carry a redemption date.
4. Dividends are paid only from available profits. However, when profits are available a dividend need not be paid. It is for the directors to recommend whether to pay out profits by way of dividend or to retain the profits in the company to finance expansion or to reduce borrowing. Shareholders can vote to reduce the directors' dividend recommendation, but they cannot vote to increase it.	Interest is a debt and is payable irrespective of whether profits are available.
5 In inflationary times companies can sometimes increase prices, and hence profits and turnover. Thus the share price may increase with inflation and dividends may also grow. Much depends on the choice of the company and timing of purchase of shares but the possibility of growth exists.	(a) The interest remains the same irrespective of inflation. Interest therefore declines in purchasing power. (b) The loans are normally redeemed at par at maturity. Thus there is no scope for capital gains unless the stocks are purchased below par.
6 Capital gains are subject to CGT.	Capital gains on fixed interest stocks are free of CGT.

Considerations when contemplating an investment in company loan stock or company debentures, and how these investments compare with gilts

Apart from an investor's own tax position and his own investment aims, the main considerations are as follows:

● Compare the interest yield and redemption yield with yields on gilts for a similar redemption date. If the loan stock has a comparatively high yield, it may indicate undue risk. Alternatively, a high yield may simply mean that the market has not realized that the loan stock is out of line, thus creating an anomaly situation;

● Does the company appear to be capable of covering interest payments and redemption of the stock on the due date? Consider the prospects of the industry and look at the accounts of the company to assess its financial strength, profit record and future prospects. Ideally, the company should have a stable record in an industry with consistent, if steady, growth prospects. Security of earnings is more important than growth;

● Is the loan or debenture secured? Are there any other loans that take priority?

● Check the articles of association for the terms of the issue;

● Check the trust deed for details of any sinking fund that may exist;

● Compare the rates of interest on bank deposits and other fixed-rate investments;

● Are there any conversion rights to the loan stock?

● Calculate capital and income priority percentages and overall cover.

Comparison of company loans with gilts

● Company loans are only as secure as the company, whereas gilts are guaranteed by the Government. Obviously, loan stocks in companies such as banks are virtually as secure as gilts, but this is not the case with all company loans.

● Charges on dealings in gilts are much lower than commission rates on company loan stocks. Indeed for smaller sums (say under £10,000), the charges for gilts purchased on the Bank of England Brokerage service are even lower than the commissions on those purchased via a broker.

● Gilts are all easily marketable, but very 'thin' markets exist in some company loan stocks.

The conclusion from all this is that a private investor should only contemplate an investment in a company loan or debenture that has a redemption yield above that of a gilt with a similar redemption date. Even then the company must be 'sound' and the investor should not be intending to sell the stock, but hold it until redemption because the dealing costs of selling along with the wider bid-offer spread will reduce the return to the investor.

9 Convertibles

Convertible loan stock

A convertible loan stock is a fixed-interest loan stock that carries the right to convert into ordinary shares on the terms and conditions set out in the articles of association. The stockholder has the right, but not the obligation, to convert within the stated time. If conversion rights are not exercised by the expiry date, the stock will revert to a conventional dated loan stock.

Convertible preference shares

A convertible preference share is similar to a convertible loan stock, in that it carries the right to convert into a preset number of ordinary shares at, or between, a set future date or dates. If the conversion rights expire, the shares revert to straightforward preference shares.

With convertible preference shares, the holder receives a fixed rate of dividend payable out of post-tax profits. With a convertible loan stock, the holder receives a fixed rate of interest payable out of pre-tax profits. In both cases, once the conversion rights are exercised, the holder receives the dividend paid to all ordinary shareholders.

The 'best of both worlds'

The holder of a convertible loan stock has a legal right to receive his fixed interest in the same way as any other creditor is entitled to money owing. In addition, the loan stock is of course an external liability that must be met in full in any liquidation before the shareholders receive a penny. Thus income and capital of a convertible loan are more secure than those for ordinary shares. However, should the company prosper, the loan stockholder can obtain an equity stake by converting.

(Note: if the convertible is not a loan stock but a preference share, there is no legal right to the dividend, thus the income and capital are not as secure as with a convertible loan stock.)

The classic example of 'having your cake and eating it' occurs when the trustee of a will trust buys convertibles to help to maintain the income of the life tenant, while retaining the possibility of capital growth through exercise of the conversion rights on behalf of the reversionary interest after the life tenant's death.

Usually a convertible loan stock will be priced above a comparable 'straight' loan stock because of the attraction of the conversion option. However, if the prospects for the shares seem to be poor, the convertible loan stock price should be supported at the level of a comparable fixed interest stock. This support level is known as the 'bond support price'. A similar situation occurs with convertible preference shares.

To sum up, income from a fixed-interest stock will generally exceed the dividend income from shares in the short term, but in the longer term there is scope for growth in the dividend income and market price of shares.

A convertible enables the investor to take advantage of the higher fixed income in the short term, while retaining the option to benefit from growth of capital and income from the shares in the long term. If the shares do not perform very well he will simply retain the convertible as a straight fixed-interest stock or a straight preference share, depending on the type of convertible purchased.

Example of a convertible

Williams Holdings plc have an 8p Convertible Preference share 2018 that gives the holder the right to convert at the rate of 0.3175 ordinary shares for every 8p convertible preference share converted. The conversion right can be exercised between 3 and 31 May in each year up to and including 2008. If the final date for conversion passes and holders have not exercised their conversion rights, the preference share will become a straightforward 8p preference share redeemable in 2018. Until the conversion, the holder will receive a dividend of 8p net of basic rate tax for every one convertible preference share held. The shares are cumulative and redeemable.

As with many convertible issues, the terms of issue state that if 75% (or other preset %) or more of the originally issued convertible is converted, the company has the right to convert the remaining convertible preference shares upon giving 28 days' notice in writing to the shareholders concerned.

Note: the details would be the same for a convertible loan stock, with the exception that the rate of interest would be % not pence.

Weighing up the merits of convertibles

Choice of company

The golden rule is to choose a convertible only in a company that is likely to be successful. If the company is unsuccessful, the share price will fall and the conversion rights will become worthless. If matters become even more desperate, the value of the convertible could even fall below the bond support price because of fears of default.

Length of option period

If you like the company, then the next consideration is the length of the conversion option. The longer the conversion period the more chance there is for the investor to benefit, because there is a greater time during which the share price could 'take off'.

Conversion premium (or discount)

The conversion premium represents an amount or percentage by which the 'conversion price' exceeds the current market price of the shares at the time the convertible is purchased.

Sometimes the market price of the shares can rise very quickly, and there can be a time lag before the convertible follows suit. In such cases, purchase of the convertible can be a cheap way of obtaining the shares because the conversion price is at a discount to current market price of the shares.

Taxation

Tax considerations also apply, however, because the highest rate of income tax is now 40%, and capital gains are taxed at the investor's marginal rate of income tax after the £7,100 allowance, so there is little to choose between high income and capital gain for the investor. However, there are no tax consequences when simply exercising the conversion rights.

Information

For the private investor, information is hard to come by. However, some brokers provide 'newsletters' giving details of conversion premiums or discounts, prices, yields, and opinions on whether or not to exercise the conversion option.

Convertible calculations

Assume that today's date is 21 April 2000. A customer has received notification of impending conversion dates in respect of two convertibles he holds:

- ABC plc 12% convertible unsecured loan stock 2009 is convertible into 25p ordinary shares on 25 May each year from 1995 to 2007 inclusive at the rate of 30 shares for every £100 stock. The market price of the ordinary shares is 280p. The market price of the convertible stock is £105. Net dividends per ordinary share in respect of the year ended 31 March 2000 totalled 9.8p;

- XYZ plc 3.5p convertible preference share 2004 is convertible into 25p ordinary shares on 28 May each year from 1988 to 2000 inclusive at the rate of 38 shares for every 100 preference shares. The market price of the ordinary shares is 370p. The market price of the convertible is 142p. Net dividends per ordinary share in respect of the year ending 31 March 2000 totalled 7.77p.

Conversion premium/discount

ABC plc

> £100 nominal costs £105
>
> £100 nominal converts to 30 shares
>
> Therefore 30 shares cost £105 if obtained via the convertible
>
> Therefore one share obtained via the convertible costs 350p (£105 ÷ 30)
>
> The premium is $(350 - 280) = 70p$
>
> As a percentage the premium is $\dfrac{70 \times 100}{280} = 25\%$

XYZ plc

> 100 preference shares cost $(100 \times 142p) = £142$
>
> 100 preference shares convert to 38 ordinary shares

Therefore 38 ordinary shares cost £142 if obtained via the convertible

Therefore 1 share obtained in the convertible costs 374p (to the nearest penny)

The premium is $(374 - 370) = 4p$

As a percentage the premium is $\dfrac{4 \times 100}{370} = 1.08\%$

Monetary calculations on conversion implications

(i)   ABC plc

	Market value (£)	Gross income (£)
£100 nominal stock	105.00	12.00
30 shares at 280p	84.00	3.27
	21.00	8.73 **

Capital loss on conversion is £21 or $\dfrac{(21 \times 100)}{105} = 20\%$

Income loss on conversion is £8.73 or $\dfrac{(8.73 \times 100)}{12} = 72.75\%$

For ABC there would be a great loss of both income and capital on conversion. Bearing in mind the long time left before expiry of the conversion right, it would be best to retain the convertible for the time being, provided ABC's prospects seem sound.

**   To compare like with like, compare the gross dividend (x 100/90) with the gross interest (coupon x nominal).

(ii)   XYZ plc

	Market value (£)	Gross income (£)
100 convertible preference shares	142.00	4.38
38 ordinary shares	140.60	3.28
	1.40	1.10

Capital loss on conversion is £1.40 or 0.99%.

Income loss on conversion is £1.10 p or 25.11%.

For XYZ the loss of capital on conversion would be very small, and while gross dividend income is below the fixed dividend rate on the preference share, this could soon be eliminated by dividend increases.

As the deadline for the conversion option is fast approaching, action must be taken otherwise the convertible will fall to its bond support level. The investor must therefore convert or sell, depending on the prospects of XYZ.

Note: the 'large' capital loss on conversion for ABC plc and the 'small' loss for XYZ plc are also reflected in the two conversion premiums of 25% and 1.08% respectively.

Reasons for a company to issue convertibles

Takeovers

When a company wishes to take over another company, it may offer its own convertible loan stock or convertible preference shares in exchange for control of the shares of the company being bid for.

Such a stock can be very attractive to potential vendors of shares in the 'victim', because as we have seen convertibles can give the best of both worlds. In addition, the issue of a convertible defers equity dilution in the bidding company. This enables it to bring the company that has been taken over under the new ownership without problems from possible hostile shareholders of the company that has been taken over. Effectively, this method provides a breathing space.

Lack of security

Sometimes there are insufficient assets available to offer as security for a new issue of a fixed interest loan stock. The extra benefits from a conversion option may persuade otherwise reluctant investors to subscribe.

Coupon or dividend rate

The convertible can be issued at a lower coupon than that of a comparable 'straight' loan stock. Likewise, the fixed dividend on a convertible preference share can be lower than that on a straightforward preference share.

As an alternative to a rights issue

A convertible can be an alternative to a rights issue. If the current share price is below nominal value, a company cannot make a rights issue because the subscription price must be at least equal to nominal value.

Long-term financing

Convertibles can be used as a means of financing long-term projects. Subscribers would require a guaranteed income in the first few years while the profit levels were likely to be low. In later years the investor could convert if the project had been as successful as had been anticipated.

Redemption and conversion

If the company prospers, redemption of the convertible will be unnecessary because the stockholders will all exercise their conversion rights.

Note: the disadvantage of convertibles, especially of convertible loan stocks, from the issuer's point of view is that:

● If the company prospers, conversion will dilute the control of current shareholders;

● If the company does not prosper, conversion will not take place and the company will probably be seen as 'over-borrowed'.

10 Local Authority Loans

The different types of local authority loan

There are three types of local authority loan:

● Fixed loans
● Yearlings
● Local authority stocks.

Fixed loans (also known as local authority bonds, town hall bonds, or mortgages)

These are fixed capital investments where the rate of interest is fixed at the outset and the loan cannot usually be repaid early. However, some authorities will allow early encashment against a penalty charge. There is no secondary market.

The return therefore consists entirely of income, which is paid net of basic tax in the same way as interest on gilts or other quoted loan stocks. A non-taxpayer can reclaim the tax deducted.

These fixed loans are really suitable only for basic-rate taxpayers who require income and who can afford to tie up their capital for the period of the loan. Higher-rate taxpayers probably prefer capital gains rather than income.

Yearlings (local authority negotiable bonds)

Despite the name 'yearlings', they can have a life of one or two years. The minimum investment is £1,000. There is a secondary market and the yearlings can be bought and sold at any time at the current market price.

If the investor buys a new issue there will not always be any capital gain or loss if he holds the yearling until maturity, because many 'yearlings' are issued at par. However, a capital gain or loss will normally occur if he buys or sells on the secondary market. Interest is paid net of 20% tax, and a non-taxpayer can reclaim the tax deducted.

Local authority stocks

These are traded on the stock market and prices are quoted in the *Financial Times* under the heading 'Other Fixed Interest'. Interest is paid in the same way as for all local authority stocks, thus non-taxpayers can reclaim the tax deducted.

Security of local authority stocks

The assets and rates of the local authority are charged as security for these loans, and the Government-backed Public Works Loans Board has a statutory duty to lend to a local authority to enable it to meet its commitments.

11   Permanent Interest Bearing Shares (PIBS)

These are fixed-interest shares that were first issued in June 1991 by building societies. They are issued and traded on the stock market to provide capital, which counts towards their capital adequacy ratio. 'Permanent' means that the shares have no set redemption date, i.e. they are undated.

PIBS are not protected by the Deposit Protection Board because they are quoted securities, not accounts with a building society. Settlement for a PIBS transaction is three working days (T+3) after the date of dealing and the price of PIBS is quoted 'clean'. Accrued interest is calculated separately and is added to or subtracted from the settlement total in the same ways as accrued interest is dealt with on gilts.

Unlike other securities quoted on the Stock Exchange, each PIBS specifies a minimum amount that can be purchased. The minimum on the issue varies; for example the minimum on the 13% Britannia PIBS is £1,000 and on the 13% Bradford and Bingley PIBS £10,000.

PIBS holders, subject to the rules of the society, are members of the society and are entitled to attend general meetings. However, voting powers are limited to one vote per holder, regardless of the size of the PIBS holding, in common with the rights of all other building society shareholders.

The interest rate on PIBS can be fixed or a margin over a specific market rate of interest (although all the early issues carry a fixed rate of interest).

PIBS are non-cumulative and do not participate in the profits of the building society. On winding up, PIBS rank after all other debts and share accounts (other than deferred shares) for repayment of interest and principal. If a building society converts to plc status (i.e. becomes a quoted company), the PIBS will be changed into subordinated unsecured loan stock of the company.

From an investor's point of view, PIBS are similar to non-cumulative, undated preference shares in a company. PIBS are not identical to unsecured loan stock in a company, because failure to pay the interest on PIBS does not mean the building society would be wound up, whereas failure to pay interest on a loan stock will result in liquidation proceedings starting.

12   Derivatives

Derivatives are financial contracts whose price relates to the price of a particular asset. There are a very wide range of derivatives which are used mainly for managing financial risk. However for the purposes of this book we are restricting this area to warrants and traded options.

Warrants

What are warrants and why are they issued?

Warrants in a particular company give the holder the right to subscribe for ordinary shares in that company on the terms set out in the articles of association. Holders of warrants are not entitled to any dividend or voting rights, and if the subscription has not been exercised by the expiry date, the warrant becomes valueless. However, some companies appoint a trustee who will exercise the warrants, sell the shares in the market and remit the sale proceeds minus expenses to the warrant holder. In such a case, on expiry of the warrants, the holder will receive cash, provided the trustee decides that it is worthwhile to exercise the warrants and sell the shares. If he decides it is not worthwhile, the warrants become valueless.

Warrants are dealt with on the Stock Exchange in exactly the same way as any other quoted security. The holder will receive a certificate that usually sets out the number of warrants held, and the terms on which ordinary shares can be purchased.

Companies have often issued warrants as part of a 'package deal' whereby the warrants and a loan stock were issued together to make the loan stock more attractive. On completion of the issue formalities the warrants and loan stock were then quoted and dealt in as separate entities.

Some companies, for example BTR plc, have issued warrants free to shareholders in order for the shareholders to be able, at set future dates, to 'enhance their future participation in BTR'. The company benefits because it receives new money when the warrants are exercised.

Investment trusts are the main category of company that issues warrants. A quick glance at the Investment Trust sections of the 'London Share Service' page of the *Financial Times* will confirm this fact.

The benefits to the company from the issue of warrants

Reducing the financial burden

No dividends or interest are paid on the warrants themselves. The company has the benefit of the proceeds of the issue of warrants (which are shown as a capital reserve in the balance sheet) at no cost to itself until and unless conversion takes place.

Taking advantage of an overvalued share price

If a company believes its share price to be overvalued, it can sell warrants to outsiders. If the company's share price does indeed fall far enough to make exercising unattractive, the warrants will not be exercised and the capital reserve will have been acquired at no cost. However, to prevent abuses, the Stock Exchange insists that a new issue of warrants can be offered to outsiders only with the consent of the existing shareholders.

Warrants and investment trusts

By law, new issues of shares in an investment trust must be priced at their asset value. However, prices on the market often fall to a discount. Thus warrants are sometimes an essential 'sweetener' to accompany a new issue of investment trust shares. Once the issue has been made the warrants and shares are dealt with separately.

Enhancing the attraction of other issues in the 'package'

In cases where the warrants are issued as part of a 'package', the accompanying loan stock may be issued at a lower coupon because of the added attraction of the warrant. Once the issue is complete, the loan stockholder can sell the warrants in the market, or choose to hold them with the intention of exercising the warrants at a later date.

An example of a warrant

In February 2000, Omega plc warrants 2001-02 were priced at 102p, and its ordinary shares at 365p. The exercise terms gave warrant holders the right to subscribe for one ordinary share for each warrant held at a subscription price of 380p between 2001 and 2002 on any of the 30-day periods each commencing on the dates falling one day after the date of posting of the annual report and accounts and the interim results of Omega plc in those years.

If we ignore dealing costs, we can see that the price of obtaining the shares via the warrants is at a premium of 32.05%. The cost of a warrant is 102p which, when added to the subscription price of 380p, makes a total cost of 482p. This means that the shares cost 117p (482 – 365) more when obtained via the warrants, and there is a premium of:

$$\frac{117 \times 100}{365} = 32.05\%$$

Premiums and discounts

Generally speaking, the premium on a warrant will be higher the longer the unexpired period for subscription, although much must depend on the prospects of the underlying shares. There have been instances, however, where the warrant price has not moved as quickly as the underlying share price, and in these instances a discount can arise.

As the warrant nears the end of its life the premium will tend to disappear because the warrants either be exercised or be allowed to lapse.

Time value and intrinsic value

The 'intrinsic value' of a warrant is the amount, if any, by which the current share price exceeds the subscription price. If we look back at the Omega warrant we can see that its intrinsic value is nil (365 – 380). A warrant can never have a negative intrinsic value, because the holder will simply let the warrant lapse if its subscription price on expiry is above the current market price.

The 102p warrant price consists of nil intrinsic value and 102p 'time value', which can be described as the price paid now for the opportunity to acquire the shares at a later date at a predetermined price. Perhaps a clearer name for the concept of 'time value' would be 'speculative potential'.

When the subscription price exceeds the current share price the warrant is said to be 'out of the money', whereas the term 'in the money' applies when the warrant has some intrinsic value.

Gearing

The concept of gearing is best explained by considering a cyclist. When the going is good with a favourable wind and a downward slope, the benefits will be magnified by a highly geared cycle. However, as the wind changes direction and the cyclist starts to climb a hill the difficulties posed by these two factors will again be magnified by a highly geared cycle. In short, gearing exaggerates the effect of both the ups and downs of both cyclists and investors.

Let us now consider a warrant with the following features:

- Warrant price   29p
- Share price   160p
- Subscription price   177p (on a one for one basis)
- Expiry date   2002

Suppose the underlying share price were to double to 320p by 2002, then we could certainly expect the warrant price to settle at its intrinsic value at least. Thus the warrant could be expected to stand at 143p (320 – 177). (Indeed if the share price were to reach 320p well before 2002, then the warrant price would certainly acquire a time value on top of its intrinsic value of 143p.)

However, if the warrant reaches only 143p, its increase in percentage terms is:

$$\frac{143 - 29}{29} \times 100 \quad = 393\%$$

This shows how gearing on a warrant can magnify the benefits of a rise in the underlying share price.

If we look at the converse and assume the share price never rises above 177p, the warrants would be valueless by the expiry date. This would mean that there had been a 100% loss on the warrants whereas the underlying shares could have increased in value by anything up to 10.625%.

$$\frac{177 - 160}{160} \times 100 = 10.625\%$$

This hypothetical example shows how gearing on a warrant can magnify the effects of the movement in the underlying share price.

Capital fulcrum point

We have just seen how gearing exaggerates the effect of the underlying share price. In our example we saw that a rise of 10.625% or less in the share price at the expiry date would result in a 100% loss in warrant value, whereas a 100% rise in the share price would result in a 393% rise in the warrants.

The capital fulcrum point can be defined as the annual percentage equity growth required (between purchase date and expiry date of the subscription rights in the warrant) for an investor to gain equally, in terms of pure capital gain, whether he buys the warrants or the shares. While there may be some obscure mathematical formula for this calculation, in practice the quickest and easiest method is by trial and error.

Example of capital fulcrum point for a warrant

The details of a warrant's subscription rights are as follows:

- Time to expiry date   8 years
- Subscription price   153p
- Today's warrant price   38p
- Today's share price   149p

If the share price grows by 4% per annum compound, after eight years it will rise to 204p. (A simple check is to multiply 149 by 1.04 or by 104% then multiply the result by 1.04 or 104%, repeating the operation eight times in all.) At the expiry date, the warrant price will consist purely of its intrinsic value, which will be (204 − 153) = 51p.

If the warrant grows at the same 4% per annum compounded, it will indeed reach 52p after eight years. (Check as before by multiplying 38 by 1.04 or 104% repeating the process eight times in all.)

In the above example the investor will make a marginally better capital gain on the warrants over eight years if the growth rate of the shares exceeds 4% per annum compound. Obviously the lower the capital fulcrum point, the greater the attraction of the warrant as opposed to the equity.

Points to bear in mind when evaluating a warrant

Takeovers

If there is a likelihood of a takeover, the warrant holder could suffer very badly if the warrant is 'out of the money'.

Under the terms of the issue of almost all warrants there is a clause stating that in the event of a successful takeover of the company, the subscription expiry date will be brought forward to coincide with the bid. The successful bidder must then offer the intrinsic value of the warrants calculated on his offer price to the ordinary shareholders. However, there is no obligation to compensate the warrant holders for lost 'time value'.

Let us revert to our previous example of a warrant, and refresh our memories on the salient points:

- Warrant price   29p
- Share price   160p
- Subscription price   177p
- Expiry date   2002

The warrant is 'out of the money' because the subscription price exceeds the current share price.

Suppose there is a successful takeover at a general offer price of 180p. The warrant expiry date would be brought forward, and the successful bidder would have to offer the intrinsic value of the warrants, i.e. 3p (180 – 177).

The conclusion from all this is that when a warrant's price consists mainly of time value, the warrant holder should sell his warrant on the first news of a takeover bid, unless the offer price is vastly above the current share price. Having no votes, warrant holders cannot exercise any influence on the outcome of the takeover.

Capitalization issues and rights issues

The warrant holder can view such issues with equanimity, because the Stock Exchange requires the company to protect warrant holders from suffering any loss due from a fall in the ex capitalization or ex rights price.

Liquidation

The rights of a warrant holder in liquidation will depend on the terms of the issue. In any event a warrant is classed as capital, and the warrant holder will rank behind all external creditors.

Capital fulcrum point

The lower the capital fulcrum point, the more attractive the warrants.

Expiry date

The longer the expiry date the better, because there is a greater chance of a favourable movement in the price of the underlying shares. The current market price of the warrant could well contain a large 'time value' in recognition of the value of a long timescale.

The company

As with convertibles, the golden rule is not to buy warrants unless the investor expects the company to be successful.

Capital gains tax

Warrants do not constitute a 'wasting asset' for CGT purposes, thus an unexercised warrant becomes valueless on expiry of the subscription period, and is classed as a loss for CGT purposes. If the warrant is exercised, the cost of the shares for CGT purposes is the exercise price plus the cost of the warrants.

Conclusion

Because of the gearing factor, warrants are really suitable only for investors who can afford to risk their capital in the hope of a great reward. Remember there is neither dividend nor voting rights unless and until the subscription is made.

13   Traded Options

Traded options are traded on the London International Financial Futures and Options Exchange (LIFFE). Traded options are a type of derivative (i.e. their value derives from that of another asset) and, as their name implies, can be bought and sold at any time during their lives. Alternatively they can be exercised or abandoned.

A 'call' traded option gives the purchaser the right, but not the obligation, to buy the underlying shares. A 'put' traded option gives the purchaser the right, but not the obligation, to sell the underlying shares.

Traded options can be arranged only in certain securities. At present there are traded options available in approximately 90 classes, some of which include index options in FTSE 100 and Eurostyle FTSE 100, as well as shares such as Asda, Barclays Bank and RTZ. Details of the classes available can be found in the *Financial Times*.

Traded options run for three-, six- and nine-month periods and are standardized contracts. Although the price of the option and the exercise price are quoted for a single share, each contract, which is indivisible, relates to 1,000 shares.

If a traded option is bought and sold on the market, gains or losses are allowed for CGT purposes. If the traded option is actually exercised, the position for CGT is that the cost of a call option is added to the purchase price and the cost of a put is deducted from the sale proceeds.

Note: these rules are applicable only to the private investor. Professionals investors pay income tax or corporation tax.

Traded options can be exercised at any time and settlement is for 'cash', thus payment is due on the next working day.

How prices of traded options are quoted

Let us examine details of a typical traded option in Orange shares.

Note: assume today is 2 November.

Option	Exercise price	Calls			Puts		
		Dec	**Mar**	**June**	**Dec**	**Mar**	**June**
Orange	1450	85$\frac{1}{2}$	135$\frac{1}{2}$	188	471	81	118
(*1478$\frac{1}{2}$)	1500	57	108$\frac{1}{2}$	164	71	104$\frac{1}{2}$	143

* underlying share price

Explanation of price of the Orange traded option

The price of a traded option, which strictly speaking is called the option premium, is set by supply and demand. However, the theoretical components of the price of traded options are:

● *Intrinsic value*: Amount by which the share price exceeds the exercise price for a call, or amount by which the exercise price exceeds the share price for a put. This figure can be given an exact value. As with warrants, there can never be a negative intrinsic value.

● *Time value*: This value is subjective. Generally speaking, the longer the option has to run, and the more volatile the price of the underlying share, the greater the chance of the underlying share price moving in favour of the holder of the option.

Examples from the above

For 85$\frac{1}{2}$p you can purchase a call option to buy Orange shares at 1450p, any time up to 4 December. For 135$\frac{1}{2}$p you can buy the shares at 1450p any time up to 4 March. For 188p you can buy the shares at any time up to 4 June at 1450p.

The call option premiums are made up as follows:

	December	**March**	**June**
Intrinsic	28$\frac{1}{2}$	28$\frac{1}{2}$	28$\frac{1}{2}$
Time	57	107	159$\frac{1}{2}$
Option premium (price)	85$\frac{1}{2}$	135$\frac{1}{2}$	188

(Intrinsic value is calculated: 1478$\frac{1}{2}$ -1450).

If we look at the bottom line of put options, we can see that the prices are made up as follows:

	December	March	June
Intrinsic	$21\frac{1}{2}$	$21\frac{1}{2}$	$21\frac{1}{2}$
Time	$49\frac{1}{2}$	83	$121\frac{1}{2}$
Option premium (price)	71	$104\frac{1}{2}$	143

Note: an option contract relates to 1,000 shares. The cost of only one December put traded option contract would be £710 (excluding commission).

The concept of 'in the money' options and 'out of the money' options applies in just the same way as for warrants. For example, the December $47\frac{1}{2}$ put is 'out of the money' because the exercise price of 1450p is below the current share price of $1478\frac{1}{2}$p. 'Out of the money' traded options are more speculative than 'in the money' ones and thus can be said to be 'higher geared'.

If the exercise price is approximately equal to the underlying share price, the option is said to be 'at the money'.

Traded option terminology

Exercise price

This is the price at which the traded option can be exercised. Statistically, only approximately 5% of traded options are ever exercised. The majority of traded options are either sold in the market or allowed to expire, thus becoming worthless.

Writers

These are the organizations, approved by the Stock Exchange, that will guarantee to honour any traded options that may be exercised.

Premium

The premium is the price of the traded option.

Premium = time value + intrinsic value.

Expiry dates and series

The expiry date is the last day on which a traded option can be exercised. Expiry dates are fixed at three-monthly intervals, and there are three possible expiry cycles:

- January, April, July, October
- February, May, August, November
- March, June, September, December

When a traded option is written on the shares of a company it is allocated to one of the above three cycles. It is rare for the allocated cycle to be changed. At any one time only three of the four months specified in the cycle will be quoted.

All options on a particular security that have the same exercise price and exercise date are known as a series.

Option premiums for traded options

The prices are published in various newspapers, such as the *Financial Times*. However, the prices are based on the settlement prices of the previous day, and there is always a spread between 'bid' and 'offer' prices.

Other charges on traded options

Commission rates are negotiable between investor and broker. One example of the rates quoted is 1.5% of the option premium, plus £1 per contract subject to a minimum of £20, although commission is usually charged at half these rates on closing deals.

Index traded options

Index options are not based on individual shares, but on an index. The indices used are the FTSE 100 Index and Eurostyle FTSE 100 Index.

If an index option is exercised, the buyer will receive cash equal to the difference between the index value on the day of exercise and the exercise price of the series being executed, multiplied by £10.

These options are quoted with a large range of index values, and with four-month, not three-monthly expiry dates. Thus they expire at monthly intervals.

Taking today as 2 November 1999.

FTSE 100 Index (*6284)
* this is the underlying index number

CALLS	5800	5900	6000	6100	6200	6300	6400	6500
Nov	$520^1/_2$	427	340	$250^1/_2$	176	112	62	$28^1/_2$
Dec	568	484	$403^1/_2$	$330^1/_2$	$260^1/_2$	$198^1/_2$	142	$99^1/_2$
Jan	656	577	498	$419^1/_2$	349	$284^1/_2$	220	$172^1/_2$
Feb	$715^1/_2$	636	557	$478^1/_2$	414	$350^1/_2$	$288^1/_2$	$239^1/_2$
PUTS	5800	5900	6000	6100	6200	6300	6400	6500
Nov	15	22	33	$43^1/_2$	70	107	$159^1/_2$	229
Dec	$51^1/_2$	75	83	109	$138^1/_2$	$169^1/_2$	$226^1/_2$	$284^1/_2$
Jan	$106^1/_2$	127	$148^1/_2$	$170^1/_2$	$201^1/_2$	$237^1/_2$	276	$329^1/_2$
Feb	$164^1/_2$	180	196	$213^1/_2$	243	274	308	357

The minimum contract size is 1,000. To purchase a call option expiring in November, with the expectation that the index will have risen to 6,500, the cost will be $1,000 \times 28^1/_2 = £285$ excluding dealing costs.

If the index rises to 6500, the November call will be exercised. On exercising the option the amount received is £2,160 (calculated 6500 – the underlying index number of 6284 = 216 x £10 = £2,160), thus a net profit of £1,875 (£2,160 – £285) before dealing costs will have been made.

There are two distinct types of option with index options, the European option that was introduced on 1 February 1990, and can be exercised only on its expiry date, and the American option that was introduced on 3 May 1984, and can be exercised on any normal business day.

Index options are particularly useful for providing protection for a portfolio against adverse movements in share prices. If a fund manager expects the market to fall, he will buy a put option to protect the portfolio. If the index does fall, he will receive cash to compensate for the fall in the value of the portfolio.

Hedging a portfolio of equities using index traded options

'Hedging' is the term for using a specific tool such as a traded option to protect an investment against a fall in value. Hedging can be likened to a form of insurance.

If an investor has a portfolio of equities and expects the market to fall in the next few months he can do one of two things to protect the capital value – either he can sell all the shares or he can use a put index traded option. Selling all the shares will incur heavy dealing costs on a large portfolio and may also give rise to a capital gains tax liability. If he is wrong about the movement of the market and it rises, he has lost out on the rise in value that would have occurred in the portfolio.

The purchase of a put index traded option protects against a fall in share prices because as the market falls the put index traded option rises in value. If shares prices rise the put index traded option will fall in value, thus the cost of the option is lost but the rise in the value of the portfolio will compensate for the loss. A gain on a traded option is liable for CGT, but the gain is likely to be far lower than that from selling the whole equity portfolio.

Provided the investor can find an index option that reflects his portfolio, he can provide a hedge against falls that protects against the downside risk but enables him to benefit from the upside movement. Consider an example of a portfolio, using the FTSE 100 index put option figures given.

The investor has a portfolio of blue chip equities valued at £230,000 today. He feels which the market may have reached its peak and will fall back by 10%. He wishes to retain the right to sell the market at 5900 for three months. He will purchase a February 5900 put option at 180 index points. The cost of the February 5900 put at 180 is:

● Buy 4 x February 5900 at £180 each = £720 (plus dealing costs)

Calculation

Each index point is worth £10

Each put covers £59,000 (5900 x £10)

Thus he will purchase ($\frac{£230,000}{59,000}$ = 3.9) 4 puts to cover his position.

If the market falls to 5310 (5900 less 10%) the option will be exercised. He will receive (4 puts at £5,900 each) £23,600 (less dealing costs), which gives him a net profit of £22,880 (£23,600 – £720). The portfolio will have fallen by 10% from £230,000 to £207,000, a loss of £23,000. This is not entirely covered by the net gain on the index option, but hedging the portfolio has protected most of the value.

In reality, the portfolio may fall by more or less than the fall in the market, unless the chosen index and the portfolio exactly mirror each other in weighting and number of holdings of shares.

If the market rises during the period the option may not follow suit, and the closer February is, the less likely it is that the option price will also rise. Thus a rise in value of the portfolio will be offset against the cost of buying this particular put index traded option.

Conclusion

The traded option market has expanded very quickly over the last few years (students should study the *Financial Times* to examine the number of classes and series of traded options available). However, the complexities of this market mean that it must remain the domain of the professional who wishes to speculate or to hedge his position, or alternatively of the speculator who can afford to risk his capital in pursuit of great potential rewards available from the gearing factor.

14   Risk and the Reverse Yield Gap

From a study of this unit and the earlier units, you will readily appreciate that some investments are more risky than others. For the moment, let us omit warrants and options from our considerations, and simply compare gilts, local authority quoted stocks and company securities.

The order in degrees of risk would appear to be as follows:

● Equities (most risky)

● Preference shares

● Unsecured loan stock

● Secured loan stocks

● Local authority stocks

● Gilts (least risky).

Risk and return

The prime rule of investment is that the greater the risk, the greater the return must be. If we were to demonstrate in graph form we would expect the position to look like Fig. 8.1.

Figure 8.1

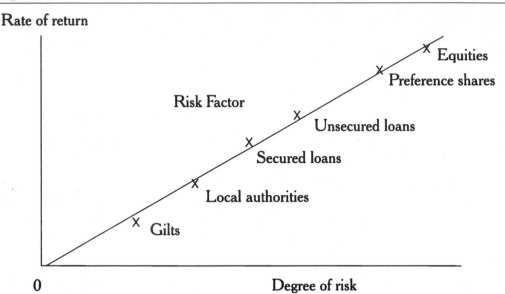

Rate of return

Risk Factor

X Equities
X Preference shares
X Unsecured loans
X Secured loans
X Local authorities
X Gilts

0   Degree of risk

Note: the graph is for illustration purposes only and is not intended to be drawn to scale.

Obviously a secured loan stock in a speculative company could be more risky than an unsecured loan stock in, say, a bank, but the graph assumes that we are comparing different classes of security in the same company with gilts and local authorities.

Why the reverse yield gap makes the above graph seem untrue

The graph in Fig. 8.1 is correct except for one major discrepancy – the returns on equities compared with fixed-interest stocks. In theory, the return on equities should be much higher than that on gilts, because gilts have the backing of the Government. In practice this is not so, when comparing dividend yields and redemption yields. As this is the 'reverse' of what you would expect, so the term 'reverse yield gap' has been coined.

Since 1959 equities have yielded less than gilts (when comparing dividends) for one basic reason – their scope for growth. Inflation erodes the purchasing power of fixed-interest payments in real terms, and that income cannot increase whatever the rate of inflation. Likewise, the capital value of a fixed-interest stock is always set at a fixed amount, usually at par, with a known redemption date (or dates). Thus the capital value of a fixed-interest stock will also be eroded by inflation. (Index-linked gilts are, of course, the exception here.)

Equities, on the other hand, give scope for both growth of dividends and growth of capital. Share prices in general have out-performed inflation over the long term. In view of this, an investor is prepared to accept a lower initial dividend yield from equities than he will accept from gilts. This factor was recognized by the institutions at that time, whereas they had previously invested almost exclusively in the fixed-interest market, they began to switch their emphasis to equities.

It must be remembered that the return from equities consists of two elements, dividend and capital growth. Investors in equities require a higher total return from equities than is required from gilts. However, a lower initial dividend yield is acceptable.

How the reverse yield gap is measured

The two 'benchmarks' that are used for comparison purposes are:

- The gross dividend yield on the FTSE Actuaries All Share Indices;

- The gross redemption yield on the British Government high-coupon long-dated benchmark gilt.

This information can be found in the *Financial Times* and students must be aware of the current rates at the time of the examination. In November 1999 the gap is 2.4%, with gilts yielding 4.74% and equities 2.34%. The gap has narrowed since mid-1997, when gilts yielded 7.07% and equities 3.35%, giving a gap of 3.72%.

If the yield gap widens, gilts would appear to be relatively cheap in price in relation to equities and it can be taken as a sign to buy gilts. If the yield gap narrows, this may be taken as a sign to buy equities since it means gilts prices are rising more quickly than those of equities.

Gilt/equity yield ratio

The principles involved are similar to those of the reverse yield gap, in so far as the returns on gilts and equities are compared using gross redemption yields and gross dividend yields. However, instead of measuring the gap in absolute terms (i.e. gilt yield minus equity yield) a ratio is calculated thus:

$$\frac{\text{gross redemption yield (long dated benchmark gilt)}}{\text{gross dividend yield on FTSE Actuaries All Share Index}}$$

Gilts usually yield between two and three times as much as equities. If the ratio falls, this is a signal to buy equities, and if it rises it is a signal to buy gilts.

Summary

Now that you have studied this unit, you should be able to:

- describe the main features of ordinary shares;

- describe the main features of preference shares;

- describe the main features of company loan stocks and debentures;
- describe the main features of convertibles;
- describe the types of local authority loans available;
- describe the nature of permanent interest bearing shares;
- describe warrants;
- describe traded options;
- calculate the time value and intrinsic value of traded options;
- explain traded option terminology;
- describe index traded options;
- explain the nature of risk and return;
- show how the reverse yield gap relates to risk and return.

9

OTHER FORMS OF DIRECT INVESTMENT

Objectives

After studying this unit, you should be able to:

● understand what overseas investment is, its advantages and disadvantages;

● define and describe the main features of overseas bonds and Eurobonds;

● define and describe bearer securities, marking certificates and depository receipts, including American Depository Receipts;

● understand the principles of investment in unquoted companies;

● explain the advantages and disadvantages of investing in property, both for residential use and as an investment, and understand the various methods of financing the purchase of property;

● define chattels, give examples of chattels used for investment purposes and describe the advantages and disadvantages of investing in chattels.

1   Introduction

Apart from gilts and company securities there are various other forms of direct investment available to an investor. Some of these investments are in stocks and shares of UK and non-UK companies and other bodies which can be purchased in a variety of methods detailed in this unit. Other investments are investments in tangible assets such as property.

2   Overseas Equity Investment

An investor who puts his money purely into UK-based companies that have all or most of their profits arising in the UK loses out on the potential available in overseas markets. Obviously there are many problems involved as well. It can be difficult enough to keep track of the UK stock market, let alone the Japanese stock market. Even so, there is sufficient potential overseas to make such investments suitable for inclusion in many portfolios.

Advantages of overseas investment

The London Stock Market is the third largest in the world, behind New York (USA), which is the largest, and Japan (Tokyo), which is the second largest. These three markets are the world's major markets. They are commonly known as the 'golden triangle', and because of time differences one of these three is always open.

The European markets are all smaller than the UK (London), with France, Germany, Holland, Spain, Sweden and Switzerland representing some of the other European markets. Effectively the major markets are overseas, with Europe, including the UK, representing about 20% of the market.

Because different markets are at different stages of economic growth at any one time, there is potential for large gains (and losses) by investing in these markets. There are also newer markets in the old communist countries, and markets in other Latin American, Asian and European countries that are now being recognized as 'emerging markets'.

The 'emerging markets' account for around 12% of the world's stock markets by market capitalization, and the emerging markets consist of approximately 16 countries. These markets have only a relatively small number of stocks and shares quoted, thus a major buy or sell order can move the market dramatically. The performance of some of the emerging markets is measured by the Emerging Markets: IFC Investable Indices.

Currency movements vis-à-vis sterling and the overseas currency can generate higher profits when sterling falls against the overseas currency.

It is possible to invest in sectors that do not exist in the UK, or that are very few and far between. Two very good examples of such areas are gold mining and diamond mining.

Disadvantages of overseas investment

While currency movements can work in favour of the investor, they can also work against him. It is not unknown for a rise in the value of sterling against the particular currency involved to wipe out all the profits made. This is called the exchange risk.

There is a 'political risk' involved in certain countries. Although a country may appear to be politically stable when an investment is made, changes may take place that wreck that stability.

Although the UK does not have any exchange control regulations at present, other countries do have them, or could easily introduce them. If this occurs it may be impossible for an investor to remove his money from that country, and no amount of profit made by that investment is of any use if it cannot be brought back to the UK.

Certain countries have made double taxation agreements with the UK. Where this has happened the UK resident, who is of course liable to UK tax on his overseas investments, will receive a credit to offset against his UK tax liability if the investment has also been subject to tax in the overseas country. For example, if the overseas dividends are subject to a 20% 'withholding tax' levied by the overseas government, the UK tax liability will be reduced by the same amount. The maximum amount of double taxation relief available cannot exceed the UK tax liability of the investor. Thus a withholding tax of 40% is only allowed for up to 10% on dividends interest for a basic-rate taxpayer, the investor 'pays' the extra 30% himself in effect to the overseas government. In the main the investors who suffer most from any withholding tax are non-taxpayers, because in many cases it is not possible to reclaim the withholding tax from the overseas government.

The levels of accountancy policies, disclosure requirements and controls abroad do not always match up to the UK standards. Where this is the case an investor may not be aware of any adverse trends or unhealthy situations until it is too late.

It is very difficult to obtain information about overseas companies from the UK press, thus monitoring performance becomes very difficult. However, in 1987 the *Financial Times Actuaries World Indices* commenced. These indices allow an investor to follow the general progress of overseas markets in terms of sterling, US$ or local currency. (See Unit 17 for details of all *Financial Times* Indices.) It is more difficult to find information about companies in the smaller, emerging markets. Any press comment will be in their own national press thus, unless the investor is fluent in a specific language, problems arise! However, there is now comment regularly in the *Financial Times* about the emerging markets, plus the Emerging Markets: IFC Investable Indices to help to judge performance.

Different stock exchanges have different settlement periods, and some exchanges deal only in 'board lots', i.e. shares are sold only in multiples of, say, 1,000 shares. For example, in Japan, 90% of quoted stock is available only in lots of 1,000 shares.

Some countries, or even some companies, restrict the proportion of shares that can be held by overseas investors. In such cases, these limited holdings may command a premium price compared to domestic holdings. This higher price may make the shares less attractive to investors, particularly because there is no difference in the amount of dividend paid to national and overseas investors.

Many foreign stock exchanges not only limit the number of shares held by overseas investors, but also prohibit the overseas investor from having any voting rights.

Dividends are received in foreign currency, thus the cheque will have to be converted to sterling. The costs associated with such a transaction will greatly reduce the value of the dividend.

There are several alternatives available to investors interested in overseas equity investment. Some methods are safer than others, and much depends on the amount of risk the investor is willing to take.

Purchasing shares of an overseas company on an overseas stock exchange

This operation is done by approaching a stockbroker in the UK who will make the necessary arrangements to purchase the shares on the overseas stock exchange. This is the most risky method of investing overseas because it carries all of the disadvantages mentioned above, and is also an expensive operation because the UK stockbroker has to contact the overseas market himself, thus incurring heavy dealing costs. This method of overseas investment is suitable only for the institutional investors who have very large amounts to invest, and the necessary expertise available to monitor the risks involved.

Purchasing shares of an overseas company quoted on the London Stock Exchange

Certain shares are available that are quoted both on the stock exchange in their own country and on the London Stock Exchange. Some of these shares are quoted fully on the London Stock Exchange. In the *Financial Times* you will find details of American, Canadian and South African shares under those headings, along with other companies that are included under headings such as 'Oil Exploration and Production'.

The advantages of purchasing overseas shares by this method is that it reduces the problems of exchange risk, because the shares are bought and sold in sterling (although the dividend received may well be in foreign currency). It is also easier to obtain information about these companies from sources such as the financial press because the London Stock Exchange requires all listed companies to supply certain information as a prerequisite to obtaining a quotation.

Purchasing shares of a UK company with large overseas interests

There are quite a few UK multinational companies whose profits depend quite heavily on their overseas operations. Companies such as ICI and BP Amoco not only export goods, but also have operations in overseas countries. The success or otherwise of these activities will be reflected in the profits of that company.

This method of investment not only reduces the exchange risk but also the problems of accountancy, disclosure and control requirements, because these companies are subject to the UK requirements laid down by the Companies Acts 1985 and 1989 and the Stock Exchange's 'Continuing Obligations'. In addition, this method also removes the problem of finding enough information in the financial press.

Indirect investment in overseas equities

Even this method does not overcome the problem that the majority of investors do not possess the time and expertise necessary to manage direct equity investment, and some investors who would like an element of overseas exposure do not have enough money available for direct equity investment on a large enough scale. To overcome these problems, indirect investment overseas is the answer, and the two methods that are available are unit trusts and investment trusts.

Minimum amounts for direct investment in overseas equities

Direct investment in overseas equities should only be considered for portfolios in excess of

£1 million. The minimum amount per share for cost effectiveness is £5,000 per share.

3 Overseas Bonds

A bond is an interest bearing certificate of debt, issued by large companies, governments, banks, supranational organizations (e.g. The World Bank) and by nationalized industries. Most bonds carry a fixed rate of interest, are repayable at or between set future dates and can be traded at any time up to maturity.

Bonds issued by the UK government are called gilt-edged securities, bonds issued in the US are 'Treasury Bonds' or 'T' bonds, in France they are called OATs (*obligation à trésorerie*) and in Japan JGBs (Japanese Government Bonds). The standing of these bonds depends greatly on the standing of the issuing authority.

Commonwealth securities

There have been many times when Commonwealth countries have borrowed from UK residents by issuing securities that are quoted on the UK Stock Exchange. The status of such securities is not, as you would expect, automatically high. Obviously countries such as New Zealand are as stable as the UK, but some of the old Eastern Bloc countries, sadly, are not.

Foreign government bonds

As with all government securities, the standing depends very much on the government issuing them. Some foreign government securities have virtually 'gilt-edged' status, such as Finnish and Swedish stocks, whereas others are virtually worthless except as collector's items. An example of one such stock is the pre-revolution Chinese Boxer issue that can be purchased for less than £10 per nominal £100 stock, because the likelihood of a modern Chinese government offering any terms at all for repayment is virtually nil. However, the certificates themselves are collected for their artistic merit and thus have a value in themselves.

Some foreign governments have defaulted or deferred on interest payments. In such cases the Council of Foreign Bondholders will exert pressure on the defaulting government to make it pay. The council's main weapon is that eventually defaulting governments will need to raise fresh capital, and when this happens it has enough power to insist upon agreement being reached with existing creditors before the new loan can be agreed.

A number of foreign government securities have been issued in London in sterling and these have been nicknamed 'bulldog bonds'. Interest is payable in London in sterling on these bonds. Issues in foreign currency are affected by the exchange risk, and the fluctuations of the currency must be taken into account when investing.

Eurobonds

A Eurobond is a loan to a government, public body or company underwritten by an international syndicate of banks and sold in countries other than the country of issue. Interest rates can be fixed or floating. A floating-rate note Eurobond denominated in US$ has the interest linked to the Interbank rate for Eurodollars, and this linking to market rates should make the bond price stable.

The principal currencies of issue are sterling, dollars, yen and euros.

Eurobonds are issued in bearer form and, as with all bearer shares, interest is claimed by submitting a coupon. It is safer to keep the certificate in safe custody, and Euroclear provide safe custody facilities for Eurobonds, in addition to the usual UK banks' facilities.

There is no withholding tax on Eurobond interest, but such income must be declared on the investor's tax return. Income tax is payable and any capital gain is subject to CGT.

4   Bearer Securities

These are stocks and shares issued mainly by overseas companies, public bodies and governments. The issuing authority does not maintain a register of ownership, whereas with virtually all UK stocks and shares there is a register. Ownership of these securities passes by mere delivery, unlike registered stocks and shares where ownership is transferred by the system described in Unit 5. There is no owner's name shown anywhere on the certificate.

Some gilts have part of the issue available in bearer form, one example is 3½% War Loan. A few UK-registered companies also have part of their share capital in bearer form, two examples being RTZ and Shell Transport.

Ownership of a bearer security vests in the holder of the certificate, and ownership passes by mere delivery. A problem here arises if the share certificate is stolen, and a bona fide transferee for value purchases the certificate from the thief. If this occurred the original owner would lose all his rights to the shares. To safeguard against this occurrence, a bearer certificate should be kept in a safe place such as a bank. Many of the banks, such as Citibank and Barclays Bank, act as global custodians, whereby they hold bearer securities and claim all dividends due for onward remittance to the owner of the shares.

Keeping a bearer certificate with a bank has other advantages also. Because there is no register of holders, the issuing authority does not know where to send notice of meetings, circulars and dividends. Such items are always preceded by advertisements in the financial press or the Bond Holders' Register. In the case of dividend payments the advertisement will inform holders which coupon to submit in order to claim the dividend.

Coupons are attached to the certificate and are numbered. Each time a dividend is claimed the relevantly numbered coupon is detached and sent to the issuing authority. At some time the coupons will run out and the next set of coupons in numerical order will be claimed by submission of the 'talon', which is the last coupon and is larger than the other coupons. Obviously for the private investor it can be easy to miss the dividend notice, and failure to claim the dividend can lead to forfeiting that dividend. If the certificate is lodged with a bank then there is no likelihood of this happening because the bank is geared up to checking for such items. Another advantage here is that the bank will amalgamate all the coupons and make one claim. The cheque received is in foreign currency and must be converted into sterling for distribution to the individual holders. The cost of this is divided between all the holders and it is less than the cost to an individual holder with one cheque to convert into sterling. See the Robeco bearer shares for an example of a bearer share, coupons and talon (see Figures 9.1 and 9.2).

In order for a bearer certificate to be sold it must be 'good delivery'. This means that the certificate must be in good condition and all coupons that should be attached must be attached. If there is any doubt as to whether the certificate is 'good delivery' then application must be made to the Council of the Stock Exchange who will rule on the matter.

The final area that can be a problem with bearer securities is the danger of forged documents. Obviously as ownership can pass by mere delivery it is quite feasible that a forged document could escape careful scrutiny, resulting in a purchaser holding a worthless piece of paper. Here again the bank would be in a position to verify the genuineness of the certificate purchased.

Figure 9.1:

Figure 9.2:

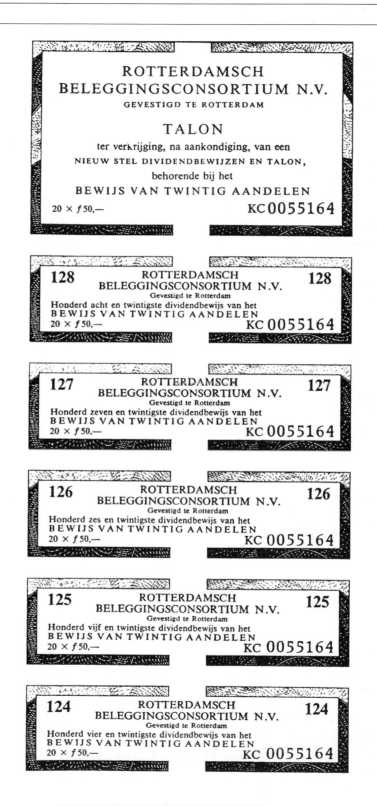

5 Marking Certificates (Shares Registered in a Recognized (or Good) Marking Name)

These are shares issued mainly by American and Canadian companies. They are registered shares. (There are also a few Dutch companies that issue these shares.) The name of the registered holder appears on the front of the certificate and the company maintains a register of holders in exactly the same way as for any registered share.

The difference between marking certificates and ordinary UK registered shares is that the transfer form on the reverse of the share certificate is blank endorsed. This means that the registered holder signs the form in front of a witness, who also must sign, but then leaves the rest of the form blank. This has the effect of making title pass by mere delivery, i.e. the certificate acquires most of the characteristics of a bearer security. (See Figures 9.3 and 9.4, the BellSouth Corporation certificate.)

Figure 9.3:

The registered holder is called the 'marking name' and appears in the issuing company's books as the holder of the certificate. The marking name receives all correspondence, rights and capitalization issue details and dividends. The marking name must then account to the

---

true owner for all of these. It is usual for the marking name to be a member firm of the Stock Exchange, bank or the financial institution recognized as being of impeccable standing by the Stock Exchange. Such a marking name is classified as a 'good marking name' or 'recognized marking name', and shares registered in a 'good or recognized marking name' command a higher price than ones in a 'bad marking name', i.e. in the name of someone or somebody not recognized by the Stock Exchange for this purpose. The 'good marking name' will give the Stock Exchange an undertaking to pay interest and dividends to the true owner when he claims them. Interest and dividends are paid in the currency of the issuing company's country and the 'good marking name' also undertakes to the Stock Exchange to convert the currency cheques at the approved rate of exchange.

There is no reason why the true owner of a marking certificate should not have the shares registered in his own name. To do so he will complete the form on the back of the certificate, showing himself as assignee. He will then send the certificate and the required fee to the issuing authority who will delete the 'good marking name' from its books as holder and insert the true owner's name. It will then issue a new share certificate showing him as registered owner on the front of the certificate. However, it is inadvisable for the true owner to carry out this operation for four reasons:

- The shares will command a lower price in a 'bad marking name', i.e. in a private individual's name, as opposed to being in a 'good marking name';

- There is a fee to be paid to carry out this operation;

- The shareholder will receive a foreign currency cheque and will have to pay the full cost of converting this into sterling. If his holding is not very large, or the dividend is small, he may find that the charges virtually take the whole of the value of the cheque. The issuing authority itself also deducts a charge for paying a dividend to an individual;

- It takes a long time for ownership to be transferred, one reason being that you are dealing with a company abroad, and postal times can be long.

In conclusion it can be seen that it is better to retain the shares in a good marking name. Because the shares are blank endorsed they are effectively bearer shares, and for safety should be kept in the bank. The bank will claim the dividends due, and in the same way as with true bearer shares, the costs of changing the dividend cheque into sterling is divided between all the holders, thus the true owner will effectively receive a higher dividend than he would if he transferred the shares into his own name.

These certificates have the name 'marking certificates' because in the past each time the dividend was claimed the certificate was marked. However, most banks now do not mark the certificate every time the dividend is claimed.

If a shareholder has a marking certificate registered in his own name, it is recommended that he has the shares registered in the name of a good marking name. The major benefit of having the shares transferred into a good marking name is that all dividend cheques are converted to sterling at a lower fee than charged by most banks.

Figure 9.4:

THIS CERTIFICATE ALSO EVIDENCES AND ENTITLES THE HOLDER HEREOF TO CERTAIN RIGHTS AS SET FORTH IN A RIGHTS AGREEMENT BETWEEN BELLSOUTH CORPORATION AND AMERICAN TRANSTECH INC., AS RIGHTS AGENT, DATED NOVEMBER 27, 1989 (THE "RIGHTS AGREEMENT"), THE TERMS OF WHICH ARE INCORPORATED HEREIN BY REFERENCE AND A COPY OF WHICH IS ON FILE AT THE PRINCIPAL EXECUTIVE OFFICE OF BELLSOUTH CORPORATION. UNDER CERTAIN CIRCUMSTANCES, AS SET FORTH IN THE RIGHTS AGREEMENT, SUCH RIGHTS WILL BE EVIDENCED BY SEPARATE CERTIFICATES AND WILL NO LONGER BE EVIDENCED BY THIS CERTIFICATE. BELLSOUTH CORPORATION WILL MAIL TO THE HOLDER OF RECORD OF THIS CERTIFICATE A COPY OF THE RIGHTS AGREEMENT, WITHOUT CHARGE, WITHIN FIVE DAYS AFTER RECEIPT OF A WRITTEN REQUEST THEREFOR. UNDER CERTAIN CIRCUMSTANCES, AS PROVIDED IN THE RIGHTS AGREEMENT, RIGHTS ISSUED TO OR BENEFICIALLY OWNED BY ACQUIRING PERSONS OR THEIR ASSOCIATES OR AFFILIATES (AS DEFINED IN THE RIGHTS AGREEMENT) OR ANY PURPORTED SUBSEQUENT HOLDER OF SUCH RIGHTS WILL BECOME NULL AND VOID.

BELLSOUTH CORPORATION
Relative Rights and Preferences of Classes of Stock of the Company

The Company is authorized to issue one or more series of preferred stock, and the shares represented hereby will be subordinate to each of such series with respect to dividends and amounts payable upon liquidation. The Company will furnish to any shareholder, upon request and without charge, a full statement of the designations, preferences, limitations and relative rights of the common and preferred stocks of the Company and the variations in the relative rights and preferences between the shares of each series of preferred stock insofar as the same have been fixed and determined. The Board of Directors of the Company is authorized to fix and determine the relative rights and preferences of each series of preferred stock at the time of its issuance in the manner provided in Georgia Business Corporation Code Section 14-2-61, as amended, and the Articles of Incorporation. Requests may be addressed to the Transfer Agent named on the face of this Certificate or to the Secretary of the Company in Atlanta, Georgia.

The following abbreviations, when used in the inscription on the face of this certificate, shall be construed as though the words set forth below opposite each abbreviation were written out in full where such abbreviation appears:

TEN COM — as tenants in common
TEN ENT — as tenants by the entireties
JT ENT — as joint tenants with right of survivorship and not as tenants in common

UNIF TRANS MIN ACT — _____ Custodian _____
(Cust)   (Minor)
under Uniform Transfers to Minors
Act _____
(State)

Additional abbreviations may also be used though not in the above list.

For Value received, ____ hereby sell, assign and transfer ____ Shares represented by the within Certificate unto

PLEASE PRINT OR TYPE
SOCIAL SECURITY NUMBER OR TAXPAYER IDENTIFYING NUMBER, NAME AND ADDRESS, INCLUDING ZIP CODE, OF ASSIGNEE

SHARES

PLEASE PRINT OR TYPE
SOCIAL SECURITY NUMBER OR TAXPAYER IDENTIFYING NUMBER, NAME AND ADDRESS, INCLUDING ZIP CODE, OF ASSIGNEE

SHARES

and do hereby irrevocably constitute and appoint ____

____ Attorney

to transfer the said shares on the records of the within named Company with full power of substitution in the premises.

Dated, ____

IMPORTANT { BEFORE SIGNING, READ AND COMPLY CAREFULLY WITH REQUIREMENTS PRINTED BELOW.

THE SIGNATURE(S) TO THIS ASSIGNMENT MUST CORRESPOND WITH THE NAME(S) AS WRITTEN UPON THE FACE OF THE CERTIFICATE IN EVERY PARTICULAR WITHOUT ALTERATION OR ENLARGEMENT OR ANY CHANGE WHATEVER. THE SIGNATURE(S) SHOULD BE GUARANTEED BY A COMMERCIAL BANK OR TRUST COMPANY, OR BY A MEMBER OF THE EXCHANGE(S) ON WHICH THIS STOCK IS LISTED WHOSE SIGNATURE IS KNOWN TO THE TRANSFER AGENT

Director.

Comparison of bearer shares and marking certificates

There is often confusion as to where bearer shares end and marking certificates begin. Because they are both bearer in nature does not mean they are totally identical. Marking certificates acquire only some of the attributes of bearer shares, and the differences and similarities are best seen by the following table of comparison.

Common points

● All bearer or marking certificates should be kept in a bank in safe custody for the following reasons:

➢ Title passes by delivery and a thief could pass on a good title to a bona fide transferee for value;

➢ Banks are geared up to claiming dividends from the company/issuing authority – if a dividend is missed it may be lost forever;

➢ Because the bank amalgamates all the claims it receives only one foreign currency cheque, thus the costs involved in collecting the cheque are much lower and are divided pro rata among all the companies.

● When either security is bought it is dearer than buying a registered security because there are handling fees charged on top of the broker's commission.

● Secrecy – no one knows that you own these certificates (apart from the bank who will never disclose the fact).

6 American Depository Receipts (ADRs)

An American Depository Receipt is a certificate issued by a depository bank stating that a specific number of a company's shares have been deposited with that bank. Some British companies have used the American stock market to raise funds through primary issues of ADRs, notable names being Saatchi and Saatchi, Cadbury Schweppes and BT.

ADRs represent a means by which shares of foreign companies listed on foreign stock exchanges can be traded in dollar denominations and in bearer form in the US stock market. 'Foreign' in relation to ADRs means companies that are not American.

An ADR is created when the shares of a company are purchased on the US stock exchange system and then held in safe custody in a bank. The certificate issued by the bank represents the shares that have been purchased. The holder of the ADR certificate has all dividend rights belonging to the shares, and he has the right to vote at company meetings in the same way as he would if he had purchased the shares direct and held them himself.

From the point of view of the company, which can have anything up to 20% of its equity in ADR form, problems arise because it is unable to trace the beneficial owners of its share capital. This is because the ADRs effectively turn registered shares into bearer shares. It can be vital to a company to know who owns its share capital in the event of a takeover bid, and it is not impossible that a prospective purchaser of the company could acquire a sizeable holding via ADRs without the knowledge of the directors of the company.

Although ADRs are an American creation, some UK institutional investors have purchased shares of UK companies through ADRs in New York rather than on the UK Stock Exchange. ADRs are usually retained in the name of the depository bank but, like marking certificates, they can be transferred into an individual's name.

Other depository receipts

Apart from ADRs, other countries have very similar depository receipts. The various types available are called by their initials, for example BDRs are Bearer Depository Receipts and EDRs are European Depository Receipts. In each case the shares concerned are issued in a country, or in the case of EDRs a continent, other than the one issuing the depository receipts. An example of a BDR is the Ford Motor Company, an American company, and the BDR is issued by a UK bank, NatWest Bank plc. Various Japanese securities are available in depository receipt form, e.g. Nitto Boseki have depository receipts issued by Citibank in EDR (European Depository Receipt) form, and Itoh and Co Limited have depository receipts issued by Hambros Bank in BDR form.

Details of some of the available depository receipts can be found in the Bondholders' Register.

7 Investing in Unquoted Companies

Unquoted companies are ones whose shares are not traded on the Stock Exchange. From the investor's point of view this means any companies whose securities are not dealt in on the Stock Exchange's Main Market or AIM.

In most cases deals are done only on a matched bargain basis (i.e. a buyer and seller must have been found who will deal with the same amount of stock).

Disadvantages of investing in unquoted companies

It is not impossible for an investor who has recently come into a large sum of money to be approached with a view to investing in an unquoted company. This may occur if the company he is employed by sees an opportunity of raising some much needed new finance, or it may just be a friend who makes the suggestion. Whatever the means by which the approach is made, the investor needs to look very carefully at the many disadvantages that apply to this form of investment.

● If the company is desperate to raise new capital, what is the state of the balance sheet? A full analysis needs to be carried out to ascertain whether the company is a 'sinking ship' or whether it is sound, but in need of a capital injection for, say, some major expansion.

- What is being offered in return for the investment? Is it a directorship, debenture stock, loan stock or shares? Does the investor really need what is being offered to complement his position? It is more than likely that the money invested will not produce the right sort of investment for that particular individual.

- Private company shares can be very difficult to sell. The articles of association of the company may restrict the transfer of its shares, and in such a case it may be impossible to find a purchaser who will meet these regulations.

- There is no straightforward valuation available for unquoted shares. For quoted shares valuation is simple, just a matter of obtaining the prices from the *Financial Times*, but for unquoted shares the price to a large extent is what a prospective investor is willing to pay.

- Because of the two problems directly above it may be impossible for the investor to realize his shares when he wishes to, and this is especially difficult if he needs the cash from his investment for a particular purpose.

- Unlike quoted shares, private company shares are not attractive to banks as security against a loan. This is because the bank may not be able to sell the shares if it needs to exercise its power of sale in event of the loan being in default. If the articles of association of the company restrict the transfer of the shares, the power of sale is virtually worthless.

- If the investor is also an employee of the company, and the company goes into liquidation, then his loss will be compounded. He will not only lose his job, but, depending on the class of capital he contributed, he could also lose the cash he invested in the company.

8 Property

Investment in property is the main aim of the majority of wage earners. Owning your own home is seen as attractive although not every homeowner realizes that he has made an investment. For the majority of people their home is the only valuable asset they own and, apart from a few pounds or so in a bank or building society, it will remain their only real investment. At the other end of the scale you find the insurance companies and other institutional investors who own many of the large office blocks and retail shop properties found in our towns and cities. When looking at property as an investment there are two distinct areas to consider: home ownership and investing in property to let.

Home ownership

Property is a very emotive investment. The saying that an Englishman's home is his castle is very true. A house is a real asset, one that will not suffer from the problems that can surround paper assets such as stocks and shares, for example liquidation of the company causing loss of the investment.

However, home ownership does have problems that are unique and that must be guarded against, such as fire, subsidence, theft and any resultant damage. All these risks should be covered by insurance. These problems are though far outweighed by the advantages of home ownership.

Advantages of home ownership

A house is usually purchased using a mortgage. Housing prices tend, over the long term, to rise at a greater rate than inflation.

For example a house costing £30,000 in March 1982 could, in 1999, be worth around £59,000 if the value simply rose in line with the RPI. However, depending on location, such a house could be worth £90,000 or more today.

Mortgage repayments remain fairly static in money terms over the life of the mortgage, while pay increases and inflation reduce them in real terms.

Capital gains on the sale of an owner-occupied house are free of CGT for the main residence and it is usually easy to obtain a mortgage for up to 90% of the value of the property, so the initial sum invested is within the reach of many people. However, care needs to be taken that the mortgage repayments can be comfortably afforded.

When an investor retires it is possible to use the house to generate an income. This is called a mortgage annuity scheme (also called a home income plan) and is available only to investors over the age of 70 (sole owner) or 76 each for joint owners.

If the owner needs at some time in the future to borrow money, a house is a very acceptable form of security.

Disadvantages of home ownership

The costs of purchasing and selling property are high. It is necessary to use solicitors whose fees also include stamp duty on the purchase of property. If a mortgage is used to finance the purchase the lender will require surveyors' reports that must be paid for. The use of an estate agent also adds to the cost if the investor is selling his property.

Building insurance is compulsory if a mortgage is used to purchase the property, but even if the house is purchased without a mortgage, the property should be fully insured, and this is an expensive annual cost. In addition to this, all repairs and maintenance are the responsibility of the owner.

If the investor has taken out the maximum mortgage he can afford he may find problems making ends meet if interest rates rise above the level of his salary increases. If he is made redundant he may no longer be able to afford the house and be forced to sell. This may well occur at a bad time, especially if he lives in an area where many people have been similarly affected. This will depress the prices of the houses in the area, and selling becomes difficult.

Property valuation is difficult. Two estate agents valuing the same house at the same time can give prices that are very different.

Conclusion

Homeowners who have enough cash to repay their mortgages early may wish to remove the 'burden' of a mortgage. While on a straight comparison of interest earned on cash deposited compared to cost of interest (and repayments on a repayment mortgage), it may seem to be attractive to repay early, care must be taken. Mortgage lenders often levy quite high charges for early repayment. Prior to deciding to repay a mortgage early, the cost of these charges must be considered because it may make early repayment less attractive.

There are advantages and disadvantages to all investments, and home ownership is no exception. However there is far more to be said for owning a property than against. If the decision is made not to buy, accommodation will have to be rented. The rent paid is 'lost' money because you never receive any lasting benefit, and there is the feeling expressed by many people who do live in rented accommodation that 'the house is never your own'.

Types of mortgage available

There are various types of mortgage available to investors, all of which attract relief as detailed above.

Repayment

Monthly repayments consist of part repayment of capital and part interest. Life cover is required in case of death prior to the mortgage being repaid.

With-profits endowment

The proceeds of the policy should not only repay the loan, but also produce a lump sum for the investor.

Note: in the past virtually all mortgages have been at a floating (variable) rate. However, many mortgage lenders also offer fixed-rate mortgages. These mortgages have a guaranteed rate of interest fixed for a preset period that can be from two to 25 years. The term of the fixed rate is set at the outset. These mortgages are mainly linked to endowment mortgages.

Pension mortgages

These work in a similar way to an endowment mortgage, but the mortgage is repaid by commutation of part of the pension on retirement. Up to 25% of the available pension can be commuted (i.e. withdrawn in cash), subject to a maximum of £150,000.

The pension mortgage is the most tax efficient, but there is no guaranteed minimum sum available on retirement. In theory the borrower would need to make good the shortfall from his own resources if the pension did not generate sufficient funds. In practice this is unlikely to happen.

The 'extra' tax efficiency of a pension mortgage over an endowment mortgage arises because the pension contribution is eligible for tax relief at the investor's marginal rate of income tax.

Occupational and SERPS pensions cannot be used for pension mortgages, only personal pension plans.

PEP and ISA mortgages

PEPs are Personal Equity Plans; ISAs are Individual Savings plans. ISAs have now replaced PEPs, but there are PEP mortgages still in existence, and these will be supplemented by ISA investments in order to provide the capital due on repayment. These mortgages are often linked to unit trust investment via a PEP or an ISA. The maximum annual investment in unit trusts via a PEP was £6,000. The maximum annual investment in an ISA is £5,000. For high earners this is attractive, especially because the spouse can also take out a plan, effectively doubling the maximum loan. Term life cover is needed in the event of early death.

The tax advantages, especially to high-rate taxpayers, arise because PEP and ISAs proceeds are free of all taxes. The plan can be encashed at any time without penalty, and the proceeds used to repay the mortgage.

Investing in property to let

Purchasing property to let can take the form of purchasing the freehold of the property or by the purchase of leasehold property. If the property purchased is leasehold then it is usually of a commercial nature, i.e. shops or offices which are then sublet. If the property consists of a flat, this is also usually purchased in leasehold form. If private property is rented for full value, this is (technically) called 'rack rent'.

Rack rent

If the property is let to a tenant for its full value, the rent charged is called 'rack rent'. The maximum term of such leases is 50 years. This type of investment can have major problems if the property is let to people to live in. Legislation has been enacted to protect such tenants from unscrupulous landlords who could at one time evict the tenant without notice for no reason at all. For the investor owning such property this legislation has become a nightmare, because it is now an extremely lengthy, and often expensive, business to evict unsatisfactory tenants, even if they have failed to pay the rent due for a long period. The legislation also makes it difficult to raise rents, and in some cases the tenant can have the rent lowered by appealing to the Rent Tribunal.

This legislation has caused many problems for perfectly fair landlords, and has caused a major decline in private rented property as investors find that the problems do not justify the return they receive on their capital investment.

In order to try to overcome the problem of lack of rented accommodation, the Housing Act 1980 brought in legislation covering a new type of tenancy: protected shorthold tenancies.

Protected shorthold tenancies are for not less than one year and for not more than five years. Such a tenancy applies only to a new tenant and cannot be imposed on an existing tenant. Protected shorthold tenancies provide protection for both the landlord and the tenant as follows:

●   The tenant

> ➤ Provided the rent is paid, and any other terms of the tenancy are complied with, the tenant cannot be evicted;

> ➤ The rent can still be subject to a fair rents tribunal.

● The landlord

> ➤ At the end of the tenancy the landlord can compel the tenant to vacate the property upon giving three months' written notice;

> ➤ If the tenant fails to comply with the notice at the end of the period, eviction proceedings are quick and easy.

Advantages of investing in property to let

Property is a good hedge against inflation in the long term, even though commercial property saw major falls in value and fewer tenants able to rent the property during the recession. As the recession has ended, there are now tenants available for office properties.

Rents may be fixed at a sufficiently high level to gain a good income for certain types of letting where there are no problems with rent tribunals, e.g. assured (not protected) tenancies created by the Housing Act 1988. Upward only reviews are usually allowed for in the lease.

Property is a real asset and there is a certain amount of satisfaction to be gained from holding real assets as opposed to paper representing financial assets. One advantage that let property has over financial assets is if the tenant goes into liquidation, the owner of the property still has his main asset and it can be re-let. If a company in which the investor holds shares goes into liquidation he will probably lose everything.

Disadvantages of investing in property to let

Capital gains on the property are subject to capital gains tax at the investor's marginal rate of income tax on gains over £7,100. The gain is calculated after allowing for the costs of selling, i.e. estate agents' and solicitors' fees.

Any income is classed as investment income and is subject to income tax. Any costs involved in the collection of the rents, maintenance, repairs or insurance are allowable against the rent in the computation of the amount of taxable income.

All property maintenance falls to the landlord unless the property has been let on a full repairing lease. Commercial properties let in the period from around 1980 onwards are virtually always on full repairing leases. Older leases leave the internal decoration and repairs to the tenant and the external decoration and fabric maintenance to the landlord. The rent charged will reflect that type of lease is used. For private properties the tenant is expected to leave the internal property in the same repair as it was in when he took it over.

With property let to tenants for residential purposes the landlord then runs up against some very special problems created by the Leasehold Reform Act 1967, among other Acts. A tenant has the right to apply to a rent tribunal if he feels his rent is too high. The tribunal will rule in the case and their decision is binding. This can result in the rent being lowered to a figure below the level required by the landlord.

The other major problem caused by the various Acts is that it can be very difficult to evict an unsatisfactory tenant, even if he is in arrears with his rent. Eviction orders are not quickly and easily obtained in many cases, and they always require the aid of solicitors to obtain them. This means a twofold cost: loss of rent plus the expenses of employing a solicitor. However, the newer protected shorthold tenancies overcome this problem, and virtually all new leases to new tenants are of this type.

The purchase and sale of property plus the costs of drawing up the lease are high. Solicitors' fees, estate agents' fees and other fees such as planning permission are expensive, and while they are allowable against the gain on sale for the computation of the capital gains tax liability, they have to be paid out at purchase and during the letting period. These fees are far in excess of the costs involved in buying stocks and shares.

The length of time involved in buying and selling property renders it a highly illiquid investment. The purchase may take two to three months to complete, while a sale can take a far longer period if a buyer is not readily available.

Unlike stocks and shares, which are easily valued, property valuation is very much a matter of opinion. Purchase cost is not a reliable guide to the selling price. Much depends on the market for property at the time, and the condition of the property being sold, which may be better or worse than the original condition.

With commercial property the usage may be limited by local bylaws. While the investor may have purchased a retail shop in a prime site, if the trade the tenant wishes to carry on in that property is different from the original trade, planning permission may not be forthcoming. This results in the investor holding a property that is empty, thus not generating income, and empty property is a prime target for vandals, which will cause even more problems and expense.

A private investor will need a very large sum to purchase just one property. In certain areas of the country this can be in the £25,000-30,000 range, but in the south and London the figure can easily be £150,000 plus. Even this £25,000-30,000 will buy only a small terraced style or small commercial property, which will not be in a prime area. To have a good investment in property requires prime site properties in various centres, and the costs involved here are outside the range of the vast majority of investors. It is really only the institutional investors who have the requisite amount of money for the scale of investment needed to provide a good spread of properties.

In conclusion it must be said that investing in property to let is really outside the range of the majority of private investors. Only the institutions really have the time, expertise and funds to manage property investment successfully. For the private investor who wishes to have a property element in his portfolio, indirect investment is a much more attractive option. There are three main ways in that to invest indirectly in property; property shares, property bonds, and property unit trusts.

Property shares

Property shares are quoted on the Stock Exchange and they are bought and sold in exactly the same way as any other share. The property companies invest in large commercial properties, usually in prime sites in towns and cities. The underlying assets of these companies are the properties, and at times this can cause problems.

Despite the fall in commercial property values, property shares have (in the main) risen in value. The property share does not suffer from the illiquidity of direct property investment, and more institutional investors have moved into property shares and out of direct property investment.

Property bonds and property unit trusts

The other two major alternatives mentioned are somewhat different from property shares. Property bonds are insurance company products, while property unit trusts are collective investments.

9   Chattels

Otherwise called 'alternative investments' or 'collectibles', chattels are defined for tax purposes as tangible moveable assets. They include antiques, pictures, jewellery, china and wine among others, but do not include motor vehicles (which are classed as 'wasting assets' for CGT purposes), or gold, silver or other precious metals except when made into items such as jewellery.

Chattels prices can be very volatile, and valuation can be difficult because there is no standardized market. Prices are set by how much the buyer and seller agree upon, or the highest bid made at auction.

Advantages of investing in chattels

Very large capital gains are possible, especially if you are able to predict the next trend in 'collectibles' and are able to purchase an item at a low price just before the market blossoms. There is a favourable tax treatment for CGT purposes that is explained also below.

The bulk of chattels are attractive to own and can bring great pleasure to the owner. As Keats said, 'A thing of beauty is a joy forever'.

Disadvantages of investing in chattels

Although large capital gains can be made, chattel values can fluctuate wildly. To a certain extent the strength or weakness of the dollar is an influence on prices, because Americans are very heavy investors in the UK chattel market. A strong dollar will make UK chattel prices even more attractive, thus pushing up UK prices. When inflation levels in the UK are low, as is now the case, chattels tend on the whole not to rise very quickly in price. It should also be noted that they generate no income whatsoever.

Valuation is difficult. The purchase price of the chattel is not a good guide to its value, especially as some chattels carry $17^1/2\%$ VAT that is not part of the true cost of the item.

Dealers' buying and selling prices vary a great deal, and different dealers will quote different prices for an identical item, so it is necessary to 'shop around' to obtain the best price.

Some items such as paintings will require specialist storage to ensure they are kept in good condition. This will either have to be installed, or the painting will have to be kept in a specialist store, each of which adds to the cost of the item.

Chattels are valuable items, thus insurance to protect against damage, fire and theft is essential. For some very valuable items, insurance companies may insist on special alarm systems being installed before they will provide insurance cover. Again this adds to the cost of the item.

Many of these items are quite easy to forge, and it takes an expert to detect forgeries. In the art world, forging Old Masters is more difficult, although one artist, Tom Keating, was such an expert forger in this field that several major art galleries and museums paid the going price for the genuine 'Old Master', only to find out later that it was a Tom Keating forgery. The paintings they had paid hundreds of thousands of pounds for were virtually worthless. In fact this particular forger has now become so notorious that his forgeries command a price in their own right, which while well below the price of the genuine article, is nonetheless at a high enough level to make his paintings 'collectibles'.

Many chattel prices are subject to fashion, certain items becoming fashionable to collect, pushing prices up rapidly. If last year's fashion has now gone out of date prices will consequently fall.

Taxation treatment of chattels

Sale proceeds of chattels are subject to capital gains tax, at the investor's marginal rate of income tax on sale proceeds (not the gain) of over £6,000 per item. The £6,000 applies to each person, thus a chattel jointly owned by husband and wife has a £12,000 exemption. Indexation allowance and taper relief apply as described in Unit 6.

The £6,000 exemption applies to items that are not part of a set, and while a set is not defined legally, items made as a pair, such as a pair of candlesticks, or an item such as a canteen of cutlery, would be regarded as one item only. If the items form such a set and are sold to the same or associated persons, the £6,000 exemption limit applies to the whole set regardless of the number of items it contains.

If an investor owned a set of items but wished to sell only part of the set and retain the rest, he would be able to claim the exemption if he did not subsequently sell the remainder to the same or associated persons. However, he would have to bear in mind that items made as a set command a far higher price than do the individual parts. He may well end up with a larger after-tax gain by selling the set as a whole and paying CGT than by breaking it up to gain the exemption.

How to reduce the risks involved

Having looked at the many problems surrounding chattel investment an investor may feel that he would still like exposure to the chance of gains to be made in this area, but not wish to have all the problems associated with physical ownership. In this case the main way of gaining this exposure is to purchase the shares of a company that deals in chattels, e.g. Sotheby's. This will give the investor exposure to the rise in value of chattels, but because the companies deal in more than one chattel there is a degree of diversification, especially in the case of Sotheby's who will auction many items apart from chattels, and whose profits depend on the prices paid at auction.

Summary

Now that you have studied this unit, you should be able to:

- describe the advantages and disadvantages of investing in overseas equities;
- describe the methods of investing in overseas equities;
- explain who issues overseas bonds;
- Describe the problems associated with investing in:
  - ➣ commonwealth securities
  - ➣ foreign government bonds
  - ➣ eurobonds;
- describe the nature of bearer securities;
- describe the nature of marking certificates;
- compare and contrast bearer shares and marking certificates;
- describe ADRs and other Depository Receipts;
- explain the problems that arise with investing in unquoted companies;
- explain the benefits and problems of investing in property for home ownership;
- describe the different types of mortgage available and the advantages and disadvantages of each type;
- explain the advantages and disadvantages of purchasing property as an investment;
- explain the use of property shares and property bonds as methods of indirect property investment;
- define what is meant by 'chattels';
- describe the advantages and disadvantages of investing in chattels;
- describe the taxation treatment of chattels;
- describe how to minimize the risk of investing in chattels.

10

ASSESSMENT OF COMPANY SECURITIES 1: FROM THE COMPANY ACCOUNTS

Objectives

After studying this unit, you should be able to:

- assess the information in published accounts from the point of view of a shareholder;
- define 'shareholders' funds', 'net asset value' and 'capital cover';
- calculate a liquidity ratio and understand its significance;
- calculate earnings per share and understand its significance;
- calculate the price/earnings ratio and understand its significance;
- understand the significance of:
  - ➤ dividend yield and dividend cover
  - ➤ income cover
  - ➤ income priority percentages;
- know the meaning of cash flow and understand its importance;
- interpret information published in the *Financial Times* on company performance;
- define gearing and understand its significance to future company prospects.

1   Introduction

In this unit we consider how a company's financial accounts can be used to assess the immediate past performance of a company. We shall see how the private investor, and the student, can find the relevant information.

2   The Information to be Found in a Balance Sheet

A balance sheet is a list of the book values of assets and liabilities of a company at a particular date. Obviously assets such as good labour relations or an expanding customer base cannot appear in the balance sheet because there is no direct monetary asset value. Conversely, liabilities, such as product obsolescence, cannot be shown because they do not have a direct monetary claim on the company in the way that a creditor would have.

Shareholders' funds

Here is a simplified balance sheet which shows clearly what constitutes shareholders' funds and what does not.

ABC plc balance sheet as at 31 December 199-

	£000	£000	£000
Fixed assets			1,020
Goodwill			100
Current assets			
Stock	562		
Debtors	1,094	1,656	
Current liabilities			
Creditors	1,032		
Tax	80		
Dividend	64	1,176	480
			£1,600
Represented by:			
800,000 £1 ordinary shares			800
Reserves			200
10% Mortgage debentures			200
12% Unsecured loan			160
9.16% Preference shares			240
			£1,600

Total shareholders' funds can be calculated in two ways:

- Total assets, apart from intangibles such as goodwill, less all external liabilities; or
- All classes of share capital

    plus reserves

    plus any credit balance on profit and loss in balance sheet

    less any intangibles such as goodwill.

Calculations of total shareholders' funds from ABC balance sheet

Note: total shareholders' funds relates to all types of shareholders. Take care when reading a question that you distinguish between total shareholders' funds and ordinary shareholders' funds.

Total assets apart from goodwill, less creditors

	£000	£000
Fixed assets		1,020
Current assets		1,656
		2,676
Less: current liabilities	1,176	
10% mortgage debenture	200	
12% unsecured loan stock	160	1,536
Total shareholders' funds		1,140

Alternative method

	£000
Ordinary share capital	800
9.16% preference shares	240
Reserves	200
	1,240
Less: goodwill	100
	1,140

The calculation of net asset value per ordinary share

Note: net asset value is also called 'break-up value' or 'balance sheet asset value'.

If we take for the moment the balance sheet value of the assets as being synonymous with forced sale values, and if we assume that ABC went into liquidation as at the balance sheet date, then we can calculate the theoretical amount per ordinary share payable on liquidation.

All external liabilities must be paid out in full before shareholders can receive anything, and we can assume in the absence of information to the contrary that preference shareholders must then be paid off at nominal value. Any surplus after satisfaction of all these claims will vest in the ordinary shareholders in proportion to their share holding.

Thus on the basis of our previous calculations, we can see that total funds available to preference and ordinary shareholders are £1,140,000. From this we deduct the nominal value of the preference shares and the residue is the amount available to ordinary shareholders.

	£000
Total funds available to all shareholders	1,140
Less: preference shares	240
Ordinary shareholders' funds	900

The figure could be calculated in another way

	£000
Issued ordinary share capital	800
Reserves	200
	1,000
Less: goodwill	100
	900

Thus there is anticipated surplus of £900,000 to be divided among 800,000 ordinary shares, giving a net asset value per share of 900,000 ÷ 800,000 = £1.12$\frac{1}{2}$p per share. (The number of ordinary shares can generally be found in the balance sheet.)

Note: although the dividend shown in the current liabilities will be paid to the shareholders, do not adjust your calculations. The dividend in practice would be paid out very soon after the balance sheet date.

Why might net asset value calculations be unrealistic?

The £1.12$\frac{1}{2}$ calculated in the previous balance sheet is the theoretical amount per share payable in a liquidation of the company. However, in practice this amount is unlikely to be realistic because balance sheet values of assets may well differ from forced sale values. If fixed assets such as property are shown in the books at original cost, there could well be a surplus on sale. On the other hand, a specialist factory of a failed business may have to be sold below cost, especially in a recession. In addition, there is always a considerable delay while property sales are finalized. Any borrowings that existed at the balance sheet date would continue to be liable for interest until they had been paid off, or until the commencement of any liquidation.

Similar considerations apply to other assets. Stock is notoriously difficult to value accurately and debtors may not pay in full. The expenses of liquidation must also be borne in mind.

Furthermore, published balance sheets are not normally available until well after the balance sheet date. Thus the make-up of assets and liabilities could have changed between balance sheet date and publications date.

The current assets may now consist of more stock and fewer debtors if sales have fallen, some capital expenditure may have occurred, or any one of a host of changes may have taken place. Whatever the changes, the published balance sheet will not reflect the profits made, or losses incurred, since its date.

The relevance of net asset values to investors

Net asset values should be compared with the current share price. As a generalization, a low net asset value compared to the share price means that the company is using the assets effectively, whereas when net asset value is above the current share price assets are being inefficiently used.

This generalization must be examined in more detail because, as with all balance sheet analysis, the results must be considered in the light of the company concerned.

Companies in the 'people' business such as advertising or public relations companies can be expected to have low net asset values per share compared with the share price. Such companies do not require large factories or vast amounts of plant and machinery; rather they require a highly motivated, professional staff. Thus the main asset of such a business is the 'people' who are employed. Such assets do not appear in the balance sheet.

For other companies with large property portfolios, such as a retail consortium, the net asset value mainly depends on when the properties were last valued and on whether the valuation has been incorporated into the balance sheet.

Lastly, manufacturers would be expected to have a fairly high net asset value compared with share price, because of their large investment in factories, plant and machinery, and stocks.

When are net asset values particularly significant?

Net assets per share are important in the following sectors:

● Investment trusts (for full details please see Unit 13);

● Takeover targets:

   – One of the criteria a potential bidder will consider before fixing the price of his bid is the bidder's assessment of the net asset value of the target's shares.

   – It frequently happens that a successful bidder's strategy will be to recoup some of the cost of the bid by selling off assets or subsidiaries or divisions of the target. The term 'asset stripping' is used to describe this process when subsequent asset disposals are planned to recoup most or all of the cost of the bid.

- Generally speaking this net asset value forms a 'back-stop', i.e. the lowest bid that might be successful. Other factors such as synergies usually mean that the actual offer is above this net asset value back-stop value;

● Oil or mining companies, where the net asset value based on proven or probable reserves is a vital factor. Once the reserves have been exploited there will be no earnings, only a 'hole in the ground';

● Real estate companies. By this we mean companies whose main business is dealing in and renting of property, as opposed to companies such as Marks and Spencer that operate from expensive high street sites. Since the main income of the company will be derived from the sale and letting of its properties, the net asset value is very important. Real estate companies such as A and J Mucklow plc invest in housing land, industrial estates, trading estates and office blocks. Their profits derive from rents received and any sales of land made. Real estate company shares are often at a discount to their net asset value.

Net asset values and profit potential

Apart from the sectors specified in the previous section, a high net asset per share figure compared to a low earnings per share figure can mean:

● The assets appear in the balance sheet at book value, but the true 'forced sale value' will be less because of the poor profitability generated by the assets;

● With a manufacturer, the assets figure has recently been increased by capital investment, but the increased profits from this investment have not yet 'come on stream';

● Poor management has resulted in low profits so that the assets are being underutilized. In such a situation there could be a takeover bid, because the buyer may well acquire the company's assets cheaply.

3 Capital Cover and Capital Priority Percentages

What is capital cover?

An individual lender is more concerned with the security of his own particular loan than with the indebtedness of the company as a whole. Capital cover is a means of deciding by how much the assets available to a particular lender exceed his debt.

The word 'capital' in this context usually applies to loan stocks, debentures or preference shares, or to medium/long-term bank loans, i.e. the providers of medium- to long-term capital.

Example of capital cover calculation

To save you turning back to find it, we repeat the balance sheet of ABC plc.

	£000	£000	£000
Fixed assets			1,020
Goodwill			100
Current assets			
Stock	562		
Debtors	1,094	1,656	
Current liabilities			
Creditors	1,032		
Tax	80		
Dividend	64	1,176	480
			£1,600
Represented by:			
800,000 £1 ordinary shares			800
Reserves			200
10% Mortgage debentures			200
12% Unsecured loan			160
9.16% Preference shares			240
			£1,600

The conventions for calculating capital cover are as follows.

● Assume that all current liabilities will be paid off in full before any repayment of loan capital or preference shares. In practice things may not work out like this, but an assumption must be made to enable calculations to be completed on the same basis.

● Calculate the money available to all the providers of loan or share capital. This figure is known as capital employed.

The figure can be calculated in two ways:

	£000
Fixed assets excluding goodwill and intangibles	1,020
Net current assets	480
Capital employed	1,500
or	
800,000 £1 ordinary shares	800

Reserves	200
10% mortgage debentures	200
12% unsecured loan stock	160
9.16% preference shares	240
	1,600
Less: goodwill	100
Capital employed	£1,500

Note: if there had been a deficit in the working capital (current liabilities in excess of current assets), the net deficit would have to be deducted from the fixed asset totals to calculate the capital employed for our purposes.

Rank the various classes of capital in ABC plc's balance sheet in order of priority in liquidation.

Work out the cover for every capital item, except for ordinary shareholders' funds.

The significance of capital cover

In the example just completed, the forced sale value of the assets could drop 7.5 times before the debenture holders were affected in any liquidation, and 4.2 and 2.5 represent the same falls that could occur before the unsecured loan stockholders, or preference shareholders would suffer.

Remember that the presumption is that loan stockholders and preference shareholders will be able to claim the nominal value of their respective securities in liquidation.

Capital priority percentages

This is simply an alternative way of presenting the same information, and it shows what percentage of the available assets belong to that class of capital.

For ABC plc the capital priority percentage table is as follows:

Capital	Amount £000	Cumulative total	Priority %	
10% mortgage debentures	200	200	$\frac{200 \times 100}{1,500}$	= 0 – 13.3%
12% unsecured loan stock	160	360	$\frac{360 \times 100}{1,500}$	= 13.3% – 24%
9.16% preference shares	240	600	$\frac{600 \times 100}{1,500}$	= 24% – 40%

Capital	Amount £000	Cumulative total	Priority %	
Ordinary shareholders' funds	900	1,500	$\dfrac{1,500 \times 100}{1,500}$	$= 40\% - 100\%$
	£1,500			

This supplies the same information as for capital cover. Asset values in liquidation could fall by (100 – 13.3) 86.7% before debenture holders suffered any loss. The relative figures for unsecured loan stocks and preference shares are 76% and 60% respectively.

There is an alternative way of calculating capital cover from this table. Simply divide the priority percentage into 100.

Capital cover for 10% mortgage debenture	= 100/13.3	= 7.5 times
Capital cover for 12% unsecured loan stock	= 100/24	= 4.2 times
Capital cover for preference shares	= 100/40	= 2.5 times.

Liquidity ratio

The purpose of a liquidity ratio is to help to assess whether a company has sufficient cash for its immediate trading needs. If there is a short-term shortage of cash, the classic method of overcoming the problem is a bank overdraft. It should be noted that a short-term cash budget is far more useful than these ratios for the purpose of analysing liquidity.

Liquidity ratios are of two kinds:

● Current ratio

● Quick asset ratio.

Current ratio or working capital ratio

The formula is:

$$\frac{\text{Current assets}}{\text{Current liabilities}}$$

For ABC plc question, the current ratio is:

$$\frac{1,656}{1,176} = 1.41$$

Generally the current ratio should be not less than 1.5, but there are wide variations between different companies. Perhaps of more significance is the change in the ratio over a series of years for the same company.

Do not be misled into thinking that a 'high' ratio is a good sign. Too high a working capital ratio can indicate wasted resources, with too much capital tied up in stock and debtors.

Indeed one of the first acts to be taken when a company has a liquidity crisis is to try to 'squeeze' working capital to generate cash.

Obviously too low a working capital ratio can indicate an imminent liquidity crisis. Generally speaking, a manufacturer who has a substantial time lag between receipt of order and receipt of funds will require a higher working capital ratio than a retailer of fast-moving consumer goods.

Quick assets ratio or acid test ratio

This ratio is similar to the current ratio, but it excludes stock, the most illiquid of current assets and the one most difficult to value.

The formula is:

$$\frac{\text{Current assets} - \text{stock}}{\text{Current liabilities}}$$

For ABC plc the ratio is:

$$\frac{1,656 - 562}{1,176} = \frac{1,094}{1,176} = 0.93$$

The normally accepted minimum is 1, but, as with working capital, there are many exceptions, the major example being supermarkets. These organizations can exist on tiny acid test ratios because they buy on credit but sell for cash.

4   Earnings Per Share (EPS)

Earnings per share defined

So far in this unit we have examined the security of capital from the balance sheet. However, even in today's somewhat uncertain economic circumstances liquidations of quoted public companies are rare. Thus capital cover and capital priority percentages are not really as vital as earnings, if we assume that a company will continue as a going concern.

Earnings are found not from the balance sheet but from the annual profit and loss figures, and they represent the net profits of a company available to ordinary shareholders. Earnings can either be paid out to the ordinary shareholders by way of dividend, or they can be retained within the company. The earnings figure remains the same whether or not any dividend is declared. Obviously earnings per share is simply total earnings divided by the number of ordinary shares.

The significance of earnings

Earnings are vital to the share price. If earnings are ploughed back into the company, the reserves or retained profits figure in the balance sheet will rise. Thus the total shareholders' funds will increase, along with a corresponding increase in net asset value per share. This should result in a rise in the market price of the shares. Earnings are said to have 'quality' when the company shows steadily increasing earnings, the management is sound, the product range is diversified, and profits are in line with forecasts.

If earnings are paid out by way of dividend, all things being equal the dividend yield will rise, thus making the shares more attractive and causing their price to rise. The decision as to how much of the earnings should be paid by way of dividend is extremely complex. Usually shareholders in companies in mature industries expect that dividends will be constant in real terms or will rise in real terms over time. However, shareholders in companies in fast-growing areas, such as Internet stocks, will be looking for capital growth and low dividends will normally be acceptable in such cases.

Obviously, the other providers of the capital benefit from increased earnings, because higher earnings will mean more cover for the respective interest payments or preference dividend. Growth of EPS year by year is often a stated financial objective of a listed company.

When we wish to compare earnings of two companies from the point of view of an ordinary shareholder we need to relate EPS to current price of a share. The normal way to relate EPS to price is to calculate a price earnings ratio.

The prospect of growth of earnings is an important influence on the share price. When earnings grow at a faster rate than inflation there is said to be real growth.

Price earnings ratio (P/E ratio)

This ratio shows the number of times the current share price exceeds earnings per share. The formula is simply:

$$\frac{\text{Current share price}}{\text{EPS}}$$

The P/E ratio is shown for all shares quoted in the 'London Share Service' page of the *Financial Times*. Estimated price earnings ratios in the *Financial Times* are based on the latest annual reports and accounts, and, where possible, are updated on interim figures. The EPS is calculated on the net basis, being profit after corporation tax.

The significance of P/E ratios

The main use of a P/E ratio is for comparing one share with another. Sectors with the best growth prospects have relatively high price earnings ratio, e.g. 'Pharmaceuticals' compared with those of, say, Water. A high P/E ratio will often indicate that a share is attractive even if it has a relatively low gross dividend yield. Alternatively, a P/E ratio can be relatively high if the last reported earnings have fallen but the share price has not because recovery is anticipated.

Students should keep abreast of current P/E ratios by studying the information in the *Financial Times* FTSE Actuaries Share Indices.

The P/E ratio of a particular company can be compared with the average for its sector, and appropriate conclusions can be drawn.

One method of valuing a company (or of assessing the 'intrinsic value' of its shares) is to try to forecast the earnings for the next accounting period. These earnings can then be multiplied by the average P/E ratio for the sector to calculate an estimated company value (also known as estimated market capitalization). This figure can be divided by the number of ordinary shares to calculate the estimated 'intrinsic value' of a share in that company.

Fully diluted earnings

Dilution of earnings applies when a company has issued convertible loan stock, convertible preference shares, warrants or share option schemes. All of these can at some future date at the holder's option be converted into ordinary shares of the company. Until they are converted into ordinary shares these instruments do not qualify for ordinary share dividends. However, as conversion is at the holder's option, it is normal practice for a company that has issued such securities to calculate earnings per share in two ways. First the method shown above is used, and then the calculation is reworked assuming that the securities have been converted into ordinary shares. Obviously this fully diluted method will result in a lower earnings per share figure, because there will be a larger number of ordinary shares. However, where loan stocks or preference shares have been converted the total earnings figure will be increased by the after-tax amount of interest or preference dividend saved.

Note in the case of warrants, the correct term is to 'exercise' rather than to 'convert'.

Going back to ABC plc, assume that £200,000 of the 10% debenture stock was in fact 10% convertible loan stock. The capital structure would show:

	£000
800,000 ordinary £1 shares fully paid	800
Reserves	200
	1,000
12% unsecured loan	160
10% convertible loan stock	200
9.16% preference shares	240
	1,600
Less goodwill	100
	£1,500

If the loan stock could be converted on the basis of 100 shares per £100 nominal stock and undiluted earnings were, say, 15p per share, this would mean that earnings were £120,000 (800,000 shares x 15p).

The fully diluted earnings would be:

Saving on loan stock interest

> = (£200,000 x 10%) – 30% corporation tax
>
> = £20,000 – 30%
>
> = £14,000

Therefore fully diluted earnings

> = £120,000 + £14,000
>
> = £134,000

Although the company saves the net of tax cost of the loan stock interest, it will have to pay out the fully diluted earnings of £134,000 to 1,000,000 shares (800,000 + 200,000 convertible), reducing the earnings per share from 15p to 13.4p.

5   Dividend Yield, Dividend Cover

How dividend yield is calculated

Dividends are the actual amounts from profits paid out to the shareholders in cash. As we have already learned, the dividend is paid net of 10% tax.

The formula is:

$$\frac{\text{net dividend per share x } 100}{\text{current share price}}$$

The resultant figure is a percentage and shows the net dividend as a percentage of current share price.

When comparing dividend yields on shares in two companies in the same sector of the market, do not assume that the one with the higher dividend yield is better value than the one with the lower dividend yield.

The higher dividend yield may have arisen because:

●   Prospects of future dividend rises are considered small;

●   Investors believe that earnings are likely to fall in the future.

In either case, the market will have lowered the share price to reflect future prospects. Hence a past dividend is being compared to a current price that discounts future prospects.

Conversely, low dividend yield and high price earnings ratios can often go hand in hand, because the current 'high' share price reflects future prospects whereas the relevant dividends and earnings reflect the past performance.

Dividend cover

The formula is simply:

$$\frac{\text{earnings per share}}{\text{net dividend per share}}$$

The resultant figure represents the number of times the dividend could be paid out of earnings. A high dividend cover indicates that the dividend rate could probably be maintained in the future even if profits were to fall by a small amount.

6 Income Cover and Income Priority Percentages

The purpose of the calculations

The principles on which these concepts are based are similar to those for capital cover and capital priority percentages. The purpose of these two calculations is to show the extent to which profits could decline without resulting in the interest or dividend payments being uncovered by profits.

Once again, each provider of capital is concerned with the cover for his own particular interest or dividend payment, so the calculations are worked on a cumulative basis.

How to calculate overall cover and priority percentages for income

(a) Calculate the net of corporation tax cost of all interest, remembering that the full interest is charged to the profit and loss account before tax is assessed.

(b) Calculate the total net cost of the preference dividends and ordinary dividends.

(c) Add back the net of corporation tax cost of the interest payments to the profits after tax and interest. This total represents the profits available to meet interest and dividends.

(d) Set out the various forms of interest and dividend in order of priority and assess overall cover and priority percentages on the same basis as for capital priority percentages.

Specimen calculations

You are given the following information from the profit and loss accounts of Electra plc. Assume corporation tax to be 30%.

Profit and loss account	£000	£000
Trading profit		4,880
Less: depreciation		1,535
Pre-tax profit		3,345
Less Interest on quoted debt		515
Pre-tax profit after interest		2,830
Corporation tax for year (say)		933
Profit after tax and interest		1,897
Ordinary dividend	720	
Retentions for year	1,177	
	£1,897	

(a) From the information given above, calculate:

(i) The income priority percentages;

(ii) The overall income cover.

(b) What are the investment implications of both these calculations?

Answer

			£000
(a) (i)	After-tax cost of interest =	$\dfrac{515 \times 70}{100}$ =	360

N.B. the £360 as been rounded up to the nearest £'000.

(ii) Net cost of ordinary dividend is £720,000.

		£000
(iii)	Profit after tax and interest is	1,897
	Net of tax cost of interest is	360
	Profit available to meet interest and dividends	£2,257

(iv) Income priority % and overall cover:

Capital	Net cost of interest /dividend	Cum total	Income priority %	How calculated	Overall cover
Quoted debt	360	360	0-15.95%	$\dfrac{360 \times 100}{2257}$	6.27
Ord. Dividend	720	1,080	15.95-47.85%	$\dfrac{1080 \times 100}{2257}$	2.09
Retained profits	1,177	2257	47.85%-100%	$\dfrac{2257 \times 100}{100}$	-

£2,257

Note: overall cover is simply the total profits available to meet interest and dividends divided by the cumulative total.

(b)   The investment implications are as follows:

(i)   Interest. The available profits must fall by 84.05% before they are insufficient to cover the interest (100-15.95).

Alternatively, available profits cover interest 6.27 times. Thus interest looks very secure.

(ii)   The ordinary dividend. Available profits could fall by 52.15% before the dividend was uncovered or, alternatively, the dividend is covered 2.09 times by available profits.

7   Cash Flow

This figure is a monetary amount. It is not a ratio, nor is it a percentage.

The formula is: retained profit for the year + depreciation written off in that year.

For Electra plc the figure is:

	£000
Retained profit	1,177
Depreciation	1,535
	£2,712

In theory this monetary amount is the cash generated from trading operations, and the figure should be compared with the projected capital expenditure for the following year. A more accurate comparison can be made if we consider the capital reductions required by proposed and current bank and hire purchase facilities over the forthcoming year.

If the cash flow is insufficient, then some other sources of funds may be needed to service the borrowings, the obvious choices being rights issues or sales of assets. If the funds are to be borrowed as a medium-term loan, cash flow should be compared to the cost of servicing the loan.

Even if the cash flow appears sufficient to service the various facilities over the next year, we still need to bear in mind the following reservations:

● The cash flow is from a past period – a projected cash flow is of more use;

● The cash flow does not equate with actual cash generated, because some of that retained profit can have manifested itself in increased stock and debtors, rather than in cash;

● Cash flow is more accurately calculated on the basis of FRS 1 (shown below). Some investment analysts, however, still use retained profit plus depreciation.

Cash flow statements in published accounts

Under the first Financial Reporting Standard (FRS 1) of the Accounting Standards Board, all companies with turnover in excess of £2m and net assets in excess of £975,000 will have to produce cash flow statements as part of their published accounts.

A specimen cash flow statement follows.

XYZ Limited

Cash flow statement for the year ended 31 March

	£000	£000
Net cash inflow from operating activities (note 1)		6,889
Returns on investments and servicing of finance		
Interest received	3,011	
Interest paid	(12)	
Dividends paid	(2,417)	
Net cash inflow from returns on investments and servicing of finance		582
Taxation		
Corporation tax paid		(2,922)

Investing activities

Payments to acquire intangible fixed assets	(71)	
Payments to acquire fixed assets	(1,496)	
Receipts from sales of tangible fixed assets	42	
Net cash outflow from investment activities		(1,525)
Net cash inflow before financing		3,024
Financing		
Issue of ordinary share capital	211	
Repurchase of debenture loan	(149)	
Expenses paid in connection with share issues	(5)	
Net cash inflow from financing		57
Increase in cash and cash equivalents		£3,081

Notes to the cash flow statement
Reconciliation of operating profit to net cash inflow from operating activities

	£000
Operating profit	6,022
Depreciation charges	893
Loss on sale of tangible fixed assets	6
Increase in stock	(194)
Increase in debtors	(72)
Increase in creditors	234
Net cash inflow from operating activities	6,889

The purpose of this format is to provide an accurate statement describing how the company's cash or cash equivalents have altered during the year. Cash equivalents are investments with less than three months to maturity at the time they were acquired.

From the above it can be seen that:

● Cash flow from operating activities adjusts the traditional calculation of operating profit to take account of funds absorbed by extra stocks or debtors or in reduced creditors. This overcomes one major drawback from the traditional 'cash flow' calculations, namely that when profits increase, in most businesses cash is absorbed by increased working capital and the actual cash flow is less than the reported cash flow;

- Net cash flow from investing activities shows the new cash flow resulting from capital expenditure less asset disposals;

- Net cash flow from financing shows the amount of money raised from external borrowing or from new issues, and also shows the amounts of loan reductions made over the year;

- Net cash inflow from returns on investments and servicing of finance covers interest and dividends paid or received. Any interest that has been omitted from the reported profit and loss account because it has been capitalized must still be reported here. (An example of such capitalized interest would be where a property developer is charged interest on a loan to develop a property, but that interest is simply added to the capital value of the asset in the balance sheet instead of being charged as an expense to profit and loss.);

- Taxation is the actual amount of tax paid to the Inland Revenue by cheque during the year.

The cash flow statement will provide a useful guide to a company's short-term situation. The 'profit' figure in reported accounts can be very subjective, and very misleading. However, cash flow is not subjective and it has been described as 'the most difficult parameter to adjust in a company's accounts'.

8   The Statistical Information in the 'Financial Times London Share Service'

Extract of the information (Tuesday to Saturday)

Let us examine the information available for a particular share in the *Financial Times* in a Tuesday to Saturday edition. The edition is 5 January 2000.

			52 week				
Notes	Price	+ or-	High	Low	Volume	Yield	P/E
B.T. (♣) †	1,423xd	-90	1520³/₄	838	11,392	1.5	39.1

Under the column headed 'Notes' various symbols can appear and the reader should refer to the *Guide to the London Share Service* key that appears each day at the end of the London Share Service. For BT the symbol (♣) shows that the company is a member of the 'Free Annual Reports Club' and gives details of how the latest BT published reports can be obtained. In addition the notes show that BT's interim dividend has since increased or resumed, so that investors can see that the dividend seems set remain constant or to increase.

Additional information is available in the key, extracts of which are as follows:

- The price is the closing mid-market price shown in pence unless otherwise stated;

- High and low prices are based on intra-day mid-prices over a rolling 52-week period;

- Trading volumes are end of day accumulated totals rounded to the nearest 1000 trades. When there is an unusual increase in volumes, this may well be a sign that the market expects some major change in the company's prospects, such as a takeover bid;

● Yields are the net dividend yields based on mid prices;

● P/E as previously mentioned is the price earnings ratio based on EPS taken from the latest annual reports and accounts, updated on interim figures.

Extract of information – Monday

On a Monday the information published in the *Financial Times* differs from that in the Tuesday to Saturday editions. The reason is that no business is conducted on a Saturday, thus information would merely be a repeat of the Saturday edition.

The headings for the information in the FT of 3 January 2000 edition was:

Notes Ch'nge	Price cov	Wk % Cap £m	Div xd	Div line	Mkt	Last	Cityline
BT (♣)†	1513 xd	5.3	21.0	1.7	98,435	29.12	1925

The *Guide to the London Share Service* 'notes' are basically the same as for the Tuesday to Saturday editions. In addition:

● Wk % change is the change in the share price in percentage terms over the previous week;

● The dividend is shown as pence per share and dividend cover is calculated on a net basis;

● The market capitalization is the number of shares issued multiplied by the price per share. Market capitalizations are calculated separately for each line of stock quoted;

● Last xd is the date that the shares last went ex div. You will recall that the significance of ex div is if the shares are sold during the ex div period the next dividend will be paid to the seller;

● Cityline is the phone line providing information about that specific company's share. Details are provided in the key.

NB There are frequent changes in the information to be found in the *Financial Times* London Share Service. Readers are recommended to purchase a current *Financial Times* and to note any changes.

9 Gearing

What is gearing and what effect does it have?

We have already discussed the concept of gearing in connection with options and warrants.

In this context we said that gearing magnifies the gains or losses in the underlying securities.

With companies, a highly geared share is one where the company has a high ratio of fixed interest capital in relationship to ordinary shareholders' funds.

The effect of high gearing, as we shall see, is not only to magnify the effect of profit increases for the ordinary shareholders but also to exaggerate the effect of profit reductions.

Capital gearing

As the name implies, capital gearing is calculated from the balance sheet. There are many different ways of calculating capital gearing, but for our purposes the following should suffice:

$$\text{Capital gearing ratio} = \frac{\text{loan capital and preference shares}}{\text{capital employed}}$$

From the following balance sheet, the capital gearing ratio would be calculated thus:

Alpha plc Balance sheet as at 31 December 19-

Assets employed	£000	£000	£000
Fixed assets			
Land, buildings, plant at cost	20,500		
Less: accumulated depreciation	8,000		
			12,500
Current assets			
Stock and work in progress	8,800		
Debtors	6,800		
Cash at bank and in hand	2,900	18,500	
Current liabilities			
Creditors	5,600		
Taxation	1,170		
Dividends proposed	480	7,250	
Net current assets			11,250
			£23,750
Represented by:			
Future taxation, deferred liabilities and provisions			2,350

Quoted loan capital		
5.83% debenture stock	3,000	
6.81% unsecured loan stock	5,000	8,000
5% preference capital		2,000
Ordinary shareholders' funds		4,000
Reserves		7,400
		£23,750

$$\frac{\text{Loan capital and preference capital}}{\text{Capital employed}} = \frac{3,000 + 5,000 + 2,000}{12,500 + 11,250 - 2,350^*}$$

$$= \frac{10,000}{21,400}$$

$$\text{Capital gearing ratio} = 0.47$$

* Future taxation, deferred liabilities and provisions of £2,350 are not classed as capital because they represent possible depletion of capital in the future.

Notes

Preference shares are included as fixed interest capital, because no dividend can be paid on the ordinary shares unless the preference dividend has been met.

As a 'rule of thumb' the ratio should not usually exceed 0.50. However, much depends on the type of business as to whether this 'rule' need be of any concern. Generally speaking, the greater the industry risk and the operating risk the lower the gearing should be. For example, capital goods manufacturers (a risky industry) with high fixed costs (high operating risk) need low gearing.

Nowadays many bank lending agreements contain clauses, known as covenants, that state that the borrower will be in default if the gearing ratio exceeds a stated figure. In the recession of 1990-92, several companies experienced major problems because their gearing ratio exceeded the limits set out in the covenants. As the recession ended there was a spate of rights issues made to reduce gearing and give companies room for financial manoeuvre.

Some analysts calculate the gearing ratio as:

$$\frac{\text{long-term debt}}{\text{shareholders' funds}}$$

Whatever method is used, the principles and conclusions to be drawn are the same.

Where companies have medium-term bank loans, these should be included in both the numerator and in the denominator. For some companies, medium-term bank loans perform the function of debentures or loan stocks.

One of the objectives of financial management is to ensure that a company's gearing is at the optimal level so as to minimize a company's weighted average cost of capital. For most listed companies, the weightings of debt and equity are based on market values, rather than on book values, for the purpose of assessing the optimal proportions of debt and equity in the capital structure.

Debt is normally cheaper than equity because lenders will accept a lower return in exchange for the lower risk that debt holders have in comparison with the risks of shareholders. However, as the gearing ratio rises, the overall risks to both shareholders and debt holders also rise. When gearing exceeds a certain level the weighted average cost of capital will rise. Figure 10.1 illustrates this.

Figure 10.1:

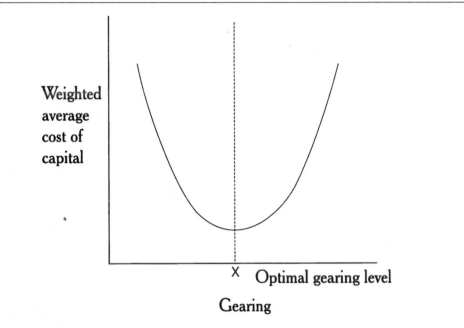

Note: interest is tax deductible, whereas dividends are paid from after-tax income.

Income gearing

This can be defined as the number of times total available profits exceeds the fixed interest on loan stocks. The generally accepted formula is:

$$\text{Income gearing} = \frac{\text{profit before interest and tax}}{\text{gross interest payments}}$$

If we glance back at the profit and loss account of Electra plc (reproduced here again for the reader's convenience), we can see that the income gearing is:

Electra plc

Profit and loss account	£000	£000
Trading profit		4,880
Less: depreciation		<u>1,535</u>
Pre-tax profit		3,345
Less: Interest on quoted debt		<u>515</u>
Pre-tax profit after interest		2,830
Less: Corporation tax for year (say)		<u>933</u>
Profit after tax and interest		<u>1,897</u>
Ordinary dividend	720	
Retentions for year	<u>1,177</u>	
	<u>£1,897</u>	

$$\frac{3,345}{515} = 6.5 \text{ times}$$

The resultant income gearing figure shall not generally be less than 2:1 according to *Money for Business*, published by the Bank of England. However, as with the capital gearing 'rule', the optimal level varies from company to company.

It is the author's personal opinion that the income priority percentages and overall cover are of more relevance from an investment point of view, because they take account of the preference dividend. However, income gearing is a useful tool for a lender, as opposed to an investor, because lenders can estimate the potential income gearing ratio when deciding whether or not to grant facilities. Nowadays lenders often prefer to use a cash-flow based ratio for interest cover. This would compare the forecast cash flows available to service debt over the relevant period against the cash cost of servicing the debt over that period.

Lenders are not concerned with the preference dividend, which is not even an enforceable debt. Ordinary shareholders, on the other hand, must concern themselves with the preference dividend, because the ordinary dividend cannot be paid while the preference dividend is in arrears.

Why the concept of gearing is important to ordinary shareholders

The easiest way to illustrate the general concept is to study a simplified example. Suppose that the capital employed of LMN plc and CDE plc, and profit records, are as follows:

	LMN plc	CDE plc
	£000	£000
Issued ordinary share capital	500	500
Reserves	500	1,500
10% Loan stock	1,000	Nil
Total capital employed	2,000	2,000
	£000	**£000**
Net profit before interest – year one	200	200
Net profit before interest – year two	400	400
Net profit before interest – year three	150	150

For simplicity and clarity we shall ignore taxation and we shall also simply assume that the capital employed remains unchanged over the three years. In real life such assumptions must not be made, but for the purpose of illustrating the concept of gearing, these assumptions are quite valid.

Let us now look at the distribution of those profits:

	LMN plc Year one £000	CDE plc Year one £000
Net profit before interest	200	200
Less: Interest	100	nil
Available to ordinary shareholders	100	200

	LMN plc Year two £000	CDE plc Year two £000
Net profit before interest	400	400
Less: Interest	100	nil
Available to ordinary shareholders	300	400

	LMN plc Year three £000	CDE plc Year three £000
Net profit before interest	150	150

	LMN plc	CDE plc
Less: Interest	<u>100</u>	<u>nil</u>
Available to ordinary shareholders	<u>50</u>	150

From the above we can see:

Percentage increase/decrease in profits available to ordinary shareholders between:

	LMN plc	CDE plc
Year one and two	+200%	+100%
Year two and three	-83%	-63%

The above illustrates the point that a shareholder in a highly-geared company will benefit from gearing when profits rise, but he will suffer from gearing when profits fall.

10   Advance Corporation Tax (ACT)

This tax has been abolished, but as ever there are complex transitional arrangements, which involve concepts such as 'shadow ACT'. These complexities are outside the scope of this text, and interested readers are recommended to study a specialist taxation publication for further details. From an earlier edition of this book, some readers may have come across the terms 'nil', 'net' and 'full' in the context of earnings and P/E ratios. These terms arose, in the main, as a result of ACT and thus they are not now included in the current edition of this book.

Summary

Now that you have studied this unit you should be able to:

- describe the information contained in a balance sheet and profit and loss account;
- calculate shareholders' funds;
- calculate net asset value per ordinary share, explain why this may not be a realistic figure, and understand why NAV may be different for different types of business;
- calculate capital cover and explain its significance;
- calculate capital priority percentages and explain their significance;
- describe the purpose of calculating the liquidity ratio and be able to calculate both the current ratio and acid test ratio;
- calculate the price/earnings ratio and describe its significance;

Investment

- calculate dividend yield and dividend cover and explain the significance of each of these figures;

- calculate income cover and explain its significance;

- calculate income priority percentages and explain their significance;

- calculate cash flow and understand its significance;

- understand the information in the *Financial Times* relating to shares;

- explain the concept of gearing.

11

ASSESSMENT OF COMPANY SECURITIES 2: ANALYSIS OF VARIOUS ASPECTS OF COMPANIES

Objectives

After studying this unit, you should be able to:

- identify the various sources of information on company performance;

- explain the purpose of beta coefficients;

- understand the role of management in determining future profitability and growth;

- understand the main features of fundamental analysis and technical analysis;

- understand the principles of:

  - Dow Theory

  - Hatch Theory

  - the random walk hypothesis

  - the efficient market hypothesis;

- differentiate between systematic and non-systematic risk;

- appreciate the basic principles of portfolio theory.

1 Sources of Information

Extel on-line and CD-Rom systems

Extel has an on-line system that carries information on stocks and shares, company data, financial news, and financial systems plus a system that enables accountants and financial accountants to calculate investor's tax liabilities utilizing on-line information.

Datastream

This is a screen-based source of information that carries more information than Extel. In addition to the analysis of the accounts, data relating to the company, its industry and economic prospects are constantly updated. Charts of share price movements plus a wealth of other information, such as a share's beta (b), are provided.

Financial Times

We have already discussed some of the details that can be found in this publication. Other information includes:

   Details of interim and final results with comments;

   News of rights issues, capitalization issues, takeovers, management changes and industry developments;

   List of active stocks, new highs and lows, and major price changes.

Stock Exchange daily official list (SEDOL)

The SEDOL is published by the Stock Exchange on each working day. It lists every stock and share that is quoted on the Stock Exchange. (Not every quoted share appears in the *Financial Times* London Share Service because not all companies are willing to pay the annual fee.)

Details shown in SEDOL include:

- Particulars of the last dividend paid, in pence or %;

- The date the share was last quoted 'ex div';

- The date of the next dividend payments;

- Separate sections for AIM shares, Rule 4(2), miscellaneous warrants, traded options, suspended securities and takeover disclosures;

   The quotation column on the date of the SEDOL contains the prices of particular stocks or shares, and these prices are used as a basis of the quarter-up method for inheritance tax calculations by the Inland Revenue in connection with lifetime gifts, or with disposals on death;

   Business done, i.e. the range of prices at which deals have been made during the day, including a symbol against intra-firm deals;

- Notice of any selective marketing (placings) of securities;

   The US and Canadian dollar rates at 4.30 p.m., the FTSE 100, FTSE Eurotrack 100 and FTSE Eurotrack 200 indices at close of business;

   The SEDOL code number which is a six figure digit. This number appears on contract notes with a prefix number that denotes the type of security, e.g. 0 is for securities quoted in the UK and Eire, while 2 is for securities quoted in North and South America;

● The companies involved in takeovers as notified by the Takeover Panel.

Stock Exchange Year Book

Published annually, it gives details of every quoted company. It provides details of all information recorded at Companies' House, but does not include details of the accounts.

Other sources of information

The *Investors Chronicle* and *The Economist* often give in-depth analysis of the prospects of particular companies or industries.

Teletext and Ceefax provide up-to-date information on television relating to share prices, stock market movements, company news and other important information relating to operations in the City of London.

There are also a wide range of web sites that provide information. Some of this information is free, but more in-depth information is available only by subscription. A list of some of these web sites is shown in Appendix 2.

2   Beta Coefficients

The beta coefficient purports to measure the riskiness of a particular share relative to the stock market as a whole. If a share has a beta coefficient of one, the share is considered to be no more or no less risky than the stock market as a whole. The higher the beta coefficient, the more risky the share is considered to be.

We need not be unduly concerned as to the method by which the beta coefficient is calculated. Suffice it to say that a computer will compare the total return on a particular share (dividend and capital gain) over a given number of periods with the return on the stock market as a whole for these periods. The volatility of the share's return can be compared with the volatility of the return on the stock market as a whole, and for simplicity a beta coefficient can be used to express that comparative volatility in a single number.

Other things being equal, shareholders will expect a higher average return from a high beta stock than from a low beta stock, because volatility of returns is usually equated with riskiness.

Generally speaking, a highly-geared share will have a higher beta coefficient than a low-geared share. A 'bullish' investor will look for shares with high beta coefficients, whereas a 'bear' would prefer shares with low beta coefficients.

If a share has a high beta coefficient it is said to be 'aggressive', whereas one with a low beta coefficient is said to be 'defensive'

The beta coefficient of each quoted share can be obtained from Datastream.

Some writers are not convinced that the beta of a share is an appropriate criterion for the measurement of its risk and hence its expected return relative to other equities. For instance, research has shown:

● Some low beta securities earn higher returns than high beta ones – the opposite of what would be expected;

● Betas change over time. For example, the beta of Marks and Spencer measured from quarterly returns between 1990 and 1999 is 0.68. However, the beta for this company as measured during 1999 based on various 30-day periods of daily returns has varied between 0.1 and 1.4;

● Many studies suggest that alphas (returns different from those implied by the beta of a share) can be significantly different from zero. In theory, alphas for individual shares should quickly return to zero as investors buy on excess returns and sell underachievers to bring prices and returns back to those implied by the beta. In practice, this is not always the case.

3 Management

So far we have looked at figures as an aid to assessing the past performance and potential performance of a company. We now consider an intangible factor, management.

If a company's rate of growth has consistently exceeded those of similar companies, then the reason could well be management. Management changes can therefore be an important factor affecting future performance of a company and its shares.

The requirements of good management are an ability to spot the potential markets of the future and the skill to enable the company to change its operations so as to be able to meet the demands of such markets. In a takeover, the quality of the management in the two companies can sometimes be a decisive factor in the outcome.

4 Examples of Information Available to Managers

The managers of any UK domiciled company with equity lines of stock listed on the London Stock Exchange will be provided with free access to the Stock Exchange Company Report Service. This is a secure website that provides high-quality interactive reports of the company's market performance, covering share price, trading and market value movements over the previous month and in the last 12 months. It allows the managers to select up to 5 key competitors/peers to benchmark their company's performance against. Obviously, any capable management team will exploit such information as a powerful tool for strategy development.

5 How the Professional Analysts Assess the Prospects of a Company

Fundamental analysis

The purpose of fundamental analysis is to suggest whether a share is cheap or dear compared with its intrinsic (or 'true') value.

In order to assess the 'true value' of a share, the fundamental analyst will make a detailed study of the company's accounts over a number of years so as to study the trends. He will then examine the prospects of the industry and the economy in general, and against this background he will study the company's strategic plan. Naturally, the analyst's opinion of the calibre of the management will have an important bearing on his decision as to whether or not he believes the plan to be viable.

The end result of this detailed study will be a prediction of future profit levels of the company, and perhaps also future dividends. If profits and dividends can be predicted, a projected price earnings ratio can be calculated, based on the current share price. This projected P/E ratio, adjusted for risk by means of a beta coefficient, can then be compared with the projected P/E ratio for the sector as a whole.

If the projected P/E ratio of the company appears to be lower than that which would be expected, then the share is 'cheap'. The current market price must be below the 'intrinsic price', and thus the share is a 'buy'.

There are other means of calculating whether a share is 'cheap' or 'dear'. One method is to predict the likely amount of the next dividend and future dividend growth rates. This predicted dividend stream can then be discounted at the rate of return thought appropriate for the riskiness of that company. The resultant net present value is said to represent the intrinsic value of the share. The obvious problems are how to predict dividends and their growth. This method is known as the Gordon Growth Model.

The formula for the Gordon Growth Model is:

$$P = \frac{D}{(r-g)}$$

where: P = intrinsic value of the share

D = next dividend

r = investor's required rate of return

g = dividend growth rate

Example: The next dividend on ABC's shares will be 21p. Future dividend growth is forecast at 5% p.a. and the required rate of return is 12%. The intrinsic value of the share is:

$$\frac{21}{*(0.12 - 0.05)} = \frac{21}{0.07}$$

Intrinsic value of share $= 300p$

*   Note: 12% expressed as a decimal is 0.12 and 5% is 0.05.

Fundamental analysis involves predicting the profits or dividends of a company and comparing these predictions with a prediction of the 'average' profitability of the sector or of the market as a whole. Alternatively, fundamental analysis can involve forecasts of free cash flows, discounted to a present value at an appropriate discount rate.

Unfortunately for the fundamentalist, the price of a share is set by market forces, not by any 'intrinsic value'. Usually fundamental analysis is aimed only at a long-term scale of investment. In the short term, the intrinsic value of a share may be totally overcome by speculative market forces, and in the long term the fundamentals themselves may change before the share price has reached its 'true value'.

Nevertheless, fundamental analysis must have a successful track record judging by the number of such analysts employed in this capacity in the various City organizations

Technical analysis

Technical analysts, or 'chartists' as they are often called, state that the price of a share is determined by supply and demand, and they totally disagree with the fundamental analyst's view. A chartist predicts future share price movements by plotting charts of the share price movements over a period of time. From these charts of price movements, they then claim to be able to see trends which foretell where the share price will move next.

There are three different types of chart that the analyst can use. They are:

●   Line charts

●   Bar charts

●   Point and figure charts.

Line charts

Figure 11.1: Line chart

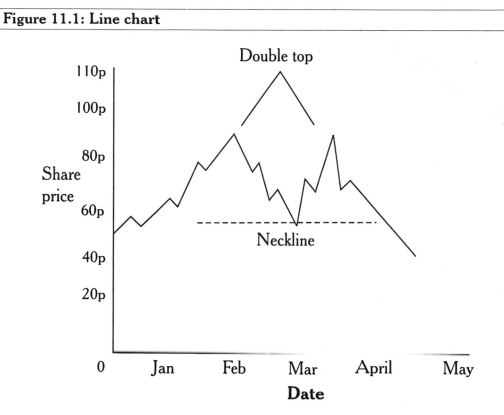

This is the type of chart more commonly understood. It simply plots the closing price of the share each day.

Fig. 11.1 shows a line chart with a trend called a 'double top'. This arises when the share price has risen sharply followed by a limited profit taking, which causes the share price to fall. The share then rallies around the previous high figure but again meets resistance. Investors decide that the peak has been reached and they take their profits, causing the price to fall again. The neckline is the support level above or below which the pattern forms. Any breakout through the neckline should be noted. If the price falls below the neckline the shares should be sold; if it rises above, then they should be purchased.

The opposite trend is called 'double bottom'.

Bar charts

This is more sophisticated than the line chart because it shows the high and low trading prices for the day, joined by a vertical line. The closing price is marked by a horizontal line across the bar (see Fig. 11.2).

Figure 11.2: Head and shoulders formation

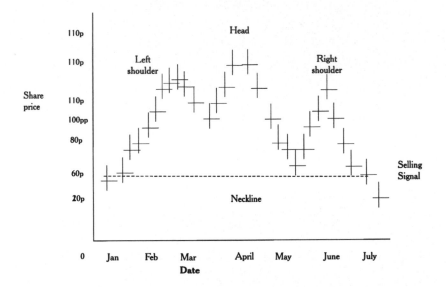

Fig 11.2 also shows the 'head and shoulders' formation. This formation develops when a share price rises quite quickly, falls back because of profit taking (the left shoulder), rises again sharply to a new high because investors think they missed out on the first rise (the head), falls again due to profit taking, rallies again (the right shoulder) then falls because of profit taking. Once the right shoulder has been reached the share price drops quickly, and once it falls below the neckline this is a signal to shareholders to sell.

Point and figure chart

This is a chart with no fixed timescale, although the horizontal axis does represent time. The object of this chart is to show significant price movements. Significant upwards movements are marked by a row of Xs, and downward movements by a row of Os, not both. The rule on starting a new column is that the chartist ignores the highest X in the previous column, but fills all the other squares while the price continues to fall. Once the price rises again a new column of Xs is commenced that starts one square above the lowest O. This can be seen clearly by studying Fig. 11.3.

Figure 11.3: Point and figure chart

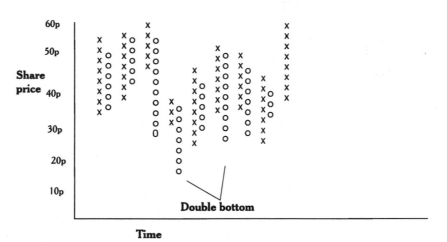

Time

Other patterns

When reading charts certain patterns emerge. One that always seems to occur is after a sharp upward price movement. The following period often has the share price hovering around at a similar level while investors evaluate their next course of action. This period is called 'consolidation' by chartists. If the price then climbs again a 'continuation' pattern forms; if it falls the pattern is called a 'reversal'.

The Triangle

Figure 11.4: The triangle

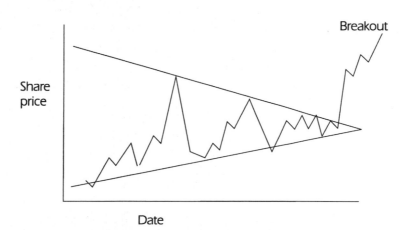

This forms after there has been a strong rise or fall in the share's price. It may produce either a continuation or a reversal pattern when the breakout from the formation occurs. The breakout is always a strong price movement either upwards or downwards.

The flag

Figure 11.5: The flag

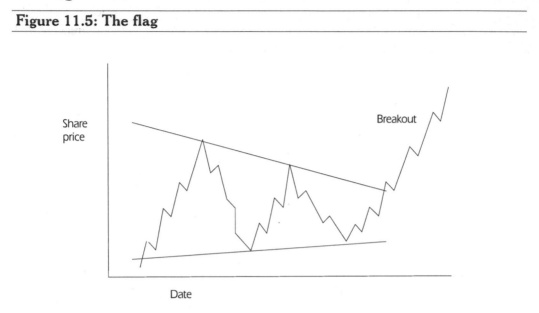

Although this appears similar to a triangle, it has two distinguishing features. First, it always signals the continuation of a trend, and second it forms more quickly than the triangle.

Figure 11.6: The rectangle

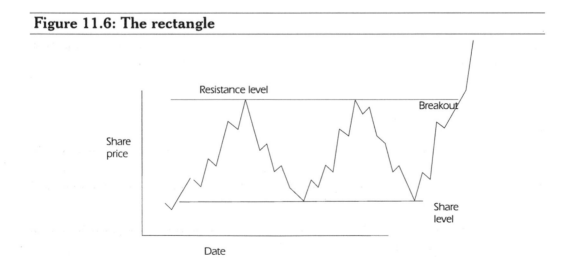

The rectangle-like shape arises when a share's price swings between two points above which it is reluctant to rise, the resistance level, and below which it does not want to fall, the support level.

The resistance level is created when investors feel that they have made enough profit and they decide to take that profit. This will cause the share price to fall. The support level arises because investors feel that the share is now cheap, and buying pushes the price up again. As with the breakout on the other patterns, this can be an upward or downward breakout and signals the end of that particular pattern at that time.

Figure 11.7: Trend lines

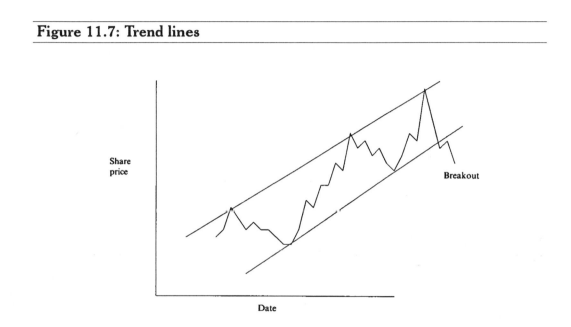

A trend is simply the overall direction taken by the share price. In Figure 11.7 the price is moving up and down in the trend lines, but the overall movement is upwards.

Trends

Chartists watch for three trends developing as an aid to their art:

● The primary trend means that the chartist is looking at the share price movements in the long term. In a bull market the primary trend is upwards; in a bear market the trend is downwards. The chartist then looks for any changes in the overall pattern that will indicate a new trend;

● A secondary trend is one that lasts for a few weeks, but does not have any effect on the overall primary trend;

● A tertiary trend is only a minor movement that lasts for just a few days.

Comparison of fundamental and technical analysis

Both types of analysis try to predict share price movements as a whole. The fundamental analyst compares the share price with indicators such as the level of interest rates, inflation, the index of employment. He also delves into the company's balance sheet and looks at the industry itself. From this the fundamental analyst claims to be able to say whether to buy or sell a particular share from the point of view of a medium- to long-term investor.

The fundamental analyst may also use cash-flow based methods, such as the dividend growth method or discounting of forecast free cash flows, for valuation purposes.

Technical analysts on the other hand disagree with the fundamental analyst's view because they claim that reliance on past performance is a hindrance in judging future prospects. Technical analysts consider that the share price is fixed purely by supply and demand and past performance as evidenced by the company's accounts is no guide whatsoever. Not surprisingly, the fundamental analysts disagree violently and they compare chartists to astrologers or palmists! Chartists aim to say when to buy, sell or hold a share. Their time scale is short-term, whereas that of fundamental analysts is long-term.

Neither fundamental nor technical analysts have ever been able to prove that they are 100% right and that the other is wrong, and even more confusion reigns because different chartists will sometimes interpret the same chart in different ways.

The Dow Theory

This theory depends on the plotting of daily price indices on charts. It originates in America, and in its pure form is related to two US stock market indices, Industrials and Rails. Before any conclusion may be established, the one index must confirm the other. In the UK there is no Rails index, but advocates of the theory claim that it can be successfully applied to other indices.

In essence, it is maintained that there is a primary movement in the market at all times lasting for one or more years. There are also secondary movements usually lasting for a few weeks or months. The daily movements that comprise the secondaries are ignored.

The Hatch System

This system is based on the argument that if an investor sells at 10% below the top of the market and buys at 10% above the bottom of the market, he is going to do as well as he can reasonably expect. It can be applied to an index, a group of shares or an individual share. There are various ways of operating the system but once the method has been decided upon ~~t~~ be adhered to, and the signals obeyed.

investor purchased a share in March for 250p he would immediately subtract or 'exit' price of 225p (250p − 25p). If in April the share price had calculate a new selling (exit) price of 234p (260p − 26p). If in May len to 258p, the exit price would remain unchanged because the share price is above the 234p. If in June the share price fell to 230p he would have sold his holding as soon as the price reached 234p. The Hatch operator would then work out a purchase or 'entry' price of 230p + 10%, i.e. 253p, that would be adjusted downwards if the price had fallen on subsequent review days. Whenever the share price rose to the automatic purchase price, he would buy.

A refinement of this system would be to calculate the control selling or buying price using the average price for the previous month, rather than the selling price on a fixed day. The advantage of this system is that it prevents selling too soon in a bull market, or buying too early in a bear market. However, in order to make a profit using this system the market price must rise by at least 20% (in order to cover dealing costs).

Filter rules (that is, systems such as the Hatch System)

These are designed to isolate primary trends from minor price changes caused by random factors. The problem with this method is deciding upon the size of the filter. If it is small, say 3-5%, the investor is constantly buying and selling, thus incurring heavy dealing costs. If it is too large, say 20-25%, much of the price movement will have taken place before the investor acts. (See Fig. 11.8.)

Figure 11.8: Filter method

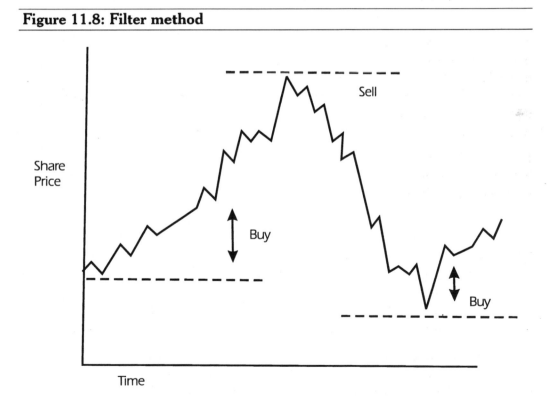

6   The Random Walk Hypothesis

The random walk hypothesis states that stock markets are highly efficient and that at any one time, therefore, share prices reflect all the available information about companies and economies, including the best guess of millions of investors about what the future holds. In these conditions prices will change for one reason only: that new information has become available, including any facts or ideas that alter perceptions of the future.

Because new information is unpredictable, future share price movements are unpredictable. Yesterday's share price represented the collective view of yesterday's information. Every day starts out fifty-fifty, so that prices could move up or down depending on the market reaction to new information. The current share price is the best estimate of tomorrow's price, because it reflects all known information and all the estimates that investors have made as regards the future.

Efficient Market Hypothesis (EMH)

The efficient market hypothesis developed from the random walk hypothesis. It takes three forms.

Weak form of EMH

This weak form seeks to expose the vulnerability of technical analysis by stating that whatever information may be conveyed by charts has already been recognized in the current share price. Thus the current share price already takes account of past price trends and therefore the chart of a share price cannot help in predicting the future share price. One derogatory quotation concerning charts says 'Markets have no memory', referring to the previous comment that every day starts out as fifty-fifty.

The semi-strong form of EMH

This theory goes on to say that not only is the chart of the share price reflected in the current price of a share, but that all other publicly available information has been taken into account in the current share price.

The justification for this semi-strong EMH is that all leading companies are under constant examination by a large number of fundamental and technical analysts. Therefore the prices of the shares in these companies reflect the consensus of this expert advice to investors. In addition to investors who deal in a share on the basis of expert advice, there will be non-experts who will buy or sell the shares. However, statistically there is a fifty-fifty chance that a non-expert will be bullish or bearish about a share and therefore the view of the non-experts should cancel out, leaving the expert advisors as the ones whose views move the share price.

As new information becomes available the market will react to it. Thus the new information will change the market's view of the fundamentals and the share price will therefore immediately adjust to its new intrinsic value.

Strong form of EMH

This strong form states that not only is all publicly available information reflected in the share price of leading shares, but that so too is all privately known 'insider information'. Most 'insider information' in leading companies is quickly available to the analysts because it can be anticipated from other sources. Thus the shares in leading companies are considered to be valued fairly because all information (both public and 'private') is reflected in the present share price.

The strong form of EMH explains and backs up the random walk hypothesis. Leading shares are priced at their current intrinsic values, and their prices will fluctuate in line with changes in information. Changes in fundamentals cannot be predicted, hence share prices will move in a random manner.

Implications of the EMH for investors

Diversify to reduce risk exposure

Financial commentators have been known to select a portfolio by sticking a pin or dart into the *Financial Times*. The performance of such a randomly chosen portfolio has compared no better and no worse than a carefully selected fund. Thus the investor should simply invest equal amounts in all the leading shares, because every leading share is priced at its intrinsic value. The performance of the portfolio would then represent that of the stock market as a whole, and the investor would be subject to less risk than if he had invested in a single share.

Further research has shown that it is not necessary to invest in every leading share, but that equal amounts invested in 15 different shares from different sectors, chosen at random, will give most of the benefits of diversification, and will prove to be a satisfactory substitute for the 'market portfolio'.

Once the portfolio has been selected, follow a buy-and-hold strategy

There is nothing to be gained by switching once the portfolio of shares has been selected. Switching will involve dealing costs and, possibly, advisory fees. The EMH implies that the shares an investor holds (at whatever price they stand in relation to the original purchase price) are currently valued at their intrinsic value based on currently available information.

Exceptions can arise when changes in market values of the constituent equities mean that particular sectors have become under- or over-represented as a proportion of the total portfolio value. It may then be necessary to switch investments to restore the balance of the portfolio so as to gain maximum benefits of diversification. In addition, it may be beneficial to dispose of certain shares to establish a loss for capital gains tax purposes.

A buy-and-hold strategy may seem to be an inadequate policy when there are market peaks and troughs that signal timely opportunities for active dealing. However, in practice such opportunities become apparent only with the benefit of hindsight. Indeed, very few actively managed portfolios have outperformed the stock market indices consistently over any given period of time, presumably because of transaction costs. The rise in popularity of indexed funds, whereby funds portfolios merely replicate the stock market index, has come about as a consequence of the acceptance of EMH.

The paradox regarding expert market analysts and advisors

If the current market price represents the intrinsic value of a share, there is little point in individual investors trying to use experts to 'beat the market'. On the other hand, the continuing efficiency of the market may well depend on the efforts of those analysts which will ensure that price movements continually reflect new information.

The balance of the evidence for and against the EMH

The crash of October 1987

During October 1987, the stock markets of the world experienced a price fall of around one-third. Many writers asked what new information had come to light to cause such a dramatic fall.

In the USA, interest rates had risen, thus driving up the return available from risk-free investments such as Treasury Bills. Share prices had to fall so that dividend yields could rise to compensate. In addition, there was a proposed 'merger tax' from the US Congress that would have ended the merger boom. The stocks that fell in price just before the main falls on 'Black Monday' were shares of potential takeover targets.

Some writers claim that the fall was a result of a rational assessment of new information, but others blame mass hysteria, herd instinct, or program trading whereby initial falls in price triggered off automatic computerized sell orders that escalated the price crash.

Monday blues

Some writers quote statistics to show that share prices in general have fallen on Mondays because of sales of shares by private investors. The argument states that private investors make investment decisions over the weekend and then execute these decisions on Monday. Generally speaking, so the argument goes, the private investor is more pessimistic than the institutional investor, and thus the net effect will be to generate sell orders.

Supporters of the EMH would say that if this were true, then other investors would incorporate this information in the investment decision making and would buy on Monday when shares had become temporarily depressed.

The January effect and sell in May and go away

Some writers claim that prices in general have risen in January but have fallen in May. They say that such changes are irrational.

Stabilization techniques for new issues

Issuing houses sometimes make it known that they will buy back a new issue if the price falls in the wake of the launch. Clearly, this means that the price will be artificially supported.

Where does all this leave the EMH?

There is no single 'correct' answer that can prove or disprove the validity of the EMH. The strongest argument against the EMH is the crash of October 1987. Was this caused by new information or was it the result of mass hysteria and program trading?

On the other hand, the failure of professionally managed funds significantly to outperform the market over a long period of time would tend to support the EMH.

Against this, consider the implications of three hypothetical portfolios chosen at random (by throwing darts at the *Financial Times* London Share Service). The progress of the three 'portfolios' was measured by the *Investors Chronicle* from 30 October 1987 to 31 October 1991. Not one of these portfolios, each of 25 shares, came anywhere near to beating the performance of the FTSE Actuaries All Share Index.

Some would argue that the semi-strong version applies to the shares of major listed companies (i.e. those in the FTSE 100 index), because of the number of analysts following these shares. The EMH, however, is said to be less in evidence in the shares of smaller listed companies which are followed by fewer analysts.

7 Directors' Share Dealings

Directors' dealings in the shares of their companies are being looked on as a useful signal to the prospects of that company. Although directors cannot deal on 'inside information' (a criminal offence), they are in a good position to know just how good or bad the companies' prospects are. 'Insider dealing' is a criminal offence and occurs when a person has inside knowledge of happenings, e.g. a prospective takeover bid, and buys or sells shares in order to make a profit from that information. To prevent any problems the Stock Exchange rules prevent directors from dealing for two months prior to the announcement of interim or final results. Information is available about purchases and sales made by directors, and these can be interpreted to be 'buy' or 'self' signals for the shares.

'Buy signals'

This is taken as a more significant signal than when a director sells. If he is buying, he is putting his own money 'on the line'. Usually a director will buy because he believes the share price will rise; occasionally he buys as a 'damage limitation exercise' when he feels that the share has been badly depressed and needs bolstering up to aid recovery.

'Sell signals'

These can be misleading, especially if only one director is selling. He may be selling simply to meet personal expenditure such as a large tax bill, or a new house, or a divorce settlement. However, if several of the directors are selling at approximately the same time and in large size transactions, then a 'sell signal' is more likely.

Accuracy of this system

Information about directors' share dealings is now freely available. The analysts in this field expect that 75% of the directors' dealings that are interpreted as significant prove to be worthwhile buy or sell signals.

Directors' share dealings are not to be taken in isolation when deciding whether to buy or sell a share, but they are one of the factors professional investors take into account when trying to determine the likely direction of a share price.

8   Systematic and Unsystematic Risk

Risk can be classified under two headings, as follows.

Systematic risks

Most investments are affected by one of the systematic risks:

Interest rate risk

This applies to gilts or to any marketable fixed-interest investment. If interest rates in general rise, the price of the stock will fall.

The longer dated the gilt, the more its price will be affected by interest-rate levels. Therefore short-dated stocks can be bought to minimize the risk, because their price will tend to be near to par. Alternatively, bank and building society deposits pay interest linked to market rates and their capital value is not affected.

As a generalization, higher interest rates, or persistent rumours that interest rates are about to rise, usually result in a fall in equity prices, as well as in a fall in fixed-interest stock prices. One reason for this fall in share prices could be that the higher interest rates mean that equity investors will require higher returns from their shares. Thus shareholders will discount forecast dividends or free cash flows at a higher discount rate. Higher discount rates mean lower net present values in any discounted cash flow calculation, and lower NPVs equate to lower share prices.

For example, compare the intrinsic value of a share as calculated by the dividend growth method. As we have already seen:

The formula for the Gordon Growth Model is:

$$P = \frac{D}{(r - g)}$$

where: $P =$ intrinsic value of the share

$D =$ next dividend

r = investor's required rate of return

g = dividend growth rate

If the next dividend on ABC's shares will be 21p, if future dividend growth is forecast at 5% p.a. and if the required rate of return is 12%, the intrinsic value of the share is:

$$\frac{21}{*(0.12 - 0.05)} = \frac{21}{0.07}$$

Intrinsic value of share = 300p

However, if the required rate for return by equity investors rose from 12% to 14%, the intrinsic value of the share based on the dividend growth model would fall to:

$$\frac{21}{*(0.14 - 0.05)} = \frac{21}{0.09}$$

Intrinsic value of share = 233p

Inflation risk

Rising inflation is usually equated with falling securities prices. The capital value of bank deposits or gilts at maturity will be eroded by inflation, as will the purchasing power of payments under an annuity, or fixed-coupon gilt. Inflation equates with uncertainty in the eyes of equity investors, and this usually results in share prices being marked down.

Currently most fixed-interest investments give a 'real' rate of return for basic and non-taxpayers: in other words the monetary return exceeds the rate of inflation. In the long term, equities also have given a 'real' return as shown by the unit trust statistics in Unit 12. However, the only sure way not to lose from inflation is to buy index-linked NSCs, or index-linked gilts.

The market risk

The performance of the stock market as a whole generally affects the prices of individual shares.

Within the context of direct equity investment, a portfolio of non-durable consumer shares will be less affected by market movements than a portfolio of shares in capital goods producers.

Non-durable consumer goods producers generally have low beta coefficients (i.e. are less volatile than the market as a whole). If the shares are low geared, then there is even less risk.

The only other way to avoid market risk is to invest in overseas shares. However, such shares are vulnerable to changes in their own markets.

In the short run, i.e. up to nine months, investors can buy traded put options on the FTSE 100 or 250 index. If the market as a whole falls, the drop in value of the investor's portfolio will be compensated for by the profit on the traded option.

Unsystematic risks and how to reduce their effect

These are risks that apply to a particular investment, usually an equity investment.

Management risk

Bad decisions can result in poor profits.

Try to buy shares in companies with proven management.

Financial risk

Highly-geared companies, or those with heavy liabilities in overseas currency, are at risk here.

Study the balance sheets to assess the risk.

Industry risk

Some industries become fashionable. The investor needs to be aware of the current 'fashionable' areas, because they often become tomorrow's failures. At the time of writing, some concern has been expressed about over-inflated values of 'Internet stocks'. These IT-based equities are in the main shares of recently formed companies that have not actually made a profit and in many cases have paid out little or no dividend. Investors had purchased these stocks as 'growth stocks' and the main motivation was capital gain, as opposed to dividend income. However, some commentators have expressed reservations regarding the length of time before the growth potential will be realized in the form of cash, profit and dividend generation, and others have expressed the fear that low barriers to entry will inevitably erode future profit margins anyway. It will be interesting for readers to compare the prices of such stocks on 30 December 1999 with their prices in a year's time to see whether the doubts were valid or not.

Reduction of unsystematic risk in a portfolio of shares

Use a mixture of fundamental and technical analysis to select the shares, and spread the risk by buying a minimum of 15 different shares in different sectors. To be cost effective, you need to invest a minimum of £2,000 in each share otherwise the performance of the share will have to be exceptional simply to cover the dealing costs.

Research has shown that most of the unsystematic risk can be avoided by investing equal amounts at random in 15 -20 different shares in different sectors. According to the strong form of EMH, the current share price reflects all information, whether public or private. Thus the current price of any share should equate to its intrinsic value, and new information will affect individual shares in different ways. However, the effects on the performance of the individual shares in a diversified portfolio will tend to cancel each other out, and the portfolio will tend to generate the average return of the market.

Unit trusts and investment trusts with professional management and diversification are a means of eliminating most of the unsystematic risk. Buy three or four units and/or investment trusts under different managers for maximum benefits of diversification.

Note that diversification among equities cannot remove the systematic risk. Only diversification into other markets and/or into other forms of investment (such as chattels) can remove the systematic risk.

General points on risk reduction

A basic portfolio should include an emergency cash reserve, gilts for guaranteed income, equities with scope for growth of income and capital, and tax-free investments for high-rate taxpayers. In addition, large portfolios benefit from a property element that should be provided by indirect methods such as property bonds. This structure spreads the risk across a range of different types of investment, thus increasing diversification.

9   Modern Portfolio Theory: Background

The view shared by most academics is that the only way persistently to beat the average return generated by the market is to assume more risk than the market average risk. Portfolio theory seeks to explain how portfolio diversification may help the investor to achieve an above market average return without exceeding the average market risk.

The usual way to measure the risk associated with investment in particular share is via calculation of the *probable variability of future returns*. In other words risk may be measured in terms of the *variance* or *standard deviation* of the expected return. *The higher the variance/ standard deviation, the higher the risk.*

For example, let us assume that the average return on a particular share over a period of time, say one year, had been 10%, and that the standard deviation of the returns had been 3.5%. This means that:

- Around 68% of actual measured returns on the share will have been within one standard deviation of the 10% average return;

- Around 95% of actual measured returns on the share will have been within two standard deviations of the expected return;

- Around 99.73% of actual measured returns on the portfolio will have been within three standard deviations of the expected return.

Therefore, for this particular share:

- measured returns will have been between 13.5% p.a. and 6.5% p.a.(10 +/- 3.5) for around 68% of the time;

- measured returns will have been between 17% p.a. and 3% p.a.(10+/-7) for around 95% of the time; and

- measured returns will have been between 20.5% p.a. and -0.5% p.a.(10+/-10.5) for 99.73% of the time.

Thus, concentrating on the downside risk, if we assume that the future will follow past trends, there is about a 16% chance of return falling below 6.5%, (100- 68) ÷ 2, but only around a 2.5% chance, (100-95) ÷ 2, of the return falling below 3% p.a., and less than a 1% chance of the return falling to minus 0.5% p.a.

From the above we can conclude that a security generating a stable return with little possibility of that return deviating from the expected level will involve little risk and will have a very small (or even zero) associated standard deviation. This would apply, for example, to a short-dated gilt-edged stock, or to a three-month treasury bill.

However, an investment in the equity shares of a high-risk company would involve the acceptance of possibly quite variable returns (and in some years losses). As the actual return might vary considerably from the expected average return on a year-by-year basis, the associated variance/standard deviation of the return on the risky equity would tend to be high.

The relative variability of returns on two securities is known as their *covariance*.

● Where the returns on the two securities have a very close positive correlation (i.e. the returns move up and down together in response to particular events), the covariance of the returns on the securities is high and positive.

● Where the patterns of variability in returns have a fairly random relationship, the covariance of the two securities is small and may be positive or negative in sign.

● Where there is a near perfect negative relationship between the variability of the returns on the securities, the covariance is high and negative.

10 Modern Portfolio Theory: Basic Application

If the returns on two securities have a high negative covariance, it is possible to eliminate much of the risk faced in holding each individually by instead holding both securities in a portfolio. Consider the following example:

Security	X	Y
Returns in years with hot weather	30%	-10%
Returns in years with cold weather	-10%	30%

Let us assume X is an ice cream manufacturer and Y is a central heating company.

Assuming that the weather is either 'hot' or 'cold' (and hence that all possible outcomes are covered):

● Investing in Security X produces a good return in years when the weather is good, but generates a loss in the years when the weather is bad. If an investor holds just Security X, then a series of years of bad weather could be very damaging financially;

● Investing in Security Y produces a good return in years when the weather is bad, but a poor return when the weather is good;

● By dividing investment funds evenly between Securities X and Y, the investor will receive:

➢ a return of 10% when the weather is good – i.e. (0.5 x 30% return on Security X) + (0.5 x –10% return on Security Y); and

➢ a return of 10% when the weather is bad – i.e. (0.5 x –10% return on Security X) + (0.5 x 30% return on Security Y).

Therefore, irrespective of the weather, by holding the two-security portfolio an investor receives a constant return from year to year. Compare this to the outcome of holding just one or other of the securities, when the return will be volatile. In this purely theoretical case it would appear that the risk associated with the return on the two securities has been eliminated entirely and the standard deviation for the returns on this two-share portfolio would be nil.

In reality it is most unlikely that the returns on two securities would be so perfectly matched as to eliminate entirely the risk associated with their respective returns. However, so long as the returns on the securities held within a portfolio respond in different ways to developments or economic events, the risk embodied in the portfolio is reduced through diversification.

Thus by adding to a portfolio a security the return on which has a negative covariance with the returns on the securities already held, the risk associated with the portfolio as a whole will be reduced.

Obviously, holding just two different securities does not constitute a diversified portfolio. Fifteen or more different securities is normally thought of as being the minimum number of securities required to achieve significant risk reduction.

The key to selecting a diversified portfolio is to be found in selecting securities that are influenced by different sets of economic and financial variables, or are affected differently by particular economic and financial variables. In practice, this means that risks can be reduced by selecting securities from companies in different business sectors.

In practice all portfolios of securities, irrespective of the diversity of their content, carry with them some risk. Selecting low-risk shares, which have returns with negative covariances, may reduce the variability of returns, but it does not eliminate the chance that in any given year losses will be made.

The calculation of standard deviations and the other statistical methodology associated with betas (b) and Modern Portfolio Theory is beyond the scope of this text. Indeed whole text books have been devoted to these topics. For a very readable yet in-depth study of the EMH, beta, Modern Portfolio Theory and related areas, readers are recommended to study *A Random Walk Down Wall Street*, published by W.W. Norton and Co and written by Burton G. Malkiel.

Summary

Now that you have studied this unit, you should be able to:

○ describe various sources of information:

➤ Extel

➤ Datastream

➤ *Financial Times*

➤ SEDOL

➤ Stock Exchange Year Book;

● describe the use of beta coefficients in measuring risk;

○ understand the importance of judging the quality of a company's management;

○ understand the criteria used by fundamental analysts to assess a company's shares;

○ understand how technical analysts assess shares from the share-price movements;

○ draw freehand, and be able to interpret:

➤ line charts

➤ bar charts

➤ point and figure charts;

● recognize and explain the following chart patterns:

➤ double top and double bottom

➤ neckline

➤ head and shoulders

➤ consolidation

➤ continuation

➤ breakout

➤ triangle

➤ flag

➤ rectangle

➤ resistance level

➤ support level

➤ trend lines;

○ distinguish between primary, secondary and tertiary trends;

○ compare and contrast fundamental and technical analysis;

- explain the Dow theory and Hatch system;

- describe the random walk hypothesis;

- describe the efficient market hypothesis and its weak, semi-strong and strong forms;

- explain how directors' share dealings can be a guide to deciding whether to buy or sell shares;

- categorize risk into systematic and unsystematic;

- understand how to reduce risk.

- Appreciate the basic principles that underpin portfolio theory.

12

UNIT TRUSTS AND OPEN-ENDED INVESTMENT COMPANIES (OEICs)

Objectives

After studying this unit, you should be able to:

- define and describe a unit trust;

- understand the roles of managers and trustees;

- explain how unit trusts are regulated;

- describe (briefly) the role of the Association of Unit Trusts and Investment Funds (AUTIF);

- understand the pricing of unit trusts;

- describe the different types of unit trusts;

- explain the benefits of unit trusts and how investors should evaluate the various unit trusts available;

- explain the nature of open-ended investment companies (OEICs).

1   Introduction

Direct investments are ones that are selected and reviewed by the investor himself, with or without the assistance of professional advice. On the other hand, with indirect investments individuals hand over their money to professional managers who manage the pooled funds on behalf of their investors. In this unit and in Units 13 and 14 we look at the major forms of indirect investment: unit trusts, investment trusts, OEICs, pension funds and insurance products.

2 What is a Unit Trust?

A unit trust is a fund into which investors pool their money. This money is invested by professional managers in cash, shares, gilts, loan stocks, property, warrants, futures and options.

When an investor contributes money to the fund he will receive a number of units of the fund in exchange for his investment. All units of the same fund rank equally, and at any one time the value of a unit reflects the total value of the funds under management divided by the number of units in existence. We shall examine the pricing of units in more detail later on, but for now suffice it to say that the price of a unit will be based on the net asset value of that unit.

Unit trusts are 'open ended' so that when new monies are received by the managers new units are created. When investors withdraw their money from the pool the units are cancelled in exchange for their cash value, which is returned to investors.

Obviously when new monies exceed redemptions the managers will have additional cash to invest, but if redemptions exceed new monies then it may be necessary for managers to liquidate some of the fund's underlying investments to meet these redemptions.

The unit trust 'industry' has approximately 13.9 million unit holder accounts and funds under management valued at approximately £237.772 billion. This makes it a vital part of the UK investment scene. These figures relate to authorized unit trusts as at December 1999.

Who are the managers and what are their functions?

The role of the managers is to invest the unit holders' money in accordance with the stated objectives of the trust. They are also responsible for calculating the bid and offer prices of the units, the bid prices being the price at which the managers will buy units and the offer being the price at which they will sell them.

Most individual fund managers are part of a management group that controls a number of different trusts. Generally speaking, there is an overall group philosophy with regard to liquidity levels, the number of securities in which a trust should invest, the size of companies invested in and how actively the fund is to be managed. This philosophy will be influenced by the group's collective view of the UK and overseas economies. The individual fund manager will normally invest in accordance with the parameters laid down by the group as a whole. Fund managers are not necessarily expected to subscribe fully to the group view, but it is unlikely that any radical departures would either arise or be tolerated. This is why performance of an individual trust will tend to reflect the performance of the other trusts under the same management group.

Who are the trustees and what are their functions?

Trustees are substantial financial institutions, and indeed the Financial Services Act 1986 lays down strict requirements regarding minimum capitalization of trustees. They are also of the highest financial standing and integrity; companies such as Royal Bank of Scotland, General Accident and Barclays Bank Trust Co act as trustees.

The role of the trustee involves the following:

- Safeguarding the assets of the unit holders. All cash and securities in the fund are held in the trustee's name so that there is no possibility of misappropriation by the managers;

- Issuing certificates to the unit holder;

- Ensuring that the relevant unit certificate has been duly cancelled before any proceeds are released to meet the sale of units;

- Collecting the dividend income of the trust and distributing the income by way of dividend to the unit holders;

- Supervising the register of unit holders;

- Ensuring that the trust is managed within the terms of the trust deed (a formal document that lays down investment guidelines for managers);

- Vetting any advertisement to ensure that it is not misleading and checking that the advertisement states that unit trust prices can fall as well as rise.

How trustees supervise the investments made by the managers

The trustee must ensure that the investment aims of the trust are complied with, and because all investment is to some extent subjective, there can be different interpretations of how the investment policy should be supervised.

Some trustees take this duty to the point of being prepared to veto any investment that they feel conflicts with the unit holders' interests. Other trustees take a more relaxed view and are prepared to veto an investment only where it contravenes the terms of the trust deed.

Payment of trustees

The fee is fixed by negotiation between the trustees and the managers.

3   The Role of the Financial Services Authority (FSA)

Under the Financial Services Act 1986 only unit trusts that are 'authorized' by the Financial Services Authority are allowed to advertise.

All authorized unit trusts are governed by a trust deed that must be approved by the Financial Services Authority (FSA). This deed will cover such matters as maximum management fees, the precise method of calculating the bid and offer prices, and the provisions enabling new investors to join.

As regards the investments made by the managers, an approved trust deed must contain the following minimum requirements:

- Investments must be in securities that are quoted on a recognized stock exchange (although up to 25% of the funds can be invested in shares of companies quoted on the Alternative Investment Market (AIM)), of which 10% may be held in unlisted securities or non-British recognized stock exchanges;

- No single share holding can be acquired that, at the time of its purchase, would represent more than 5% of the value of the whole of the trust's portfolio;

- There can be problems regarding the '5%' stipulation if a particular investment increases rapidly in value after acquisition, but as long as its value does not exceed 7½% of the fund the trustees will not be obliged to intervene;

- A unit trust may not hold more than 10% of the share capital of one particular company;

- No direct investment in commodities is permitted. (Investment in shares of companies dealing commodities is allowed.)

The Financial Services Authority insists on these minimum constraints, although there is nothing to prevent a more restrictive trust deed being drawn up. These constraints ensure that the investments are readily realizable. Thus the managers can buy or sell units at any time and can easily obtain cash if it is required to meet net redemptions.

4 The Association of Unit Trusts and Investment Funds (AUTIF)

This Association is yet another example of the City of London's desire to keep its own house in order by self-regulation.

The objectives of the association are:

- to make representations to the UK Government on legislative, regulatory and taxation matters that affect the business interests of its members;

- to liase with the Financial Services Authority and other organizations in the UK and Europe on regulatory matters and other important issues;

- to increase public awareness and understanding of investment funds;

- to seek to improve the standards of training in the industry;

- to seek to integrate personal finance education into the school curriculum;

- to add value to member companies by providing them with information, guidance and assistance in matters related to their business;

- to offer an information service to external parties interested in the activities of the UK investment funds industry.

AUTIF is a powerful force in the financial services industry, working closely with the regulatory and tax authorities in the UK, the EU and around the world, as well as the other major trade associations and leading financial journalists.

Membership of the association is open to any management company of a unit trust that is authorized by the Financial Services Authority. The work of the association is financed by contributions from members based on the volume of funds managed by each particular group.

One of the most valuable functions of AUTIF is the provision of information. Monthly statistics regarding the number of unit trusts and value of funds under management are published, and any significant developments are chronicled. The association is only too pleased to answer any general enquiries on unit trusts, although it cannot advise on the merits of individual trusts.

5 PIA and IMRO

PIA (Personal Investment Authority) regulates the marketing and advertising of unit trusts to the general public. It is responsible for seeing that full disclosure of commission paid to agents/intermediaries is made available.

IMRO (Investment Management Regulatory Organization) regulates the fund management firms' side of the unit trust operations.

6 Summary of the Various Bodies

The Treasury is the overseer body for the industry, but most of its powers are devolved to the FSA (Financial Services Authority), which covers the authorization of unit trusts. The FSA also sets out the basic formula for valuing unit trust units.

PIA (Personal Investment Authority) covers the marketing, advertising and commission side of the unit trusts.

IMRO (Investment Management Regulatory Organization) covers the investment management side.

AUTIF (Association of Unit Trusts and Investment Funds) concerns itself with the role of promoting understanding of unit trusts and investment funds, lobbying on behalf of its members, and the provision of statistics and other information.

The PIA Ombudsman deals with complaints that have not satisfactorily been dealt with (in the complainant's eyes) by the other bodies mentioned. The PIA Ombudsman covers the unit trust and investment funds industry as well as the insurance industry.

7   Pricing of Unit Trust Units

Net asset or creation value as a basis of prices

We have already noted that the value of a unit at any one time will be based on its 'net asset value'. If a fund's assets (i.e. its investments at current valuation together with accrued income and the brokerage costs) totalled £10 million and if there were five million units in existence, then the net asset value per unit would be £2. This net asset value is more correctly called the creation price. If the value of those assets were to increase to £15 million, then the creation price of the units would become £3 per unit, provided there had been no new units created and no redemptions. If a unit holder wished to redeem his units when the assets had increased to £15 million, he would receive around £3 per unit. Likewise, a new investor would expect to pay around £3 per unit if he bought units at this time.

Prices are published in the financial press. There are two prices, the higher offer price at which managers will sell to the public, and the lower bid price at which they will buy the units back. The formula for valuing unit trusts is laid down by the FSA. The *Financial Times* does not use the terms 'bid' and 'offer', instead using the clearer names 'selling price' for 'bid price' and 'buying price' for 'offer price'.

The bid and offer price

In practice some adjustment is necessary to the creation price before the units can be priced by the managers. Administration, dealing costs, trustees' fees, and the manager's own fees have to be paid for. These expenses are allowed for in the spread between the bid and offer prices. The manager's fees consist of the initial charge, which is incorporated in the bid offer price spread of the units, and an annual management fee of, on average, 1-1½%. Most trust deeds specify that the managers can make an initial charge (known as a front-end loading charge) of a percentage of the value of the units purchased, but this charge is incorporated in the spread between bid and offer prices. The average initial charge is about 5%. Under FSA rules, the maximum spread between bid and offer prices would work out at around 10% – but even this is not a statutory maximum figure. However, most managers work to a spread of around 6% between the two prices, because a larger difference may well reduce the attractiveness of the units. Some unit trust managers have reduced the front-end loading charge to around 1% to make the trust more attractive to investors.

In practical terms the significance of the spread to an investor is that the units must rise by the amount of that spread before he can recoup his original investment. In the simplest possible terms, if the offer price of units is 100p and there is a spread of 6%, the investor would buy from the managers at 100p, and if he sold them back the same day he would receive only 94p per unit.

There are no commission charges for lump-sum investments made direct with the managers, but an annual management fee of around 0.75-1.5% is deducted from either the dividend paid out to unit holders or the value of the fund. Increasingly, the annual fee is levied on the value of the fund,. When the annual fee is deducted from the value of the fund, the published dividend yield will be higher than if the fee is deducted from income. The apparently higher yield, however, is obtained at the expense of capital erosion.

Historic and forward pricing

In essence, the price of unit trust units is based on creation value with a margin allowed for managers' fees and costs. Pricing can be on one of two methods, historic or forward:

- Historic pricing. This is the price calculated on the price set at the most recent valuation. Investors will deal at the price shown in today's newspaper;

- Forward pricing. The price for the units is the price to be set at the next valuation. Investors will not know the exact price at which they have dealt until the next day.

Some unit trusts use only historic pricing, some only forward pricing, some use historic up to a set time then go onto forward pricing, and some switch between the two depending on the mood of the market. The pricing basis is indicated in the financial press for each trust.

Investors purchasing or selling units priced on the forward basis are effectively 'dealing blind'. The previous day's price acts as a guide and the movement in the stock market from the previous day should give some indication as to whether the unit price will be higher or lower than the previous day's price.

The managers must deal at a forward price on request and may move to forward pricing at any time.

Prices quoted on a bid basis, prices quoted on an offer basis and the cancellation price

If the trust is expanding with new monies exceeding redemptions, the managers will usually quote their prices on an offer basis, but conversely when there are net redemptions a bid price basis is often used.

When a price is quoted on an offer basis it means that the managers sell units to investors at the maximum offer price using the FSA formula with the bid price being set at around 6% below this.

If prices are quoted on a bid basis the managers will set the bid price at the lowest possible amount using the FSA formula and will then set the offer price around 6% above this figure. Some management groups are now reducing the bid/offer spread from around the 6% mark to around 1% in order to encourage investors into the trust.

Example of offer and bid price calculations

Offer price

Suppose the total value of securities held by a fund, based on the lowest available market dealing offer prices, is £5 million and suppose there are five million units. The value of the securities divided by the number of units is £1.

The calculation of the maximum offer price under the FSA formula is:

	Pence
Unit value of securities (£5m ÷ 5m units)	100.00
Add brokerage (say 0.25%)	0.25
Add accrued interest dividends and cash (say)	0.75
Creation price	101.00
Add Manager's initial charge (say 5%)	5.05
Maximum offer price	106.05

Bid price

Suppose the total value of these securities was £4.9 million when valued at the highest available market dealing bid price. The unit value of a single unit on this basis would be 98p.

	Pence
Unit value (£4.9m ÷ 5m units)	98.000
Deduct brokerage (say 0.25%)	0.245
	97.755
Add accrued income as above	0.750
Minimum bid price/cancellation price	98.505

The maximum spread here is 7.545p, about 7.11% of the offer price.

However, we have already said that market forces will tend to restrict the spread to around 6%. Thus if the managers were dealing on an offer basis their prices could be:

● offer 106.05p

● bid 99.687p.

If the pricing were on a bid basis, it would probably be:

● offer 104.7925

● bid 98.505p (6% below offer).

Notes

1. The cancellation price is the lowest price at which the managers would be allowed to repurchase units from investors. This price in the above example would be 98.505p,

which equates to the lowest price under the terms of the FSA formula. When dealings are on a bid basis, the cancellation price and the bid price are the same.

2.   The figures have to be adjusted by rounding up or down, because unit prices are usually quoted to two decimal places. The method of rounding up or down is governed by the FSA formula.

3.   The manager's initial charge/front-end fee is set out in the trust deed relating to the units. Clearly the higher this charge, the greater the spread. However, the FSA formula imposes limits on the maximum front-end fee.

4.   In practice, managers often quote their bid/offer prices somewhere in between the bid or offer basis. In the above example, the bid/offer prices might have been 99p and 105.32p.

Why bid and offer price basis is important to the investor

There is nothing in law to stop the managers changing their basis of pricing overnight, provided the prices are within the figures calculated from the FSA formula. A sudden change in market sentiment could make the managers decide to switch from a bid to offer basis on bullish news and from an offer to bid basis if a bear market seemed imminent. This means that someone who bought units priced on an offer basis could in theory find their 'resale' value had fallen by 10% overnight if the basis of pricing had been changed to bid.

In practice the managers would try to smooth the transition over a week or two, but this is not always possible.

Another point for the private investor to bear in mind is that advertisements can be misleading if they quote the unit prices at the start and end of a period on an 'offer to offer' basis. If a unit trust unit started the period at 100p and finished it at 115p priced on an offer to offer basis, the investor who wished to realize his gain could only sell at the bid price of around 108p. Thus the true gain, ignoring any dividend income, is 8%, not the 15% shown.

The significance of the bid and offer price to the managers

Unit trust managers can buy their own units, so the concept of 'box management' can be applied when a fund is expanding. However much the net purchases of units by investors, the traffic will be two-way with new purchases exceeding redemptions. The managers can therefore make a tidy profit from buying the units at the bid price and then reselling immediately at the offer price, without the need to disturb the underlying fund as regards these transactions.

The converse applies at times of net redemptions. However, net redemptions usually occur when the market as a whole is in decline so the net asset basis will be falling continually.

Conclusions regarding spreads

Although the spreads are important, market forces have tended to bring most spreads into line. In any event, unit trust units should normally be considered as a long-term investment and in this context it is the investment performance of the units that matters, not their spread.

8   Distribution and Accumulation Units

The differences between these two kinds of unit

The income earned by the trust must be distributed to the unit holders, after deduction of the annual management fee of 1-1½%. Such distributions generally take place twice a year, but some trusts pay out the income more often.

If the trust is a distribution trust, which is the commonest type, the dividend is distributed in cash. The tax position of the investor is the same as for any other dividend in that a 10% and basic-rate taxpayer has no further liability. However, non-taxpayers CANNOT reclaim the tax deducted from the gross equivalent, and higher-rate taxpayers pay the difference between 32.5% and 10%, i.e. 22.5% on the gross equivalent. When dividend yields are quoted for unit trusts, they are quoted on a gross basis and are calculated in the same way as the gross dividend yield on a share, i.e. grossed up by 100/90.

Accumulation funds work on the basis that the trust is split into two: one that distributes the income and an accumulation fund. Two different prices are quoted for the distribution and accumulation funds.

For example, the Lloyds Bank unit trust managers use this basis for their accumulation units and the price of the two is different, as shown from the following figures taken from the *Financial Times* of 9 September 1997.

LloydsTSB Trusts

	Selling price	Buying price
High Income – income	110.66	114.68
High Income – accumulation	139.36	144.42

An investor who held funds in the distribution part of the fund would receive 110.66p per unit (bid price), whereas the holder of accumulation units would receive 139.36p per unit. The holder of accumulation units would have the same number of units at all times (assuming no sales or purchases are made), but his accumulated dividend is reflected in the higher unit price.

At first sight this may seem a wonderful way of avoiding income tax, but in practice this is not the case. The unit trust will issue every unit holder with a tax certificate showing the amount of money retained in the fund on his behalf. The sum shown will be the net of 10% figure, so that the investor will face exactly the same tax consequences as would apply to a cash distribution.

There is one particular advantage of accumulation units. The new units created in lieu of a cash dividend are issued below the published offer price because the administration required is less complex than that needed to create new units for new unit holders.

The significance of 'xd' (ex distribution) on distribution unit trusts

Apart from the final six weeks before income is due to be paid to unit holders, the offer price of a unit trust includes the accrued income since the last distribution. The price quoted in the *Financial Times* is always the 'cum distribution' price unless the letters 'xd' are shown.

The day after its accounting date a trust goes 'ex distribution', and anyone buying units on this date or during the next six weeks will not receive the next distribution. To compensate for this the unit price falls on xd day by the exact amount of the net of 10% tax distribution due.

9 Taxation

Income tax position on dividends paid to the investor

The distribution paid will have tax deducted in exactly the same way as dividends from shares – 10% tax is deducted. This satisfies the 10% and basic-rate taxpayer's liability. Non-taxpayers CANNOT reclaim the tax deducted and 40% taxpayers must pay a further 22.5% (32.5% – 10%) tax on the gross equivalent distribution (gross up 100/90).

Capital gains tax position

The position is:

- As regards the trust itself: unit trusts themselves are entirely exempt from capital gains tax. Thus the managers can buy or sell shares or other securities on their investment merits, without the need to consider CGT;

- As regards unit holders: investors are, however, subject to CGT on disposals of the units. CGT is levied on capital gains on disposals of units in exactly the same way as it is levied on disposals of shares or of any other securities;

- From the point of view of the small investor it should be perfectly possible to avoid CGT on unit trusts altogether, simply by using the £7,100 exemption limit and by taking advantage of the indexation allowances.

Corporation tax as regards the trust itself

Unit trusts pay corporation tax at the lower rate of 20% on all income. Dividend distributions carry a tax credit of 10% and interest distributions (from funds investing in fixed interest bonds) are paid net of 20% tax.

10 Dealing in Unit Trust Units

Unit trust units are purchased from the managers at their offer price and sold back at the bid price. There is no secondary market. When a new trust is being created it is usually advertised in newspapers, with a fixed price until the closing date of the offer. Funds received prior to the deadline will be allocated units at the set price. Any funds received after that closing date will be allocated units at the offer price ruling on that date.

Prices of authorized unit trusts are quoted daily (except Monday) in the *Financial Times*, and the addresses and telephone numbers of the managers are also printed there.

It is quite possible to obtain units through an agent such as a bank, solicitor, stockbroker, accountant or unit trust broker. Generally speaking, the unit trust managers will pay a share of their front-end loading fee as a commission to the intermediary, but the investor himself will still only pay the offer price. However, the trend may change and the student must ascertain his own bank's policy on this matter.

The position is quite different when an investor sells unit trusts. Managers will not pay commission on redemptions, and if an intermediary is used to effect the sale he will usually make a separate charge for his services to be borne by the seller. The moral is simple. If you wish to sell your units, deal direct with the managers.

As regards the mechanics of dealing, the process is very simple. On purchase of units an investor receives a contract note specifying the number of units bought, the price per unit and the consideration. Settlement is on 'cash' terms and the certificate will be received in six to eight weeks.

To sell units the investor signs the form of renunciation on the back of the certificate and then sends the certificate to the managers. The proceeds of the sale should be received within a week.

11   Unit Trust Information in the *Financial Times*

Baring Fund Managers Ltd (1200) H

	Init. Chg%	Notes	Selling price	Buying price	+ or-	Yield Grs
UK Growth	5		199.80	212.90	-5.40	0.9

ACM Investments Ltd. (0830) F

	Init. Chg%	Notes	Selling price	Buying price	+ or-	Yield Grs
Gilt Income	11		51.93	52.74	+0.10	5.00

Explanation of columns

- Initial charge: Manager's 'front-end loading fee' (5% charge or 11%).

- Selling price: The manager's buying or 'bid' price (i.e. price the seller of units receives – 199.80p or 51.93p).

- Buying price: The manager's selling or 'offer' price (i.e. price the buyer would pay for units purchased – 212.90p or 52.74p).

- + or -: Price movement since last price calculation (-5.40 or +0.10).

- Gross yield: Equivalent to gross dividend yield on equities, the estimated annual pre-tax yield expressed as a percentage of the quoted offer price (0.9% or 5%).

- Time quoted: The time at which the managers' prices are set (8.30 a.m. or 12 noon)

- H or F: The pricing basis – H for historic, F for forward.

In addition there are four symbols that may occur against individual funds: heart, club, diamond or spade. These symbols indicate that the fund is revalued at a different time from the time shown against the manager's name.

Heart	0001-1100 hours.
Club	1101-1400 hours.
Diamond	1401-1700 hours.
Spade	1701-midnight.

The 'Notes' column carries one of two letters:

'C' indicating that the manager's periodic charge (management fee) is deducted from capital;

'E' indicating that there is an exit charge on sale of the units. This can apply to funds that do not levy an initial charge, although a few funds do charge both an initial charge and an exit charge. An exit charge is designed to dissuade investors from selling the units and persuading them to become long-term holders.

The information shown above is to be found in the Tuesday to Saturday edition of the *Financial Times*. On a Monday the only change is that there is no '+ or -' column. It is replaced by the 'Cityline' column, which is the phone number to ring to establish the current unit trust price.

12   Categories of Unit Trust

The role of AUTIF

AUTIF (Association of Unit Trusts and Investment Funds) has placed the different unit trusts into 33 categories so as to help the investor to narrow down the choice. Because there are currently around 1,800 authorized unit trusts and OEICs (see Section 18), this segmentation is of great service to unit holders and potential unit holders.

Perhaps of even more importance is the fact that AUTIF regularly publishes the performance of a 'median' (unidentified) fund in each of the categories. The investor can obtain such information from AUTIF.

Thus investors and potential investors can regularly monitor the performance of their chosen fund against the 'median' for the sector as a whole. Naturally it is of much more benefit to compare a fund with its sector, rather than with trusts as a whole, because there will be times when that sector as a whole compares very well with unit trusts in general, and there will be other times when the reverse is true. At least with this method the investor is able to obtain an impartial benchmark for comparing like with like.

The 33 categories are:

- UK Gilt
- UK General Bonds
- Global Bonds
- Managed Income
- UK Equity & Bond Income
- UK Equity Income
- Global Equity Income
- UK All Companies
- UK Smaller Companies
- Japan
- Far East Including Japan
- Far East Excluding Japan
- North America
- Europe Including UK
- Europe Excluding UK
- Cautious Managed
- Balanced Managed
- Active Managed
- UK Equity & Bond
- Global Equity & Bond
- Global Growth
- Global Emerging Markets
- Property
- UK Money Market
- Guaranteed/Protected Funds

- UK Specialist

- North American Specialist

- European Specialist

- Japanese Specialist

- Far East Specialist

- Global Specialist

- Index Bear Funds

- Pensions.

AUTIF also provides graphical examples of the returns from £1,000 invested in various types of unit trust compared to £2,500 minimum invested in an average Building Society Instant Access account on a net and gross interest basis. The examples take returns over various periods from 1 to 20 years.

AUTIF also provides graphical statistics on 'The power of monthly saving'. The graph compares the performance of £50 per month saving for 5, 10 and 15 years in an Instant Access Building Society account (net interest) to the performance of the UK Equity Income sector – net interest reinvested and to the same trust held in a PEP or ISA. These comparisons are on an offer to bid basis with net and gross income reinvested.

The monthly savings show that £50 per month produces the following returns:

	Building Society Gross Income	Building Society – Net Income	UK All Companies net income re-invested	UK All Companies gross income re-invested
5 years (£3,000 invested)	3317	3206	4150	4186
10 years (£6,000 invested)	7488	7124	11826	12119
15 years (£9,000 invested)	14243	12697	25808	27128

Notes on unit trusts that invest overseas

The general internationalization of the securities industry has resulted in an upsurge in overseas investment by unit trusts.

This move into overseas shares ensures that investors can spread their risk even further and enables their portfolios to be weighted to take account of the markets that look strongest worldwide.

A factor of equal, if not greater, importance than the selection of the individual shares is the movement in the exchange rates. If the pound weakens considerably against the overseas currency, then the value of the portfolio in terms of sterling will rise, and vice versa.

Other sources of statistics for unit trusts

Apart from the information carried in the *Financial Times* and other newspapers, or supplied by AUTIF, the other main source of performance statistics can be found in *Money Management*.

Money Management gives the top five unit trusts in each sector. *Money Management* does not use the same sectors as AUTIF. The sectors in *Money Management* are:

- UK All Companies
- UK Smaller Companies
- Managed Income
- UK Equity and Bond
- UK Equity and Bond Income
- UK Equity Income
- UK Gilt
- Global Growth
- Global Emerging Markets
- Global Equity Income
- Global Equity and Bond
- Global Bond
- Cautious Managed
- Balanced Managed
- Active Managed
- UK General Bonds
- North America
- Property
- Guaranteed/Protected Funds
- Europe Including UK
- Europe Excluding UK
- UK Specialist
- European Specialist
- Japanese Specialist

- Far East Specialist
- Global Specialist
- North American Specialist
- Japan
- Far East including Japan
- Far East excluding Japan
- Money Market
- Index Bear.

Figures are also provided in each of the above sectors for each authorized unit trust in that sector as follows:

- £1,000 invested for one, three and five years in the best and worst trusts;
- Sector volatility over one month, six months, one, two, three, five and ten years;
- Under each sector heading, all the trusts in that sector are listed with details of:
  - launch date
  - buying price
  - fund size £ms
  - dividend yield and month of payment
  - fund's volatility and monthly performance relative to its peers over 36 months. Five is best, one is worst
  - £1,000 buy-to-sell, net income reinvested and ranking over six months, one, two, three, five and 10 years
  - percentage compound annual return, offer to bid, income reinvested over five and ten years
  - volatility – expressed as a standard deviation of monthly total returns over the last 36 months
  - averages/total funds
  - on some sectors the relevant index returns are also given.

This information is invaluable for measuring the performance of a specific trust against its sector and relevant index where one is available.

Money Management also provides performance figures for annuities, insurance rates, investment trusts, insurance funds, pensions funds, sterling-converted offshore funds and guaranteed income bonds.

Money Management can be particularly useful for comparing the performance of unit trusts and investment trusts, which is difficult to do from any other printed source.

13   Types of Unit Trust Schemes Available

Savings plans

The investor signs a banker's order to make monthly transfers, usually for a minimum of £20 per month, to the unit trust managers. The managers allocate units to the investor on the basis of their current offer prices.

Regular savings plans are an ideal savings vehicle. Because there is no contract, the banker's order can be modified or cancelled at any time without any tax or other consequences. The units can be sold back to the managers at their current bid price, with little likelihood of capital gains tax because of the current £7,100 exemption.

Investors must be careful to select a trust that does not levy penalty charges. By law the managers could retain the first three months' instalments to cover their charges (i.e. there would be no units purchased until the fourth month), but not all unit trust managers do this.

The benefit of regular investment is 'pound cost averaging'. The average cost of the units is below the average price, because more units are bought when prices are low. This also ensures that all the investors' funds are not committed when the market is at a temporary peak, a danger that can apply to lump-sum investment.

The taxation of dividends, whether distributed or accumulated, is exactly the same as for dividends on lump-sum investments in unit trust units.

The benefits of pound cost averaging

Because a fixed sum is invested in units every month, it follows that the average cost of the units to the investor will be below the average price for any given period. This is because the fixed sum buys more units in a month when prices are low, and less in a month when prices are high.

Let us take a simple, exaggerated, example to illustrate the point. Suppose the investor makes a monthly transfer of £20 for three months. Let us calculate the consequences for a given set of prices.

	Offer price	Number of units bought
Month 1	100p	20
Month 2	166p	12
Month 3	200p	10

Average offer price 155p

Average cost £60 ÷ 42 = 143p

The basic effect of what may seem to be a statistical quirk is that your money is never committed at the top of the market, although you can never effect all your purchases at the bottom. Thus, pound cost averaging does bring more stability to the investment.

Share exchange schemes

Virtually all unit trust managers offer these schemes. Anybody who owns shares direct may be able to take advantage of this type of scheme, whereby the managers would take over ownership of the shares and issue units in exchange. Naturally, the managers reserve the right to refuse any shares that they feel are unsuitable.

The benefits for the investor are:

● A reduction in, or possibly total elimination of, the brokers' commission that would normally arise on a sale of shares;

● The trust could simply acquire the shares directly from the shareholder by taking from him the certificates and signed stock transfer forms;

● The managers may be prepared to credit the shareholder with the offer price value of the shares, and use this as the basis upon which to calculate the number of units to be issued in exchange.

Note: the share exchange scheme will still count as a 'disposal' of the original shares for CGT purposes.

Exempt unit trusts

Exempt unit trusts are trusts that are available only to tax-exempt bodies, i.e. registered charities, pension funds and friendly societies. Exempt unit trust holders tend to retain their holdings for much longer than the average unit trust investor, thus this stability means less work for the managers on the buying and selling side of the units. This lower level of administrative work is reflected in lower annual management fees. In addition, the exempt unit trust is exempt from corporation tax, and the investors can reclaim the tax deducted from their dividends.

Ethical unit trusts

Some investors prefer not to invest in companies that take part in activities of which these investors disapprove. Examples of such companies are those that operate in South Africa, those involved in armaments, drinks, tobacco, exploitation of workers, animal products, pornography, nuclear industry, pharmaceuticals, depletion of the rain forest, and exploitation of third world countries.

Certain unit trusts offer ethical units where the underlying shares are in companies that do not pursue what are considered by these investors to be unethical activities.

In practice it has proved difficult for ethical unit trusts to find many companies that are

100% ethical. To overcome this problem ethical trusts will invest in either companies that have only 5-10% of their business in unethical areas or in companies that have made a positive effort to reduce the unethical part of their operations. According to Friends Provident, there are 400 quoted UK companies that are believed to satisfy ethical criteria.

Indexed funds

Many fund managers (unit trusts included) have failed to produce returns that match the average as measured by whichever index is deemed most suitable, e.g. FTSE 100 or FTSE Actuaries All Share Indices. As a result there has been a growth in indexed funds. These funds are aimed at both professional and private investors, and some unit trusts have introduced index-tracking funds.

A computer will design and run a portfolio to match a particular index (e.g. FTSE 100). Most indexed funds only partly replicate (reproduce) the chosen index. They use various techniques to provide an overall portfolio with a beta factor of one, i.e. no riskier than the index chosen.

The more common name for funds that partially replicate a chosen index is tracker funds.

Many tracker funds are available to private investors as well as to institutional investors. Some funds track overseas indices, or a chosen part of the FT World Index Series, e.g. Japan, or the index in that chosen country, e.g. Japan's Nikkei index.

The benefits of indexed funds are:

- They are cheaper to run than a 'managed' fund – *The Economist* quotes the cost as being one-third;

- Performance will match that of the index.

The only 'decision' to make is which index to match. However, indexed funds will under-perform the chosen index slightly because of the dealing costs involved in switching the shares to keep the correct weightings.

The performance will, by the very nature of the funds, be only 'average'. However, as many fund managers have failed to obtain even an 'average' performance, this method may well produce better results. Care needs to be taken in choosing a tracker fund, because statistics show that they have virtually all under-performed their chosen index. The major factor for under-performance is the level of the front-end fee.

Emerging markets

The emerging markets are markets in those countries that have only in more recent years begun to have a regulated stock market. Many of these countries' shares are small in market capitalization and there are only a few quoted shares of companies of modest size. Such markets are very volatile because large buy and sell orders in one stock can move the market dramatically. In addition to this the accounting standards may not be of the same level as those in the UK. Unit trusts investing in the emerging markets provide a diversified portfolio, while still being able to benefit from rises in the market.)

14   Guidelines for Unit Trust Selection

There are around 1,800 authorized unit trusts and this number tends to increase every month. Despite the fact that unit trusts are one form of collective investment that provides investors with a simple doorway to the stock market and professional investment management, the choice of trusts must be bewildering to the average unsophisticated investor. However, he can make a rational choice by using the following considerations.

Deciding whether he should invest in unit trusts at all

The investor must have an existing emergency cash reserve invested in a bank or building society before he can even contemplate investing in unit trusts.

The rate of growth in unit trusts is not steady and the investor should be able to choose the moment when he sells, rather than being forced to do so when the market is temporarily depressed. An emergency cash reserve will, it is hoped, prevent the investor from becoming a forced seller.

Linked with this point is the timescale of the investment. Although high short-term gains can be seen, unit trusts should be regarded from the outset as a long-term investment.

Deciding on the investment objective (assuming unit trusts are appropriate)

The investor must choose a trust that mirrors his own objectives. The simplest way is to ascertain which of the AUTIF or Money Management categories would be most suitable. His objectives may be for high income, capital growth or a mix of both. He may prefer to stay mainly in trusts investing in UK equities, or may be willing to take a higher degree of risk by choosing some of the new emerging markets such as Latin America.

Selecting a trust from those within the appropriate category

Factors to consider are:
● Past performance
● Consistency of management
● New trusts
● Size
● Redemptions/new monies position.

Past performance and management

It is possible to obtain details of the performances of other trusts in the required category so that their progress can be compared with the median fund. Information on the various trusts' performances is available in the *Unit Trust Year Book*, the financial press, *Money Management*, or from the managers themselves. The fund's performance can also be checked against that of a median fund from statistics provided by AUTIF.

It is likely that management companies showing a good performance record for all their trusts over a one-year period will also exhibit a better performance record in the long term. This can be attributed partly to the probability that trust managers with a good past performance record can point to proof of their expertise and are therefore keen to try to maintain these results.

Consistency of management

Maintaining a good performance is partly dependent on continuity. Frequent changes in investment management can bedevil overall group performance because of changes in investment policy.

New trusts

A new trust has a virgin pool of cash that can be invested in accordance with current market conditions, which will have been carefully researched. Existing trusts, however, are to some extent committed to their past investment decisions. It is not easy in practice to liquidate a large holding of shares that has already fallen in value because this would convert a 'paper loss', which could possibly be recovered, into a 'cash loss', which would be irrecoverable.

In addition, new trusts often waive or reduce the front-end loading charges to encourage new investors by the attraction of a lower initial offer price. They sometimes offer a discount if investors respond by a set date.

Investing in a new trust at a time when the market appears bullish can be an excellent means of achieving a good result, provided the bullish expectations of the market are fulfilled. Naturally, the investor will wish to check the past performance of the management group.

Size

In theory, a small fund should be able to respond more quickly than a large one to changing market conditions. In practice there is little statistical evidence to support this theory. What evidence there is suggests that very large funds very rarely appear at the top or at the bottom and tend to perform around the average for trusts of that type.

An investor who did not wish to take an above-average risk should invest in a large fund as opposed to a small fund.

Redemptions/new monies position

Because unit trusts are open ended, the managers will eventually have to sell some of the underlying investments if there are net redemptions for a long period. Forced sellers of equities frequently find that market conditions are not ideal for the sale of the equity concerned, and so the sales could be at a temporarily depressed price.

In addition, the mere prospect of forced sales of the underlying assets may influence the managers to switch from an offer price base to a bid price base. Someone buying such units just before the change of pricing could see a fall of 10% from the offer price at which he purchased to the current bid price.

Invest in more than one unit trust

Bearing in mind that the minimum lump-sum investment is around £200-500, it would be better to split a larger lump sum available into three or four equal amounts, with each part being invested in a suitable trust under a different manager. Even a good manager can have a bad year, and this diversification cushions the investor against such an occurrence. This will provide the maximum diversification.

15   Benefits of Unit Trust Investment

Diversification

Research has shown that an investor should spread his investments among 15 different shares in different sectors of the market to avoid the unsystematic risk. The minimum economic investment in a single share is around £2,000 (because of the minimum broker's commission), hence £30,000 would be the absolute minimum to invest in a directly held, diversified, equity portfolio.

With unit trusts the minimum lump-sum investment can be as low as £200, and this gives the investor an indirect interest in a diversified portfolio. Most unit trusts invest in between 50 and 100 different shares.

Professional management

Most private individuals lack the time or expertise to manage a portfolio. Decisions on which shares to buy, which to sell and whether to take up a rights issue are taken by professional managers who have access to detailed research by their own analysts or stockbrokers.

Elimination of paperwork

The investor merely records the purchase or sale of the units on his tax return, together with the dividends. All other matters, company reports, bonus issues, rights issues, and takeovers are dealt with by the managers.

Overseas investment

Dealing costs with direct investment in shares quoted on an overseas stock market are very high. Unit trust investment is one of the most economic ways of obtaining a diversified portfolio of overseas investments.

The professional managers can keep in touch with overseas market developments and can monitor the exchange risk.

16   Commodity Unit Trusts

As the name suggests, these funds invest in commodities. Under FSA rules such trusts cannot be authorized, because the underlying investment is not liquid enough to meet a sudden spate of net redemptions.

Commodities are very wide ranging and include items such as metals, sugar, soya beans, coffee, wheat, barley and pigs.

It is as well to remember that an authorized unit trust, while being unable to invest directly in commodities, can invest in the shares of companies dealing in commodities.

17   Offshore Unit Trusts

From the point of view of a UK investor, an offshore unit trust based in the Channel Islands, the Isle of Man or Bermuda should be as secure as an authorized one, provided the managers are UK clearing banks or their subsidiaries or some other reputable City institution. These three countries are classed as 'designated territories', i.e. the UK regulatory authorities consider that their investor protection laws are equivalent to those of the UK. Funds in these countries can apply under the Financial Services Act to market their funds in the UK as 'authorized offshore funds'.

Other offshore unit trusts should be regarded with caution, unless the managers are well known and undoubted. Offshore funds can invest in almost anything, but currency deposits or even high-interest sterling accounts are common.

Suitable offshore funds appeal to expatriates and other non-residents because there are potential tax benefits. However, such benefits do not apply to UK resident investors.

The problems of unauthorized unit trusts

One major problem is that the trustee may have very little power. The 1983 collapse of Westgrove Property Unit Trust illustrates this point only too well because the trust deed was drawn up in such a way that the trustee, National Westminster Bank, was powerless to intervene until too late.

Another problem is that when the managers of the unauthorized trust are asked for information, their response is not restricted by AUTIF or the FSA. Yields on some unauthorized gilt-edged unit trusts have been quoted at higher figures than those for an authorized gilt trust, purely because the basis of the calculation formula was more favourable to the trust than the strict rules laid down for advertisements for authorized unit trusts. The moral is plain: make sure the managers are reputable.

18   Open-Ended Investment Company (OEIC)

The OEIC is in many ways a cross between a unit trust and an investment trust. They are pooled investments that are legally a company but have the ability to create or cancel shares, i.e. an OEIC can expand and contract as supply and demand for its shares determines.

Thus as a unit trust is open-ended it can create and cancel units, whereas an investment trust is legally a company thus cannot expand or contract the number of shares. Under the specially written company law covering OEICs, they can expand or contract the number of shares issued.

Both OEICs and Investment Trusts (see Unit 13) issue shares, whereas unit trusts issue units. However the pricing of OEICs is different to both unit and investment trusts. Unit trusts have dual pricing, i.e. a bid and an offer price, investment trust shares also have dual pricing – the market maker's bid and offer price. OEICs have a single price, i.e. buyers and sellers pay/receive the same price. This does not mean that there are no dealing costs or manager's fees, just that these are shown separately.

OEICs prices are based on net asset value, as is the case with unit trusts, thus there will be no discount/premium to NAV as is seen with investment trusts.

Summary

Now that you have studied this unit, you should be able to:

- describe what is meant by a unit trust;
- describe the role of the managers;
- describe the role of the trustees;
- describe the role of the FSA;
- describe the role of AUTIF;
- detail the various bodies involved in the unit trust industry;
- explain how unit trust units are priced;
- explain the relevance of net assets value and creation price to pricing;
- explain what is meant by bid and offer pricing;
- explain what is meant by historical and forward pricing;
- explain the significance of bid and offer pricing to the investor and managers;
- distinguish between distribution and accumulation units and describe the tax treatment of dividends received;

- describe the tax treatment of the unit trust itself;

- explain how unit trusts are dealt with;

- understand the *Financial Times* information on unit trusts;

- detail the categories of unit trusts;

- describe how the following schemes work:

  - savings plans, including benefits of pound cost averaging

  - withdrawal plans

  - share exchange schemes;

- explain the features of:

  - exempt unit trusts

  - ethical unit trusts

  - indexed funds;

- explain the guidelines an investor should use when selecting a unit trust;

- describe the benefits of unit trust investment;

- explain what is meant by 'unauthorized unit trusts' and the problems that may accompany investment in them;

- be able to describe OEICs and draw comparisons with unit trusts.

13

INVESTMENT TRUSTS AND VENTURE CAPITAL TRUSTS

Objectives

After studying this unit, you should be able to:

● explain what an investment trust is and describe its legal structure;

○ understand the taxation treatment of investment trusts;

○ understand discounts and gearing;

○ explain methods of removing discounts;

○ define and describe limited-life and split-level trusts;

● understand warrants;

○ describe investment trust savings schemes;

● explain (briefly) the role of the Association of Investment Trust Companies;

○ interpret information on investment trusts published in the financial press;

○ compare a unit trust with an investment trust;

○ differentiate between a unit trust, investment trust and OIEC;

○ describe the nature of a venture capital trust (VCT).

1 The Legal Structure of an Investment Trust

An investment trust is a limited company with a fixed share capital whose shares are listed on the Stock Exchange. The capital of the investment trust is invested in quoted shares, unquoted shares and overseas shares. Thus an investment trust offers its shareholders an indirect interest in a professionally managed portfolio of securities.

Investors deal in the stocks and shares of an investment trust via a broker in the usual way that any securities are dealt with. The exception is the savings scheme run by some trusts.

As with any limited company, an investment trust is allowed to have loan capital or other forms of capital, and we have already seen in Unit 9 how the warrant market is dominated by investment trusts.

Thus the underlying assets of an investment trust are similar to those of a unit trust but the legal position of the shareholders is quite different from that of unit holders.

2 Taxation and Investment Trusts

The position of an investment trust shareholder

The investment trust shareholder will be treated for tax purposes in the same way as a shareholder of any other limited company. Dividends will be paid net of 10% tax, however non-taxpayers CANNOT reclaim the tax and 40% taxpayers are liable to extra tax at 22.5% (32.5% – 22.5%).

Capital gains on disposal of investment trust shares are liable for CGT in exactly the same way as are gains on any other share.

The tax position of the investment trust itself

Capital gains

As with unit trusts, all capital gains made by the trust itself are totally tax free of CGT (Finance Act 1980). In order to qualify for this exemption, the investment trust must be 'approved' within the terms of s.359, Income and Corporation Taxes Act 1970 as amended by s.93, Finance Act 1972.

For approval to be granted, the investment trust must:

● Be resident in the UK;

● Be listed on the UK Stock Exchange;

● Derive its income wholly or mainly from shares or securities;

● Not invest more than 15% of its assets in any one company (except in another investment trust);

● Not retain more than 15% of its income from stocks and shares;

● Not distribute any capital profits from the sale of its investments as a dividend to shareholders.

3 The Importance of an Investment Trust being Closed-ended as Opposed to Open-ended

An investment trust is a closed-ended fund, unlike a unit trust which is an open-ended fund.

Purchases and sales of the investment trust's shares on the secondary market do not result in cash coming into or out of the investment trust itself. Thus, because their capital is fixed, investment trusts have the benefit of continuity, and investment trust companies can plan their investment strategy on a long-term basis.

Investment trusts therefore can take a very long-term view of the underlying investments without needing to worry about short-term performance. Thus this investment medium benefits from a relatively stable structure and lower stock turnover.

4 The Significance of Discounts on Investment Trust Shares

What is meant by 'discount' in connection with investment trust shares

In Unit 10 we explained the concept of net asset value of a share which, briefly summarized, can be defined as total shareholders' funds divided by the number of shares.

We have also explained that share prices are set by market forces, and that for most successful companies the current share price should be above net asset value. However, for investment trusts, the share price is generally below (i.e. at a discount to) net asset value.

Why are most investment trusts priced at a discount?

A number of factors cause this apparently strange position to arise.

- If the investment trust were to liquidate itself, it might not be possible to realize the full net asset value. Unlisted shares may not fetch their expected value, and there will be the usual brokers' and other selling costs to bear. In addition, there may be a penalty to pay for early redemption of any fixed-term loans taken out by the trust.

- The stock market still generally expects to see investment trust shares priced at a discount to net asset value. If the discount narrows or is eliminated, investors begin to feel that the share price is too high. The resultant fall in demand for the investment trust's shares will make their price fall, without any effect at all on their underlying net asset value.

- The annual management expenses and corporation tax on unfranked income reduce the flow of income from the underlying investments to the investment trust's shareholders. In other words, the shareholders would receive a slightly higher income if they could invest directly in the underlying assets, rather than investing indirectly via the trust.

What is the effect of the discount?

There are two major points an investment trust shareholder should bear in mind.

Increased income

Suppose an investor buys 1,000 shares in an investment trust when the share price is 200p and their net asset value is 266p.

The cost to the investor would be:

	£
Consideration 1,000 x 200p =	2,000.00
Commission at 1.65% (say)	33.00
Stamp duty	10.00
	2,043.00

In the above example, £2,043.00 acquires assets of 1,000 x 266p = £2,660. These assets are earning income for him.

This can be contrasted with a unit trust where the investor would expect to obtain £1,941 of assets for an investment of £2,043 (£2,043 less a 5% spread). Other things being equal, which they rarely are, the same amount of money should generate more income from investment in an investment trust than would be received from a unit trust investment.

Additional capital gain in a rising market and additional losses in a falling one

Discounts on investment trust shares tend to narrow in a rising market, and to widen on a falling market. Hence in a rising market the net asset value will rise, but the share price will rise even more as the discount narrows. Conversely, as the market as a whole falls, the discount will widen, hence the share price will fall at a greater rate than net asset value falls. Thus the discount can be said to contribute a gearing factor.

What causes the discount to change?

As was previously stated, discounts tend to narrow on a rising stock market, and they will also narrow when a particular trust is expected to perform better.

Instances of this would occur when:

● The trust is invested in a particularly popular sector of the market, e.g. the emerging markets;

● There is a change in management or of investment policy that is likely to improve performance;

● There is a fall in interest rates that makes the returns on equities look more attractive. The classic illustration of this would be a narrowing of the reverse yield gap;

● There is a possibility of a takeover that would make the shareholders anticipate that they were likely to receive the net asset value of the shares in the near future;

● Investment trust savings schemes have had the effect of narrowing the discount. Although the amounts saved are small in relation to the value of the investment trust sector, there has been a stabilizing influence from this growth of small investors. Small investors prefer to retain their share holding, so this has the effect of stabilizing the share price. Institutions, however, tend to trade actively, which can have a destabilizing effect on the share price.

Discounts will widen when performance is expected to worsen. Examples are:

● If there is a sale of a large number of the shares by a single large investor, this will depress the share price and widen the discount;

● If there are only a few shareholders, there tends to be a narrow market in the shares, and this usually results in a wider discount.

Gearing and discounts

We have already said that an element of gearing is introduced by the discounts on investment trusts. However, the major factor that determines how highly geared the shares are is the amount of fixed-interest capital compared to shareholders' funds.

Investment trusts can borrow money, subject to the usual restrictions imposed by the memorandum and articles of association, in just the same way as can any other limited company.

As with any share, on a rising market gearing should beneficially exaggerate the share performance of the underlying assets in its effect on the share price and dividends of the investment trust share. However, the usual downside still applies in that gearing will also exaggerate the fall in share price and dividends in a bear market.

Investment trusts can 'gear up' by way of preference shares, debentures, loan stocks, bank loans, or foreign currency loans.

Methods of removing the discount – liquidation and split level trusts

Liquidation

This would entail the trust winding itself up with the shareholders' approval. The assets would realize at full market value less dealing costs, around net asset value. Problems arise with this option because it is a disposal of shares for CGT purposes and shareholders may not be overkeen on a CGT liability.

Turning into a split-level investment trust

This type of trust has a set redemption date at which it will be wound up. Investors receive a package of income and capital shares.

Although conventional split-level investment trusts have been in existence since the 1950s, these newer versions have more than two types of share to offer their shareholders. A package of up to five different types of shares, plus warrants have been offered by some investment trusts opting for this route.

5   Special Types of Investment Trusts

Limited-life trusts

These trusts consider it desirable that the shareholders have the opportunity to decide whether the company should continue or be liquidated. The articles of association accordingly specify that at periodic intervals (usually five years) the shareholders must vote on whether or not to liquidate.

Split-level trusts (split-capital trusts/dual trusts)

The operation of split-capital trusts

The ordinary share capital is usually subdivided into three or four classes: income shares, zero-dividend preference shares, stepped preference shares and capital shares.

There is a set date, or predetermined period, when the trust must be wound up.

Zero-dividend preference shares

These shares, known as 'zeros', are issued at a price below their par value. On redemption date the trust will redeem the zeros at the pre-determined redemption value, provided there are sufficient assets available. Redemption of the zeros will take priority over redemption of the other classes of shares, but they are not repaid prior to any loan capital the company may have issued.

'Zeros' provide a fixed capital return in the form of a redemption value. They do not provide any income.

Stepped preference shares

These shares offer dividends that rise at a preset rate plus a guaranteed redemption value on winding up.

Income shares

During the life of the investment trust all or most of the income accruing to the trust is paid out by way of dividend on the income shares. At the liquidation date the income shares are redeemed at a predetermined capital value, which may be the nominal value but need not be.

Capital shares

The capital shareholder receives little or no income during the life of the trust, although there are few exceptions to this point. On winding up they receive all the remaining money after all prior loans and classes of shares have been repaid.

Capital fulcrum point or 'hurdle rate'

This is the annual average growth rate of the underlying fund that the trust must achieve in order to repay the zeros at their face value on redemption. A negative capital fulcrum point or 'hurdle rate' indicates the annual amount in percentage terms by which assets could fall and yet cover the commitment to redeem the zeros.

An analysis of split-level investment trust

M & G Equity	Date for liquidation	Repayment terms	Price	Gross div yield	NAV	Discount
Income shares	2011	At par	401	9.8	-	-
Capital shares	2011	All surplus assets	251	-	77.1	66.9%

Because the redemption date is eleven years away (taking the date now as 2000), the price of the income shares is heavily influenced by the amount of dividend they will generate. However, as 2011 approaches the price of the income shares will tend to approach par, with an allowance for accrued dividends. The same principles apply as apply to short-dated gilts just prior to redemption, provided the value of the trust's portfolio is sufficient to cover the redemption commitment.

Turning to the capital shares, their price was at a discount of 66.9% to their net asset value. At this stage of the trust's life these shares are speculative. No income is generated so the price is dependent purely on the market's view of the net asset value in 2011. There are few analysts who would even attempt to predict so far ahead, so a large discount applies to take account of the uncertainty.

As redemption date approaches, the discount on the capital shares will narrow; the price will then stabilize at a small discount unless there are major price movements expected in the market as a whole.

Conclusion

For an investor who requires a high and growing income for a long period, and who can accept a capital loss in the long term, income shares of a split-level capital trust are an ideal vehicle provided the redemption date is well ahead.

Conversely, a higher-rate taxpayer, who prefers capital gains to income, would prefer a capital share. If he wished to speculate, he would buy a long-dated capital share, but if he required a safer investment, a capital share with a shorter redemption period, or a zero-dividend preference share with a relatively low fulcrum point or 'hurdle rate' would be preferable.

Warrants

Investment trusts may issue all types of capital, including warrants. In fact, a number of investment trusts have issued warrants, and indeed the warrant market is dominated by investment trusts.

Warrants issued by conventional investment trusts can be exercised for ordinary shares in the trust.

Warrants issued by split-level capital trusts will specify the class of capital into which they are exercised, e.g. a capital share or zero-dividend preference share.

Suitability of the different types of share capital for different investors

Consider the following table.

Share capital	*Type of investor*
1. Zero-dividend preference shares.	Investors who need a fixed capital sum at a set future date. The investor would tend to be a little risk averse, but willing to invest in these shares in preference to gilts that are safer but offer a lower guaranteed return. Also may be a 40% taxpayer who prefers gains to income.
2. Stepped preference shares.	An investor who wants a growing income that is to grow at a preset rate, along with a guaranteed capital sum on winding up.
3. Income shares.	Investors who need a high level of income, but are willing to take a loss on capital on winding up. Also 40% taxpayers who wish to put these shares into a ISA and withdraw the income tax-free.
4. Capital shares.	Investors who do not want or require income but are willing to take a higher risk, in which all prior claims and classes of capital must be repaid before they can receive any money. The investor is likely to be a 40% taxpayer who prefers capital gain to income.

Investment trust savings schemes

These work in a similar way to unit trust savings schemes and have the same advantage of 'pound cost averaging'. There has been a rapid growth of investment trust savings schemes since their introduction.

The schemes start with monthly contributions as low as £20, and dividends can also be reinvested with the same effect and tax consequences as unit trust accumulation units. Some schemes also accept lump-sum investment from as little as £250.

The money is pooled and the investment trust purchases its own shares in the market and allocates them to the new shareholders. This is a cheap way of purchasing shares for the private investor because dealing costs are shared among all the investors pro rata rather than each saver having to pay brokers' commission at top rates on his own dealings. The cost works out at about 0.2% of the amount invested against broker's commission of around 1.5-1.65%.

Most schemes also offer the facility to sell shares purchased through this scheme at similar, low rates of commission.

For the trust it has the added advantage of reducing the discount to net asset value. This reduces vulnerability to takeover because the trust is increasing its shareholders while retaining its original share capital.

Share exchange schemes

Some investment trusts have introduced share exchange schemes whereby an investor can give any shares he owns to the investment trust, and in return he will receive investment trust shares. The system operates in much the same way as share exchange schemes with unit trusts (see Unit 12).

6 The Role of the Association of Investment Trust Companies (AITC)

This body performs a similar function for investment trusts to that performed by AUTIF for unit trusts. Advice will be given on all aspects of investment trusts. Although the AITC cannot advise on the selection of an individual trust, it is prepared to supply, free of charge, a list of firms of brokers who are prepared to offer advice and handle investment trust shares for private investors.

7 The Future of Investment Trusts

Although there has been a rise in popularity of investment trusts, they cannot yet fully compete with unit trusts. While there are approximately 1,800 unit trusts to choose from there are only around 500 investment trusts available. Thus an investor requiring a specialized type of investment may not be able to find sufficient choice in the investment trust sector.

For this reason, unit and investment trusts will find a place together in many portfolios.

Investment trusts are categorized by **Money Management** into 29 types:

● UK General
● UK Capital Growth
● UK Income Growth
● North America
● Far East – Including Japan
● Far East – Excluding Japan (General)
● Japan

- Far East – Excluding Japan (Single)
- European (General)
- European (Single)
- Commodity and Energy
- Emerging Markets (General)
- Emerging Markets (Single)
- Smaller Companies UK
- Smaller Companies International
- High Income
- Property
- Closed-End Funds
- Venture and Development Capital
- Split Capital – Capital Shares
- Split Capital – Income Shares
- Split Capital – Income and Residential Capital Shares
- Split Capital – Zero-Dividend Preference Shares
- Split Capital – Stepped Preference Shares
- Split Capital – Capital Indexed Shares
- International – General
- International – Capital Growth
- International – Income Growth
- Warrants.

While this comprehensive categorization enables an investor to look at the performance of an investment trust against the average for its type, some categories have very few companies. For example 'Property' consists of just four trusts, and 'Split Capital Indexed Shares' consists of just one trust.

8 Investment Trust Information in the *Financial Times*

The **Financial Times** classifies investments trusts into two different categories:

- Investment Companies

- Investment Trusts – Split Capital.

The format of the information provided is identical for each category.

Extract details in Tuesday to Saturday Editions

Stock	Notes	Price	+ or -	52 week High	52 week Low	Yield grs	NAV	Dis or Pm(-)
Candover		1089½	+½	1090	803	2.3	975.9	-10.4
Bankers'		300	-9	309½	234½	2.0	344.5	14.8

Explanation

- Stock: Name of the stock.
- Price: The closing mid-market price on previous trading day.
- + or -: Change in price from previous trading day.
- High/low: The highest and lowest price the share has reached over a rolling 52 week period.
- Yield: Net dividend yield. This is based on the mid price.
- NAV: Net Asset Value. This is in pence per share. It assumes prior charges at par value, convertibles converted, and warrants exercised (if applicable). This should be compared to the share price to establish the premium or discounts.
- Dis or Pm (-): Discount or premium in relation to the closing share prices.

  Thus the price is at a discount when the NAV exceeds the current share price, and at a premium when the share price exceeds the NAV.

Difference between details in Monday's edition to the rest of the week

There are slight differences in Monday's edition, because no trading has taken place on Saturday. The differences are listed below.

	Monday edition	*Tues-Sat edition*
1	Stock	Stock
2	Notes	Notes
3	Price	Price
4	Wk % change	+ or -
5	Div	52-week high
6	Dividends paid	52-week low
7	Market cap £m	Yield

8	Last xd	NAV
9	Cityline	Dis or Pm (-)

Note: Investment trusts never have a price/earnings ratio as it would be meaningless because of the nature of their business.

Differences

- Wk % change: The percentage changes in the share price are over the week.

- Div : The dividend per share in pence.

- Dividends paid: The months in which the company pays its dividends.

- Market Cap £m: This is the market capitalization. In the Monday **Financial Times** the market capitalization figures all refer to individual securities and are not necessarily a company's total market capitalization, because a company may issue other securities not shown in the **Financial Times**.

- Last xd: The last date the shares went ex div.

- City Line: The number to ring to access the particular share price of the company.

9   Investment Trusts versus Unit Trusts

As far as private investors are concerned it is difficult to choose between an investment trust and a unit trust. For investments of under £1,000 the unit trust is more suitable, because the 'spread' between bid and offer price is usually less than the dealing costs for purchase and sale of £1,000 worth of investment trust shares, although this may not be the case if a discount stockbroker is used.

For the large investor, investment trusts tend to provide better returns, taking into account their gearing and discounts. However, this is by no means certain because the performance at the end of the day is influenced by the success or otherwise of the manager's investment policy.

For small investors, the investment trust savings schemes offer both monthly savings and lump-sum options. These provide excellent value for the small saver.

The FTSE Actuaries Share Indices contain an index that measures the performances of investment trust shares as a whole. **Money Management** also provides performance statistics grouped according to the aims of the trust.

Although it may be unfair to compare a single trust's performance against an average of other trusts which may have different aims, the index does give an approximate guide to general performance. **Money Management** gives a better picture of performance measurement of similar types of trust.

10 Summary of Main Differences Between Investment Trusts, Unit Trusts and OEICs

	Investment Trusts	*Unit Trusts*	OEICs
1.	Control is exercised by directors, subject to the normal approvals required from shareholders at meetings and subject to the memorandum and articles of association.	A unit trust is a trust where each unit holder is entitled to share in the assets of that trust in proportion to the number of units owned. Control is exercised by managers, subject to approval by trustees within the terms of the trust deed.	As for unit trusts.
2.	An investment trust is closed-ended. The shares of the investment trust are dealt with on the secondary market. Hence the purchases or sales of the trust's shares do not result in cash payments to or from the trust managers. No new shares are created, nor are any liquidated, because of dealings on the secondary market.	A unit trust is open-ended. Sales or purchases by unit holders result in cash payments to or from the managers. Hence net redemptions of units will mean that the managers have to sell some of the trust's underlying investments to meet such redemptions. Some units will then be liquidated. Conversely net new monies cause new units to be created and increase the underlying investments.	Open-ended (as for unit trusts), but *shares* not units are issued and dealings are via the managers.
3.	The shares are bought or sold on the Stock Exchange in the same way as any other shares. Hence, dealing costs are based on the usual brokers' commission, stamp duty, and PTM levy.	Unit holders buy and sell units from the managers. There are normally no commission charges as such, the 'cost' to the investor is the difference between the bid and offer prices.	As for unit trusts.

Investment Trusts	*Unit Trusts*	*OEICs*
4. The price of investment trust shares is not laid down by any formula, but in the same way as for other share prices, the level depends on market forces.	The price of units is based on the net asset value, with a maximum spread between bid and offer prices as set by the FSA formula.	The price is based on the net asset value, but there is only a single price.
5. Dual pricing.	Dual pricing.	Single pricing.
6. Generally the price of an investment trust share is at a discount to net asset value.	See 4 above.	As for investment trusts.
Investment trusts can have different types of capital. If investment trusts have loan capital, then the concept of gearing applies.	Unit trusts can have only one class of unit for each trust. Every unit is treated equally. The concept of gearing cannot apply. (The only time that there can be two classes of unit is where there are accumulation units as well as distribution units. Both types rank equally.)	As for unit trusts.
Investment trusts cannot invite the public to buy their shares through advertising. (There is an exception to this in the case of a new issue of investment trust shares.)	Authorized unit trusts are permitted to advertise to invite the public to purchase units.	As for unit trusts.
Annual management fees tend to vary between 0.5% and 1% of the value of the assets under management.	Annual management fees are usually 0.75% – 1.5% of the value of the funds under management.	As for unit trusts.

11   Venture Capital Trusts (VCTs)

Venture capital trusts were created in the Finance Act 1993 as a method of enabling new and unquoted companies to raise money from investors. They are very similar in legal structure to investment trusts.

VCTs hold at least 70% of their investments in shares or securities they have subscribed for in qualifying unquoted companies trading wholly or mainly in the UK.

Other rules

- At least 30% of the holdings must be in ordinary shares;

  No single holding can be more than 15% of the total investment;

  Loans or securities that are guaranteed are excluded;

  At least 10% of the total investment in any company must be in ordinary shares;

  Companies quoted on AIM qualify for inclusion in a VCT providing they are carrying out a qualifying trade;

  The maximum permitted investment is £100,000 per annum;

- The VCT must not retain more than 15% of it income from shares and securities;

  The money raised by the VCT must be at least 70% invested after 3 years and the maximum amount that can be invested in one company in one tax year is £1m.

Because the VCT does not have to invest its funds immediately, the money received can be invested in high-interest accounts, Government stocks (gilts) and fixed-interest securities until the funds are invested.

The VCTs shares are traded on the Stock Market as with any other quoted company.

The underlying investments have a higher risk than quoted companies because of their size and/or age. To encourage investment, the Finance Act 1993 has given special tax breaks to investors:

  Investors receive tax relief at 20% on their initial investment up to £100,000 per annum. (This relief is claimed from the Inland Revenue);

  If the shares are sold within 5 years (other than to the holder's spouse or on the holder's death), tax relief will be withdrawn;

  Dividends are free of the higher rate of income tax, but the 10% tax credit on dividends cannot be reclaimed;

  Capital gains rollover relief is given to investors re-investing up to £100,000;

  There is no liability to CGT.

Main exclusions from the definition of qualifying trades:

- Companies dealing in land;

- Finance, legal and accountancy services;

- Property development;

- Farming and market gardening;

- Forestry and timber production;

- Hotels and nursing or residential care homes.

In addition the total gross assets of the company must not exceed £15m immediately before the VCT purchased the holding, nor £16m immediately afterwards.

VCTs are a high-risk investment, suitable only for a high-rate tax payer who already has a large, well diversified portfolio and who is willing to take a higher risk than average. Jonathan Fry, managing director of Premier Asset Management, suggested that an investor should have no more than 5% of his portfolio in a VCT (**The Daily Telegraph**, 4 March 2000 page B14). Valuation of a VCT is difficult because most of the shares are not freely traded. Many shares on AIM have a very thin market, thus the bid-offer spread will be very large. There is little secondary market trading in VCTs because most investors are holding them for the five-year period to gain maximum tax benefits.

There are currently four main types of VCTs:

- Traditional, investing in expanding and developing companies;

- Specializing in management buy-outs;

- AIM trusts;

- Technology-based trusts.

Summary

Now that you have studied this unit, you should be able to:

- describe the legal structure of an investment trust;

- explain the tax position of:

  ➤ an investment trust shareholder

  ➤ the investment trust itself relating to capital gains and income tax;

- explain the meaning and understand the implications of an investment trust being a closed-ended fund;

- explain what is meant by a discount and premium in relation to investment trust shares;

- explain why most investment trust shares are at a discount;

- describe the effect of the discount;

- explain the factors that cause the discount to change;
- explain how gearing relates to discounts;
- explain the effect that liquidation would have on shareholders of an investment trust;
- describe limited life trusts;
- describe split-level trusts;
- explain how investment trust savings schemes operate;
- describe the role of the Association of Investment Trust Companies;
- describe the future prospects for investment trusts;
- explain the information provided in the **Financial Times** relating to investment trusts;
- differentiate between unit trusts, investment trusts and OEICs;
- be able to describe the features of a venture capital trust (VCT).

14

INSURANCE, PENSIONS AND FRIENDLY SOCIETIES

Objectives

After studying this unit, you should be able to:

● describe the functions of life insurance companies as providers of policies that offer protection and/or investment;

● understand the range of products available from life insurance companies, their main features/benefits and their tax treatment;

● understand the principles of pensions;

● explain the basic state scheme, SERPS, occupational pensions and personal pensions;

● describe the functions of friendly societies, their main products and tax treatment of these investments.

1   Introduction

One thing that insurance, pensions and friendly societies all have in common as an investment is that they are all able to provide the investor with a vehicle whereby money invested now provides a future return usually at a known date. With insurance products this varies according to the specific product; with pension plans a pension is paid upon retirement; with friendly societies a sum is payable on maturity or earlier death. Each type of institution is different and the insurance industry has a very wide range of products. This unit covers the various types of products that are offered by insurance companies, pension funds and friendly societies.

2   Insurance Products

Insurance products cover a wide range from life insurance, both qualifying and non-qualifying policies, to annuities.

The taxation treatment of life insurance companies and life insurance policies

The life insurance company

All life insurance companies pay tax. The insurance company pays a special corporation tax rate of 23% on income. It also pays a special CGT rate of 23% on all capital gains realized.

When a life insurance policy matures the insurance company will make a deduction from the gross proceeds in respect of its own CGT liability. This deduction cannot be reclaimed by investors who are not subject to CGT.

The life insurance policy

The proceeds of all qualifying life insurance policies are totally free of all income and capital gains tax in the hands of the investor because the insurance company itself has paid tax on its profits and capital gains.

Rules for qualifying life policies

For a policy to be classed as a 'qualifying policy' it must adhere to certain rules:

- Premiums must be payable for a minimum of 10 years, except in the case of term life policies;

- Premiums must be paid annually or more frequently, and those paid in one year must not exceed twice those paid in another year, nor must they exceed one-eighth of the total over the first 10 years;

- The sum assured under an endowment policy must be no less than 75% of the total premiums payable during the term of the policy, although these rules are relaxed when the life assured is over 55 years of age;

- The sum assured under a whole life policy, which carries a surrender value, must be no less than 75% of the total sum payable if death occurred at the age of 75;

- The life insurance company must have an office in the UK and be trading there also. (Some insurance companies, e.g. Sun Life of Canada, are not UK-based companies, but because they have an office in the UK, their policies can be qualifying policies.)

Change in tax relief on premiums

The 1984 Finance Act changed the position regarding tax relief on qualifying life insurance premiums. Prior to 13 March 1984 life insurance premiums were eligible for tax relief of 15% of the premium provided the premiums were paid annually or more frequently for a minimum period of 10 years. The tax relief also had a ceiling of one-sixth of taxable income or £1,500 per annum whichever was the higher for the taxpayer.

Policies taken out after 13 March 1984 do not attract any tax relief on premiums for the investor. This has made life insurance a less attractive savings vehicle.

If an investor is paying premiums on a qualifying policy taken out before 13 March 1984 he should make every effort to continue paying the premiums because he will retain tax relief at a rate of 12½% – Finance Act 1988. (The rate of LAPR (Life Assurance Premium Relief) was lowered from 15% to 12½%, by the Finance Act 1988.) The tax relief is deducted from the gross premium payable to the insurance company, which means that the investor only pays £87.50 for every £100 of cover purchased. The insurance company reclaims the 12½% from the Inland Revenue.

Non-qualifying life policies

If a life policy does not qualify for tax relief under the rules it is classed as a non-qualifying life policy. Most of these non-qualifying policies come under the umbrella heading of 'single-premium bonds'.

The difference between protection and investment

With the investment syllabus the products that are of interest lie on the life assurance (or insurance) arm of the insurance industry's products, rather than on the house insurance and car insurance products.

There are a variety of life insurance policies available to suit an investor's needs Some simply provide a sum of money if the life assured dies before a set date but nothing if he survives, and they are pure protection policies also known as term life policies. Others are mainly a savings vehicle, but provide protection in the event of premature death. Endowment policies are examples of the latter.

With life insurance there are three parties to the policy: the proposer, the life assured and the beneficiary. The proposer is the person who pays the premiums to the insurance company. The life assured is the person on whose life the policy is based, and it is that person's age and health that determines the level of premiums to be paid by the proposer. If the life assured dies prior to maturity of the policy then the proposer pays no more premiums, and the insurance company will pay out the sum due to the named beneficiary. It is quite common for all three parties to the policy to be one or two persons only. In these cases the proposer and life assured will be the same and the beneficiary will be either the same person or a third party. This is most commonly seen when a husband takes out life cover on his own life, payable on his death to his wife, or vice versa.

From the point of view of giving investment advice when a customer asks for it, one of the questions must be whether he or she has adequate life cover. What may seem adequate to a customer is not necessarily adequate from the viewpoint of the professional adviser. The minimum amount of life cover a customer should have is enough to pay off his mortgage and any other debts if he should die before the final payment is due. If the customer is married, then on top of this an extra provision should be made for his or her family in the event of his or her early demise.

Husband and wife should both have their lives insured, first so that they can at least afford to cover funeral expenses, which are quite high, and even more importantly if there are children, to be able to provide help in the home to look after them in the event of the early demise of a parent. This type of advice may seem morbid, but without adequate life cover an investor's family would be in great trouble if he or she died young.

For a young couple with children the sum assured (i.e. the amount that is guaranteed to be paid out on death) should be at least 10 times the annual salary of the life assured, so for someone earning £15,000 p.a. the sum assured should be £150,000. This may sound a large amount, but company and state pensions are not very high for younger couples with children, and it is advisable to provide enough money so that the same standard of living can be maintained.

If the children are young, say pre-school age, it must be remembered that they will be at school until they are at least 16 years of age, and expenses are very high during this period. It is equally important for the wife and the husband to carry adequate life insurance, for if he or she dies leaving a young family, the spouse will either have to stop working with the resultant lowering of the standard of living, or employ people to run the house and care for the children. With adequate life cover the second option would be available.

From the savings side the investor is looking to provide himself or herself with a lump sum at a set future date. In the event of death before this date a guaranteed sum will be paid out, but the real purpose is to provide a lump sum in the future to coincide quite often with a known event, say a child's eighteenth or twenty-first birthday, or retirement. In this case the investor would choose the life insurance vehicle that provided a guaranteed minimum sum plus profits at the required date. This is called a 'with-profits endowment policy' and is described fully below. In this case the investor is relying on the expertise of the insurance company in investing his money in a good spread of underlying assets that will generate good profits. Some insurance companies are more successful than others, and the investor would be well advised to look at the league tables of results published in the financial press from time to time. There is a vast difference between the amount he would receive from the top and bottom performers.

Types of life insurance policies available

There are three distinct types of life assurance:

- Protection
- Investment/protection
- Investment.

As regards protection, life insurance is unique, but life insurance should be compared with unit trusts and investment trusts as regards its investment merits.

- Protection only is provided by term life and whole life policies.

● Investment/protection is provided by the various forms of endowment policy available.

● Investment is provided by single-premium bonds, where the protection aspect is very small compared to the investment potential of the policy.

Term life insurance

This is the cheapest form of all life cover available. The policy pays out only if the life assured dies before a set date. If he or she survives this period then nothing is paid out. Premiums are paid for the term of the policy and, if the life assured dies during this term, the beneficiary will receive a preset guaranteed sum. Donors who make potentially exempt transfers under inheritance tax should take out a seven-year term assurance written in trust to cover the potential inheritance tax liability.

These term life policies are purely protection policies, and are often found marketed under different names, the most common being mortgage protection policies and family protection policies.

Mortgage protection policies are usually needed when an investor takes out a repayment mortgage with a bank or building society. The lender will insist on such cover being held to pay off the mortgage if the borrower dies before the end of the term of the mortgage.

Family protection policies are marketed to provide the surviving spouse with enough capital to carry on living at the same standard, and provide any necessary extras should the other spouse die before a predetermined date. Whatever the name a term policy is marketed under, the protection provided is always the same.

Whole life insurance

This type of policy pays out a guaranteed sum upon the death of the life assured. There is no payout during the time the life assured is alive, and thus it is not a savings policy that benefits the life assured. However it is a way of providing for the family after the death of the life assured. The cost of this form of life cover is more than for term cover, because the insurance company will have to pay out at some time, but the premiums are lower than those for endowment policies.

A whole life insurance policy can be with or without profits.

Endowment policy

There are four forms of endowment policy, with or without profits, unit-linked and unitized with profit endowment. In the case of a with/without profits policy a guaranteed minimum sum is paid out after a set period, or on death of the life assured, whichever occurs first. The money is paid out to the named beneficiary of the policy. Approximately 10% of the premium paid is used by the insurance company to cover its costs and provision of the death benefit in the event of the life assured dying before the policy is due to mature. The remaining amount is invested by the insurance company to provide the sum paid out on maturity.

Without-profit endowment policies

These are the cheaper of the two types of straight endowment policy because they pay out only a set sum upon maturity or earlier death. The premiums are higher than for a whole life policy, because the guaranteed sum has a known payout date (assuming no prior death).

With-profits endowment policies

These policies pay out a guaranteed sum plus profits on maturity. At the end of the term the guaranteed sum is paid out plus profits. In the event of death prior to the preset maturity, payment will be made on the death of the life assured.

The profits are added to these policies in the form of two types of bonus: reversionary and terminal. With both bonuses, their size depends on the level of profits made by the insurance company. (Profits refers to the profit the insurance company has made on the underlying investment fund. A with-profits endowment policy shares in these profits.)

The reversionary bonus is added to the policy each year and is based on the sum assured. Once the reversionary bonus has been declared (i.e. added to the policy) it cannot be withdrawn. The level of the reversionary bonus does not always reflect the level of the insurance company's profits for that year. If the profits were high, the company could retain some profits to enable it to at least maintain the level of bonus in a year when profits were poor. The level of the reversionary bonus usually increases steadily each year.

The terminal bonus is paid out on maturity of the policy and it is a reflection of the success of the insurance company's investment policy over the life of the policy. Terminal bonuses have on occasion been cut when the insurance company has had a poor profit performance. The last time this happened on a large scale was in 1974 when the property market collapsed. Because insurance companies are one of the largest owners of commercial property the collapse seriously affected their profits. For similar reasons, but to a much lesser extent, some life companies cut terminal bonuses in 1990. Terminal bonuses are not guaranteed.

One very important factor an investor must take into consideration when investing in a life policy is whether or not he will be able to afford the premiums throughout the period of the policy. If a premium is not paid then the life cover is invalidated. If by unhappy circumstances an investor does find that he can no longer afford the premiums he has one of three options available to him if the policy is a whole life or endowment policy. He can either surrender the policy, which means that the insurance company will pay him a cash sum in return for the policy, or he can sell the policy, or he can have the policy made into a paid-up policy. With the first option there is no guarantee that the investor will receive back the amount he has invested.

During the early years of a policy the surrender value is very low, and is always less than the premiums paid (typically for the first 18-24 months). This is because the insurance company has heavy costs to cover in setting up the policy, and in organizing a surrender, and these costs must be covered from the premiums paid before paying out anything on surrender. However, if the investor is desperate for cash this may be one option available. An alternative is to take out a loan against the surrender value of the policy, and this can be obtained from the insurance company itself. Provided the premiums can still be met this is the better option. Up to 90% of the surrender value can be borrowed and the capital is repaid from the proceeds of the policy on maturity.

If the investor does need cash from his life policy, a better way of increasing the amount received is to sell the policy at auction via one of the firms that specializes in this area. However, if it is impossible to meet the premiums but a cash sum is not required, the policy can be converted into a paid-up policy. No more premiums will be due, and the policy will mature on its due date. Even this option is not usually attractive because the conversion terms do not favour the investor. However, it does still supply the element of life cover that may be necessary.

Before an investor starts to pay premiums on a life insurance policy, and more specifically on a with-profits endowment policy, he must choose the life insurance company carefully. Not all companies are the same. Some have far superior profit records, thus the amount paid out on a with-profits policy is much higher if a top-performing company is chosen.

One area that affects the pay-out on the policy is whether or not the insurance company pays fees to intermediaries for introducing customers. Some top-performing companies refuse to pay commission to intermediaries, while others pay a relatively low rate of commission. The low intermediary commission has been a major factor in these companies' success, especially when you consider that other companies pay up to 100% of the first year's premiums as commission. In the case of the top performers, the majority of insurance brokers and financial advisers will not recommend such companies simply because there is no financial advantage to the broker from such recommendations.

However, the investor can simply approach the company direct to obtain life cover, thus avoiding intermediary commissions. If for any reason he needs to obtain life cover from a company paying commission to intermediaries, the investor should still approach the company direct and enquire whether he would receive a better deal as no intermediary is involved. In some cases the insurance companies that pay intermediary commission will give better value if approached directly.

Unit-linked and unitized with-profit endowment policies

Unit-linked endowment

Strictly, unit-linked policies are not endowments as such. They have similar purposes, however, and are often grouped in the same portfolio as with-profits policies. Both with-profits policies and endowment policies are commonly used to repay the capital on a mortgage.

The sum payable on maturity of a unit-linked endowment policy depends on the performance of the underlying fund, which is run like a unit trust. There are no bonuses added to unit-linked endowment policies.

Approximately 10% of the premium paid is used to purchase term life cover, the remainder is invested in the underlying fund. On death there is usually a guaranteed minimum sum paid out (which comes from the percentage of the premium used to purchase term life cover). If the value of the units in the underlying fund exceeds this sum, that extra value is also paid out on top of the guaranteed sum.

For an investor who survives the term of the policy, the sum paid out will depend on the value of the units. If the investor purchases a policy with a fixed maturity date then it is possible that he could receive back less than he has invested. This would occur if the stock market had fallen badly on the maturity date, because the value of the policy is calculated on the value of the underlying fund. The investor can guard against this occurrence by taking out a policy with a flexible maturity date, thus if the market is low he can retain his policy until a more favourable time.

The main advantage of these policies ceased with the abolition of LAPR in the 1984 Finance Act. Prior to 13 March 1984 all unit-linked endowment policies were eligible for tax relief on premiums. This of course improved their performance because the tax relief increased the sum available for investment, but with the abolition of LAPR these policies are not as attractive as they once were. Policies that were issued before 13 March 1984 still qualify for LAPR at 12½%. If an investor wishes to invest in a savings scheme, and does not require life cover, he should consider a unit or investment trust savings scheme or an ISA. These schemes offer more flexibility because payments can be stopped at any time without the problems associated with lapsing insurance policy premiums.

Unitized with-profits endowment

The other type of unit-linked policy is called a unitized with-profits endowment policy. This policy operates in much the same way as the unit-linked endowment but there are bonuses added to the policy. These are safer than unit-linked policies, but do not have the potential for such large gains (or losses).

Comparison of unit-linked endowment policies and a direct unit trust savings plan

Unit-linked policies

1. The insurance company makes a deduction from the proceeds in respect of its own CGT liability.

2. Policies taken out prior to 13 March 1984 attracted 15% tax relief on premiums (now reduced to 12½%).

Unit trust savings plans

1. Unit trusts managers are not liable to CGT.

2. There has never been any tax relief on the amount invested.

Comparison of unit-linked endowment policies and a direct unit trust savings plan (cont.)

Unit-linked policies

3. The proceeds of a qualifying policy are free of income and capital gains tax in the hands of the investor.

4. Missing a premium invalidates the life policy.

5. The policy can only be surrendered, sold or made fully paid.

6. A guaranteed minimum sum paid out on the death of the life assured prior to maturity of policy. Policies automatically pay out on death of the life assured.

7. If the life assured survives the term of the policy, the proceeds are paid out, with the payment value being based on the value of the underlying units. It may not be possible to defer payment if the stock market is low, thus the return may not be very good in such a situation. Hence investors should purchase only those unit-linked policies that have a flexible maturity date.

Unit trust savings plans

3. The proceeds of a unit trust savings plan are subject to income tax on the dividends and capital gains tax on the gains in the hands of the investor.

4. Missing a premium merely means that no units are purchased that month.

5. Units can be sold at any time while continuing with the plan.

6. Only the value of the units is paid out on death. Alternatively, the units can be left to a beneficiary. Death does not mean that the units are automatically sold.

7. The value of the units depends on the price quoted by the managers. However, the unit holder is free to sell the units when he so desires.

Comparison of unit trusts, investment trusts and life assurance as a savings vehicle

Life assurance

The 1984 Finance Act abolished the tax relief on premiums of all new insurance policies. Any policies in existence prior to the 1984 Finance Act are a good investment because they attract the 12½% tax relief, which is a valuable bonus on the sum invested.

However, for an investor considering life assurance as a vehicle for new savings the position is different. Life cover is vital for all investors, and term, whole life or without-profit endowment should be used according to the investor's needs. League tables of the best performing companies are published and investors should choose the best company for all forms of life cover. As a savings vehicle, life insurance must be compared to a regular monthly unit trust savings plan and investment trust savings plans. With-profit endowment policies are the savings vehicle.

Life assurance – with-profits endowment	*Unit trust savings plan*	*Investment trust savings plan*
1. Guaranteed minimum sum payable on death or maturity. Sum paid out on death/maturity will be at least equal to amount paid in, plus any bonuses accrued. (Provided not a unit-linked policy where the problems are similar to unit and investment trust savings schemes).	1. Sum paid on encashment depends on the price of the underlying securities. Thus less than the money invested could be paid out.	1. When the shares are sold, the price is set by supply and demand on the stock market. The investor could get back less than he paid.
2. The insurance company make a deduction in respect of its own tax liability, but the proceeds of the policy are free of all taxes in the hands of the investor.	2. The unit trust is not itself liable to CGT, but the proceeds of the sale of the units are subject to CGT in the investor's hands, and interest subject to income tax.	2. As with unit trust savings plan.
3. Professional management and diversification of underlying investments.	3. Same.	3. Same.
4. Missing a premium invalidates the life cover.	4. Missing a payment merely means no units are purchased that month.	4. As with unit trust savings plan.

Continued

Life assurance – with-profits endowment	*Unit trust savings plan*	*Investment trust savings plan*
5. Payments should be kept up for 10 years to get a good return. If payments cease in the early years the sum repaid may be less than the sum invested due to deduction of insurance company costs.	5. Payments can cease at any time. Obviously sales should be made only when the market is high to avoid a loss.	5. As with unit trust savings plan.
6. With one or two exceptions insurance companies pay co-mmission to insurance brokers who introduce business. If a new client comes direct, these insurance companies keep the commission for themselves.	6. Many unit trust com-panies pay commission to intermediaries which reduces sum available.	6. Some investment trusts pay commission to intermediaries. If this is the case, then the sum available for investment is reduced.
7. No costs (apart from 6) involved in investing in life insurance.	7. Front-end loading charges and annual management fees are deducted from investments.	7. Broker's commission and PTM levy are charges on purchase of shares – but all purchases are made once or twice a month, thus the broker's commission is very low. These charges are divided between all investors. No front-end loading charges, but annual management fees are charged.

3   Single-Premium Bonds – Non-qualifying Life Policies

These are non-qualifying life policies where the investor pays a lump sum to the insurance company. A small percentage (around 10%) is used to purchase life cover, and the remainder is invested in units in the underlying fund. The units reflect the value of the assets held in the fund, plus the accumulated income of the fund. When the bond is encashed the proceeds depend on the value of the underlying fund.

The life cover element provides only a basis on which to calculate the amount payable on death, it is not used to calculate the value of the bond on encashment. Some life companies purchase term life cover that gives a guaranteed minimum payment on early death of the bondholder, whereas others use the life cover element on death to ensure that the bondholder's estate receives at least the same amount as was originally invested in the bond. In the second case the formula used to calculate the sum due on death uses the life cover element as its basis, but the exact formula varies from company to company.

The minimum investment in single-premium bonds varies from company to company, but is around £500. There is no income paid during the life of the bond, but the investor can withdraw 5% cumulative per annum of the capital sum invested for up to a maximum of 20 years. This facility is free of income tax at the time of withdrawal and capital gains tax on the partial withdrawals, but the total encashed is added to the value of the bond to calculate the investor's tax liability.

There are several types of single-premium bond available:

Property

Managed – of which there are the following types:

> Balanced Managed

> Cautious Managed

> Defensive Managed

UK Equity Income

UK Equity General

UK Smaller Companies

Guaranteed Funds

Distribution Bonds

International

International Fixed Interest

UK Gilt and Fixed Interest

- Index-Linked Gilts
- Money Market
- Europe
- North America
- Australasia
- Far Eastern Including Japan
- Far Eastern Excluding Japan
- Japan
- Emerging Markets
- Stockmarket Managed
- Currency
- Commodity and Natural Resources
- Friendly Societies – Tax Exempt.

Although an investor may make his initial investment in, say, the money market fund, he can at any time move his investment into one of the other bonds within the same company without cashing the bond. The switching between funds is done on a bid price to bid price basis.

The insurance company deducts an initial sum of around 5% of the amount invested (depending on the company) which is the 'front-end loading charge'; it also charges an annual management fee of around ¾% that is not fixed but can be raised at the company's discretion.

The investor should look very carefully at funds mentioned earlier and compare them with the performance of unit trusts in the same field. Investment in the index-linked gilt fund should be compared to direct investment into index-linked gilts. For a money market fund, comparison should be made with direct investment into building society and money fund accounts. In the case of many of the funds listed above down to 'Balanced managed funds', the investor will almost certainly be better to use the alternative vehicles, one major reason being that the insurance company will make a deduction from the value of the bond on encashment in respect of its own CGT liability, whereas the investor will have his annual exemption to offset gains made on the alternative forms of investment that produce taxable capital gains. In addition direct investment into money-market or fixed-interest stocks are free of CGT, whereas the insurance company has to deduct money for its own CGT liability.

Taxation treatment of single-premium bonds

The tax treatment of single-premium bonds in the hands of the investor is different from the treatment of qualifying life policies.

The Inland Revenue treats the proceeds of single-premium bonds as income, not capital gains. The bond is deemed to have suffered basic rate income tax because the insurance company has paid tax itself on its income at 23%. The proceeds are free of capital gains tax because the insurance company has paid the liability on the gains it has made.

Partial encashment

An investor can withdraw 5% cumulative per annum of the initial investment in the bond for a maximum of 20 years free of tax. If in year one no withdrawals are made, then in year two, 10% can be withdrawn. If in years one and two no withdrawals have been made then in year three, 15% can be withdrawn and so on.

On final encashment

Ascertain the total profit (encashment proceeds plus any partial withdrawals, less the original cost of the bond).

If the bondholder's marginal tax rate is 40%, in the year of encashment, he will be liable to income tax at 17% on the whole of the gain (the rate is the marginal tax less basic rate of 23% (40 − 23 = 17%)).

If the bondholder's marginal tax rate is less than 40%, calculate the total gain above and divide it by the number of years the bond has been held. This average gain is then added to the investor's taxable income to see if it takes him into the next tax bracket. The amount unused of the 23% tax threshold is used up, and the remaining amount times number of years held, in excess of the 23% tax threshold, is taxed at 17% (i.e. 40% − 23%). There is no point in averaging the gain if the bondholder's marginal tax rate is 40%, because this is currently the highest rate of income tax.

If the investor's marginal tax rate is 23% after adding the 'averaged gain' to his taxable income, he will not pay any tax at all on the gain.

Non-taxpayers and lower-rate (10%) taxpayers cannot reclaim the tax deducted from the proceeds of the bond.

Example of top slicing calculation

An investor purchases a single-premium bond for £10,000. He holds it for five years then surrenders it, receiving £25,000. He has withdrawn 5% of the purchase value of the bond each year. Calculate whether he has any further tax liability on encashment of the bond in the following circumstances:

(a) He has a total taxable income of £10,000

(b) He has a total taxable income of £45,000

(c) He has a total taxable income of £27,000

First the total profit is calculated:

	£
Sale proceeds	25,000
Plus 5%, withdrawals (£500 x 5)	2,500
	27,500
Less original cost	10,000
Total profit	17,500

(a) Because he has a total taxable income of £10,000 he is a basic-rate taxpayer. The profit must be annualized, and added to his taxable income to see if he becomes a 40% taxpayer.

Annualized profit $\qquad = \qquad \dfrac{17,500}{5} = £3,500$

Total taxable income $\qquad = \qquad £10,000 + £3,500$

$\qquad\qquad\qquad\qquad = \qquad £13,500$

Thus, he remains a basic-rate taxpayer and has no further tax liability.

(b) With a total taxable income of £45,000 he is a 40% taxpayer. Thus the whole of the profit is subject to top slicing i.e. 40% – 23%.

Income tax payable on profit $= £\dfrac{17,500 \times 17}{100} = £2,975$

(c) The annualized profit of £3,500 is added to his total taxable income of £27,000.

$$= 27,000 + 3,500$$

$$= £30,500$$

Thus the profit takes him into the 40% tax band. The tax payable is calculated thus:

Unused part of basic rate tax band $\quad = £28,000 – £27,000$

$$= £1,000$$

Annual profit $= £3,500 – £1,000 \quad = £2,500$

Tax at 17% (40% – 23%) on £2,500 x 5 years

$$= (2,500 \times 5) \times \dfrac{17}{100}$$

$$= 12,500 \times \dfrac{17}{100}$$

Income tax payable $\qquad = £2,125$

4   Property Bonds

A property bond is a single-premium insurance bond where the underlying assets consists of a range of commercial and industrial property. These bonds provide the investor with an indirect interest in a professionally managed portfolio of properties which are situated on prime sites and are let to first-class tenants.

The minimum sum that can be invested in property bonds is £500 and for the investor who wishes to have property in his portfolio, these bonds are one very good way of providing it. The tax position is as described earlier, and for a high-rate taxpayer property bonds are an attractive addition to a balanced portfolio.

Disadvantages of property bonds

There are, however, certain disadvantages with property bonds that must be considered before investing.

● The value of the bond depends entirely on the value of the underlying property. If the property market collapsed as it did in 1974 and 1990, the underlying assets could be so reduced in value that the investor would make a loss.

● Valuation of property is subjective. Different experts will give widely different values on the same property at the same time. This makes accurate valuation of the underlying fund difficult, although the property bond holder can easily obtain a valuation of his bond as the bid and offer prices are published in the **Financial Times**.

● The percentage of the initial sum used to purchase pure life cover will not give as high a sum assured as would using the same amount to purchase a term life policy directly from the insurance company. However, there is no way that the bondholder can avoid the deduction for life cover from his initial premium.

● If too many bondholders encashed their bonds simultaneously the insurance company could be forced to sell some of the property to repay the bondholders. This could depress the property market and start off a downward spiral of property values.

5   Managed Bonds

These are also single-premium bonds and have all the characteristics of such bonds. The underlying fund is invested four ways: fixed-interest stocks, equities, property and cash. The investment principle behind managed bonds is that the insurance company can switch from a fund that is performing badly to one that is doing well. However, this advantage is more theoretical than practical. The time to leave an investment is when it is doing well and the investor has made a good gain. Likewise he should invest in new areas when the investment is just starting to look attractive. This is called 'good timing'. The theory behind the managed bond completely reverses this policy and is one that should not be pursued. Another problem arises if it is the property fund that is doing badly. Property takes a long time to sell, and the value of the insurance company's property holding would fall dramatically if it sold a large part because the sales at such a level would reduce property values.

One advantage that a managed bond has over a property bond is that the managed bond has one of its funds invested in cash, thus a large number of bondholders simultaneously encashing their bonds will not depress the value of the bond as much. At certain times it can be advantageous to have a high level of cash, particularly when interest rates are high and the stock market is depressed. The cash part of the bond is as actively managed as the other three elements of the managed bond.

6   Suitability of the Various Insurance Products for Various Investors

Figure **14**.1: *Insurance products compared*

Investors requiring protection rather than investment		Investors mainly concerned with investment	
Young, with families	Wealthy with potential inheritance tax liability on death	Basic-rate taxpayers fairly risk averse	Higher-rate taxpayer willing to take some risk
Term assurance or possibly whole life policy	Term assurance with the policy writen in trust	Endowment policies – with- or without- profits, especially if linked to a mortgage	Single-premium bonds, particularly managed or property bonds. Unit-linked life policies

Figure 14.1 is a brief summary in connection with term life cover, endowment policies, single premium bonds and unit-linked life policies.

Note: a basic-rate taxpayer would normally find endowment policies attractive when linked to a mortgage. However, if he is looking for investment rather than a mortgage repayment vehicle, he would be better advised to consider a unit or investment trust savings scheme because of the flexibility of these schemes compared with life policies. (See Units 13 and 14.)

7 Guaranteed Growth, Guaranteed Income Bonds and Guaranteed Capital Bonds

A lump sum is invested in an insurance company at a fixed interest for terms of one to 10 years. The rate of return is guaranteed at the outset, and in the case of income bonds the income is paid out net of basic rate tax and with growth bonds it is rolled up in the bond. At the end of the term the investor receives back the capital sum invested, and with the growth bond the accumulated interest. Whether the interest is accumulated or paid out is irrelevant for tax purposes, it is treated as being paid net of basic rate tax. Non- and lower-rate taxpayers cannot reclaim the tax. The bonds are treated as single-premium bonds for tax purposes, thus are subject to the top-slicing rules.

The returns can be attractive for basic-rate taxpayers, provided they can afford to lock up their money for a fixed period. In most cases the investor is unable to withdraw the sum invested early, and the bonds that do allow early encashment carry heavy penalties for such an operation. The average minimum investment is £2,000.

An example of the average interest rates paid compared to gilts is given below, all rates being quoted in December 1999.

Guaranteed	1-year term	4.9% net basic tax
income bonds	2-year term	5.1% net basic tax
	3-year term	5.2% net basic tax
	4-year term	5.5% net basic tax
High coupon	1 year to maturity	5.5%
gilt gross redemption	2 years to maturity	6.4%
yield	3 years to maturity	6.6%
	4 years to maturity	6.5%

From this table it is obvious that the income bonds can give the better return to a basic-rate taxpayer (gross up income bonds 100/80). The two advantages of gilts are that they are marketable, thus can be quickly sold if the capital is needed, and secondly that a non-taxpayer can either reclaim the tax paid on the interest, or have the interest paid gross. It may not be advisable, however, for a basic-rate taxpayer to take out a bond for over four years because the interest rate remains fixed. Thus the general level of interest rates and inflation may rise over a longer period, eroding the purchasing power of both interest and capital. A higher-rate taxpayer has to pay tax calculated under the 'top-slicing rules' on the income.

The principle behind these bonds is quite simple. The insurance company purchases a large amount of fixed-interest stock and sells off slices as income or growth bonds. The maturity date of the bond and the stock is the same, hence the guaranteed return.

Another variation on the guaranteed growth bond is a guaranteed capital bond. This bond guarantees capital growth of 110% of the increases in the FTSE 100 Index (less management fees), or 100% money-back guarantee if there is no rise in the FTSE 100 Index (or whichever index the bond is linked to).

This type of bond could be attractive if the stock market rises over the preset period (usually five years), but will result in a loss in real terms if the market falls because the investor will receive back only his initial investment. However, inflation will have eroded the purchasing power of the investment.

8   Annuities

An annuity is a lump-sum payment to an insurance company that in return guarantees to pay out a set sum for a guaranteed period or until death, whichever is later. The sum paid to the insurance company is never returned unless the annuity is a capital protected annuity.

The guaranteed sum is paid at regular intervals yearly, half-yearly, quarterly or monthly, and the more frequent the payments the lower they are. The amount paid out depends on the age at the commencement of the annuity and sex of the annuitant, and whether there are any special provisions involved. Men have a lower life expectancy than women, thus men receive a better return. The other deciding factor in determining the amount paid out is the general level of interest rates at the time the annuity is taken out. The higher the general level of interest rates, the higher the annuity. This type of annuity is called a 'level-term annuity'.

Special provisions available

On a sole life paying a fixed sum per annum until the death of the annuitant. This method gives the highest level of income.

The variations available are:

- The income will be paid for a guaranteed minimum period, usually five or 10 years. If the annuitant dies during this period the income continues to be paid into his or her estate or to a named beneficiary until the period ends;

- Escalator annuities. These start with a lower initial income and the income rises each year by a set percentage or by the rate of inflation;

- Joint and last survivor annuities are taken out on the joint lives of husband and wife. They continue paying until the last survivor dies. The income paid out is lower than for a basic annuity because the insurance company is committing itself to what may possibly turn out to be a larger payment over the term of the annuity.

Taxation treatment of annuities

The tax treatment of annuities is favourable. Part of the payment is treated as return of capital and is tax free, the remainder is classed as interest and is subject to tax at the 20% or 40% rate depending on whether the taxpayer is a 10%, basic or 40% taxpayer. The capital element of the payment is at levels laid down by the Inland Revenue, and the greater the age of the annuitant on commencement of the annuity, the greater the capital element for tax purposes.

Example of returns available on annuities

An indication of the amounts received under annuities purchased for £10,000 is given below.

	Male aged **70**	*Female aged* **70**
Level term annuity	£1,000	£900
Escalator annuity, escalating at 5% p.a.	£690	£560

Joint and last survivor

(male 75/female 70)   £767 (no reduction on first death)

£909 (reducing by 2 on male death)

From the above rates it may seem that the return for age 70 is reasonable compared to gilts, however the returns are fixed, the capital cannot be repaid and as the individual could easily live for 20 or more years, the fixed return will be severely depleted in real terms by inflation.

However, the returns improve as the individual ages. For example, a level-term annuity would provide a man aged 80 on commencement of the annuity with a return of around £1,340 p.a. and a woman aged 80 at that time with a return of around £1,070. Effectively, the minimum age for an individual to consider an annuity is 70.

Disadvantages of investing in an annuity

Unless special provisions are made that will reduce the amount paid under the annuity, the initial sum invested is lost completely to the heirs on the annuitant's death.

The annuitant can never reclaim the sum paid to the insurance company.

Unless the annuity allows for the annual income to keep pace with inflation, the purchasing power of the annuity is eroded by inflation. If the annuitant lives to a very old age inflation can effectively wipe out the purchasing power of the annuity.

To get a good return the investor needs to be at least 70 years old at the time an annuity is taken out. To receive back the amount invested, the annuitant needs to live for around five years from the date of purchase. From the investor's point of view he or she should be in good health to enjoy the annuity for many years. However, it is possible to get better rates for 'impaired life' e.g. for a smoker or someone with a chronic life-shortening illness.

Conclusion

For an elderly investor aged at least 70 and in good health the investment is attractive because he or she should be able to live long enough to reap its benefits. From a flexibility angle, however, the investor should not commit all of his or her capital to an annuity because later on a capital sum may be needed for unexpected expenses. For an investor over 70 who has no need to utilize the capital spent, it is worthwhile to consider committing part of his or her capital to an annuity and invest the remainder in a balanced portfolio. Portfolio planning is covered in Unit 16.

9 Mortgage Annuities or Home Income Plans

For many investors their only asset of real value is their home, yet they need to be able to boost their income. A mortgage annuity (also called a home income plan) allows them to do this provided they are over 70, own an owner-occupied house free of mortgage and worth at least £15,000. For a joint and survivor mortgage annuity the joint ages must be at least 150. These limits are laid down by the companies operating these schemes.

The lender takes an interest-only mortgage over the house and the investor uses the sum raised to purchase an annuity. The amount lent against the value of the house varies from 65% to 80% depending on the company. The maximum loan is usually £30,000 but the interest paid on the loan is subject to MIRAS (Mortgage Interest Relief At Source) on only the first £30,000 of the loan up to 5 April 2000. After which date mortgage interest does not receive MIRAS. Thus the investor pays only the net of basic rate tax amount of interest to the lender. The annuity payment is treated as part repayment of capital, which is tax free, and the remainder as income that is subject to tax at the investor's marginal rate. The annuitant is allowed to retain up to 10% of the sum lent in cash and the remaining 90% must be invested in an annuity.

The loan is repaid only on the death of the annuitant by the sale of the house. Any excess of sale proceeds over the loan amount is paid into the deceased's estate. This does pose one problem for many elderly people, in that they will not be able to leave the whole value of their house to their heirs, but for those whose heirs have no need of the house, or for pensioners who are childless, the mortgage annuity scheme enables them to unlock capital tied up in their home. One advantage a mortgage annuity/home income plan has over a straight annuity is that as the value of the property increases it is possible to take out further top-up annuities, thus enabling the annuitant to increase his income.

Note: it is advisable only to take out a fixed-rate mortgage. A floating-rate mortgage may be cheaper in times of low interest rates but if interest rates become high, the interest on the mortgage may exceed the amount of the annuity payment, thus causing severe financial difficulties.

For individuals who receive housing benefit care must be taken because the extra income from this investment could reduce the entitlement to benefit.

10 Home Reversion Schemes and Roll-up Loans

Home reversion schemes

All or part of the house is sold to a company specializing in this area, and the house becomes the property of the company. In return a cash sum is paid that can be invested as the individual wishes. There is no loan involved and thus no interest to pay, and the company sells the house on the death of the occupier (or if the occupier moves permanently into a nursing home).

While this may seem a better scheme than a mortgage annuity, there are some important disadvantages:

- The house is no longer owned by the person/couple, thus cannot be left to their heirs. The person/couple only retains the right to live in the house until their death;

- The amount paid for the house is substantially below its market value, 50-65% below market value is not uncommon. Any rise in value belongs to the company.

Shared appreciation mortgages

The homeowner takes out an interest-free mortgage equal to a percentage of the value of the house. In return the homeowner gives up a substantial part of any increase in the value of the property when it is sold or they die. There is no risk of losing the home because only the initial loan has to be repaid from the sale proceeds.

11 Pensions

A pension is a method whereby an individual pays into a pension scheme a proportion of his earnings during his working life. These contributions provide an income (pension) on retirement that is treated as earned income and is taxed at the investor's marginal rate of income tax. The contributions to the pension are deducted from the investor's income before arriving at taxable income, thus gaining tax relief at the investor's marginal rate of tax. The rate of Class 1 National Insurance is determined according to whether or not the pension is contracted in or out of SERPS.

Example: A single investor whose gross earnings are £34,000 contributes 5% of his earnings to a pension scheme. His marginal rate of tax is 23% calculated:

	£
Gross income	34,000
Less: Pension contributions	
(5% of £34,000)	1,700
	32,300
Less: basic personal allowance	4,335
	27,965

This is within the 23% tax band of up to £28,000.

Without the pension contributions his marginal rate of tax would be 40%. So it is a very tax-efficient saving for retirement.

A variety of schemes are available, detailed in this section.

Occupational pension schemes

These are schemes run by employers and they come in two basic types: 'contracted-in' and 'contracted-out'. The maximum annual contributions are generally limited to 15% of earnings. A tax-free lump sum of up to 1.5% times final salary up to a maximum of £150,000 salary can be taken in cash, and a reduced pension received if the scheme was joined before 14 March 1989. After that date the figure is £135,900.

Contracted-in schemes

A 'contracted-in' scheme is contracted in to SERPS (State Earnings Related Pension Scheme), and does not have to give any minimum guarantees. These schemes can be based either on 'final salary' or on 'money purchase'. A 'final salary' scheme means that the pension will be an amount based on a proportion of your salary, the proportion depending on the number of years worked in the company. A 'money purchase' scheme is not related to employee earnings but to the success of the pension fund managers. All contributions to pension schemes receive full tax relief.

Contracted-out schemes

A 'contracted-out' scheme is so named because it has contracted out of SERPS. This has a guaranteed minimum pension equal to at least what would have been received via SERPS. A contracted-out money purchase scheme is also known as COMPS. A contracted-out scheme means that the employee receives a company pension and basic state pension only. The employee pays a lower rate of Class 1 National Insurance on this scheme.

Should an employee stay in or opt out of a company scheme?

An employee has the right to opt out of his company scheme into a personal pension plan (PPP). Before he changes he should consider the following points:

- Is the company scheme a money purchase or final salary scheme? All PPPs are run on a money purchase basis, but if the company scheme is a final salary scheme it may be best to stay in (bearing in mind the next two considerations);

- Is the employee likely to move jobs? If so, a PPP may be more suitable than a frozen pension from a series of past employers;

- Does the employee want a flexible retirement age? PPPs allow for retirement at any time between the ages of 50 and 75 whereas company schemes tend to be much less flexible;

- If the employee transfers to a PPP how much, if anything, will the employer contribute, bearing in mind the employer has no obligation to pay into a PPP? If employers will not contribute to a PPP it will probably be better for the employee to stay in the occupational scheme;

- Is the scheme a COMPS one? Employees under 45 (male) or 40 (female) will probably be better off staying in the COMPS scheme. For those over these ages it will probably be better to stay in a SERPS scheme.

Personal pension plans (PPPs)

These are not available to anyone who is already in an occupational scheme unless there are earnings from other sources.

All contributions to a PPP are tax deductible, and therefore attract tax relief at the investor's marginal rate of income tax. The maximum contribution that can be made is on a sliding scale according to age and varies between $17\frac{1}{2}\%$ and 40% of 'net relevant earnings'. 'Net relevant earnings' are defined basically as pre-tax salary for the employed, and taxable profit for the self-employed. The contribution limits are subject to a maximum salary of £90,600 gross for 1999-2000 and are:

Age at **6** *Apr*	*% of net relevant earnings*	*Effective maximum contribution i.e. of* **£90,600**
35 or less	17.5%	£15,855
36-45	20%	£18,120
46-50	25%	£22,650
51-55	30%	£27,180
56-60	35%	£31,710
61 and above	40%	£36,240

This increasing scale means that older employees can boost the size of their pension fund, which is tax advantageous, so that they can enjoy a greater pension and tax-free lump sum on retirement if they wish.

Note: the income limits (% of net relevant earnings) are given on the exam paper.

The pension fund itself pays no tax except for the 10% tax credit on dividends, thus the potential investment return is higher when compared to alternative investments.

Finally, on retirement a lump sum is available. Up to 25% of the available sum can be commuted, i.e. taken as a tax-free lump sum, but the maximum amount of the tax-free lump sum is limited (see Unit 11). The remainder is used to provide a guaranteed income for life.

The scheme is set up by the investor directly with a pension fund. The employer is not bound to make any contribution into a PPP as he is with the SERPS or occupational schemes. So why should an employee opt for a PPP? If he/she is likely to stay with the same employer all their life then the company scheme will be more likely to be beneficial, especially if it is a final salary scheme. However, many people nowadays change jobs regularly and with a company scheme the pension can be frozen, which means in real terms that it may be worth very little on retirement. A PPP operates on a money purchase basis, so the employee needs to have a long period before retirement to build a good fund.

The employee can arrange a 'buy-out' plan whereby his company scheme is transferred to a PPP. This does not mean that the employee will have the same value transferred in relation to the number of years service with the company, but a reduced number.

PPPs are more flexible in relation to retirement age. The benefits can be drawn from the age of 50 onwards, unlike company schemes where the age will be 60 or 65. For anyone planning early retirement a PPP is more flexible. They are also the scheme to use if the individual concerned is self-employed.

The right of the self-employed or people in non-pensionable employment to utilize previous years for contributions to **PPPs**
It sometimes happens that someone who could have invested in a PPP has failed to do so, and instead has built up a capital sum from investment in another asset, for instance unit trust units.

Such people are entitled to 'carry forward' contributions over the previous six years. This means that a single lump sum, which is tax deductible, can be paid into a PPP. The amount can equal the total contributions that could have been made over the last six years, using the age-related percentage rate of annual net relevant earnings rule. The only proviso is that the total sum calculated in this way must not exceed the level of the taxable earnings for the current year.

Let us consider a practical example. A self-employed builder who has always been a basic-rate taxpayer retires at the age of 65, after selling his business for a considerable sum. Over the last six years he could have made total contributions of £21,000 within the 'net relevant earnings' rule. Provided the level of taxable profits in the fiscal year in which he sold the business was running at £21,000 or more per annum, the builder could invest a lump sum of £21,000 in a pension plan. Assuming he is a basic-rate taxpayer, the net cost of that lump sum would be £16,170 (£21,000 less tax at 23%). He would receive a tax rebate from the Inland Revenue of £4,830 for tax overpaid due to the carry-forward.

The lump-sum contribution would have purchased a pension fund of about £20,000 after charges, and up to £5,000 (25%) could be commuted as a tax-free lump sum. The remaining £15,000 could purchase an income for life.

However, it is better to invest in a PPP on a regular basis, if possible, because the money can then be invested in a tax-free pension fund which should outperform other investments.

SERPS (State Earnings Related Pension Scheme)

The amount received is paid for out of higher National Insurance contributions and the benefits are directly linked to earnings. For older employees (men over 45 and women over 40), if they are already paying into the SERPS scheme, then they will be better to stay in. The employer is bound by law to contribute to an employee's SERPS scheme. Younger employees are better off out of this scheme which is being reduced in value after the year 2000.

If the individual opts out of SERPS into a PPP, the plan must be an appropriate Personal Pension Plan as certified by the Occupational Pensions Board.

Appropriate PPPs relate only to schemes that result from transferring from SERPS. All other PPPs are classed as 'Approved' PPPs.

Position of self-employed, of those employed in pensionable employment, and those relying only on SERPS

Self-employed people have always been allowed to contribute to pension plans, subject to the age-related $17^1/_2$%-40% of net relevant earnings rule.

Those employed in company pensions will have the right to transfer any pension rights accumulated in a company scheme into a PPP. Alternatively, the employee could let his company pension scheme continue, but make additional voluntary contribution into the company scheme or into an FSAVC (see Unit 11).

Rights of those in SERPS

Individuals have the right to contract out of SERPS. They will then qualify for a rebate of the National Insurance contributions that would normally have gone into SERPS. The Department of Health will pay this rebate directly into the nominated PPP. Alternatively, an individual should be able to continue in the SERPS scheme, but make regular payments to a PPP.

Topping-up pension schemes

Most employees pay around 5-6% of their gross earnings into a pension scheme, but the maximum actually allowed is 15% of gross earnings for occupational schemes and a sliding scale with a minimum of $17\frac{1}{2}\%$ for PPPs. If an individual wishes to increase the value of his pension fund he has three options – AVCs, FSAVCs or a PPP.

AVCs (additional voluntary contributions)

These are extra payments made into the company scheme by the employee. Depending on the scheme, the employee may be able to increase his monthly contributions, purchase full years or put in lump sums as and when convenient. The terms vary between the schemes. The total contribution to the occupation pension plus AVC must not exceed 15% of net relevant earnings.

FSAVCs (Free-standing AVCs)

These are individually set up schemes not paid to the company scheme but purchased directly from a pension fund. The employee continues to pay the usual pension contributions to the employer's schemes, but pays FSAVCs elsewhere. This route would be chosen if the individual did not find the company AVC scheme suitable. FSAVCs are money purchase schemes.

PPPs (Personal Pension Plan)

These schemes can also be useful if an employee has non-pensionable earnings from other sources, e.g. royalties or fees.

The pension funds are run by a variety of institutions such as insurance companies, building societies, banks and unit trusts. In all cases the tax position is identical. The fund itself is free of tax, except for the tax credit of 10% deducted on dividends, and the contributions receive tax relief at the investor's marginal rate of income tax. On receipt of the pension it is treated as earned income and taxed at the investor's marginal rate of income tax.

Using **PPP**s to fund mortgages (pension mortgages)
'Pension mortgages' work along the following lines:

- The lender (say, a bank) agrees to lend a sum of money for house purchase. The house is mortgaged as security for the loan;

- The borrower takes out a PPP with agreed contributions. The projections should show that the tax-free commutable sum at retirement will equal the loan. In addition, term life cover is taken out, and the premiums for this will qualify for tax relief if they and the pension contributions do not exceed the age-related percentage rule;

- The borrower pays interest only on the bank loan, and pays the pension contributions. Normal PPP benefits apply, so the contributions are tax deductible and the PPP itself is free of all taxes;

- As with all house purchase loans, there is no MIRAS relief after 5 April 2000;

- On retirement the commutable lump sum pays off the mortgage, and there is money left over to purchase an income for life.

Comparison of 'pension mortgages' with 'endowment mortgages'

An endowment mortgage is an interest-only loan with the capital to be repaid from the maturity proceeds of a life policy.

The performance of the underlying investments will presumably be similar if the PPP is managed by an insurance company.

There is no tax relief on the life policy premiums, however, and the insurance company will be subject to a special corporation tax rate of 23%. Thus the same total contributions will be much more beneficial if a PPP rather than an endowment policy is used.

Comparison of repayment mortgages with pension mortgages

Repayment mortgages are where the borrower pays a monthly instalment that covers both interest and capital reduction. The interest element is tax deductible on the first £30,000 of the amount lent until 5 April 2000, as it is with all the house purchase mortgages so far described.

There is no tax relief on the capital repayments. Hence, pension mortgages should always be a better alternative, unless there is a stock market collapse that would affect the value of the pension. If the borrower were ultra cautious, he could use a deposit-based pension plan, that would be a 'safer' pension, but would miss out if the stock market did prosper. (Deposit-based plans have the contributions invested in a bank or building society high-interest account.)

SIPPS (Self Invested Pension Plans)

This new type of pension plan is aimed at wealthier, more experienced investors, who have at least £100,000 in their pension fund or who can afford large annual pension contributions. The pension holder can decide on the investments to be held in a SIPP rather than pay a fund manager to do so.

The pension provider usually charges an up-front fee of between £500 – £700 and an annual fee of around £400.

The main eligible investments are:

- Stocks and shares listed on a recognized stock exchange;

- Futures and options traded through a relevant exchange;

- Unit trusts – authorized, subject to regulation by the Financial Services Act or US mutual funds recognized by the Financial Services Authority;

- Investment trusts;
- OEICs;
- Insurance managed funds;
- Deposit accounts;
- Commercial property (with certain limitations).

SIPPS allow the investor flexibility in planning for retirement. At a younger age the investor may look for higher-risk investments, but 5 to 10 years prior to retirement he may decide to change his strategy to a more conservative one in order to lock in the gains (as far as is possible).

The inclusion of commercial property is particularly attractive to the businessman who trades from his own property. He can place the property in his SIPP.

12   Friendly Society Bonds

A friendly society is a tax-exempt body (except for the tax credit on dividends) which gives it a major advantage over life insurance companies. All returns on a friendly society bond are tax-free, thus the combination of the tax-free status of the society and the returns in the hands of the investor make these bonds very attractive to any investor who can afford to tie up his money for 10 years. The policy must run for at least 10 years with the premiums paid for a minimum of 10 years. If the premiums cease during the first 10 years the most that will be returned is the amount paid in.

Policies taken out prior to 13 March 1984 receive the $12^1/_2$% tax relief on premiums, as do life insurance policies taken out prior to that date. Policies taken out after 13 March 1984 do not qualify for tax relief on premiums. The maximum sum assured is £2,050 and maximum monthly premium is £25. If the premiums are paid annually the maximum is £270 p.a. Husband and wife can each have friendly society bonds. It is possible to make a lump-sum payment into a friendly society bond, and this amount is around 20% lower than the cost of 10 years premium, i.e. the sum is £2,160. The interest earned by the friendly society on the sum deposited makes up the shortfall, although the interest itself is subject to income tax at the investor's marginal rate.

A more tax-efficient way to produce the necessary premium from a lump sum is to take out a temporary annuity. This is identical in tax treatment to an annuity, the word 'temporary' meaning that the annuity ceases after a set term, in this case 10 years. For a high-rate taxpayer this scheme is attractive because part of the payment is classed as return of capital and is tax free, the remainder being treated as income and thus taxed at the investor's marginal rate of tax.

With all friendly society bonds the investor has four options open to him at the end of the 10-

year period:

- He can encash the bond free of all tax;
- He can partially encash the bond as and when desired, leaving the remaining sum to grow;
- He can leave the entire sum in the bond to continue growing tax free;
- He can continue to make payments.

Although the amounts invested are small, these bonds can be attractive to high-rate taxpayers. For a basic-rate taxpayer who is certain that he can afford to tie up his money for 10 years the returns are also very attractive. It is possible for an annual premium of £270 over 10 years to realize in excess of £6,000, which is a growth rate of approximately 9% per annum.

Many friendly societies have now brought out plans aimed at parents, grandparents or other adults who wish to save money for a child. The advantage of these plans is the same for the beneficiary (whether child or adult) in that they are totally tax free.

Friendly society bond funds invest in a wide range of investments – building society accounts, UK and overseas government stocks and shares.

Summary

Now that you have studied this unit, you should be able to:

- describe the taxation treatment of insurance companies and life insurance policies;
- differentiate between qualifying and non-qualifying life policies;
- understand the difference between protection and investment in relation to life policies;
- Describe the types of qualifying life policies:
  - ➤ term
  - ➤ whole life
  - ➤ endowment (with- and without-profits, unit-linked and unitized);
- describe which types of policy offer protection only, a mix of protection and investment, and mainly investment;
- compare and contrast unit trusts, investment trusts and life assurance as savings vehicles;
- compare and contrast unit-linked policies with unit trust savings plans;
- describe the various types of single-premium bonds;
- calculate tax liability under the top slicing rules;
- describe the advantages and disadvantages of property bonds as an investment;
- describe the advantages and disadvantages of managed bonds as an investment;

- understand which type of investment product is suited to a specific type of investor;
- describe guaranteed growth and guaranteed income bonds;
- describe the features of annuities;
- describe the tax treatment of annuities;
- describe the features of home income plans (mortgage annuities);
- describe the features of home reversion plans and roll-up loans;
- understand and describe the features of the following types of pensions:
  - occupation
  - personal pension plans
  - SERPS;
- explain how and when an investor can take out a PPP;
- understand when it may be advisable to opt out of SERPS;
- describe the ways of topping up a pension;
- describe pension mortgages;
- describe the main features of SIPPS;
- describe the features and tax treatment of friendly society bonds.

15

CASH AND TAX-FREE INVESTMENTS

Objectives

After studying this unit, you should be able to:

● explain the interest rates available on bank and building society accounts;

○ describe the features of the NSB accounts and the tax treatment of NSB account interest;

○ describe the features of the 53rd issue NSCs;

○ describe the features of the 16th issue index-linked NSCs;

● explain what is meant by 'general extension rate';

○ explain what is meant by 'reinvestment certificates';

○ describe the features of National Savings Income Bonds;

● describe the features of the Pensioners Guaranteed Income Bond;

○ describe the features of National Savings Capital Bonds;

○ describe the features of Premium Bonds;

● describe the features of National Savings Children's Bonus Bonds;

○ describe the features of ESOPs;

○ describe the features of PEPs;

○ describe the features of TESSAs;

○ describe the features of ISAs;

○ identify the investments that are totally exempt from income and capital gains tax in the hands of the investor;

○ identify the investments that provide instant to one month's access to capital;

○ identify the investments that have a withdrawal period of one month to one year;

- identify the investments that mature between one and 10 years;
- identify longer-term (five years plus) investments;
- identify investments that provide a monthly savings scheme.

1   Introduction

Cash investments

These are funds placed with:

- National Savings, representing loans to the Government;
- Banks and building societies.

These funds are generally repayable on demand or at very short notice. They are also capital guaranteed – the customer cannot make a capital loss unless the institution with which he invests becomes insolvent.

Cash investments are straightforward and are readily understandable. They offer the convenience of transactions by post or over the counter of branch offices. They usually incur few if any charges. Those charges that are made are published in a tariff by the institution in keeping with the Code of Banking Practice, to which most institutions subscribe.

Tax-free investments

These are investments that are exempt from Income Tax and Capital Gains Tax under government regulations. They include many National Savings products, Individual Savings Account (ISAs), personal equity plans (PEPs) and employee share option schemes (ESOPs).

2   Bank Accounts

Current accounts

Retail banks are the main providers of current accounts. Generally, current accounts providers pay low rates of interest (or no interest at all) on balances held, because money is available on demand. Interest-bearing current accounts pay interest on a net basis, i.e. with 20% tax deducted at source (that satisfies a basic-rate taxpayer's liability).

High interest cheque accounts

Most large banks have 'premium' rate cheque accounts, aimed principally at high net worth customers. These products usually have a minimum opening balance, with interest paid reducing to a very low rate if the balance falls below a certain level. As long as a reasonably substantial balance is held, interest rates are quite competitive. Better rates can be obtained, however, on savings and investment accounts on which cheque book facilities are not available.

Savings accounts

All banks offer savings and term accounts. Most offer instant access. The interest rates are often tiered, with larger balances attracting better rates.

Money market deposits

All banks offer these deposits, usually for amounts in excess of £25,000. The period of investment is agreed at the outset and the return is fixed for that period. Interest on balances in excess of £50,000 is paid gross and the investor is liable for tax on this. Balances below that threshold receive interest with tax deducted at source.

Money market accounts are especially useful for the investor who needs time to construct an investment portfolio, because the rates paid are about the best available.

3   Building Societies

Most building societies offer savings products that compete effectively with the offerings of the banks. There is one particular difference in that savers with a building society are members of that society.

If a society demutualizes and becomes a bank, members may receive shares in the 'building society' that are tradeable on the Stock Market.

Instant access accounts

The minimum balance for instant access varies from society to society. For some it is as little as £1, although many levy account charges on customers whose balances fall below a certain level in a given period.

Most building societies provide current accounts that offer the same benefits as those of the banks.

Interest rates on instant access accounts are usually tiered, with higher balances receiving higher interest. Generally, low-balance accounts receive very little interest – typically less than 1% net.

Term accounts

Most building societies offer notice accounts that pay a higher rate of interest in return for a period of notice of withdrawal. The terms that usually apply are:

- Tiered rates – higher balance, higher return;
- Notice of withdrawal expressed in numbers of days – for example, 30, 60, 90 days;
- Instant access offered subject to an interest penalty of the equivalent number of days notice;

- When notice is given, it is valid for a set period (otherwise the account would become instant access);
- The society may impose a minimum balance (typically £500 upwards);
- Some offer monthly income subject to a minimum balance.

Money market accounts

These operate in the same way as bank money market accounts.

Calculation of after tax returns from bank and building society accounts

Investors will need to know how much interest they receive on these accounts, after taking into account their marginal rate of tax. The following calculation shows how they calculate the rate of interest they receive after tax is deducted.

4 Taxation Treatment of Bank and Building Society Interest

Non-taxpayers can reclaim the tax deducted from interest, or they can receive the interest gross upon signing a declaration that they are non-taxpayers. The interest must still be entered on a non-taxpayer's tax return so that the Inland Revenue can establish the correct marginal rate of tax. When the interest has been entered on the investor's tax return, the Inland Revenue will gross it up and add the grossed-up figure to the investor's other income.

If the gross interest alters the investor's marginal rate of tax, there will be further tax to pay only if the investor becomes a 40% taxpayer. In this case a further 20% tax on the gross interest will be paid. A 10% and basic-rate taxpayer have no further tax liability because the 20% tax deducted at source satisfies their liability to tax.

5 National Savings Bank (NSB)

National Savings Bank Ordinary Account

The NSB accounts are opened at the Post Office. The ordinary account has a minimum investment of £10 and a maximum of £10,000. Cash withdrawals of up to £250 per day (or £500 per day if the account is classed as a 'Regular Customer Account') can be made, and standing orders can be raised to meet regular payments.

The interest paid is on two levels.

- Balances of under £500 – interest of 1.25% gross p.a.
- Balances of £500 or more that were in the account by 31 December and remain above £500 for the whole of the following year until 1 January of the next year – interest of 1.35% gross p.a.

Thus the £500 balance must be in the account on 31 December 1999 and remain above £500 until 1 January 2001 to attract the higher rate. If the account is opened during the year only 1.25% per annum is paid that year. This also applies if the balance falls below £500 during the year.

The first £70 of interest is free of income tax and a husband and wife are each entitled to £70 interest tax free, thus they can receive £140 interest tax free. The interest, while tax free, must be recorded on the investor's tax return.

Interest is paid only on each whole pound on deposit for complete calendar months. Money does not earn interest in the month it is deposited or withdrawn. This makes the timing of deposits and withdrawals very important.

- Incorrect timing: A deposit made on 1 April and withdrawn on 31 July will earn interest on only the two complete months of May and June. This has the effect of reducing the rate of interest paid.

- Correct timing: A deposit made on 31 March and withdrawn on 1 August earns interest for four complete months – April, May, June and July.

Thus, making deposits on the last day of the month and withdrawals on the first day of the month gives an extra two months' interest, yet the money has been deposited only two days longer.

For a 40% taxpayer who has deposited £500 or more for a full calendar year, and only makes deposits or withdrawals as described, the interest rate of 1.35% is equivalent to an after-tax return of 2.25% from a bank or building society. In order to keep with the £70 per annum interest that is tax free, the maximum deposit is £5,185. For this sum, the highest bank and building society rates are paying around 6% gross, which is equivalent to 3.6% for a 40% taxpayer. Given the complexity on the Ordinary Account and the poor returns quoted above, it is not worth a 40% taxpayer investing in this account. For a basic or lower rate taxpayer the Ordinary Account is very uncompetitive.

For a non-taxpayer this account should be avoided despite the interest being paid gross because the return of either 1.25% or 1.35% can be bettered by other savings accounts. If immediate access to money is needed, the instant access account in a bank or building society gives a better return because interest can be paid gross to non-taxpayers.

National Savings Bank Investment Account

This account is also available via the Post Office and offers a far more attractive return. The minimum deposit is £20, the maximum holding £100,000 plus any accumulated interest. Interest on this account is paid gross on a banded rate.

- Under £500   3.8%
- £500 to £2,499   3.95%
- £2,500 to £4,999   4.05%

- £5,000 to £9,999   4.35%
- £10,000 to £49,999   4.6%
- £50,000 and over   5.1%

The NSB pays all interest gross, unlike banks and building societies who can pay gross only to non-taxpayers. Interest is calculated on a daily basis on each whole pound deposited and is subject to tax at the investor's marginal rate. Interest on this account is paid only once a year, on 31 December. All withdrawals are subject to one month's notice, which runs from the day the application is received at the National Savings Bank in Glasgow, not at the local Post Office. Money can be withdrawn without notice, provided the amount has been in the account for at least 30 days. Thirty days' interest will be lost on the amount withdrawn.

The account is not attractive to non-taxpayers because the interest rate is between 3.8% and 5.1%. They may find a bank or building society instant access account paying higher rates. The 5.1% gross is only worth 4.08% to a 23% taxpayer, and 3.06% to a 40% taxpayer.

Remember that interest is subject to tax at 20% for a 23% taxpayer, and at 40% for a 40% taxpayer.

6   Other National Savings Investments

53rd Issue Fixed Interest National Savings Certificates

National Savings certificates can be purchased through most post offices and banks. The 53rd issue carries a guaranteed return equivalent to 4.3% compounded over five years, and the return is free of income tax and capital gains tax.

The minimum investment is £100, the maximum £10,000, purchased in units of £25. Any returns from these certificates do not have to be recorded on an income tax return.

The repayment value increases at the end of the first year and at the end of each subsequent three months. If the certificates are encashed during the first year, only the purchase price is repaid.

If the certificates are encashed early, they receive the following rates of interest.

Minimum period held	Tax free interest rate
1 year	3.90%
2 years	4.00%
3 years	4.20%
4 years	4.40%
5 years	5.01%

These rates give a return equal to 4.30% p.a. compounded if the certificates are left for the full five years.

If the certificates are encashed repayment is made within eight working days. National Savings certificates that are not redeemed at the end of the five years continue to receive interest at the general extension rate.

These certificates are attractive to 40% taxpayers because they give a gross equivalent return of 7.17%.

$$\frac{(4.3 \times 100)}{60}$$

16th Issue Index-linked NSCs

These NSCs guarantee a return that is a real return over the rate of inflation. Interest equivalent to 1.8% compounded p.a. over five years is added and this is on top of the inflation proofing. The minimum investment is £100, the maximum £10,000. The guaranteed yield p.a. above the rate of inflation is:

Minimum period held	Tax exempt return
Under 1 year	Nil
1 year	RPI + 1.20% of purchase price
2 years	RPI + 1.40% of 1st Anniversary value
3 years	RPI + 1.60% of 2nd Anniversary value
4 years	RPI + 2.00% of 3rd Anniversary value
5 years	RPI + 2.81% of 4th Anniversary value

The 'Anniversary Value' is calculated from the purchase date

These rates give a return equal to 1.80% p.a. compounded on top of the index linking if the certificates are left for the full five years.

At each anniversary of purchase the whole certificate is revalued in line with the Retail Prices Index plus the guaranteed return. If the certificates are encashed in the first year, only the purchase price is refunded; after one year the certificates receive the guaranteed return plus index linking that is calculated using the following formula:

$$\frac{\text{Purchase price} \times \text{RPI in month of encashment}}{\text{RPI in month of purchase}}$$

If the RPI on the date of purchase was 139.3, and 141.1 on the date of sale a year later, an investment of £1,000 would be worth:

$$\frac{1,000 \times 141.1}{139.3} = £1,012.92$$

For the higher rate (40%) taxpayer these certificates offer an attractive return. The 1.8% is equal to 3% gross PLUS the index linking. These certificates are attractive to basic-rate taxpayers in times of high inflation.

Note: On top of the £10,000 for the 53rd issue and 16th issue index linked NSCs, investors can invest the proceeds of any previous issues of NSCs with no maximum limit. NSCs purchased in this manner are call 'Re-Investment Certificates'.

General extension rate and reinvestment certificates

At the end of the five-year period the yearly plan, all NSCs from the 7th issue onwards (apart from the index-linked issues) receive the same rate of interest: the 'general extension rate', 2.58% p.a.

Interest is added every four months on the matured issues once the certificates have been held for one year after the end of the five-year period. If an investor decides to encash any certificates on the general rate terms he should wait until just after the four-monthly value date. For issues from the 24th onwards interest is added every three months.

Note: If an investor holds certificates in the 1st to 6th issues they should be encashed immediately because they have a lower yield than the general extension rate of 2.58% per annum.

National Savings Income Bonds

These bonds, like all National Savings and National Savings Bank investments, pay interest gross. The standard (or 'Treasury') rate is 5.45% gross on balances under £25,000, 5.7% over this amount.

The minimum holding is £2,000, the maximum £250,000, and purchases must be made in multiples of £1,000. All interest received is subject to tax at the investor's marginal rate.

The bonds pay interest on a monthly basis. This can be very useful for an investor who requires a regular income. However, the rate of interest is variable at six weeks' notice, hence it is not possible to predict the exact income received over a year or more.

If interest rates look set to rise this account is attractive for non-taxpayers who require monthly income. However, if interest rates are set to fall the non-taxpayer should consider purchasing a high coupon dated gilt that will ensure a fixed level of income until redemption.

For a basic-rate taxpayer the 5.45% gross return is worth 4.36% after 20% savings rate tax. If he requires a monthly income he should compare this to a building society 90-day account that provides this facility.

Three months' notice of withdrawal for NS Income Bonds is required. Withdrawals must be in multiples of £1,000 and at least £2,000 must remain invested, but the interest received depends on how long the bond has been held:

● Repayment in first year: Interest at half rate from date of purchase to date of repayment on amount paid;

● Repayment after first year: Interest paid in full.

A bank or building society account is more flexible than the NS Income Bond because only 90 days' notice need be given to withdraw without loss of interest, or instant access with loss of 90 days' interest is also possible.

If repayment is made during the first year, and the amount paid out as monthly interest exceeds the amount due under the 'half rate' rule, then the overpayment of the interest is deducted from the capital repaid. Interest is calculated from the date of purchase on a daily basis and is paid on the 5th of each month. The first interest payment on the bond will be made on the first interest date after the bond has been held for six weeks, and includes all interest due from the date of purchase.

Each bond has a guaranteed initial life of 10 years from the first interest date after the date of purchase. The bond will be redeemed at par either at the end of the guaranteed initial period, or on any interest date thereafter on the Treasury giving of six months' notice.

Pensioners' Guaranteed Income Bonds

As with the National Savings Income Bonds, Pensioners' Guaranteed Income Bonds also provide a monthly income. The rate of interest on these bonds is guaranteed if held for five years from the time of purchase. Early withdrawals are subject to 60 days' notice and 60 days' loss of interest. Withdrawals without notice are subject to 90 days' loss of interest on the amount to be withdrawn.

The minimum investment is £500, the maximum £50,000, and these bonds are available only to people aged 65 or over.

The rate of interest is 5.85% gross but is subject to tax at 20% for a basic-rate taxpayer and 40% for a 40% taxpayer.

National Savings Capital Bonds

Capital Bonds are designed for investors with a lump sum to invest who do not wish to receive any income. The interest paid is rolled up into the bond and on repayment the investor receives his capital back plus the accrued interest.

Interest is paid gross on the bonds at the fixed rate of 6% gross, and is added to the capital once a year but it is subject to tax (as described above) in the year the interest is added to the capital. This makes these bonds unattractive to any taxpayer because there is no facility available to defer tax until final encashment, as there is with a single-premium bond.

The minimum holding is £100, the maximum holding is £250,000. Purchases must be made in multiples of £100. The minimum withdrawal is £100. The rules regarding withdrawals and the rate of interest paid apply as those detailed for National Savings Income Bonds.

Premium Savings Bonds

These do not give any guaranteed return at all and, indeed, are not a true investment because they only guarantee capital back. However, Premium Bonds pay out prizes that are totally free of income tax and capital gains tax.

Prizes range from £50 to £1,000,000.

The minimum purchase is £100. However, the minimum holding is £1. The maximum holding is £20,000.

Each £1 unit gives the holder one chance per week or month to win a prize. The odds against winning any prize at all are in the region of 21,000 to 1. Thus, an investor with £20,000 worth of Premium Savings Bonds should, on average, receive a prize 11 to 12 times a year, but this is only a mathematical model and in practice does not hold true because the prizes are picked electronically at random.

These bonds cannot be recommended as an investment. However, if an investor wishes to have a 'flutter' and holds a balanced portfolio it is one alternative to consider among other riskier investments, the risk being loss of income and erosion of capital value.

National Savings Children's Bonus Bonds

This is a lump-sum investment of between £25 and £1,000. The rate of interest is fixed for the first five years at 5.5% per annum compounded. At the end of five years a new rate of interest is fixed. The bond can be encashed at any time, but should be encashed on the child's 21st birthday. No interest is earned after the 21st birthday.

Children's Bonus Bonds do not pay out interest – it is rolled-up in the bond. The interest is totally free of income tax and capital gains tax even when the bond has been purchased by a parent.

These bonds are useful if the parent is giving money to the child and the total interest from such gifts would exceed £100. With other investments when the income exceeds £100 p.a. gross, the whole of the income is treated as the parent's for tax purposes and taxed at the donor parent's marginal rate of income tax.

Calculation of gross equivalent from income tax and capital gains tax exempt investments

Investors must also be able to compare returns on investments that are totally free of income tax and capital gains tax with those that are taxable. To do this, the gross equivalent return is calculated for the tax-exempt investment and compared to the gross return on taxable investments. This will indicate the most attractive investments.

The following investments detailed in this unit are totally free of income and capital gains tax.

● All National Savings certificates

○ Premium Bonds

○ National Savings Children's Bonus Bonds

○ PEPs

● ESOPs

○ TESSAs

○ ISAs

Some of these investments do not give a guaranteed return; these are Premium Bonds, ESOPs, PEPs, TESSAs and ISAs. The return on these depends on other factors such as interest rates (TESSAs), performance of the stock market (ESOPs and PEPs), ISAs (performance of the underlying investment see Section 10) and 'luck of the draw' (Premium Bonds).

7   Personal Equity Plans (PEPs)

PEPs are no longer available for new investment. However, investments held in a PEP can be retained and have the benefit of tax-free income and capital gains.

The investments that can be held in a PEP are:

○ ordinary shares or corporate bonds of companies incorporated in the UK and quoted on either the London Stock Exchange on a full listing or AIM listing basis, or on the stock exchanges of the EU;

● Under PEP rules, Corporate Bonds are company loan stocks that pay out interest (zero-coupon loan stocks are not eligible investments), convertible loan stocks, convertible preference shares and preference shares.

Other rules:

○ PEPs can be run only by managers approved by the Inland Revenue;

○ Dividends from shares in a PEP are free of tax even if they are withdrawn from the plan.

Investments that cannot be included in a PEP are:

○ unquoted shares

○ permanent income-bearing shares issued by building societies

○ British Government Securities (gilts)

○ futures

○ options

○ warrants.

However all the above can be held indirectly via a unit or investment trust or OEIC that invest in these areas.

Single-company PEPs

Shares in a 'single-company PEP' can be held in addition to a general PEP. There is no requirement for the holder of this type of PEP to have any connection with the company, but it was envisaged that employees who took out ESOPs (Employee Share Option Plans) may wish to transfer their shares into a PEP.

The PEP plan managers

Because they must be approved by the Inland Revenue, the managers currently offering plans come mainly from banks, unit trusts and stockbroking firms. All the managers offer slightly different versions of the PEP, and all levy charges for their services, including initial charges and annual management fees in all cases. Some managers, however, do not levy any brokerage charges on the purchase or sale of the equities within the plan.

One aim of these plans was to encourage wider direct share ownership by 'the man/woman in the street'. Many PEP managers restrict the investor's choice of direct equities to a list of blue chip shares.

In common with other performance-related investment schemes, PEPs provide higher medium- and long-term growth potential than capital guaranteed schemes such as bank and building society accounts.

Suitability for investors

For high taxpayers who also have capital gains each year in excess of the £7,100 figure these plans are attractive.

An investor who already holds PEPs needs to consider whether to retain or transfer all or part of the PEP into an ISA (see Section 10). The drawback is that on the year of transfer the investment will count as being part of the annual amount invested into an ISA. Thus no further investment in an ISA will be possible for that year. In addition there may be costs incurred for withdrawing funds from the PEP.

The investor who holds shares in his plan will retain all the rights of an ordinary shareholder. He will receive notice of meetings, annual reports and shareholders' concessions (if any). Because PEP fees tend to be higher than unit trust fees this can make the PEP plan rather expensive in the early years. Fees tend to be around 5% of the initial investment and subsequent annual management fees are between 1.25% and 1.5%. Some managers levy a flat annual fee varying from £20 to £120.

Single-company PEP fees are somewhat lower. Some managers do not charge an initial fee, and many fees are in the 0.75-1% range. Annual management fees vary from 0.5%-1.5%.

8   Employee Share Option Schemes (ESOPs)

This is a scheme whereby employees can save a fixed sum up to a maximum of £250 per month over five years, making a total of 60 payments in all. At the end of the five-year period a bonus equivalent to 15 monthly payments is added; if the money is left a further two years the bonus paid equals 30 monthly payments. The bonus is free of all taxes, and the minimum and maximum payments are £10 and £250 per month respectively.

When the employee joins the scheme he is given the option of buying a fixed number of shares at a preset price at the end of the five- or seven-year period.

The price of the shares is effectively fixed at the outset, as is the number of shares that can be purchased. The maximum discount at which the shares can be offered on the day the ESOP option is granted must not be 'manifestly less' than 20% of the market value. The investor can either take his return as cash or use it to buy the number of shares specified. If the shares have risen in value the investor can immediately resell the shares at the current market price. If the investor chooses to do this the profit is free of income tax but subject to capital gains tax. If the shares are held there may be a liability to capital gains tax when they are eventually sold. If the investor chooses to take the cash option it is free of income tax and capital gains tax.

The scheme is a method of either benefiting from a long-term rise in the shares of the employing company or simply achieving a good tax-free return if the shares are not worth buying.

The scheme can be set up only if the employer agrees, and it must then be approved by the Inland Revenue. Minimum conditions of eligibility state that the employees must have been employed by the company for over five years and work full-time. However, companies can alter these rules to include part-time workers and those who have just joined the company.

9   Tax Exempt Special Savings Accounts (TESSAs)

TESSAs were savings schemes whereby a maximum of £9,000 could be invested over a period of five years, the interest being paid free of tax provided it is not withdrawn from the account. The interest does not have to be shown on a tax return provided, again, it is retained in full in the TESSA for five years.

Rate of return

The interest rate paid on a TESSA is not fixed (although providers can offer a fixed rate), but subject to market fluctuations. The rate is set by the bank, building society or other institution authorized under the Banking Act 1987 running the TESSA, so rates vary according to the provider.

A TESSA is suitable for retention by high-rate taxpayers who can afford to tie up the money for five years. However, interest rates vary between providers, so the investor should shop around for the best terms.

10   ISAs (Individual Savings Accounts)

ISAs are tax-free savings accounts that have replaced PEPs and TESSAs. They have been available since 6 April 1999. The maximum amount that can be invested in an ISA per annum is £7,000 for the tax year 1999/2000 and £5,000 per annum after that date. The investments held in an ISA are cash, stocks and shares, unit and investment trusts, life insurance and national savings. Basically ISAs are divided into three investment categories, cash, insurance and stockmarket.

ISAs are free of income tax and CGT. Where shares are held in an ISA, the tax credit will be paid back into the ISA account for the 5-year period ending 5 April 2004. This 'repayment' of the tax credit applies only to shares held in an ISA.

Investments held in an ISA must be listed on a recognized stock exchange, and the investments can consist of gilts, company loan stocks, unit trusts, investment trusts and OEICs. Overseas investments are allowed if they comply with these rules.

Shares from profit-sharing schemes or employee share option schemes can be transferred into an ISA within 90 days of issue, provided the total amount held in the ISA does not exceed the annual limit of £7,000 (1999/2000) and £5,000 thereafter. Shares purchased via a new issue or a demutualization CANNOT be transferred into an ISA.

CAT marks have been introduced by the Government for ISAs. This is NOT a guarantee of performance, but indicates that the ISA complies with stipulated conditions in relation to charges, access and terms. Even with CAT-marked ISAs, the tax savings may not be sufficient to cover the charges for non- and basic-rate taxpayers.

The CAT (Charges, Access and Terms) covers:

	Charges	**Access**	**Terms**
Cash ISA	No charges of any kind.	Minimum deposit/ withdrawal no greater than £10, withdrawals within 7 working days or less.	Interest rate no lower than 2% base rate, must follow base rate increase within one month.
Insurance ISA	Annual charge no more than 3%, no other charges.	Minimum premium no greater than £250 a year or £25 per month.	Surrender value must reflect the value of the underlying assets and be at least equal to premiums paid after 3 years.

(Continued)	Charges	Access	Terms
Stockmarket ISA	Annual charge no more than 1% of net asset value, no other charges.	Minimum saving no more than £500 a year, or £50 p.a. month.	Can invest in shares, authorized unit trusts, OEICs or certain investment trusts (not split-capital), units and shares must be single-priced at mid-market price.
Any ISA Provider	Decent straight-forward treatment of customers, use of plain English, no requirement to buy other linked product, no limitation of ISA investments to existing customers, undertaking to keep to the CAT standards after the investment is started.		

A basic-rate taxpayer must look at the situation regarding tax benefits and charges and compare these to the performance of the fund in order to decide whether an ISA is an appropriate investment vehicle.

ISAs come in two forms – mini and maxi.

MINI ISA – limits

	1999/2000	2000/01
Cash ISA	£3,000	£1,000
Insurance ISA	£1,000	£1,000
Stockmarket ISA	£3,000	£3,000

A mini ISA allows the investor to choose the best fund manager, bank or building society or insurance company for each element of the fund. The only restriction is that of the monetary limits per type of ISA are observed.

MAXI ISA – limits

	1999/2000	2000/01
Cash ISA	£3,000	£1,000
Insurance ISA	£1,000	£1,000
Stockmarket ISA	£7,000	£5,000

A maxi ISA has all the investments purchased from the same management company. All classes of investments are available via a Maxi ISA. There is some restriction on how the money is invested in a maxi ISA, e.g. all the £7,000 (£5,000 – 2000/01) can go into a stock market ISA.

It is important to note that an investor CANNOT have both a mini and a maxi ISA in the same tax year, the choice of ISA will depend on the investor's needs. For example, if stock market investment is the sole choice, then a maxi ISA should be used because the limit is higher.

Although the proceeds of existing PEPs can be transferred into ISAs there is little obvious benefit for so doing because switching costs would be incurred that would reduce the value of the investment. PEPs do not have a set life span. The investor cannot put any more money into the PEP, but can still change the investments within the PEP according to the PEP rules.

TESSA proceeds can be transferred into a TESSA ISA – a special account where the monetary limit of the transfer is £9,000. Because a TESSA has a life span of 5 years, this method enables the tax-free element of the savings to be maintained.

11 Summary of Savings and Investments

This section covers all the details of the various investments that are available, as detailed throughout the book, including this unit. In Units 16 and 17 we cover the construction and review of portfolios.

Investments that are totally free of income tax and capital gains tax in the hands of the investor

- All issues of NSCs
- PEPs
- TESSAs
- ISAs
- National Savings Children's Bonus Bonds
- Premium Bonds

- ESOPs
- Proceeds of qualifying life policies
- Friendly society bonds

  Note: The NSB Ordinary Account does not come under this heading because the interest must be declared to the Inland Revenue, even though the first £70 of interest is tax free.

Investments that provide instant access or access with up to one month's notice

- **Bank current accounts**
- Bank high interest cheque accounts
- Bank money market deposits at call
- **Building society instant access accounts**
- **Building society money market deposits at call**
- Premium Bonds
- National Savings Certificates
- National Savings Children's Bonus Bonds
- **TESSAs, provided only net interest is withdrawn**
- ISAs.

Investments where repayment is made in one month to one year without penalty

- Bank notice account
- Bank money market deposit for a fixed-term up to one year maximum
- **Building society 90-day account**
- Building society money market deposit for a fixed term
- National Savings Bank Investment Account
- **Short-dated gilts with one year or less to maturity provided they are held to maturity**

Investments that mature between one and 10 years

- Bank term deposits (at the end of the term)
- Employee share option scheme (five to seven years)
- Guaranteed income bond (two to 10 years)

- Guaranteed growth bond (two to 10 years)

- Local authority fixed-term loan (at the end of the term)

- Yearlings (one to two years)

- National Savings Income Bonds (one year for full interest to be paid, can be left in for 10 years)

- National Savings Capital Bonds (one year for full interest to be paid, can be left in for 10 years)

- Personal equity plan

- Short- and medium-dated gilts (one to 10 years to maturity)

- Dated company loan stocks with one to 10 years to maturity, provided they are held to maturity

- TESSAs

Long-term investments (over five years)

Return guaranteed at the outset

- Medium- or long-dated gilts held to maturity

- Dated company loan stock held to maturity

- Annuities and mortgage annuities

- Employee share option schemes (five to seven years life)

- National Savings Children's Bonus Bonds

Return variable depending on performance of stock market and/or managers

- With-profits endowment life assurance policy

- Unit-linked life policies

- Friendly society bonds

- Pension plans

- Single-premium bonds

- Unit trusts

- Investment trusts

- Equities

- PEPs

- ISAs invested in equities

High-risk investments

● Direct investment in overseas equities

○ Options

○ Traded options

● Warrants

● 'Penny' shares

● Chattels

○ AIM shares

○ 'Stagging' new issues

Monthly savings schemes

● Life assurance policies

● Pension plans

● Friendly society bonds

○ Unit trust savings schemes

○ Investment trust savings schemes

○ Employee share option schemes (ESOPs)

● PEPs

○ ISAs

Monthly income schemes

○ Building society term account (including 90-day accounts)

○ Annuities

○ Mortgage annuities

○ National Savings Income Bond

● Unit trust withdrawal plan

○ Unit trust monthly income schemes

○ Pensioners' Guaranteed Income Bond

Summary

Now that you have studied this unit, you should be able to:

- explain the interest rates available on bank and building society accounts;
- describe the features of the NSB accounts and the tax treatment of NSB account interest;
- describe the features of the 53rd Issue NSCs;
- describe the features of the 16th Issue Index-Linked NSCs;
- explain what is meant by 'general extension rate';
- explain what is meant by 'reinvestment certificates';
- describe the features of National Savings Income Bonds;
- describe the features of the Pensioners Guaranteed Income Bond;
- describe the features of National Savings Capital Bonds;
- describe the features of Premium Bonds;
- describe the features of National Savings Children's Bonus Bonds;
- describe the features of ESOPs;
- describe the features of PEPs;
- describe the features of TESSAs;
- describe the features of ISAs;
- identify the investments that are totally exempt from income and capital gains tax in the hands of the investor;
- identify the investments that provide instant to one-month's access to capital;
- identify the investments that have a withdrawal period of one month to one year;
- identify the investments that mature between one and 10 years;
- identify longer-term (five years plus) investments;
- identify investments that provide a monthly savings scheme.

16

PORTFOLIO PLANNING

Objectives

After studying this unit, you should be able to:

● list the information required from an investor in order to give advice on portfolio planning;

● understand the significance of diversification, risk and timing;

● understand how a portfolio should be constructed;

● understand the basis on which investments are selected.

1 Information Required from an Investor

Before it is possible to advise a customer as to suitable investments, the adviser must elicit information that will aid the correct choice of investments. The portfolio of investments recommended to a customer will be based upon accurate use of all the information provided by the customer.

In an examination question the sum available will be given, but there may be little or no information regarding the customer. Before repeating parrot fashion a whole list of questions, you must read the information given and then ask only the questions that are pertinent to the customer. For instance, if the question states that the customer has two children aged 11 and 13, then you do not ask whether the customer has any children! Think carefully about what is relevant to the situation.

In the examination, all portfolio planning questions should be answered from the viewpoint of an independent adviser not a tied agent.

The questions to be asked

An investor is an individual and thus has specific ideas about what he does or does not want or require. Having said that, there are general guidelines by which a portfolio is constructed.

Before starting to invest money certain information must be elicited from the investor to aid portfolio planning.

● What is the customer's marginal rate of tax? (If the question already gives his salary then the question must not be asked and you would instead calculate his marginal tax rate from his salary and any other income, and state the rate in your answer.)

- Marital status. Is he willing to transfer freely any assets into his wife's name for her beneficial use, if this would be advantageous for tax purposes?

- Age of the customer (this will give an indication of the customer's time horizon; obviously a 90-year-old has a somewhat shorter time horizon than a 30-year-old). Usually young married people require income from their investments, as do retired people. Middle-aged investors whose children are no longer dependent on them often require capital growth to build up capital prior to retirement.

- Is the customer employed? If so, is his job secure?

- Does he have an adequate pension scheme? If not, could he make AVCs or is he eligible to take out his company's scheme or freestanding AVCs, or is he eligible to take out a personal pension plan?

- Does he have adequate life insurance, and if married or living with his partner, is his wife's or partner's life also insured?

- Age of any dependent children. Any other dependants, e.g. aged parents, that he supports? The age of children may identify specific dates, e.g. eighteenth birthday, when a capital sum may be required.

- Does he have any other income apart from his salary?

- Does he have any other investments?

- Does he own his own home? If so, is there a mortgage? What is the amount outstanding, the type of mortgage, and is there life cover on the mortgage to repay it in case of early death?

- Does he have any other outstanding debts that it may be better to repay first? This is especially important if he has loans at a high rate of interest.

- Does he wish to make any provision for his dependants?

- Are there any major purchases he wishes to make, e.g. a car or a world cruise? (This is important because the sum available will have to be adjusted when constructing a portfolio.)

- Is he a non-resident? (If so, he is not liable to any UK taxes.)

- Is he averse to risk? If he is, it will not be possible to construct the best possible portfolio because some otherwise suitable investments will have to be omitted to minimize risk.

- Are there any areas of investment he wishes to avoid, e.g. is he an ethical investor who may wish to avoid companies involved in chemical manufacture, or tobacco companies? Are there any shares he wishes to buy purely because of the concessions that are attached to them?

- Does he require income, capital growth or a mixture of these from his investment?

- Does he have any specific known future commitment to provide for, e.g. a child going to university, a wedding or his retirement? If so, suitable investments can be chosen to mature at this time.

2   Diversification, Risk and Timing

Any investor needs to understand the importance of having a balanced portfolio to guard against failure in a specific area. A portfolio should be well diversified, having the elements of liquidity, fixed-interest holdings and equity content. The three areas provide accessibility, a guaranteed income and monetary capital growth from the fixed-interest element, and scope for growth of both income and capital from the equity content. Spreading the money in this way provides protection against one holding failing. It also gives instant access to enable urgent bills or other unexpected items to be paid for without having to sell any of the investments.

Timing is a vital point to bear in mind when investing, because success or failure with timing will have drastic consequences. If an investor is forced to sell some of his holdings to meet unexpected bills, then the timing of the sales is totally wrong. Sales should be made when the investment is showing a good profit.

Obviously it is not always possible to buy just as the market is taking off and to sell just before the market begins to fall, but it should be possible to avoid buying when the market is very high and to avoid selling when the market is very low. Timing of the sum to be invested in a portfolio is vital. The whole sum should not be invested in one fell swoop just because it is available. The investor should wait for the right opportunities to present themselves. While he is waiting the money should be placed where it will gain the most interest yet remain easily accessible. A money market deposit or bank or building society high-interest account should be used. The choice is a simple one: the money is invested in whichever gives the best return after tax to the investor.

Risk relates to interest-rate risk, which is seen in the cash and fixed-interest elements of the portfolio. If interest rates fall the cash element will yield a lower income. The fixed-interest element is affected because prices rise and fall inversely to interest-rate movements. Once a fixed-interest stock has been purchased it is not possible to benefit from higher interest rates in the future. However, conversely, the investor is protected if future interest rates fall. Inflation erodes the purchasing power of capital and interest when the capital is invested in cash or fixed-interest stocks.

To minimize the interest rate and inflation risks, investment in shares is utilized. However, there is risk involved in investing in shares. The company may cut its dividend, or go into liquidation. To minimize the risk involved in investing in shares adequate diversification is needed. Research and the conclusions from the efficient market hypothesis and random walk hypothesis show that investing in 15 shares in different sectors minimizes the risk of one share performing badly and having a drastic effect on the portfolio. For cost effectiveness £2,000 per share is recommended, otherwise the share price has to move a long way simply to recoup dealing costs.

Remember that the diversification shown above should eliminate the unsystematic risk but it will not avoid the systematic risks such as a stock market crash.

3 Portfolio Construction

A general guide to the construction of a portfolio is easily learned, but it is important that the customer's own views are always taken into account. With very large sums there will be a larger number of investments available that will fit into the customer's requirements.

The tax position of the customer will also indicate various investments that are suitable, e.g. a high taxpayer will find the return on National Savings certificates attractive, while a non-taxpayer could obtain far better returns elsewhere.

It is also important to realize that anyone who has inherited or otherwise received a large sum of money may well end up paying income tax at a higher marginal rate than previously. Thus it is vital that the gross income generated by the portfolio be calculated and added to the investor's other income to ascertain his tax position.

For example, if a single person earns £18,000 per annum gross he will be a basic-rate tax payer. If he then inherited a sum £350,000 which when invested gave a gross yield of 5% he would have a total gross income of £18,000 + £17,500 = £35,500. When the basic personal allowance is deducted from this it leaves a gross income for tax purposes of £31,165. This will make his marginal rate of tax 40% (over £29,500). Obviously this will affect the type of investment that can be chosen to give the most benefit to the customer. If £20,000 were invested in a high-coupon gilt it could yield £1,400 per annum at 7% gross interest yield. After tax this would be worth only £840. If instead a low-coupon or index-linked gilt were used the income could be around £600 per annum gross, £360 after tax. However, there would be a good yield to redemption on a low coupon or an inflation-proofed guaranteed capital sum on an index-linked gilt stock because all capital gains on gilts are free of capital gains tax. This could make the low-coupon or index-linked stock more attractive for this taxpayer. However, the investor should compare the net redemption yield of the gilts to find the best return, which may not always be given by a low-coupon gilt even for a 40% taxpayer.

A portfolio for an investor with less than £50,000-£60,000 should be constructed along these lines:

- 10% liquid funds
- 30-45% fixed-interest stocks
- 45-60% equity based.

If the portfolio is large, say £75,000 plus, then the breakdown between fixed interest and equity will not be up to an equal split as for a smaller portfolio. It is quite likely that someone with £75,000 or more to invest is, or may become, a 40%, taxpayer. In such a case tax-exempt investments should be considered. These would include NSCs and ISAs.

The NSCs and ISAs would take part of the fixed-interest funds, with a maximum invested in gilts of £25,000-£30,000. If the portfolio is large enough, and professional management either provided via discretionary management (see Unit 18) or the investor manages the portfolio himself, then direct equity investment is suitable. An ISA should be used for three or four of the equities for tax efficiency.

If the customer is a high-rate taxpayer the most suitable tax-free investments should also be included. Although these investments do not give an income, the returns are very attractive to the high-rate taxpayers. In addition, the high taxpayer with a large portfolio will require a property element and an overseas element of investment. We shall shortly examine how this is achieved.

The liquid reserve

A liquid reserve of up to 10% of the value of the portfolio should be provided. It should be easily accessible and carry the best after-tax rate of interest from the available investments. It is essential to have liquid funds to enable unexpected bills to be paid, 'spur of the moment' purchases to be made, and any new investment opportunities that may arise to be taken advantage of, e.g. a rights issue. If there were no liquid reserve then the investor would have to sell some of his holdings to meet any unexpected needs, and this is not a good timing policy.

Taxpayers, irrespective of whether their marginal rates are nil, 10%, 23% or 40%, should use a bank or building society high-interest access account for their liquid funds. The rate of around 4.5% net of basic tax is the rate obtainable on readily available deposits. (The NSB Investment Account is worth only 3.04% net of basic tax. This account also requires one month's notice of withdrawal, which defeats the object of instant access.)

The fixed-interest element

There are several investments that fit the bill as fixed-interest investments. Depending on whether the taxpayer wishes to receive a high income, capital growth or a mixture of both, a suitable stock can be found.

Gilts

These are 100% secure in money terms; the only risk run is that of inflation eroding the purchasing power of the interest and capital. Even this can be avoided by investing in index-linked gilts, whose only drawback is that the low coupon makes such stocks suitable only for high taxpayers.

Local authority loans and stocks

These do not all carry the advantage of capital gain, although the returns are quite high. They are not as secure as gilts and the private investor would be advised to choose gilts. Some local authority loans are not marketable, and while the return is quite high, the money is locked up for the period involved.

Debentures and loan stocks

These are issued by companies and their security depends on the class of stock and the standing of the company. A debenture has a fixed charge over certain of the company's assets and thus will be paid off from the sale of these assets in the event of liquidation. Loan stocks are usually unsecured and rank with the other creditors regarding repayment in the event of liquidation. Although company debentures and loan stocks are saleable, there is a wide spread between the bid and offer prices, indicating the far lower level of marketability when compared to gilts that have a very narrow bid/offer spread.

For the private investor, gilts are the best option. There is a whole range of coupons and interest payments and the investor's needs can be satisfied by an appropriate gilt. If the investor is a non-taxpayer he should request the interest to be paid gross.

As the highest marginal rate of income tax is now 40%, low-coupon gilts are not necessarily the most attractive option for a 40% taxpayer. To find the best stock he should compare the net redemption yield of various stocks to find the best return.

To emphasize this point let us look at four stocks quoted in 2000 as follows:

Calculate the net redemption yields for a 40% taxpayer on the following stocks. Recap to Unit 7 if necessary.

Gross yields

			Price	Int	Redemption
7¼%	Treasury	2007	107.77	6.73	6.00
13¾%	Treasury	2000-03	104.15	13.20	6.01
3½%	Funding	1999-04	89.93	3.89	6.08
12%	Exchequer	2013-17	160.80	7.46	5.64

The net redemption yields for a 40% taxpayer are:

7¼%	Treasury	2007	–	3.31%
13¾%	Treasury	2000-03	–	0.73%
3½%	Funding	1999-04	–	4.52%
12%	Exchequer	2013-17	–	2.66%

From these calculations it can clearly be seen that neither low- nor high-coupon gilts will automatically be the most suitable for a high-rate taxpayer. In fact in this case a low-coupon gilt provided the best return and a medium-coupon gilt the second best return.

However, index-linked gilts will almost certainly be suitable for long-term investment for high-rate taxpayers, so a large portfolio would probably contain a mixture of gilts, including index-linked ones. This is especially the case at present because there are only two dated low coupon gilts now quoted, whereas the number of index-linked gilts is around 14.

Equity content

A portfolio should include some equities to provide growth of income and capital. A portfolio needs careful management and this applies especially to the equity content. To have a well-diversified direct equity holding there should be at least 15 shares, each in a different sector of the market. This will ensure adequate diversification of the unsystematic risk, although monitoring would be essential. It is not cost effective to invest less than £2,000 in one share because the dealing costs will take too long to recoup. Before a share can show a real profit the price rise has to cover the costs of both purchasing and selling, thus the larger the percentage of the dealing costs, the larger the rise in price of the share must be to cover them.

The other problem facing the private investor is whether or not he has the time and expertise necessary to manage his portfolio. In the vast majority of cases this very essential area will be outside the expertise of the investor.

However, a portfolio does need an equity content but one that is professionally managed. The alternatives to direct equity investment are unit trusts, investment trusts and single-premium bonds.

Unit trusts

There are a whole range of unit trusts available that will provide exactly what the investor requires. Higher-rate taxpayers will generally prefer capital-growth oriented unit trusts. The income is low, but is taxed at the investor's marginal rate of tax. The capital gains are subject to CGT at his marginal rate of income tax on gains over £7,100 p.a. The majority of investors are unlikely to realize enough gains, when the indexation allowance is applied, to have to pay any CGT.

For a taxpayer who wishes to strike a middle way between income and capital growth, a general trust is more appropriate. This will provide growth of both capital and income in the long term.

For an investor who requires emphasis on income, then income unit trusts are suitable. They will not only give a good level of income, but also over the long term, the level of income should grow to provide a hedge against inflation. If the investor is a non-taxpayer, the tax deducted from the dividends at source can be reclaimed from the Inland Revenue.

Investment trusts

These are quoted companies that have an underlying portfolio of stocks and shares. As with unit trusts there is a range of investment trusts available to meet the investor's needs, although there are far fewer to choose from than with unit trusts.

Dealing costs on investment trusts are competitive with unit trust dealing costs as incorporated in the bid offer spread, and the performance of investment trusts has been very good. Thus a mix of unit and investment trusts is advised for indirect equity investment.

Having said that, investment trust shares are very attractive for certain types of investor. A higher-rate taxpayer requiring capital growth would be well advised to consider including in his portfolio a capital share in a split-level investment trust. These shares do not normally provide any income at all during their life. When the trust is dissolved at the predetermined date, the income shareholders are paid back at the preset rate and the remaining gains are divided between the capital shareholders. The gains are subject to capital gains tax in the hands of the shareholders, but the indexation allowance will reduce the taxable gain. Where CGT is payable, the rate is at his marginal rate of income tax on taxable gains over £7,100 p.a.

The income shares of these trusts can be attractive to investors who require a high and growing level of income, because all, or nearly all, of the income generated by the trust is paid to the income shareholders. The disadvantage, however, is that on redemption the amount income shareholders receive will probably be less than the price they paid for the shares. The share price of the income shares is relatively high in the early years, but as maturity approaches the price will tend to gravitate down towards the preset redemption figure. This loss should be allocated on an annual basis and deducted from the expected gross dividend yield. If the resultant figure is much higher compared with the yields on an income-oriented unit trust it is worthwhile considering including in the portfolio an income share of a split-level investment trust.

Even though unit and investment trusts hold a wide portfolio of stocks and shares, a particular trust may not perform well one year, thus affecting the return for the investor. In the same way as the investor should not hold only one share, he should not invest in only one unit or investment trust. To provide adequate diversification the investor should use three or four unit and investment trusts under different managers. Each trust will, of course, have the same aims as the investor. There are tables of unit and investment trust median fund performances that can be compared with the records of the managers of any trust being considered. (Full guidance on the choice of unit trusts was given in Unit 12 and on investment trusts in Unit 13.)

Single-premium bonds

These bonds come in various forms, but the most appropriate two for inclusion in a portfolio are managed bonds and property bonds. Both will provide the property element of the portfolio. However, single-premium bonds are really more attractive to a higher-rate taxpayer who wishes to defer his income tax liability until a time when his marginal rate of tax has fallen, e.g. on retirement. The 5% p.a. cumulative withdrawal facility gives quite a reasonable return to 40% taxpayers because the withdrawal is tax free at the time it is made.

Overseas content

It is very advantageous to have an overseas content in a portfolio. It gives exposure to different markets, each of which may well be at a different stage of growth. It also gives exposure to industries that simply do not exist in the UK, e.g. the diamond industry. The many problems inherent in investing directly overseas would preclude direct investment. However, indirect investment by way of a unit or investment trust that specializes in overseas stocks will ensure that these problems are taken care of by experts. The unit or investment trusts investing overseas can be chosen for income, capital growth or general emphasis. So when including unit or investment trusts in a portfolio aimed at growth, one of the three or four trusts chosen should have an overseas content.

If a portfolio is large enough to include 15 directly held shares it will still benefit from overseas exposure, which should be obtained by including a unit or investment trust investing overseas. Even experienced, professional portfolio managers who operate portfolio management services for their clients advise unit or investment trusts for the overseas content of the portfolio.

Tax-exempt investments

These are investments whose proceeds do not have to be declared on an income tax return. They are particularly attractive to higher-rate taxpayers who will find that the returns may exceed anything they could find on other fixed-interest investments.

The tax-exempt investments have been covered in full in Unit 15 but are recalled here.

List the investments that are exempt from income and capital gains tax and compare your answer to the following text:

- 53rd Issue Fixed Interest NSCs
- 16th Issue Index-Linked NSCs
- Premium Savings Bonds
- Individual savings account (ISAs)
- ISAs
- Children's Bonus Bonds.

Note: the NSB Ordinary Account is not tax exempt; the first £70 of interest is tax free but it must be declared on an income tax return.

Higher risk investments suitable for large portfolios

If there is a large sum available for investment it is worthwhile considering some slightly higher-risk investments, because the returns can be very good. In this area the investor will generally be a higher-rate taxpayer, thus these investments are aimed more at capital growth or deferral of income tax liability until the investor's marginal rate of tax should fall. It would be advisable not to commit more than £5,000 to £10,000 (depending on the size of the portfolio) to any one higher-risk investment area, and this sum should be split between two or three companies in that area to give a further degree of diversification.

Two of the higher-risk investments have already been mentioned in this unit, split-level investment trust capital shares and single-premium bonds, both of which are really suitable only for the larger portfolio because they generate no income. Few small investors can afford to forego income entirely.

The higher-risk investments to consider are:

● Capital shares in a split-level investment trust;

● Single-premium bonds, particularly managed or property bonds;

● Unit trust funds investing directly in property;

● Unit trusts investing in the emerging markets, covering a number of countries;

● Unauthorized unit trusts;

● Shares listed on AIM.

Very high-risk investments

Some investors express a wish to use some of their capital for 'fun money', i.e. they want to invest in areas that may show phenomenal growth but that could also flop. Any investor who wishes to do this must realize that he could well lose all his money. Provided he is aware of this and already has a balanced portfolio, then the areas that are open to him are:

● 'Stagging' new issues;

● 'Shell' situations;

● Penny shares; takeover situations;

● Options;

● Traded options;

● Warrants;

● Chattels (unless for personal pleasure);

● Emerging market unit trusts investing in one country only.

The investor should be advised not to invest all his 'risk money' into one specific area. Diversification can help to offset losses, and he would be well advised to choose two or three of the above options to achieve the aim of minimization of losses.

4   The Selection of Investments

This is best covered by using specimen questions with full answers.

For continuity, the following returns are assumed in all questions dealing with portfolio planning.

Bank/building society high-interest	
instant access account	4.5% net basic tax
Gilts high coupon, say	7% gross
low coupon, say	4% gross
index-linked, say	3% gross
Equity or equity-based investment	
income, say	3% gross
capital growth, say	2% gross
overseas, say	1% gross

Note: the rates ruling at the time of the examination must be used, not the above rates.

Specimen question 1

Note: the marks shown are for guidance purposes. In the examination the maximum mark on a question is 20.

You are consulted by three customers (briefly described below) about their investment problems. In each case detail the types of investment that would be appropriate and construct a suitable investment scheme based on a selection of the types of investment discussed. Give reasons for the selection made.

All three customers have suitable houses with outstanding mortgages and none of them intends to alter these arrangements.

(a)   Customer A is a married man aged 45, with four children aged 5, 8, 10 and 14. His salary is £12,500 per annum and he has £40,000 to invest. He pays 5% of his salary into a SERPS pension. He requires maximum income to supplement his earnings. His wife does not work but has income from inherited investments of £5,000 p.a. gross.

(b)   Customer B is a married man aged 45. His salary is £15,000 per annum. His wife earns £3,500 a year. They have no children. He has £40,000 to invest and requires a capital appreciation over a 20-year period. He is paying 6% of his salary into his contracted-out pension scheme.

(c)   Customer C is a single man aged 45. His salary is £18,000 per annum. He has a non-contributory pension scheme, which is contracted out of SERPS. He plans to save £150 per month for 20 years in order to build up a capital sum for his retirement. He does not have any dependants.

Suggested answer

(a) Customer A has a gross salary of £12,500, thus he will be a basic-rate taxpayer. Even with gross interest from the portfolio of, say, 6%, he will still be a basic-rate taxpayer. Mrs A will be a 20% taxpayer after the basic personal allowance is deducted from her investment income.

Mr A tax and National Insurance

	£	£
Gross income		12,500
Less: basic personal allowance	4,335	
pension contributions	625	4,960
Taxable income		£7,540
Tax payable:		
£1,500 at 10%	150.00	
£6,040 at 23%	1,389.20	
	1,539.20	
Less: married couple's allowance		
£1,970 at 10%	197.00	
Tax payable	£1,342.20	
National Insurance:		
£3,432 at 2%,	68.64	
£9,068 at 10%	906.80	
£12,500	£975.44	

Thus he pays £1,342.20 income tax and £975.44 National Insurance.

Mrs A tax payable

	£
Gross income	5,000
Less basic personal allowance	4,335
Taxable income	£665
Tax payable = £665 @ 10% =	£66.50

There is no liability to National Insurance for Mrs A, because all of her income is unearned. She is a 10% taxpayer.

First, Mr A must have a liquid reserve to meet any unexpected bills. This must be easily accessible and give the best possible return on the sum invested. 10% of the portfolio, £4,000, should be invested in a bank or building society high-interest account paying 4.5% net of basic tax. The remaining sums should be split between fixed interest and equities. The fixed-interest stock should be gilts, and he should purchase gilts to give the best net redemption yield. The gilts should have different maturity dates to coincide with his children's eighteenth birthdays, when a capital sum could be advantageous to meet any expenses incurred then. If he were to purchase three gilts to mature in 4, 8, 10 and 13 years he could choose gilts that gave a flow of interest payments at two-monthly intervals. He will be liable to tax at 20% on the interest. All gains on gilts are free of CGT. It is most likely that high-coupon gilts yielding around 7% gross will give the highest net redemption yield.

The equity content should provide a good income with scope for growth of income and capital. To gain the benefits of diversification he needs 15 shares in different sectors, plus the time and expertise to manage them. With only £18,000 it is certainly not cost effective to invest directly. Instead he should use three or four unit and investment trusts under different managers aimed at income. Even with unit and investment trusts it is unwise to invest in only one trust. If the managers have a poor year the investor's income will suffer, thus a spread of trusts under different managers should iron out any poor performances.

Investment	Amount(£)	% Gross rate	Gross income
Bank/building society	4,000	5.63	225
High-coupon gilts	18,000	7.00	1,260
Unit/investment trusts	18,000	3.00	540
	£40,000		£2,025

$$\text{Gross yield on portfolio} = \frac{2{,}025 \times 100}{40{,}000}$$

$$= 5.06\%$$

Mr A will have an approximate gross income of £2,025 from the portfolio (£1,559 after tax).

Because Mr A requires maximum income to supplement his earnings, the fixed-interest and equity elements each account for 45% of the value of the portfolio.

By setting the portfolio out as above, all your recommendations are put together in a clear manner, and the investor can see the level of income he can expect to receive from his portfolio.

Note: bank/building society interest rate assumed is 4.5% net of 20% savings rate of tax

$$5.63\% \text{ gross} \qquad \frac{4.5 \times 100}{80}$$

(b) Mr B, with his salary of £15,000 gross, will be a basic-rate taxpayer. Mrs B, with an income of £3,500 gross will be a non-taxpayer.

Mr B tax and National Insurance

	£	£
Gross income		15,000
Less: basic personal allowance	4,335	
pension contribution	900	5,235
Taxable income		£9,765
Tax payable:		
£1,500 at 20%	150.00	
£8,265 at 23%	1,900.95	
	2,050.95	
Less: married couple's allowance		
£1,970 at 10%	197.00	
Tax payable	£1,853.95	
National Insurance:		
£3,432 at 2%	68.64	
£11,568 at 8.4%	971.71	
	£1,040.35	

He pays £1,853.95 income tax and £1,040.35 National Insurance.

Mrs B tax payable

	£
Gross income	3,500
Less basic personal allowance	4,335
Taxable income	Nil

She has no liability to income tax, and no liability to National Insurance because her gross income is below the threshold in each case.

Again, as in (a), the income generated from the £40,000 will not take Mr B into the next tax band.

Mr B will require a liquid reserve invested as in (a) of £4,000. For the capital appreciation he should consider gilts, but before suggesting a low-coupon gilt, the net redemption yields of low- and high-coupon gilts maturing in 20 years' time should be compared. He should also consider index-linked gilts if he expects inflation in the future to rise. (The portfolio assumes that a high-coupon gilt is more attractive.)

If the most suitable stock is indeed a high-coupon gilt, yet the investor requires capital growth, he can easily provide this by accumulating the interest received. When he has accumulated sufficient in an interest-bearing account to make it cost effective to purchase another investment, he should buy either another gilt or another unit or investment trust holding. He will need around £1,000 to be cost effective, and as the interest at, say, 7% gross on £12,000 of gilts will give him an income of £768 per annum after lower-rate tax, he could invest each year in one of the alternatives while keeping his portfolio balanced. For a basic-rate taxpayer, index-linked gilts are not overly attractive unless future rates of inflation are viewed to be rising. For capital growth purposes, 30% of the portfolio should be in fixed interest.

For the equity content, three or four unit and investment trusts aimed at capital growth, with one investing overseas, is a more suitable option than direct equity investment. This gives professional management and a wide diversification of holdings in the unit and investment trusts. For growth purposes 60% of the portfolio should be in equity investment.

The tax-free investments of NSCs do not offer an overly attractive return to a basic-rate taxpayer.

For a slightly riskier way of achieving capital growth Mr B could consider a capital share in a split-level investment trust. He will receive no income during the term of the trust, but will share in the gains made after the income shareholders have been repaid at the predetermined rate. Another alternative is a managed bond, which is an insurance company product with the underlying assets invested in property, fixed interest, equities and cash. This provides a property element to the portfolio. The gains on the bond are paid net of basic-rate tax when the bond is surrendered, in accordance with top slicing rules. As capital growth is the main objective, an investment of £2,000 in a managed bond and a split-level investment capital share would be appropriate.

Investment	Amount (£)	% Gross rate	Gross return (£)
Bank/building society	4,000	5.63	225
High-coupon gilt	12,000	7	840
Unit and investment trusts			
growth	16,000	2	320
overseas	4,000	1	40
Capital share investment trust	2,000	Nil	Nil
Managed bond	2,000	Nil	Nil
	£40,000		£1,425

$$\text{Gross yield on portfolio} = \frac{1,425 \times 100}{40,000}$$

$$= 3.56\%$$

As Mrs B is a non-taxpayer, with an income of £3,500 gross, there is an unused part of her basic personal allowance of £4,335 amounting to £835. It would be tax efficient for the couple for Mr B to transfer around £16,000 to his wife for her beneficial use, and for her to invest that £30,000 in the high-coupon gilt and income-oriented unit and investment trusts.

Mrs B's portfolio would yield:

	Amount (£)	% Gross rate	Gross return
High-coupon gilt	8,000	7	560
Unit/investment trusts	8,000	3	240
	£16,000		800

$$\text{Gross yield} \quad \frac{800 \times 100}{16,000} \quad = 5\%$$

Note: she could opt for accumulation units or reinvestment of dividends on the unit and investment trusts. This would boost the value, but have no extra tax consequences.

(c)   Mr C will be a basic-rate taxpayer.

Mr C tax and National insurance

	£
Gross income	18,000
Less basic personal allowance	4,335
	£13,665

Note: the pension is non-contributory, so no payments are shown as deductions against income.

Tax payable:

	£
£1,500 at 20%	150.00
£12,165 at 23%	2,797.95
Tax payable	£2,947.95

National Insurance:

	£
£3,432 at 2%	68.64
£14,568 at 8.4%	1,223.71
	£1,292.35

Note: although the pension is non-contributory, the fact that it is contracted out of SERPS is relevant to the rate of National Insurance paid. He pays £2,947.95 income tax and £1,292.35 National Insurance.

There is no mention of any liquid reserve, thus this must be provided. A reserve of around £2,000 would seem reasonable in view of his salary and stated saving aim of £150 per month. This should be accumulated with a bank or building society. He should build this up in an instant access account paying around 4.5% net basic tax. Once this has been achieved Mr C should look to provide himself with adequate pension cover. He should enquire whether he can pay any more into his company pension scheme. The extra payments are called 'additional voluntary contributions' (AVCs). If the company scheme is not attractive, or he is intending to change jobs, free-standing AVCs would be more suitable.

A friendly society bond is another attractive investment. The maximum sum payable is £25 per month, but as both the friendly society and the proceeds of the policy are not liable for tax the returns are attractive even for a basic-rate taxpayer.

The final recommendation would be a unit and investment trust savings plan. This will carry the advantage of 'pound cost averaging' and the plan can be linked to a capital growth oriented trust. The money should be invested in two or three unit trusts under different managers. He should opt for accumulation units in the unit trusts and reinvestment of dividends in the investment trust to boost his capital further. These savings plans will provide long-term growth of capital and income.

Suggested answer

Build up £2,000 liquid reserve. Once completed, the following breakdown of savings is recommended:

	£ per month
Unit and investment trust savings scheme	100
Pension plan AVCs or FSAVCs	<u>50</u>
	<u>£150</u>

Specimen question 2

You have been consulted by Mr and Mrs Jones (briefly described below) about their investment problems. You are required to set out an investment strategy for each customer.

(a) Mr and Mrs Jones are both aged 60. Mrs Jones receives a retirement pension of £1,751. Mr Jones has just retired and will receive a pension of £8,000 per annum, together with a lump sum of £14,000. In addition he has bank and building society accounts amounting to £11,000. The house is paid for and the children are independent. He estimates that he and his wife will need a net income of approximately £180 per week.

Suggested answer
(a) Mr Jones Tax position

	£	£
Pension		8,000
Less: basic personal allowance		<u>4,335</u>
Taxable income		<u>£3,665</u>
Tax payable £1,500 at 10%	150.00	
£2,165@ 23%	<u>497.95</u>	
	647.95	
Less married couple's		
allowance £1,970 at 10%	<u>197.00</u>	
	<u>£450.95</u>	

After-tax income is £8,000 less £450.95 = £7,549.05

Investment

Note: a pension is not classed as earned income, thus he has no liability to National Insurance. Because Mr. Jones is aged 60 he does NOT receive the higher basic personal or married couple's allowance even though he is retired.

b)   Mrs Jones

Because her pension is less than her basic personal allowance of £4,335 she will be a non-taxpayer.

Total net income for couple	=	£7,549.05 + £1,751
	=	£9,300.05
Annual income required	=	£180 x 52
	=	£9,360
Shortfall	=	£9,360 – £9,300.05
	=	£59.95

The investment of £25,000 will need to yield only £77.86 p.a. gross (£59.95 net basic tax rate), a yield of 0.24% gross. Thus the portfolio should be aimed to give a balance between income and capital growth, which will enable Mr and Mrs Jones to maintain their standard of living. The total sum available is £14,000 plus bank and building society funds of £11,000 = £25,000.

Ten per cent of the sum should be kept as a liquid reserve. A bank or building society high-interest account provides a return of 4.5% net of basic tax, which is the best available return on easy access money. Thus, they have too much invested here and this should be reduced to £2,500. The remainder should be split between gilts and unit and investment trusts to provide both guaranteed income from the gilts, and growth of both income and capital from the unit and investment trusts. Three or four unit and investment trusts under different managers will give good diversification. The gilts should be high-coupon, long-dated to provide the required level of income in the long term. If the income generated is in excess of their needs it should be reinvested in a unit or investment trust savings plan that complements the existing investments. The unit and investment trusts should be aimed at income. This will still give a growing income, with long-term growth of capital. If they do not require all of this income at present they can opt for accumulation units. There is not sufficient available to invest directly in equities on a cost-effective basis because 15 shares in different sectors are required for a well-diversified portfolio, plus the time and expertise to manage them.

Investment	Amount (£)	% Gross rate	Gross return
Bank/building society	2,500	5.63	141
High-coupon gilts	9,000	7	630
Unit and investment trusts	13,500	3	405
	£25,000		£1,176

$$\text{Gross yield on portfolio} = \frac{1,176 \times 100}{25,000} = 4.7\%$$

This is in excess of their needs, but the net redemption yields on high-coupon gilts tend to be more attractive to basic-rate taxpayers than that on low-coupon gilts, and the excess money can be reinvested to gain more capital growth.

It would be advisable to transfer sufficient of the capital to Mrs Jones for her beneficial use to utilize the unused part of her basic personal allowance.

Note: when answering a question that specifies either an amount per week/annum or a percentage return on the investment, it is vital to show the calculations. When a set sum is required first calculate the after-tax income that is already received, then look at the shortfall to decide on investment policy.

Specimen question 3

Your customer Mr C is a married man aged 63. His earned income is £40,000 per annum. He owns his house and he holds the maximum entitlement of the 40th issue (£10,000) of National Savings certificates. He has £30,000 available for investment and is looking for capital growth over the next two years. When he retires in two years' time he will need income from his investments to supplement his pension. Mrs C has no income of her own. Mr C is not willing to transfer assets into his wife's name.

(a) Detail the types of investment that would satisfy Mr C's requirement of capital growth over a two-year period.

(b) Discuss how a change of policy could be implemented after two years to increase income, and mention any difficulties you might expect from such a policy switch.

Suggested answer:

Tax position

	£
Gross income	40,000
Investment income at, say, 4%	1,200
	41,200
Less: basic personal allowance	4,335
Taxable income	£36,865

The married couple's allowance of £1,970 is restricted to 10% and is offset against the tax payable on the above income.

This makes him a 40% taxpayer. Thus it would be tax advantageous to transfer the £30,000 into his wife's name as she is a non-taxpayer. However, he has stated that he is unwilling to do this.

Equities are totally unsuitable for a two-year period. Equity investment should be made only on a long-term basis with a view to selling when the price shows a profit. Equity-based investments, including by definition unit trusts and investment trusts, are unsuitable for a short-term investment, which may have to be realized at an unfavourable time.

(a) Investments that give guaranteed growth over the years:

    (i)   16th Issue Index-Linked National Savings certificates gain full index-linking after one year. On top of the index-linking, interest equal to 1.8% p.a. plus 1.4% of the first Anniversary Value at the end of two years. The maximum holding is £10,000 per person. All returns are tax free;

    (ii) Index-linked gilts due to mature in two years' time will give capital growth that is free of CGT. The capital is index-linked on redemption using the RPI eight months prior to redemption and eight months prior to issue. The coupon is also index-linked;

    (iii) 53rd Issue NSCs can be encashed after two years to give a return of 4% p.a. over two years. The maximum holding is £10,000 per person. All returns are tax free.

Suggested portfolio:

	Investment Amount	% Gross rate	Gross return
40th Issue NSCs (retained)	10,000	Nil	Nil
53rd Issue NSCs	10,000	Nil	Nil
16th Issue Index-Linked NSCs	10,000	Nil	Nil
Index-linked gilts	10,000	3	300
	£40,000	£300	

He will have to pay tax only on £300 at 40%, the rest of the investments being tax free.

(b) None of the above investments will carry any charges on repayment/redemption. However, the main problem with a switch of emphasis from capital growth now to income in two years' time is that interest rates in the future are unknown. If they have fallen over the period Mr C will obtain a lower rate of income than he could have received otherwise. A policy of avoiding income in the short term is rather short-sighted, and it would be preferable to construct a balanced portfolio now that will meet Mr C's long-term requirements.

The portfolio should have 10% invested as a liquid reserve to meet any unexpected bills. The best return is from a bank or building society high interest account paying

4.5% net of lower rate tax.

The returns on the 41st and 53rd Issue NSCs and 16th Issue Index-Linked NSCs are attractive to a 40% taxpayer. However, as he already has one older issue of NSCs, the full holding of all three NSCs would leave the portfolio overweight in this section. He would be advised to retain his existing certificates until maturity and consider then whether reinvestment in either or both of the current issue of NSCs was still attractive, or whether to invest the money elsewhere.

The gilt part of the portfolio should be aimed at high income, thus high-coupon long-dated gilts can be purchased to give a guaranteed return over the long term. The emphasis should be on the best net redemption yield for the investor.

The equity content should be in the form of equity-based investment rather than direct equity investment, which requires 15 shares in different sectors plus the time and expertise to manage them. As he is a high taxpayer at the moment, £5,000 invested in a managed bond would be suitable. If in two years' time the bond shows a profit he can encash it, and provided the annualized profit does not make his gross taxable income exceed 23% it will be tax free. He can also withdraw 5% p.a. cumulative tax free if he wishes.

The remainder of the equity-based content should be invested in three or four unit and investment trusts under different managers aimed at capital growth. When he retires he will be able to switch to income units in the same management group without incurring too much cost. Most unit trusts allow switching between funds on a bid price to bid price basis. There may be a potential capital gains tax liability for the investor but as the annual exemption limit is £7,100 now, and as the taxable gain is reduced by the indexation allowance, it is highly unlikely that he will actually have to pay any CGT.

Investment	Amount	% Gross rate	Gross return
Bank/building society	3,000	5.63	169
40th issue NSCs (retained)	10,000	Nil	Nil
Gilts long dated with best net			
redemption yield	5,000	7	350
Managed bond	5,000	Nil	Nil
Unit and investment trusts	17,000	2	340
	£40,000		£859

$$\text{Gross yield on portfolio} = \frac{859 \times 100}{40,000} = 2.15\%$$

Note: the NSCs and managed bond do not pay out any income, so nothing is shown in the % gross rate and gross return columns. The gross return on the gilts of 7% assumes that this also gives the highest net redemption yield.

Specimen question 4

(a) It often happens that people come into possession of lump sums of capital on retirement either from pension commutations, maturing endowment policies, or from the sale of a business. What are the advantages and disadvantages of this aspect of financial planning from the point of view of the individual concerned?

(b) What key factors should be taken into account when formulating an investment strategy for retired people?

Suggested answer

(a) Advantages

    (i) At retirement many people feel they would like to splash out on a good holiday, refurbish their home, or even move to a more convenient home. A lump sum enables them to do this to their satisfaction.

    (ii) It is tax advantageous to build up a lump sum through pension or life policies because the proceeds are tax free in the hands of the investor.

    (iii) A lump sum in the hands of the investor provides flexibility. It can be invested to meet the needs of that individual. For example, if the income from the pension is sufficient at the present, then the lump sum can be invested to provide capital growth; if extra income is the priority then this can be achieved through a balanced portfolio.

  Disadvantages

    (i) For many people this will be the first time they have had such a large sum in their possession, and they may not invest it properly if they do not obtain expert advice. The temptation for many is just to put the money in a bank or building society account where inflation will erode its purchasing power.

    (ii) It can be difficult to persuade an investor who requires income that his interests would best be met by splitting the money between gilts and equities. Yields of 7% gross on gilts look far more attractive than 3% on equities, yet the effects of inflation must be explained and the fact that the equities should provide a rising income and long-term capital growth that will help combat inflation.

    (iii) At certain times it is difficult to know whether to invest for the long or short term. If interest rates are low it can be difficult if not impossible to meet the target income figure. A decision would have to be made as to whether to stay fairly liquid and hope that the interest rates will rise in the near future so that a suitable portfolio can be constructed then.

(b) Retired people have certain needs that do not always apply to other investors.

    (i) *Security*. The investments made must be secure. Retired people have little chance of rebuilding any lost savings because they no longer have an earning capacity.

(ii) *Income.* This is generally more important than capital growth because they will be living on a reduced level of income, and while they no longer have all the expenses that someone in employment has, they still need a good level of income in order to live comfortably.

(iii) *Protection against inflation.* Although the state pension is inflation-proofed to a large extent, an occupational pension may not be. Also the income generated by the investment must allow for it to rise, thus equity-based investment is important.

(iv) *Liquidity.* There should be an adequate emergency reserve to smooth out any irregularities in income. For example, if the investments pay dividends only twice a year there needs to be a reserve to allow withdrawals between the receipts of the dividends.

(v) *Simplicity.* Although by no means does retirement mean that the investor's mental capacity has been diminished, it is advisable to keep the portfolio straightforward so that the investor is not burdened either by having to run it himself or by paying high fees for someone else to run it. Many retired people have never had any dealings with investments, thus they require an easily understandable portfolio.

(vi) Nowadays many people are retiring at age 50 onwards. Those between 50 and 60 (women) and 65 (men) will not receive a state pension until they reach 60/65. They may, however, be able to supplement their income from employment on a part-time basis, an option that is not readily available to those in receipt of the state pension.

5 Summary of Portfolio Planning for Individuals

Each time an investor requires advice it is necessary to cover the various suitable alternatives, quoting the interest rates paid, tax situation of the investment and approximate gross income generated.

Once the options have been explained a suggested portfolio should be drafted that shows not only the average rates of interest available on gilts and equities but also the gross income generated by the portfolio, and the gross yield of the portfolio. The portfolio also shows how much is invested in each area, which is just as important a guide for the investor. After all, no investor wishes to receive a list of all the options open to him and then have to decide how much to invest in what area! He is coming to the investment advisor for guidance, and in the examination you are the investment advisor.

Why not just leave the money in a bank or building society?

You may have noticed that the gross returns on some of the portfolios drafted in this unit are below the gross return available from a bank or building society. An investor may well ask why he should bother with stocks and shares when he can get a higher return from a bank or building society.

The problems with bank and building society investments are:

○ The interest rate moves in line with the general level of interest rates and if the rate falls then the investor loses out on income;

● The capital value remains static, thus inflation erodes the purchasing power of the capital.

To overcome these problems a portfolio has three elements: liquidity, fixed-interest and equity. The fixed-interest element provides a guaranteed income until maturity, irrespective of changes in interest rates. Equity or equity-based income provides a lower initial income, but over the years the income and capital value will grow. Statistics have shown that equity investment has outstripped building society interest and rises in the RPI in the long term.

Summary

Now that you have studied this unit, you should be able to:

detail the questions you would ask the investor in order to construct a portfolio to suit his needs;

understand the need for diversification;

explain the significance of risk and timing;

understand how a portfolio is constructed;

be able to construct portfolios for monthly savers, non-taxpayers, basic-rate taxpayers, 40% taxpayers and pensioners;

be able to explain why it is unwise to leave money in a bank or building society high interest account.

17

REVIEW OF INVESTMENTS

Objectives

After studying this chapter, you should be able to:

● list and describe the main Stock Exchange indices;

● understand the problems of comparing performance of unquoted and overseas securities;

● understand some techniques by which portfolio performance can be measured;

● review a portfolio.

1   The Stock Exchange Indices

The performance of fully-quoted shares on the UK Stock Market is measured by reference to one of the following main indices:

● FT 30 Share Index

● FTSE 100 Index

● FTSE 250 Index

● FTSE 350 Index

● FTSE Actuaries All Share Indices

● FTSE Actuaries All Share SmallCap

● FTSE Fledgling.

The performance of shares listed on overseas markets is measured by reference to:

● FTSE World Index Series

● FTSE Eurotop 100 Index

● FTSE Eurotop 300 Index

● FTSE European Series

● FTSE techMARK 100

plus an overall comparison of world stock markets can be made from data on 'World Stock Markets' published in the *Financial Times* and *Investor's Chronicle*.

FT 30 Share Index

The index commenced on 1 July 1935 with a base of 100 and was originally totally industrially based. Hence its original full title was the FT Industrial Ordinary Share Index. As some industrial companies have declined and other sectors have risen, the constituents have now changed and now include retailing, and oil and gas companies. The 'Industrial' part of the title was dropped in 1984. There was a time when the industrial bias made this index unrepresentative of the market as a whole and, while this has now changed, the Ordinary Index still has a heavy industrial bias. Because of this bias the index is unsuitable as a method of measuring long-term portfolio performance comparison. Indeed, it was never intended to perform this function.

The index is an unweighted, geometric mean index of the price relatives of the top 30 leading shares, and is calculated by multiplying the price relatives of the 30 shares and taking the thirtieth root. The price relative of a share is the current share price divided by the share's price at a base date. In practice the current prices of the 30 shares are multiplied together, divided by a constant, and then the thirtieth root is taken. These 30 shares represent approximately 25% of the total market capitalization of all quoted shares.

The index is calculated hourly. The 'close' position is based on the position at the end of the day's trading at 5.15 p.m., which is taken from the final prices obtained from the market makers' offices at that time.

The ordinary share index, as published in the *Financial Times*, has the ordinary dividend yield and price earnings ratio calculated on both net and nil basis. The index also has the hourly changes and the high and low figures for the year. The volume figures for SEAQ bargains, equity turnover in £m, equity bargains and shares traded in millions (excluding intra-market and overseas bargains but including CREST turnover) are also published.

The purpose of the FT ordinary share index is to give a guide to short-term market sentiment. It can be very volatile.

One reason for such volatility is due to the method of calculation. The unweighted geometric method means that a change in the price of one share has the same effect as the same change in another share irrespective of the original market capitalization of the two companies. In an extreme case if one share price fell to zero, the whole index would fall to zero. However, this would never occur in practice because the constituents of the index are changed to take into account any decline in one constituent. When this occurs a replacement share is brought in. On the other hand, however, the geometric mean method means that the index will not rise as far, if one share rises, whereas if the arithmetical mean had been used the rise in the index would have been greater.

Although the 30 companies represented are diverse in nature, they are all blue chip shares. Blue chip shares are generally first to respond to changes in market sentiment. Hence the use of this index to measure short-term market mood.

FTSE 100 Index

This is a broader-based index than the 30 Share Index. It was introduced on 3 January 1984 with the value at that date given the index number 1,000. It is a weighted arithmetical mean index consisting of the share prices of 100 of the largest companies measured by market capitalization. This gives a far more balanced spread of companies over the different sectors and thus it is a useful guide to portfolio performance. The constituents of the index are reviewed each quarter.

Since this index is recalculated every minute (real time) it is very sensitive to the mood of the market. The FTSE 100 is nevertheless not as volatile as the 30 Share Index due partly to its broader base of constituents, and partly to the method of calculation. (An index calculated by geometric mean could fall to zero, but would not do so in practice. In addition, the effect of a rise in a single share is mitigated under the geometric mean method.)

This index was introduced for several reasons. First, the Stock Exchange is in competition with overseas stock exchanges for international business. Many large sophisticated overseas investors are used to having information on a minute-by-minute basis, especially in the US markets. The FTSE 100 provides an equivalent service to that given by the US stock markets, thus adding to the attraction of our market to overseas investors, especially to those from the USA. At the time it was introduced, the FTSE 100 was the only index able to give a minute-by-minute recalculation of the relevant figure. In the UK investors have for a long time been able to hedge against price movements in individual shares by the use of options and traded options, but they have never been able to hedge against movements in the market itself. There is now a traded option series available in FTSE 100 that provides this service. Although it may appear that only 100 shares out of a total of over 2,000 quoted shares is not representative of the market as a whole, in fact the 100 shares represent approximately 75% of the total market capitalization of all UK equities. It has been proved how representative the 100 Share Index would have been if it had existed in the period 1978-83. Research showed that the 'Top 100' companies over that time period under-performed the All Share Index by approximately 0.5% per year. As the All Share Index consists of approximately 807 shares, the difference is minute.

Worked example to compare geometric mean and arithmetical mean when the price of a single constituent share rises

Let us take a hypothetical index that consists of four shares, each of which has a current price of 50. Using the geometric mean method, the index would be calculated thus:

$$\sqrt[4]{50 \times 50 \times 50 \times 50} = 50$$

Under the arithmetical mean method, the index would also equal 50:

$$\frac{50 + 50 + 50 + 50}{4} = 50$$

Suppose one share's price rises to 60p, while the others are unchanged.

Under the geometric mean method, the index would be calculated as:

$$\sqrt[4]{50 \times 50 \times 50 \times 60} = \sqrt[4]{7,500,000} = 52.33p$$

Under the arithmetical mean method the result would be:

$$\frac{50 + 50 + 50 + 60}{4} = 52.5p$$

Hence it can be seen that the geometric mean method will understate the effect of rises in individual shares when compared with the arithmetic mean method.

Note that the geometric mean method will always result in a lower index figure than the arithmetic mean method. This applies equally if share prices are falling, except when all the figures are the same.

The FTSE 250 Index

This covers the next 250 companies by market capitalization after the FTSE 100 companies.

These companies have a market capitalization of between £280 million and £1.8 billion. It is calculated on two formats, one that includes investment companies and one that excludes investment companies. The base date of the index is 31 December 1985, and the base value is 1412.60.

The FTSE Actuaries 350 Index

This combines the FTSE 100 and 250 indices. This index is a real-time index and is the basis for the real-time figures on sector performance intended to mirror the all-share sector figures. However, the FTSE 350 higher and lower yield indices are calculated once a day at close of business. The FTSE 350 is calculated in four formats – with and without investment companies, the higher yield and the lower yield. The 'higher yield' comprises stocks with an annual dividend yield above the average yield on the FTSE Actuaries 350 Index, and the 'lower yield' with a below average annual dividend yield on the 350 Index.

The base date at the index is 31 December 1985 and the base value 682.94.

The FTSE SmallCap Index

This index measures the share price performance of around 550 smaller companies. These companies are capitalized at between £40 million and £280 million, and include the smaller 450 companies in the FTSE Actuaries All Share indices. This index, like the 250, is also calculated in two formats, including or excluding investment companies. The index is calculated daily at close of business.

FTSE Fledgling Index

This index includes approximately 800 companies too small to be included in the FTSE Actuaries Share Indices. It is calculated daily including and excluding investment companies. The index accounts for less than 2% of the UK equity market by value, but contains nearly the same number of companies as the FTSE Actuaries All Share Indices.

FTSE Actuaries All Share Indices

This is a weighted arithmetical mean index consisting of the prices of around 807 shares that represent about 98% of the total market capitalization of all UK equities. The index started on 10 April 1962 and the base value is 100. This is a 'real time' index.

The constituent shares are segmented into equity groups and subsections, the breakdown in January 2000 being:

Indices	Number of shares
Resources	15
Basic industrials	71
General Industrials	70
Cyclical consumer goods	15
Non-cyclical consumer goods	76
Cyclical services	232
Non-cyclical services	22
Utilities	17
Information technology	<u>57</u>
Non-financials	575
Financials	<u>232</u>
FT-SE All Share Indices	<u>807</u>

Its main use is as a measure of portfolio performance. Each of the above groups has subsections that have their own index figures. For example, the non-cyclical consumer goods section has its constituent groups as:

● beverages

● food producers and processors

● health

● packaging

○   personal care and household

○   pharmaceuticals

●   tobacco.

Each index has its own index. These are:

○   £ sterling number

●   day's change %

○   euro index

○   £ sterling previous day

○   index 1 year ago

●   actual yield %

○   cover

○   P/E ratio

○   ex-dividend adjustment for the year to date

○   total return.

This enables investors to compare the performance of each share against the sector index and the All Shares indices as a whole.

FTSE World Index Series

This series was introduced in March 1987 with the value given at that date of 100. The base date is 31 December 1986. It is a weighted arithmetic mean index, as are all the other indices except the FT Ordinary Share Index.

The index was introduced to provide a benchmark for measuring the performance of the growing number of overseas funds. It represents at least 70% of the total market capitalization of the world's main stock markets even though there are only 2,219 shares (25 January 2000) in the index.

It consists of national and regional markets with the number of stocks represented in each market shown. There are 29 national markets, which are: Australia, Austria, Belgium, Brazil, Canada, Denmark, Finland, France, Germany, Greece, Hong Kong-China, Indonesia, Ireland, Italy, Japan, Mexico, Netherlands, New Zealand, Norway, Philippines, Portugal, Singapore, South Africa, Spain, Sweden, Switzerland, Thailand, United Kingdom and the USA. There are 15 regional markets covering: Americas, Europe, Eurobloc, Nordic, Pacific Basin, Euro-Pacific, North America, Europe excluding the UK or Eurobloc, or UK and Eurobloc, Pacific excluding Japan, World excluding USA or UK or Eurobloc or Japan.

The number of stocks included (25 January 2000) was 2,219. The three major markets, USA (580), Japan (440) and the UK (189) provide the bulk of the stocks. (All share numbers are approximate because the constituent companies change regularly.) The index also contains a US dollar index, pound sterling index, yen index, euro index, local currency index, gross dividend yield, 52 week high/low figures and value one year previously. The index is calculated nightly in all five currencies.

There are a number of other indices published in the *Financial Times* that can be used to check the performance of shares that may not be in the main indices described above.

Overseas Stock Exchange

The *Financial Times* also publishes information relating to other countries' stock exchanges. For the following countries the information published is: local currency, largest companies, price in local currency, changes on the day high/low for the year, gross dividend yield and P/E ratio.

Countries

North America	United States
	Canada
Europe (EMU) prices:	Austria
	Belgium/Luxembourg
	Finland
	France
	Germany
	Ireland
	Italy
	Netherlands
	Spain
Europe – non EMU	Denmark
	Norway
	Sweden
	Switzerland
Africa	South Africa
Pacific	Japan
	Australia
	Hong Kong
	Malaysia
	Singapore

The *Financial Times* also shows the indices of a number of other countries as well as the details listed above.

The major markets in the world are London, New York (USA) and Tokyo (Japan); these are called the 'golden triangle', and due to time differences one exchange is always trading.

The American NASDAQ Stock Market is quoted in the *Financial Times* and covers the Nasdaq 100, LargeCap and The American Stock Exchange 100.

Emerging Markets: IFC Investable Indices

This index measures the performance of some of the emerging markets. The countries represented are:

Latin America	Argentina
	Brazil
	Chile
	Colombia
	Mexico
	Peru
	Venezuela
East Asia	China
	India
	Indonesia
	Korea
	Malaysia
	Pakistan
	Philippines
	Sri Lanka
	Taiwan – China
	Thailand
Europe	Czech Republic
	Greece
	Hungary

Europe (cont.)	Poland
	Russia
	Slovakia
	Turkey
Mideast/Africa	Egypt
	Israel
	Jordan
	Morocco
	South Africa
	Zimbabwe

The details include the index for each country, day change %, and % change on a year basis.

FTSE European Series

There are a number of indices representing Europe's Financial situation. The three main ones, which track the European large cap stocks, are: FTSE Eurotop 100, FTSE Eurotop 300 and FTSE Eurobloc 100.

Eurotop 100

This is a basket of the 100 most traded European stocks. It is a 'fixed basket' construction that makes it useful for derivatives trading.

Eurotop 300

This measures the performance of the largest companies in terms of market capitalization. It has separate sector and regional sub-indices.

FTSE 100 Eurobloc

This index includes stocks from those countries who have European Monetary Union (EMU). The top 60 are selected by market capitalization and the remaining 40 added on a basis of sector weighting. It was designed with derivative trading in mind.

FTSE techMARK 100

Launched on 4 November 1999, this index consists of technology companies with a market capitalization of under £4bn. It is designed to enable investors to track the performance of small and medium-size technology companies. Thus the large technology companies such as Vodafone and BT are excluded from this index.

2   Problems of Comparing the Performance of Unquoted Companies and Overseas Companies

Unquoted companies

Although there are indices available to measure the performance of shares with a full or AIM quotation, there is nothing available to measure the performance of unquoted companies. Unquoted shares have no comparative indices available, although the investor can at least compare the current share price with the price he paid. For a completely unquoted share there is not even a share price available for comparison, because a buyer must first be found before a share price can be obtained. This is one reason why the ordinary investor should steer clear of investing in unquoted companies.

There are various methods that can be used to value unquoted shares. Examples are net asset value, or future dividends or net present value based on projections of future net cash flows discounted at a rate adjusted for risk, or price earnings based methods. However, such methods can at best be only indicative.

Overseas shares

Although the closing prices of the major shares on the major stock markets are quoted daily in the *Financial Times* along with index figures for the main indices in the major centres, there is not the same amount of published information readily available for overseas shares as there is with UK companies. In addition to the dearth of readily available information, currency fluctuations can seriously affect the size of profit or loss made on the sale of an overseas share. A good capital gain on the share can be wiped out if the value of the currency against sterling has fallen and, vice versa, a rise in the value of the currency against sterling can increase the gain. It is not merely the dearth of readily available information that the investor has to contend with, it is the added complications of currency fluctuations. The FTSE World Series do provide some guide for measuring portfolio performance. If the shares are in Europe then the FTSE Eurotop 100 and 300 indices are useful measurement tools.

OFEX Facility

OFEX is an unregulated trading facility for share dealing in unquoted companies. It is operated by J. P. Jenkins Ltd. in association with Newstrack Ltd. OFEX is published in the *Financial Times*; however, it is not an index. It gives the company name, mid-price of the shares, days charge, market capitalization (£m) and the year's high and low figures.

3   Portfolio Management Methods for the Private Investor

Some investors take an active interest in the stock market and prefer to manage their portfolios themselves. To do this they must be able to use the available information to their best advantage. One thing they need to do is read the quality financial press on a regular basis. The *Financial Times* and *Investor's Chronicle* are invaluable sources of information. For investors in unit trusts, single-premium bonds and some offshore funds, *Money Management* provides a monthly source of performance statistics. In addition information is available from various web sites, some of which are shown in Appendix 2.

The portfolio should first be valued and the gross yield of each investment calculated. Then break down the portfolio into its constituents and compare each constituent with the average of its FT Actuaries sector where applicable. The investor should also check his marginal rate of tax and any realized capital gains against his CGT allowance.

The liquid reserve

The investor should check:

- The available interest rates to ensure that the investor is getting the best return net of tax;
- The size of the liquid reserve against the value of the portfolio. If it exceeds 10% then unless this is for a specific purpose the excess should be invested elsewhere in line with the investor's overall strategy.

The fixed-interest content

The investor should:

- Check its value and the redemption dates of the stocks noted to see if any will shortly be redeemed;
- Calculate the net redemption yield of each stock to ensure it still matches his income tax situation;
- Check the current and anticipated levels of inflation and interest rates to see if any stocks need to be switched in view of the likely trends. Switching should ideally be done just before the changes take place in order to benefit the investor;
- Ensure that the value of any individual holding does not unbalance the structure of the portfolio.

However, bear in mind that all gilts are equally secure in that they are all Government backed. A mixture of stocks is still required to ensure that there is a good spread of redemption dates.

The tax-exempt content

The investor should:

First ensure that these investments are still suitable in view of his tax position;

If any of the investments are nearing maturity, check whether they are automatically repaid or whether they continue to receive interest. If they are due to be repaid then the investor should look at any new schemes available that are suitable for reinvestment. If, as in the case of NSCs, they continue to receive either index-linking or interest at the general extension rates, these rates should be compared with those available on similar investments before a decision is taken about retaining them or not;

If tax-exempt investments are still suitable, then, provided the investor does not find a more attractive alternative for this element, check to ensure that the portfolio is still properly balanced in relation to this element.

The equity content

Direct equity investment

Note the following:

The investor should ensure that he has at least 15 shares in different sectors to provide adequate diversification;

- Each holding should be valued and the yields compared to the yields given for the Actuaries Indices for that share's sector;

The overall yield on the equity part of the portfolio should be compared to the yield on the Actuaries All Share Indices;

- Any holdings that have got too large should be scaled down. The value of holdings should be about equal, and any shares that show a good gain will unbalance the portfolio. In this case some of these shares should be sold to bring the value into line, but care should be taken that disposals are within the exemption limit for CGT purposes;

Any underweight holdings should be carefully examined. If the performance has been poor and prospects for a quick recovery are slim it would be better to cut the losses and use the proceeds along with any others realized to invest in a complementary holding;

Apart from comparing an individual share's performance with past performance, the investor should also look at future prospects for both the company and the industry. If there is a major crisis looming that will affect the company it would be better to sell the share before the price is affected, and move into a more promising sector. The key is, of course, to anticipate such events correctly.

Indirect equity investment

Note the following:

This is in the form of unit trusts, investment trusts and single-premium bonds;

In each case the holding should be valued and performance compared to the average for the type of holding;

- The holdings should maintain the balance of the portfolio;

- In the case of single-premium bonds, consideration should be given to whether or not total encashment would result in a taxation payment under top slicing rules. If this were the case the whole profit would be taxed at the investor's marginal rate less basic rate.

Other considerations to bear in mind

The investor should:

- Look at any new investment opportunities available and evaluate them to see if they will suit his needs and fit comfortably into the balance of his portfolio;

- If any investments are due to be redeemed, the trends of interest rates, inflation and the market must be considered. It may turn out that for a short period it would be advantageous to retain these funds in liquid form. If, for example, a new investment was being launched in the near future, or a particularly attractive company was being floated on the stock market, then it might be better to remain liquid for the period to enable the opportunity to be taken up.

It might be advantageous to do a 'bed and breakfast' operation to realize any capital gains to use up the current year's exemption limit.

Before making any buy, sell or hold decisions the investor could employ the techniques of either fundamental or technical analysis to guide his decision making. The fundamental approach attempts to say whether a particular share should be bought, sold, or held, whereas technical analysis attempts to say whether the timing is right for carrying out the transaction.

The investor should ensure that any major changes in taxation policy introduced in the Finance Act are taken into account when carrying out the review.

4   Portfolio Review

When a customer brings in a portfolio of investments for review there is certain information that must be obtained from him, and then the portfolio review procedure can be undertaken.

Information required

You need to ask the following questions.

- What is the investor's age? If he is young or retired, income is the more likely requirement. If he is middle-aged with no dependent children, the aim will more likely be towards building up a 'nest egg' for retirement.

- What commitments does he have? Are his children in private education? Are they in higher education? If so, money will be needed to meet their fees and expenses.

- Has he adequate life and pension cover?

○ Does he own his own home? If so, what is its value and what is the mortgage outstanding on it?

● What is his salary and other income and his marginal rate of tax? How does the income from the portfolio affect his tax position?

○ Does he have any other investments? If so, do they fit into the existing portfolio, do they complement it?

○ Is he averse to risk? If so, he will not be able to make the most suitable investments.

○ Are there any areas he wishes to avoid, e.g. breweries or tobacco companies? Or are there any shares he wishes to purchase for the concessions?

○ Is he a UK resident or a non-resident? If he is a non-resident he is exempt from UK capital gains tax on stocks and share deals. He is also eligible to receive income from exempt gilts free of income tax liability.

○ What are his requirements from the portfolio?

Assessment of the existing portfolio

This should be carried out in the following order to ascertain the suitability of each holding.

○ List the investments held to show their price, current value, and gross and net yields.

○ Compare the performance of the portfolio as a whole with the FT Actuaries All Share Indices.

● Compare the performance of each equity with the performance of the individual sector index in the FTSE Actuaries All Share Indices. If there are any overseas holdings, either directly held shares or unit or investment trusts investing overseas, compare the performance with the FTSE World Indices or FTSE Eurotop as applicable.

● Have there been any sales during the year? If so, is there a potential capital gains tax liability?

○ Is there an adequate liquid reserve invested in the most efficient manner with regard to the investor's marginal rate of tax?

○ Are the fixed-income and equity content balanced?

● Is the fixed-income element of the portfolio suitable to the investor's needs? Are any stocks due to be redeemed shortly?

● Are the coupons and yields of the fixed-interest stocks suitable for the investor's tax position? Do the maturity dates of the stocks meet his needs?

○ Are there at least 15 shares in different sectors to provide most of the benefits of diversification of the unsystematic risk?

○ Are the values of any of the share holdings very small or large? If they are small should they be built up or sold? If they are large the holding should be scaled down and the funds realized reinvested in a complementary holding.

● Small holdings of individual shares are usually not cost effective to manage.

● If the investor is a high-rate taxpayer, does he have the maximum holdings of the current tax-free issues, i.e. NSCs and ISAs?

● Would the equity content benefit by inclusion of unit trusts investing overseas, single-premium bonds or split-level investment trusts?

● Are there any new investments available that would fit the investor's needs?

Reviewing the portfolio

A customer aged 59 asks your advice on his investments, a list of which is given below. He is married, his wife is aged 61, they have children but they are no longer financially dependent on him. He is a company executive and pays income tax at the top rate. He is not averse to reasonable risk. He owns his house and has sufficient cash available to pay off the outstanding mortgage of about £5,000 but no other resources. His wife is a basic rate taxpayer.

	Approx. price	Approx. value	Flat Yield
£25,000 3½% Funding 1999/04	89.71	22,428	3.9
£40,000 7¾% Treasury 2012/15	116.54	46,616	5.8
£25,000 5½% Treasury 2008/12	96.39	24,098	5.71
£10,000 2½% Treasury 1975 or after	48	4,800	5.21
		£97,942	

Indicate the general investment policy you would recommend to your customer and state, with reasons, what changes, if any, you would suggest in his present portfolio.

General Investment Policy

(a) He has accumulated enough cash to pay off his £5,000 mortgage. If he has an endowment or pension mortgage he should retain it because he receives tax relief on the interest at 10%. If it is a repayment mortgage it will almost certainly be near the end of its term because he is 59. In this case it may be wise to repay because most of the repayments now will consist of repayment of capital, thus receiving little tax relief.

We will assume it is an endowment mortgage, thus the £5,000 is available for investment.

(b)   Check he has adequate pension and life cover.

(c)   The existing portfolio consists entirely of gilts. These do not provide for any growth of income over the long term. One of the gilts is over par and will make a capital loss on redemption. One is undated and will not produce any guaranteed capital gain.

(d)   With a portfolio valued at around £100,000 (including the accumulated cash), overseas and property elements could be included. The overseas element should be provided via unit or investment trusts investing overseas to provide growth in the long term from other expanding economies.

The property element should be provided via a property bond. This is a single-premium bond that does not pay any income. On encashment the profit is subject to top slicing rules, so that if encashment is deferred until he retires and he then becomes a basic-rate taxpayer, there will be no further tax liability.

However, with both of these investments, the emphasis is on long-term capital growth, thus it may be better to avoid these investments because he is due to retire in 6 years time.

(e)   He has not taken advantage of the various tax-free investments such as NSCs or ISAs. The NSCs mature in 5 years time when he is due to retire (presuming retirement at 65). ISAs do not have a maturity date. The returns are tax free and guaranteed on the NSCs. ISAs are free of all taxes, but the return depends on the success of the ISA managers.

(f)   Check whether his wife is going to use up her full basic-rate tax allowance. If not is he willing to transfer capital into her name to fully utilize this allowance?

Changes to the portfolio

(a)   The 3^1/$_2$% Funding matures in 4 years time and is under par, thus is suitable for his needs. All gains are free of CGT. Retain.

(b)   The other three gilts should be sold. The 7¾% Treasury and 5^1/$_2$% Treasury are both giving a reasonable return, but he is overweight in gilts. The 2^1/$_2$% Treasury is undated and is unlikely ever to be redeemed. Undated gilts are not suitable for private investors.

(c)   He should retain his cash as a liquid reserve to meet any unexpected bills. Assuming he already has £5,000 cash, this could be increased to £10,000 (10% of the value of the portfolio) if he felt that he may have some larger expenses or wish to take advantage of any new investments in the future. A bank or building society high interest account gives the best rate of return for liquid cash.

(d)   He should consider taking advantage of the tax-free investments – 16th issue index linked (1.8% + RPI) and 53rd issue NSCs (5.01%) and an ISA.

(e) He could have direct equity investment with the sum available provided it is professionally managed. He has sufficient for a holding of 15 shares in different sectors. Alternatively he could use unit and investment trusts to provide professional management and diversification. Three or four under different managers aimed at growth would provide protection against one manager having a bad year.

Note: The above assumes there is no advantage in transferring any capital to his wife.

Portfolio

	Amount £	Gross Rate %	Gross Income
Bank/Building Society High Interest Account	5,000	5.63	282
£25,000 3$\frac{1}{2}$% Funding	22,428	3.9	875
53rd Issue NSCs	10,000	-	-
16th Issue Index-linked NSCs	10,000	-	-
ISAs	7,000	-	-
15/20 Shares professionally managed – growth	48,000	2	960
	£102,428		£2,117

$$\text{Gross Yield on portfolio} = \frac{2,117 \times 100}{102,428} = 2.07\%$$

Upon retirement the NSCs, will have matured. The proceeds can then be re-invested to provide income if required.

The ISA (£7,000 in 1999/2000) complements his existing holdings. All income and capital gains are totally free of tax.

Although the portfolio is fairly heavy on fixed interest investments (gilts plus NSCs), these mature around the time of his retirement. If he then needed extra income the proceeds could be invested to provide this, without disrupting the equity holdings already chosen.

Example

The following portfolio of investments is held by a new client.

Fixed-interest		Price	Value	Int Yield	Red Yield
£10,000	Treasury 6½% 2003	97.75	9,775	6.5%	6.5%
£ 5,990	Treasury 9% 2008	£119.88	7,181	6.95%	5.7%
£ 4,700	Treasury 5¾% 2009	£100.64	4,731	6.95%	6.55%
			£21,687		

Equity		Price	Value	Div Yield
1,000	Lincat	341p	3,410	4.0
300	Railtrack	808p	2,424	3.3
400	Wyndeham Press	253p	1,012	2.6
2,500	Thomson Travel	96p	2,400	3.1
500	Rolls Royce	317p	1,585	3.0
750	Allied Domecq	227p	1,702	8.3
2,000	Express Dairies	80p	1,600	9.8
			£14,133	

You are asked to examine the portfolio and discuss the suitability for the client below. What changes, if any would you make?

(a) A 65-year-old widow whose other sources of income do not provide the standard of living that she enjoyed when her husband was alive. She owns a detached house, has no mortgage payments and has two married sons who are well established in their professional careers. The pension that she receives from her husband's former employment is inflation-linked. She is in good health and, for the time being, she wishes to be independent of her children. She was widowed 3 years ago.

Possible option

She needs to maximize her income from this portfolio. We will assume she is a basic-rate taxpayer from the information given (because she has other sources of income apart from her state pension). The fixed-interest and equity should be split equally to give her a high level of initial income with long-term capital growth.

All the gilts have good interest yields, however she is overweight in the section, thus she should retain the 9% Treasury Stock yielding 6.95% . Another, longer-dated gilt should also be purchased. This will provide a further long-term guaranteed high-income element to the portfolio.

The equity content consists of only 7 shares, whereas 15 are needed to give the maximum benefits of diversification, with a minimum of £2,000 each for cost effectiveness; all the shares have yields that are higher than the average of the FTSE Actuaries All Share dividend yield of 2.26%. The shares are all in different sectors. However the emphasis is too heavy on income at the expense of long-term growth of capital, thus they should be sold and replaced with shares giving an average yield of around 3%. Unless the lady has the time and expertise necessary to manage them, they would be better sold and put under professional management.

Unit trusts could be purchased via a share exchange scheme to minimize dealing costs. The trusts should be aimed at income and 3 or 4 under different managers chosen to give protection against one performing badly. The units will provide growth of income and capital in the long term. Investment trusts should also be used alongside of the unit trusts.

She does not appear to have a liquid reserve to fall back on in case any unexpected bills arrive and this will be provided from the sale of the 5¾% and 6½%Treasury Stock. £3,500 invested in a bank or building society high interest access account paying 4.5% net basic tax, should be sufficient for her needs.

New Portfolio

	£	Gross Interest Rate %	Gross Income Income
Bank/bldg society instant access a/c	3,500	5.63	197
*£5,990 Treasury 9%, 2008	7,181	6.94	539
High-coupon long-dated gilt	8,800	7	616
3/4 unit trusts aimed at income	16,019	3	481
	£35,500		£1,833

Gross yield on portfolio $\dfrac{1,833 \times 100}{35,500} = 5.16\%$

* When the nominal value is given calculate the gross income from coupon x nominal to give the exact monetary amount received.

Summary

Now that you have studied this unit, you should be able to:

- describe the features of the following indices:
  - > FT 30 Share Index
  - > FTSE 100 Index
  - > FTSE 250 Index
  - > FTSE 350 Index
  - > FTSE Actuaries All Share Indices
  - > FTSE Actuaries All Share SmallCap
  - > FTSE Fledgling
  - > FTSE World Index Series
  - > FTSE Eurotop 100 Index
  - > FTSE Eurotop 300 Index
  - > FTSE European Series
  - > FTSE techMARK 100;
- understand the problems of comparing performance of unquoted shares and overseas shares;
- describe the method used by a private investor to manage his own portfolio;
- detail the information needed to review a portfolio;
- review an existing portfolio and suggest alterations to fit the investor's needs.

18

PORTFOLIO MANAGEMENT SERVICES, INVESTOR PROTECTION AND TAKEOVERS

Objectives

After studying this unit, you should be able to:

- describe the portfolio management services offered by banks, stockbrokers, independent advisers and accountants;

- understand the protection schemes operated to protect investors in banks, building societies, insurance companies and financial services;

- understand the purposes and main provisions of the Financial Services Act 1986;

- understand the principles of takeovers and mergers.

1   Portfolio Management Services

Portfolio management services are offered by a large number of different organizations – clearing banks, stockbrokers, merchant banks, independent advisers and accountants. The services range from simple 'dealing only', to 'advisory' and 'discretionary' management. This unit looks at each of these organizations and the types of service they provide.

Polarization

All financial institutions have been affected by the Financial Services Act 1986 in the area of giving investment advice. They can no longer sell both their own in-house investment products (mainly their own unit trusts) and other companies' investment products. They have had to decide whether to be independent intermediaries, selling only other companies' investment products, or to be tied agents selling only their own products. From the viewpoint of this examination, questions should be answered assuming that you are giving advice as an independent intermediary, not as a tied agent. This means you would suggest investments best suited to the investor, not limiting yourself to your own bank's products.

The agency relationships are important here. Clearly, as a tied agent, the institution selling the services is an agent for the principal. If, however, the seller is independent, it is an agent acting on behalf of the customer.

2 Discretionary Management and Advisory Services

Discretionary management

Private clients who want advice tend to be steered towards discretionary management if their portfolio is below £50,000. From the manager's point of view it is much quicker and cheaper to deal with a portfolio if he can take decisions unilaterally. Discretionary management clients receive valuations yearly or half-yearly, and year-end tax summaries are issued.

Clients need to be aware of the danger of 'churning' a portfolio under discretionary management. 'Churning' is a term used to describe switching for switching's sake so that the managing broker can obtain commission income. 'Churning' is forbidden under the Financial Services Act 1986. If churning is suspected, the onus is on the firm to prove that the deals carried out were justified. For tax purposes, fixed management fees cannot be offset against taxable income, nor against capital gains, whereas brokers' commissions on individual deals are included in the CGT calculation.

Advisory services

The manager, along with the client, sets up an initial portfolio, which is then monitored by the manager. Before any deals can be done, the manager must obtain the agreement of the client.

This service will be of interest to investors who understand the stock market and wish to be involved with the management of their portfolio, but who lack the time to monitor performance on a regular basis.

3 Retail Banks

The general nature of the retail banks' facilities

All retail banks offer portfolio management services, and generally the minimum investment accepted is £20,000 to £25,000. Investors with smaller sums will normally be directed towards the bank's unit trusts.

A full discretionary service is preferred, but advisory services may be available for larger portfolios. The fees are usually ¾% per annum and these compare favourably with the annual fee charged by unit trust managers.

Banks usually deal with all the paperwork on the investor's behalf.

The major selling point for a clearing bank's discretionary management service is that it amounts to a 'total financial package' that covers CGT, IHT, insurance, pensions, wills and income tax as well as portfolio management.

In particular, banks will usually recommend investments such as National Savings Certificates that are particularly suitable for high taxpayers. An investor should ask himself whether a stockbroker, merchant bank or other City institution would recommend a tax-efficient investment such as National Savings Certificates.

Banks' discretionary management services are particularly appropriate for busy people who have no time to look after their financial affairs. The equity content, whether in equities or unit and investment trusts, will be managed on a conservative basis, and the 'total financial package' concept means that the investor's money is managed efficiently.

Every student must have a detailed knowledge of his own organization's portfolio management services. He must also have a general understanding of the services of competitors as outlined in this unit. He should then assess for himself where the strengths and weaknesses of his own bank's services lie.

It is likely that other competitors will follow the lead of brokers and other City institutions in developing the total financial package concept. Banks have great expertise in all these matters because of their long experience in trustee and tax matters. Already many of the larger building societies have entered this field, as permitted under Schedule 8 of the Building Societies Act 1986.

4   Services of Stockbrokers

The growing importance to stockbrokers of the private investor

Because commission rates are (technically) negotiable, it now depends on the standing of the investor as to how high or low dealing costs will be. For institutional investors rates will be low because of the size of their deals, thus many brokers are now looking to private clients to make up for some of the lost earnings.

Fees for advice and for dealing are likely to be separated, and brokers are aiming to segment their services into:

- A 'no frills' dealing-only service. This is simply a dealing-only service that does not offer advice. Investors who wish to deal in small sums should check the minimum commission that the broker will charge. No advice is available from the broker with this type of service;

- Dealing-only services are becoming popular with small investors, especially as many of these services are highly competitive on price, and a number of specialist firms have set up business purely for this purpose. A number of these services are available via telephone and Internet brokers;

- Advisory services involve the broker, in consultation with the client, setting up an initial portfolio, and thereafter managing it on behalf of the investor. Before any changes are made, the broker must consult the client.

Because such consultation is costly, many brokers now set a minimum amount for an advisory service.

Deposit facilities

Many brokers also arrange for clients to keep money on deposit with them, and this is a particularly useful facility when the client is 'between investments'. The brokers can pool their clients' cash so as to obtain near money market rates from a clearing or merchant bank for deposits that are made up of relatively small individual deposits.

Services for small investors

The broker constructs a basic portfolio of gilts and unit and investment trusts for investors with anything between £2,500 and £25,000 and the advice is usually given free of charge, because he will be remunerated by his commission from the unit trust managers. Obviously dealing costs on the gilts and investment trust shares will be charged to the investor.

The scheme generally operates as follows: the investor discusses with the broker his income and capital needs, and then the broker recommends a mixture of gilts and unit and investment trusts. Annual or half-yearly valuations are then issued to the client.

Financial planning

In the past brokers have considered the gilt/equity/unit trust aspects of a client's portfolio, but have not really related these matters to the total financial needs of the client.

Now all this is changing, with many brokers having financial planning departments that can advise on insurance, pensions, school fees, inheritance trusts and, above all, taxation.

Conclusions on brokers' services

It is difficult to evaluate the success of a broker's services, because different clients will each have their own individual requirements that will influence the construction of the portfolio. However, where the brokers act as unit trust managers the investor can easily compare the record of the brokers' unit trusts with that of the 'median fund' for the sector. You will recall that the Association of Unit Trusts and Investment Funds publishes the records of median funds.

It should be remembered that brokers are now very keen to obtain private client business, and that their services will develop on more and more competitive lines. A detailed list of services and charges of various brokers appears in publications such as *Investors Chronicle* and *Money Management*.

5　　Merchant Banks

Merchant banks tend to specialize in the selection of an equity portfolio geared to growth. Usually the minimum investment a merchant bank is prepared to manage is £100,000. Fees are usually in the region of 0.5% to 1.25% per annum, based on the value of funds managed.

Discretionary management is always insisted upon, because when investments of this size are switched, speed is essential to take advantage of any useful bargains.

Once again, the only rough and ready guide to the quality of service is to compare the record of the unit trusts managed by the merchant bank with that of the appropriate 'median fund'.

6 Independent Advisers

There are many independent firms that act as financial advisers.

Independent advisers can advise on virtually all financial matters, including for example:

- The best building society rates currently available
- ISAs
- Unit trust outlook
- Gilts
- Tax planning
- Insurance and pension products.

Some of these independent advisers charge the investor a fee for the advice, and will remit any commission received on, for example, unit trust deals, against the fee. This type of financial adviser may provide a better service than commission-based advisers because there is no pressure to sell services for commission purposes. Other independent advisers will provide the best advice on a range of products from different companies and earn their remuneration from the commissions received. They do not charge the investor a fee.

7 Services of Accountants and Solicitors

The larger accountancy and solicitor's firms have always offered a 'total financial package' to the higher net worth investor. Most larger firms cater for the executives of the companies that they audit.

Usually an they will not recommend specific shares for a client's portfolio, but will suggest the basic outline with the proportions of gilts and equities and possibly risk capital. Other items recommended will include pension plans and life assurance, and tax planning and executor services are available in many cases. The client will then be referred to a broker for advice on a specific equity selection. These services are fee based, not commission based.

8 Investor Protection

Banks

The Banking Act 1987 and the Bank of England authorize the various banks and other 'licensed deposit takers'. These are known as authorized institutions. They must have a paid up capital and reserves of at least £1 million. In order to use the word 'bank' in their company name the minimum figure is £5 million. There are other criteria that must be met before the Bank of England will grant authorization, but they are outside the scope of this syllabus.

The National Savings Bank and local authorities are outside the scope of this Act. Building societies will fall into the scope of the Act if they demutualize, hence take 'plc' status, in which case they legally become banks.

Deposits with authorized institutions are covered by a compensation scheme for 90% of the first £20,000 deposited with any of these organizations. Deposits for an original term of over five years or deposits in foreign currency are excluded from the scheme.

Investors should beware of making deposits in any organization that claims to be a bank but is not recognized as one authorized by the Bank of England under the Banking Act.

The building societies are part of the Deposit Protection Fund, established by the Building Societies Act 1997. It is administered by the Deposit Protection Board. In addition to the statutory scheme, societies have the option to join other schemes for investor protection, although this does not permit them to opt out of the statutory scheme.

The level of protection is 90% of the balance of the investor up to a maximum balance of £20,000. Thus a person with £20,000 invested is guaranteed £18,000 maximum.

In the event of insolvency of a building society, the Board can require societies to contribute up to 0.3% of their share and deposit base from which insolvency payments are then made to investors.

The Board can also raise funds by further calls for contributions to the Fund and by borrowing.

Once insolvency payments are made, the Board has a claim on the assets of the insolvent society.

Both personal shareholders and depositors are protected by the scheme. Depositors are creditors and have priority for payment over shareholders in the event of insolvency.

As an added layer of protection, many financial advisers recommend that their clients ensure that the society in which they invest is a member of the Building Societies Association. Very few societies today are non-members.

Authorized insurance companies

The Policyholder's Protection Act

The Policyholder's Protection Act guarantees 90% compensation to policyholders in the event of failure of the insurance company. There is a Policyholder's Protection Board that will rule whether benefits offered could be classed as 'excessive'. Such 'excessive' benefits are excluded from compensation.

Overseas insurance companies that are not 'authorized' by the Department of Trade and Industry must say that they are not authorized in any advertisements or circulars. The investor must bear in mind that not all insurance companies resident in the Channel Islands or Isle of Man are 'authorized', and he should beware of investing in any unauthorized companies.

The Insurance Ombudsman Bureau

Most complaints can be dealt with by the insurance company itself, but if a policyholder feels he has been unfairly treated, he can seek redress via the Ombudsman.

The procedure is as follows:

- The policyholder must write to the manager of the branch or office that issued the policy and explain the nature of his complaint;
- If no satisfaction is obtained, the policyholder must then write to the chief executive of the insurance company;
- If this fails he can then contact the Insurance Ombudsman, but contact must be made within six months of failure to agree with the insurance company. The policyholder must write to explain the problem and should quote his policy number and company;
- The Ombudsman will, free of charge:
  - ➤ bring the sides together in a voluntary agreement;
  - ➤ or make a recommendation rejecting the complaint; or
  - ➤ make a cash award;
- If a cash award is made it is binding on the insurance company if it is a lump sum not over £100,000, or if it is a disability pension that is not in excess of £10,000 per annum; amounts in excess of these figures need the agreement of the insurance company;
- The policyholder is, however, free to reject the award and take legal action should he be dissatisfied with the outcome.

  Note: not every insurance company is a member of the scheme. Potential policyholders should check on this at the outset. The Ombudsman cannot deal with complaints on surrender values, paid-up policy values, or bonus rates. Business insurance and overseas policies are outside the scheme.

Gilts, local authority stocks and national savings

There is no formal compensation scheme, but gilts are guaranteed by the Government and it is inconceivable that there could be any default. As far as local authority stocks are concerned, they seem equally secure.

National Savings are as secure as gilts.

9   The Financial Services Act 1986

Background

In 1984 Professor Gower produced a report on investor protection, and this report formed the basis of a White Paper that was published on 29 January 1985. The theme of the White Paper was self-regulation within a statutory framework so as to provide investor protection while allowing the UK financial services industry to operate efficiently and competitively. This White Paper formed the basis of the Financial Services Act 1986, which came into force in 1987.

The main features of the Financial Services Act 1986

The main features are:

- It is a criminal offence for any firm or individual to engage in investment business without being authorized so to do. Contracts in connection with investment business are not capable of being enforced by an unauthorized firm;

- Investments and investment business are comprehensively defined to include all types of security and include financial futures, commodity futures and options;

- The main body designated by the Act is the Financial Services Authority (FSA), covering the regulation of securities and investments;

- The FSA may delegate its regulatory function to self-regulating organizations (SROs). The following organizations have been recognized as SROs by the FSA:

  - The Securities and Futures Authority (SFA) covers Stock Exchange members and firms that advise on and deal in futures and options;

  - The Investment Management Regulatory Organization (IMRO), covering investment managers and advisers including managers and trustees of collective investment schemes and pension fund managers;

  - The Personal Investment Authority (PIA), covering independent intermediaries and the marketing of life assurance and unit trusts.

As far as commission to intermediaries who help to sell unit trusts and insurance products is concerned, the Act states that notice be given to the client that the commission to be paid to the intermediary will be within the limits prescribed by a voluntary industry-wide agreement such as the one currently covering life insurance commissions. It is compulsory for those selling regulated products to disclose the amount of commission receivable once a sale has been completed.

These limits could be set out by the unit trust managers or the insurance company in a notice provided by them.

The Act seeks to prevent a possible conflict of interest with dual capacity systems operating on the Stock Exchange. For instance, if an investor requested advice on ICI shares from a broker/dealer who also owned those shares, there could be a temptation for the broker's advice to be biased. To prevent this the Act states that:

- The broker/dealer must disclose that he owns some ICI shares;
- The broker/dealer must satisfy himself that the ICI shares are suitable for his client;
- If the client decides to buy ICI shares, the broker/dealer must obtain them at the lowest

cost. This may mean the broker/dealer has to buy them from someone else instead of merely selling his own ICI shares to the client. This is known as 'best execution'.

The operation of the various bodies

Each SRO is responsible for vetting its members for honesty, solvency and competence and for this reason any firm or individual engaged in investment business must be authorized by his appropriate SRO, otherwise a criminal offence is committed.

Before an investment adviser can give advice to a client in the last above, the customer must have signed a customer agreement letter. This gives details about the firm and its services and charges, and also gives details of the guidelines that an investment adviser must follow.

In addition, the investment adviser is obliged to 'know the customer' and must find out and put on record enough about the client's personal and financial position to be able to judge whether an investment is suitable for that client.

Investment advisers must recommend the investment that is most suitable for the client, irrespective of the intermediary commission.

Investment advisers must decide whether they are independent intermediaries who can claim to be impartial, or whether they are company agents.

The adviser must make it clear whether he is an independent intermediary or whether he is a tied agent. Polarization applies mainly to the sale of unit trusts, pensions and insurance products.

Junk mail cannot be sent out unless the sender knows enough about a client to assess whether the investment is suitable for him.

Unit trust and life assurance products can be 'cold called', but the investor has a two-week cooling off period in that he can change his mind and cancel the contract.

Any complaints by investors should be referred to the intermediary. If satisfaction is not given, the investor can complain to an ombudsman appointed by the FSA.

If an intermediary or investment dealer absconds or acts dishonestly there is a compensation fund administered by the FSA. This covers investors as follows:

● First £30,000 loss covered in full;

● Next £20,000 loss covered 90%.

Thus the maximum amount that can be received is £48,000.

In addition to the SROs, the FSA authorized certain Recognized Professional Bodies (RPBs) who licence their own members to carry out investment business. Recognized Investment Exchanges (RIEs) regulate a market and transactions on it. They do not regulate the conduct of business, which is done by the relevant SRO.

The structure is:

FSA
RECOGNIZES

3 Recognized Self Regulating Organizations (SROs)	9 Recognized Professional Bodies (RPBs)	6 Recognized Investment Exchanges (RIE)	2 Recognized Clearing Houses (RCHs)
• IMRO – The Investment Management Regulatory Organization • SFA – the Securities and Futures Authority • PIA – the Personal Investment Authority	• The Law Society (covering England and Wales) • The Law Society of Northern Ireland • The Law Society of Scotland • The Institute of Chartered Accountants in England and Wales • The Institute of Chartered Accountants in Ireland • The Institute of Chartered Accountants in Scotland • The Association of Chartered Certified Accountants • The Institute of Actuaries	• London Stock Exchange • Tradepoint Stock Exchange • The London International Financial Futures and Options Exchange • The London Securities and Derivatives Exchange Ltd • The International Petroleum Exchange of London Ltd • The London Metal Exchange • NASDAQ	• The London Clearing House • CrestCo Ltd

Membership of any of the SROs confers authorization on that person, as does certification by any of the RPBs or its members.

Personal Investment Authority (PIA)

The PIA is the regulatory authority for retail financial services companies and looks after the interests of private investors.

There is a PIA Ombudsman to deal with complaints from private investors who have exhausted a company's formal appeals procedure. If the Ombudsman finds in the investor's favour, compensation will be paid from the Investors' Compensation Scheme up to a maximum of £50,000 per person. The scheme has a maximum of £100 million per annum, thus it would be possible for the fund to be exhausted if one major firm is found to have defrauded investors of their money.

Conflicts of interest in the large financial conglomerate

Over the past few years demarcation lines in the financial services industry have crumbled, and the new financial services conglomerates now carry out all the services that were once offered separately by different organizations. After the 'Big Bang' in 1986, the last of the legal 'demarcation lines' have ceased to exist. For example, Barclays de Zoete Wedd (BZW) has become a major international investment banking group that offers:

- Fund management
- Securities dealing both as principal and as agent
- Corporate finance
- Conventional banking.

The bank's attitude is that it freely acknowledges the existence of potential conflicts of interest and will control these conflicts openly by observing appropriate rules.

Possible conflicts could arise, for example:

- The banking section will probably be the first to learn of a corporate customer's financial difficulties. This department may pass on the information to the securities dealing section;

- The broking section could then advise its private clients to buy shares in the corporate customer that the 'market maker' section wished to dispose of because of the 'tip' from the banking section.

BZW approaches the problem by physical separation of the different functions. This separation can take the form of separate incorporation, or of separate physical location in different buildings or on different floors of the same building. This separation has been called 'Chinese walls' and has been regarded by some critics as 'a fortification of doubtful value'.

In order to strengthen these 'Chinese walls', BZW has set up a compliance department, staffed at the highest level, which will have the responsibility of ensuring that in all situations where conflict could arise appropriate procedures for the protection of clients should be observed.

A senior BZW official has been quoted as saying, 'We cannot emphasize too strongly that this (passing of inside information between different departments) must not and cannot be allowed to happen, and that rigorous internal action (such as a fine or even dismissal) would be taken if it did.'

BZW point out that 'insider dealing' is a criminal offence against the 1985 Companies Act, that under the law of agency an agent must not make a secret profit, and that the FSA has formulated strict rules regarding the passing of price-sensitive information.

It is expected, in the future, that all the major conglomerates will appoint compliance officers to see that their colleagues do not abuse price-sensitive information, and that they will have to be seen to succeed. Most major broking or jobbing firms already stipulate that staff cannot deal for the account, nor can they stag an in-house new issue.

10   Takeovers

Why takeovers occur

Takeovers are intended to boost the profits of the bidder in the long term. The methods by which this may be achieved are described later in this section.

The reasons for takeovers are:

- To enable the bidder to diversify its interests;

- To obtain for the bidder an increased market share of an industry;

- To help the bidder ensure supplies by taking over a supplier;

- To enable the bidder to impose improved management on the target; thus the bidder will obtain added value by more efficient operation of the target;

- To acquire retail outlets to help distribute the bidder's products;

- To enable the bidder to take advantage of synergies that will result from combining the activities of the bidder and the target. Synergies can arise for many reasons, the most common of which is cost reduction due to rationalization of operations.

Takeovers can be classed as fulfilling the corporate objectives of the bidder in the following ways.

Horizontal integration

The takeover is made by the bidder taking over another company that is in the same industry and at the same stage of production, e.g. a direct competitor. This will increase market share and sales, thus (hopefully) increasing profits.

A problem that may arise here is when the size of the two companies exceeds 25% of the market share in that industry. The 25% figure is deemed to be a monopoly, and the bid may be referred to the Monopolies and Mergers Commission. The MMC has the power to refuse to allow the bid to continue.

Vertical integration

The takeover is made by the bidder taking over a company that is either a supplier or outlet. The benefits of a vertical takeover are that the bidder can control either the supply or sale of the products, cutting out the middleman and (hopefully) increasing profits.

It is possible that a vertical integration bid may exceed the 25% rule, and the bid will then be referred to the MMC.

Diversification

Some companies have grown by taking over totally unrelated businesses that the bidder feels are not being run efficiently.

Such a bidder may well sell off part of the company after takeover to recoup some of the costs of acquisition, and then put its own management team in to turn the company around.

Disposal synergies

As mentioned above, it is not uncommon for disposal of part of a business to occur.

In the mid-1990s it became significant that several companies moved towards the creation of separate strategic business units, set up by de-mergers.

Some takeover bids are extremely hostile, with the target company trying to fight off the bid by all legitimate routes.

There is considerable controversy in the UK concerning takeovers. Some would argue that the threat of a hostile bid will ensure that managements continuously work to maximize shareholder value. Others would say that takeovers inspire short-termism on the part of the managements of potential targets and that takeovers mean that the management of bidders are free, at shareholders' expense, to act out their empire fantasies.

The procedures for carrying out a takeover

To acquire control of a target company the bidder requires over 50% of its voting shares. Such a holding will give the bidder a majority of votes and therefore he will become the controlling shareholder. However, a company needs 75% of voting shares to be sure of passing special and extraordinary resolutions. The significant stages are shown below.

3% or more of the target company's voting shares acquired

The process of acquiring shares of the target company can be commenced by the bidder buying the shares in the open market. Under S.198 of the Companies Act 1989 any person who acquires (or disposes of) more than 3% of the voting shares of a public limited company must notify the company in writing within two working days.

The 3% figure is calculated by totalling the holdings of the bidder, his family and friends, and any others acting on his behalf in a 'concert party'. This prevents a number of associates from each acquiring 2.9% of the shares and not having to notify the target company

If the target company thinks the 3% limit has been breached it can require the suspect to confirm or deny the fact. When the holding is in the name of a nominee company, the target company can insist that the nominee discloses the name of the beneficial owner if he has acquired 3% or more of the shares.

Failure to supply the target with the required notification can eventually result in an application to the court to deprive the bidder of his voting rights, dividends and the right to sell, a rule that makes it very difficult for a bidder to acquire a substantial interest unbeknown to the target company.

10% of the target's voting shares acquired

If the bidder has acquired more than 10% of the voting shares in the 12 months before it makes a full takeover bid, then the bid must be for cash or contain a cash alternative at the highest price paid during the previous 12 months.

A bidder is not allowed to acquire 10% or more of the voting rights of the target in any seven-day period if together with shares already held they comprise between 15% and 30% of the company's voting rights except by purchasing the shares from a single shareholder or through a tender offer to all shareholders. The 10% figure is laid down by the City Code on Takeovers and Mergers and includes any shares acquired by associates acting as a concert party.

30% or more of the target's voting shares acquired

It is considered that a 30% holding is sufficient to give a bidder effective control of most public companies. If the bidder, together with any associates acting as a concert party, acquires more than 30% (laid down by the City Code on Takeovers and Mergers) of the target company's shares, he is required to make a general offer to all the other shareholders at the highest price paid in the previous 12 months.

The 'bid price' will have to be set above the current market price, or at least above the market price that prevailed before the news of the bid. The consideration offered can be for cash, for shares or other securities such as convertible loans in the bidding company, or for a mixture of the three. Often the target company's shareholders will be offered a choice of cash or securities.

Usually the shareholder will learn about the bid from his newspaper. Shortly afterwards he will receive a formal offer document from the bidder.

50% or more of the target's voting shares acquired

At this stage the bidder has gained control of the company.

90% or more of the target's voting shares acquired

Under ss.428-430 of the 1985 Companies Act, the successful bidder is allowed to acquire the shares of minority shareholders under certain circumstances.

If within four months of the offer 90% in value of the shares has been acquired by the bidder, then the bidder may, within the next two months, serve notice on dissenting shareholders requiring them to transfer their shares on the same terms as the other shareholders. The transfer must be put into effect unless the shareholders petition the court within one month, in which case the court will decide whether there is a good reason for the transfer to be blocked. (The '90%' figure is calculated as 90% of the shares not owned by the bidder when his offer was made.)

Likewise, after expiry of a successful offer that acquired 90% of the shares for the bidder, the minority shareholders may, within three months, require the bidder to acquire their shares on the same terms and conditions as the other shares were obtained.

The position of a shareholder of a target company

Agreed bids

An agreed bid occurs when the directors of the target company recommend acceptance. In such circumstances the shareholder will receive a letter from his directors recommending that the bid be accepted, as well as the formal offer document.

In these circumstances it is fairly certain that the bid will prove successful and the investor has two choices: sell his shares in the market or accept the bid by returning his share certificate and completed acceptance form to the bidder. The market price of the shares will usually be a few pence below the bidder's price, so it will usually be better to accept the bidder's terms, although the shareholder should leave acceptance until the final date indicated in the formal document, just in case a larger, rival, bid is received in the meantime.

If the bidder offers his own shares as consideration, it could pay the shareholder to sell out in the market if he expects the bidder's shares to fall in value.

The bidder must state a level of acceptances that will make his bid 'unconditional' and once the offer has become unconditional, the shareholder may as well accept. The required level of acceptances is usually reached when the bidder has acquired 50% of the share capital, so there is no possibility of another bid after this stage has been reached.

While the offer is still open the level of acceptances will be announced by the press, so the investor can watch the progress.

Contested bids or 'hostile' bids

When the board of the target company objects to the bid, the bid is said to be contested or hostile. In such circumstances the shareholder will be bombarded with literature from both parties, and he must decide:

- Whether the bid is likely to succeed at the initial offer price;

- Whether the bid is likely to be referred to the Monopolies and Mergers Commission:

- Whether the bidder will offer a higher price;

- Whether another bid may come from a rival bidder;

- Whether the target will find a 'white knight'. A 'white knight' is a company by which the target is willing to be taken over.

Normally, the market price of the target's shares will be below the offer price, and if the bid is likely to fail, it may be worthwhile accepting the terms while they are available. A reference to the Monopolies and Mergers Commission probably means that the bid will lapse, because the bidder will have reserved the right to drop the bid if such a reference is made. It is possible for a bidder to avoid a reference to the Monopolies and Mergers Commission if it agrees in advance to sell parts of the combined business so as to overcome any danger of preventing competition in a particular market.

When the target company's shares stay above the bidder's terms it means that the market expects the opening bid to be merely a 'sighting shot', with an improved offer likely.

Normally the first offer period lasts for a minimum of 21 and a maximum of 60 days from the date the offer documents are posted. During this time the bidder can revise (upwards) his terms as many times as he likes. However, because shareholders must be allowed 14 days in which to consider any new proposals, terms cannot be improved after the forty-sixth day of a 60-day offer.

The 60-day timetable can be extended subject to the agreement of the Takeover Panel if:

- A new bidder emerges;

- The target company announces potentially significant 'trading information' after day 39.

Any shareholder who has accepted earlier terms is entitled to receive the benefit of any revisions. Indeed, a shareholder who has accepted the bidder's terms can revoke the acceptance altogether, if he wishes, from 21 days after the first closing date of the initial offer. However, this right of revocation is lost if the offer has become unconditional. Conversely, if the bidder fails to obtain 50% of the shares of the target by the sixtieth day all acceptances are null and void and the bid fails.

Summary of the takeover timetable

The takeover timetable runs for 60 days. The timetable starts when the bidder sends out its first formal offer documents after making its bid intentions clear.

The deadline can be extended when a rival bidder becomes involved. The timetable is put on hold if the bid is referred to the Monopolies Commission and recommences if the Monopolies Commission does not block the bid.

Day 0	Formal documents posted.
Day 14	Target can issue a defence document up to this date.
Day 21	The minimum period under the City Code for a first offer. This is the earliest possible first closing date of offer.
Day 22	The first close. A second offer can be made.
Day 39	The defence can issue no more material of significance.
Day 46	Final terms and offer documents are posted. Closing date (day 60) specified.
Day 60	Offer closes.

The City Code for takeovers and mergers

The City Code works on the following basic principles:

- All shareholders of the same class should be treated equally. This principle is illustrated by the Code's rule that the bidder must make a general offer to all shareholders once a 30% stake has been acquired;

- Such rules prevent the old practice of making a high bid to certain large shareholders, and later acquiring the other shares at a lower price;

- Shareholders should be given adequate information to form a proper judgement. All documents issued to shareholders must be prepared to the same standards as are required for listing particulars. Profit forecasts should be prepared with great care;

- The bid must be put to the board of the target company in the first instance, and this board must seek competent independent advice in the interests of its shareholders;

- The bidding company should only make an offer that it has every reason to believe can be fulfilled;

- The creation of false markets in the shares should be avoided;

- Most forms of 'knocking copy' advertising are banned;

- When assessing whether the bidder has acquired a 50% plus controlling interest, only shares backed with immediate delivery of a share certificate can be counted.

The legal position of the City Code for takeovers and mergers

The Code was last revised in April 1985 and its official title is 'The City Code for Takeovers and Mergers and the Rules Governing Substantial Acquisitions'. The nature, purpose and legal effect of the Code can be summarized from the following extracts from Section A.

The Code represents the collective opinion of those professionally involved in the field of takeovers on a range of business standards. It is not concerned with the financial or commercial advantages or disadvantages of a takeover that are matters for the company and its shareholders, or with those wider questions that are the responsibility of the Government, advised by the Monopolies and Mergers Commission.

The Code has not, and does not seek to have, the force of law, but those who wish to take advantage of the facilities of the securities markets in the United Kingdom should conduct themselves in matters relating to takeovers according to the Code.

In 1986 the Appeal Court made the following rule in the case brought by Pru-Bache in the bid by Norton Opax for McCorquodale. A Takeover Panel decision should only be quashed if it breached the rules of natural justice or fairness. In effect the Panel's rules will now be legally binding.

Legal status of the City Code and the Takeover Panel after full implementation of the Financial Services Act 1986

The power of the Code and Takeover Panel have been strengthened by the Financial Services Act as follows:

- The Takeover Panel has the formal power to ban any investment company, including merchant banks, from taking part in takeover activity if the company has breached the Code;
- The Panel has the full resources of the Department of Trade Investigators behind it. In other words the Panel will be legally able to insist on the production of documentary evidence or computer stored information;
- The Financial Services Authority (FSA) and self-regulating organizations (SROs) are able to 'require' merchant banks and others to cooperate in Panel investigations;
- The Panel has access to 'sensitive' data that until now has been available only to the Department of Trade or the Bank of England.

'Shells' and reverse takeovers

'Shells' are quoted companies whose main asset is their quotation. Such companies are usually capitalized at under £2 million.

Sometimes a person with substantial private business interests may wish to obtain a 'back door' quotation for his business. Such an investor will take over the 'shelf' and then inject his own private business into it. This is known as a reverse takeover.

A more common operator is the stock market entrepreneur who wishes to raise some capital in the City to start a new business.

Rather than using the conventional new issue methods for his business, it can be quicker and easier to take over a 'shell' and raise capital for that 'shell'. Generally speaking, the entrepreneur will have arranged a placing to raise the necessary extra capital, or he may choose to use a rights issue for the 'shell' immediately prior to taking it over. The Stock Exchange will not automatically allow the 'shell' to retain its listing if it is unhappy about the company taking over the shell.

These reverse takeovers are usually made at a price above the 'shell's' current value, and speculators are very keen to try to anticipate potential 'shells'.

Vendor placings and vendor rights issues

With vendor placings, the purchase price of a takeover is paid for in new shares of the bidding company. However, these new shares are immediately placed with clients of the bidder's merchant bank so that the target company's shareholders are effectively paid in cash. A vendor rights issue is a term used to describe the making of a rights issue by the bidder to finance a bid.

Capital gains tax and takeovers

If the shareholder accepts a cash offer, this counts as a disposal for CGT, but if the shareholder accepts shares or other securities in the bidder, the transaction is not considered to be a disposal for CGT purposes. When the new securities are eventually sold, the taxable capital gain will be the net sale proceeds of the new securities, less the original cost of the target company's shares, with appropriate indexation allowances.

Other considerations for a shareholder in a target company to bear in mind

The shareholder should examine the formal offer document. The information in this document will enable him to compare the records of both companies, the profit forecasts and asset valuations. It should also provide information on the reasons for the bid, whether the target's board recommends acceptance, how many shares have been already committed to the bidder, whether any cash offer is underwritten, and whether the City Code has been complied with.

If shares are offered, the shareholder should decide whether the bidder's shares are likely to complement his existing portfolio. He can calculate the value of this bid by using the current market price of the bidder's shares. For example, if the bidding company 'B's' shares are quoted at 100p and 'B' offers one of its shares for every two in the target company, the bid is worth 50p a share. If the target company's shares stand at 40p in the market, then there is a premium of 10p.

If the bid seems likely to fail, the target's shares will remain around 40p in the market, but if a higher offer or counter offer seems likely the market price could rise.

Once the offer has become unconditional, the shareholder has the choice of accepting, selling in the market, or becoming a minority shareholder. His choice will depend on his perception of the way the price of the bidder's shares is likely to move, but it is unlikely to be worthwhile becoming a minority shareholder.

As was previously mentioned, accepting a cash offer could involve capital gains tax liabilities, but accepting an offer of shares does not involve any immediate CGT liability.

In most cases the success or otherwise of a takeover will be decided by the institutional shareholders.

Insider dealing

Since 1980 'insider dealing' has been a criminal offence that could result in imprisonment. This rule was confirmed by the Companies Act 1985, and extended by the Criminal Justice Act 1993.

One of the problems in proving that the offence of insider dealing has occurred is the definition of what constitutes 'price-sensitive information'. If an individual who has price-sensitive information trades on that information, or encourages another person to trade (whether or not that person knows the information is price-sensitive), he could be found guilty of insider dealing.

Summary

Now that you studied read this unit, you should be able to:

- describe what is meant by portfolio management services;
- distinguish between discretionary management and advisory services;
- describe the portfolio management services offered by:
  - ➤ clearing banks
  - ➤ stockbrokers
  - ➤ merchant banks
  - ➤ independent advisers
  - ➤ accountants and solicitors;
- describe the investor protection available to individuals in relation to their dealings with:
  - ➤ banks
  - ➤ building societies
  - ➤ insurance companies
  - ➤ gilts, local authority stocks and national savings;

- describe the main features of the Financial Services Act 1986 relating to investor protection;

- describe the SROs recognized by the Financial Services Authority and the regulatory role each SRO fulfils;

- list the recognized professional bodies (RPBs);

- list the recognized investment exchanges (RIEs);

- explain the conflicts of interest that may arise in large financial conglomerates;

- explain the effects of polarization;

- explain why takeovers occur;

- describe the procedure for carrying out a takeover:

  ➤ with agreed bids

  ➤ with contested bids;

- summarize the takeover timetable;

- describe the principles of the City Code for Takeovers and Mergers;

- describe the legal status of the City Code;

- describe what is meant by a 'shell' and a 'reverse takeover';

- explain the effect of CGT and takeovers;

- explain the considerations a shareholder in the target company should bear in mind in a takeover situation;

- explain what is meant by 'insider dealing'.

19

TRUSTEE INVESTMENT

Objectives

After studying this unit, you should be able to:

● explain what a trustee is and know the position of a trustee as an investor;

● list and describe the main provisions of the Trustee Act 1925, Trustee Investments Act 1961 and the Charities Act 1993 relevant to investment;

● understand the principles of investments by registered charities, family trusts and will settlements;

● understand probate valuations;

● explain the provisions of trust legislation relevant to pension funds.

1   Position of Trustees: General Duties

The word 'trustee' in this connection refers to trustees acting under a will or settlement, or in other capacities appointed by legislative deed. Until the present century, trustees were generally private individuals; nowadays there is also the Public Trustee Office (a Government office) as well as the trustee departments of the major banks and insurance offices.

The primary duty of a trustee is to carry out the terms of the trust. These will usually be laid down in the trust instrument by the person creating the trust, but may be provided by statutory provisions. It is essential that the trustee ensures the security of the trust property and, in so far as the trust fund does not consist of authorized investments, to invest it appropriately.

An 'investment' in the context of a trust is strictly interpreted as the purchase of an income-producing asset (*re Power's Will Trusts* (1947)) and authorization may come from the trust instrument or by statute. It is possible for the trust instrument to authorize the purchase of non-income producing assets such as works of art. However, these will not qualify as investments and thus the wording as to what exactly may be purchased must be precise.

Regardless of the extent of his investment powers, or how they arise, where there is more than one beneficiary the trustee is subject to an overriding requirement to act impartially between beneficiaries. The effect of this in an investment context is best illustrated where the trust has a life tenant, A, entitled to the income of the fund to the date of his death, and a remainderman, B, entitled to the capital on that date. Clearly, investment in assets providing a high income but no capital growth, or vice versa, would benefit one beneficiary to the detriment of the other. In such cases impartiality is best achieved by the purchase of a variety of investments of different types. The Trustee Investments Act 1961 reinforces this by requiring trustees to give due regard to the diversification of the trust investments.

2   Trustee Legislation

The principal legislation concerning trustees is the Trustee Act 1925; however, the investment powers of this Act tended to reflect the attitudes of the nineteenth rather than the twentieth century, when the value of money remained constant over long periods. Investment in equities was considered highly risky and thus inappropriate for a trustee.

As a result, the Trustee Investments Act 1961 repealed most of the investment provisions of the 1925 Act, and it is this 1961 Act that now provides the statutory provisions for trustee investments. It should, however, be noted that most modern wills and settlements usually provided for extensive powers of investment and that the investment powers of the modern trustee are likely to be based solely on the statute only where the trustee instrument is an old one, or where the trust arose as a result of an intestacy (someone who dies without making a will is intestate).

Relevant provisions of the Trustee Act 1925

Although the statutory investment powers of the 1925 Act were repealed with the passing of the Trustee Investments Act 1961, some of its provisions are still relevant to investment matters. The most important are as follows:

- Section 4 provides that trustees shall not be liable for a breach of trust by reason only that they continue to hold an investment that has ceased to be an authorized investment. This, therefore, provides for the retention of such investment, provided of course the trustees continue to consider it suitable, but it should be classed as special-range property;

- Section 10(3) permits trustees to concur in reconstructions and mergers and accept any resulting securities, as well as to subscribe to rights issues in respect of shares held.

3   The Trustee Investments Act 1961

The Trustee Investments Act 1961 can apply to family trusts, will trusts, pension funds or charities. This Act does not require a trustee to follow its provisions if he does not wish to do so, provided the trust deed grants the trustee the widest investment powers. A trustee is bound by the provisions of the Act only if he wishes to invest in equities when the trust instrument does not grant this power. A person creating a trust since the Act was passed may exclude its powers and restrict the trustees' investment powers to a far greater extent than is done by the Act.

If the provisions of the Trustee Investments Act 1961 apply, then the initial division of the fund will be into two equal parts, the narrower range and the wider range. In certain circumstances a third range, special range, may also be held.

Permitted investments

Investments permitted by the Act are set out in Parts I, II and III of the First Schedule of the Act, as amended by subsequent Orders in Council as follows:

First Schedule

Manner of investment

Part I

Narrower range of investments not requiring advice

1   In National Savings Certificates, Ulster Savings Certificates and Ulster Development Bonds.

2   In deposits in the National Savings Bank, ordinary deposits in a Trustee Savings Bank, and deposits in a bank or department thereof certified under subsection (3) of Section 9 of the Finance Act 1956.

Part II

Narrower range of investments requiring advice

1   In securities issued by the governments of the United Kingdom, Northern Ireland or the Isle of Man not being securities falling within Part I of this Schedule and being securities registered in the UK or the Isle of Man, Treasury Bills or Tax Reserve Certificates.

2   In any securities the payment of interest on which is guaranteed by the governments of the UK or Northern Ireland.

3   In securities issued in the UK by any public authority or nationalized industry or undertaking in the United Kingdom.

4   In securities issued in the UK by the government or any overseas territory within the Commonwealth or by any public or local authority within such a territory, being securities registered in the United Kingdom.

5   In securities issued in the UK by the International Bank for Reconstruction and Development, and by the Inter American Bank, being securities registered in the United Kingdom.

6   In debentures issued in the UK by a company incorporated in the United Kingdom, being debentures registered in the United Kingdom. (These include debenture stocks and bonds, whether secured on assets or not, the loan stock or notes.)

7   In stock of the Bank of Ireland.

8   In debentures issued by the Agricultural Mortgage Corporation Limited or the Scottish Agricultural Securities Corporation Limited.

9   In loans to any authority to which this paragraph applies charged on all or any of the revenues of the authority or on a fund into which all or any of those revenues are payable, in any securities issued in the UK by any such authority for the purpose of borrowing money so charged, and in deposits with any such authority by way of temporary loan made on the giving of a receipt for the loan by the treasurer or other similar officer of the authority and on the giving of an undertaking by the authority which, if requested to charge the loan as aforesaid, it will either comply with the request or repay the loan.

      This paragraph applies to the following authorities:

      (a)   Any local authority in the United Kingdom;

      (b)   Any authority all the members of which are appointed or elected by one or more local authorities in the United Kingdom;

      (c)   Any authority the majority of the members of which are appointed or elected by one or more local authorities in the United Kingdom, being an authority which by virtue of any enactment has power to issue a precept to a local authority in England and Wales, or a requisition to a local authority in Scotland, or the expenses of which, by virtue of any enactment, a local authority in the UK is or can be required to contribute;

      (d)   The Receiver for the Metropolitan Police District or a combined police authority (within the meaning of the Police Act 1946);

      (e)   The Belfast City and District Water Commissioners;

      (f)   The Great Ouse Water Authority.

10   In debentures or in the guaranteed or preference stock of any incorporated company, being statutory water undertakers within the meaning of the Water Act 1945 or any corresponding enactment in force in Northern Ireland, and having during each of the ten years immediately preceding the calendar year in which the investment was made paid a dividend of not less than 5% on its ordinary shares.

11   In deposits by way of special investment in a Trustee Savings Bank or in a department (not being a department certified under subsection (3) of Section 9 of the Finance Act 1956) of a bank or any other department of which is so certified.

12   In deposits and loans to a building society designated under the House Purchase and Housing Act 1959.

13   In mortgages of freehold property in England and Wales or Northern Ireland and of leasehold property in those countries of which the unexpired term at the time of investment is not less than 60 years, and in loans on heritable security in Scotland.

14   Perpetual rent charges on land in England, Wales or Northern Ireland, and fee farm rents issuing out of such land, and fee duties or ground annuals in Scotland.

Note: Trustee Investment (Additional Powers) Order 1977 extended the ability to invest not only in fixed interest but also in variable-interest securities under Part II.

Part III

Wider range investments

(All wider range investments require advice)

1   In any securities issued in the UK by a company incorporated in the United Kingdom, being securities registered in the UK and not being securities falling within Part II of this Schedule, i.e. in shares thereof.

2   In shares in any building society designated under Section 1 of the House Purchase and Housing Act 1959.

3   In any units, or other shares of the investments subject to the trusts of an authorized unit trust scheme.

Overriding conditions

There are certain overriding conditions that qualify a trustee's investing powers, and any potential investment must comply with all of them. They are as follows:

Suitability and diversification

Section 6(i) of the 1961 Act deals with the exercise of investment powers and governs both the statutory powers and any express powers given to the trustee. It requires the trustee to have regard to the:

● Need for diversification of trust investments;

● Suitability of the proposed investment.

In all cases, such conditions should be exercised in the context of the trust's particular circumstances.

Advice

A trustee must obtain advice on each proposed investment before the investment is made

(S.6(2)). Certain exceptions are made to this ruling and these are as contained in Part I of the First Schedule covering narrower range investments.

He must obtain periodic advice on the securities held, and the frequency of this is determined by bearing in mind the nature of the particular investment. Such advice should be obtained from 'a person who is reasonably believed by the trustee to be qualified by his ability in, and practical experience of, financial matters' (S.6(4)). The advice must be given or subsequently confirmed in writing (S.6(5)). One trustee, where qualified, can give advice to the others. However, this section has been overruled by the Financial Services Act 1986, which states that investment advice can only be given by a person authorized by the Securities and Investments Board under Schedule 2 or Schedule 3 of the Act.

Place of issue

The UK must be the place of issue and registration of any investment.

Payment in sterling

No securities are authorized if the holder can be required to accept payment of interest or repayment of capital in a currency other than sterling.

Securities to be fully paid

The securities must be fully paid or require to be fully paid within nine months of issue.

Quotation

The securities must be quoted on the Stock Exchange.

Requirements concerning company securities

Companies must fulfil the following conditions, which apply in relation to both debentures and other company securities, they must:

- Be incorporated under an act of the parliaments of the UK or Northern Ireland or by Royal Charter;
- Have a paid-up share capital of not less than £1 million nominal;
- Have paid a dividend on all issued shares for the five years immediately preceding the calendar year in which the investment is made.

    Note: a company formed for the purpose of merger or takeover will qualify if all the constituent companies have paid such dividends.

Powers of the courts

Section 15 of the Act provides for an overriding power of the courts to 'confer wider powers of investment on trustees or affect the extent to which any such power can be exercised'.

Operation of the Act
Division of the fund

The 1961 Act states that a division of the trust funds into two parts, the narrower range and the wider range, equal in value at the time of division, must be made before a trustee may use the powers in the Act to invest in wider range securities. The valuation must be made by an authorized person.

Only authorized narrower range securities may be retained in that part of the fund. Any other investments allocated to it must be sold and replaced by authorized investments. The wider range may, however, contain narrower range investments as well as authorized wider range investments. Any investment that is not authorized for either narrower or wider range must be replaced.

Transfers between the two parts of the trust fund

Once the fund has been divided, transfer of securities between the two parts may be made only if allowed or required by the Act and a compensating transfer, equal in value, is made.

This ruling would apply where securities held in the narrower range cease to be authorized, narrower range securities. This could, of course, take place only if a narrower range security was at that time held in the wider range. Otherwise the ordinary shares would have to be sold and the proceeds reinvested in an authorized, narrower range security.

Additions

If investments not previously held accrue to a trust, they must be divided equally between the two ranges. If an accrual is in the form of special range property then it goes wholly into the special range.

Additions such as a capitalization issue arising from existing holdings may be treated as being of the same range as the existing holdings. Rights issues relating to the wider range must be financed by wider range funds. If an accrual is in the form of special range property it goes wholly into the special range.

Withdrawals

Investments taken out of a trust may be any investments from any range and compensating transfers are not required except at the discretion of the trustee.

It follows, therefore, that when funds are withdrawn from a trust it is possible to reduce one range to extinction. However, this is unlikely to be advisable in most circumstances, given the overriding requirements of diversification and impartiality as between beneficiaries.

4   Express Powers of Investment

Special range property

Trustees may have powers of investment quite separate from those given by the 1961 Act, for example trust deeds may authorize investment in, or retention of, property outside the scope of authorized narrower and wider range investments. An example frequently encountered is a shareholding in a family business. Any such securities must be held in a separate, special range part of the fund, unless they are authorized, narrower range investments, in which case they must be included in the narrower range part for the purpose of the fifty-fifty split. Otherwise, the equal division between narrower and wider ranges excludes the special range.

It should be noted that securities should not be allocated to the special range simply because they are not authorized narrower or wider range investments. The purpose of the special range is to enable unauthorized investments to be held in accordance with special powers granted to the trustee. It must also be remembered that deeds made after the 1961 Act may, by investment clauses, exclude any investments authorized under the Act. For example, a clause may stipulate that tobacco shares must not be held and this would prevent a trustee from so investing if the clause is dated after 3 August 1961. Obviously, too, a clause in similar terms dated prior to the Act would prevent a trustee holding tobacco shares in the special range.

Interrelationships of special, narrow and wider range funds

The extent to which the proceeds of sale of investments held in one fund may be invested in other funds depends on the powers of investment of the trustees. As already stated, the Act provides that transfers of value between narrow and wider range funds should be compensated, but similar compensation is not necessarily required in respect of transfers between the special range fund and the other two funds.

Whether or not additional sums may be invested in special range property will depend on whether or not the trustee is merely authorized to retain existing special range property, or if he is also authorized to purchase further special range investments. In the latter case, the proceeds of sale of narrow or wider range securities would be reinvested in special range property; in the former, the proceeds of any sale of special range property should be split fifty-fifty between the narrower and wider range funds.

For example, a trustee is empowered by the trust deed to invest the whole of the funds in XYZ Ltd, a private limited company. At the time the trust was established, there were only sufficient shares available in XYZ Ltd to absorb 50% of the funds. The trustee therefore invested the other 50% of the funds by adopting the Act, putting 25% in the narrower range and 25% in the wider range. If at a later date further shares in XYZ Ltd become available, the trustee may take them up by using funds obtained by realizing an equal value of securities from narrower range and wider range holdings.

In the case of a rights issue relating to a special range investment, this may be taken up and the necessary funds raised from any of the three ranges.

If any special range securities are sold and it is not intended to use the funds for reinvestment in other special range securities in the very near future, they must be invested on a fifty-fifty basis between the narrower and wider ranges.

Investment in land

The Trustee Investments Act 1961 does not authorize the outright purchase of land, either freehold or leasehold. Thus a trustee may invest money in the purchase of land only if he is expressly authorized to do so, either by the trust instrument or by some other Act of Parliament, such as the Settled Land Act 1925 or the Law of Property Act 1925.

Section 73(1) of the Settled Land Act provides for the investment of capital moneys in land, either freehold or leasehold, with at least 60 years to run. It should, however, be noted that compared with other trustees, trustees of a settlement under this Act have diminished functions because powers of investment and management are vested primarily in the life tenant. Section 28(1) of the Law of Property Act provides that trustees for sale of land can purchase further land with the proceeds of sale, provided they have not disposed of all the land held, and thus ceased to be trustees for sale.

Authorized unit trusts, including exempt unit trusts, are eligible investments. Both types of unit trust can invest in property, thus a trustee can indirectly invest in property in accordance with the Trustee Investments Act 1961.

One exception regarding special range funds relates to registered charities, which may, if they wish, invest all their money in the Charities Official Investment Fund (COIF) which is a special range investment, run along the lines of a unit trust, but it is not actually a unit trust because it issues shares rather than units.

Summary of the Trustee Investments Act 1961

The preceding information may appear rather daunting, but as a guide the main areas can be summed up thus:

- The fund initially must be divided between narrower and wider range investments if the powers of the Act are invoked;

- Narrower range without-advice investments are, broadly speaking, National Savings investments;

- Narrower range with-advice investment, broadly speaking, consists of all types of fixed-interest securities, including gilts and company loan stocks;

- Wider range investments are, broadly speaking, all classes of UK issued share capital, unit trust units and building society accounts except building society deposit accounts, which come under the heading of narrower range with advice;

- Special range investments are any investments that are not in the narrower or wider range areas – the main one to remember is the Charities Official Investment Fund (COIF);

- For an investment to have 'trustee status', it must have been listed for five years and paid dividends in each of those years.

Criticisms of the Trustee Investments Act 1961

The Act became law nearly 40 years ago, and as a result it does not take into account the changing face of investment nowadays. The main criticisms of the Act are:

- There are no powers to invest in companies that have been privatized or demutualized, until they have been quoted and paid dividends for the statutory five years. Thus companies such as British Telecom (BT), British Gas, Norwich Union and the Halifax were not eligible investments at the time of quotation despite the fact that they were well-established, well-run major UK companies;

- The £1 million paid-up capital is very outdated. This would represent a very small quoted company. Such companies are higher risk than the majority of larger quoted companies;

- The different treatment of building society deposit accounts (narrower range with advice) and all other building society accounts (wider range) is now dated. Banks and building societies are effectively as secure as each other and hence both should be treated equally.

Note

The Trustee Investment Act 1961 is due to be repealed in 2000 and replaced by a new act governing the way that trustees can invest. Details of the contents of this new Act were not available at the time of writing.

Charities Act 1993

This Act, which relates only to registered charities, will redefine trustee investments as described above. Although the body of the Act is now enacted, the sections dealing with the definition of trustee investments have not yet been finalized. The criticisms of the Trustee Investments Act 1961 show how dated that Act now is, and the new Charities Act aims to overcome these drawbacks.

One notable change made by the Charities Act 1993 is that a registered charity can choose to split its investments 50/50 between narrower range and wider range, OR 25% narrower range and 75% wider range. A charity has to choose either 50/50 or 25/75, it cannot have proportions between these percentages. These splits relate only to the initial setting up of the fund and allocation of new monies or monies released by sale of a holding. They do not apply to the existing portfolio where no new money or sales are to be made.

5   Registered Charities (Charitable Trusts)

The rules governing charitable status were laid down by Lord MacNaughton in 1891. There are four different types of charitable trust:

- For the advancement of education;
- For the advancement of religion;

● For the relief of poverty;

● For any other purpose beneficial to the community.

The last of these categories has further additional guidelines which mean any body with any hint of political association will be refused charitable status.

If the Inland Revenue and Charity Commissioners grant a charitable trust registered status, it will not be liable to any UK capital and income taxes.

Charities often require a high level of income to fund their works, thus investment in high-yielding, fixed-interest securities is used for this purpose. To provide growth of income and capital, equity or equity-based investment is used. If the charity either does not have enough cash available to invest directly in shares, or the investment manager does not have the time to manage direct equity investments, exempt unit trusts can be used. Many the major unit trusts run exempt unit trusts that are available only to registered charities and pension funds. These unit trusts are wider range investments. Originally, exempt unit trusts and authorized unit trusts were treated differently as to CGT within the fund. Prior to 1980 only exempt unit trusts were free of CGT within the fund. Now there is no difference because all authorized trusts are free (since 1980) of CGT within the fund. This does not mean that exempt unit trusts are no longer attractive to charities and pension funds. Because the investors tend to leave the investments untouched for many years the managers can take a longer-term view on investment policy. Because of this fact fees charged tend to be lower.

Also available to registered charities is the Charities Official Investment Fund (COIF), which is a special range investment that enables a charity to place all its funds under their management. COIF issues shares rather than units.

An example of the considerations relating to charity investments is best shown by considering the following question.

Question

A charitable trust has been set up with £100,000 cash. The trustees have wide powers of investment. They intend to invest on a long-term basis and are looking for a reasonable level of income, together with growth of capital value and income. Advise the trustees on the investment strategy they should follow to achieve these objectives. Mention the types of investment that would be appropriate. Give reasons for your suggestions.

Suggested answer

Note: the trust is not governed by the Trustee Investments Act 1961, because the question states that the trustees have 'wide powers of investment'.

The fund should be divided equally between fixed-interest and equity investments. High-coupon, long and undated gilts can be purchased to give a guaranteed income. Undated gilts are suitable because the income is guaranteed in perpetuity, which will meet long-term needs. The trustees should also consider local authority and company loan stocks for part of the fixed-interest portfolio, if yields are higher than gilts, but it is not advisable to place the whole of the fixed-interest element into such stocks even if their yields are higher, because these stocks can be less marketable. This could result in a lower selling price than expected if the need arose to liquidate stocks.

For the equity content equal amounts should be invested in at least 15 shares in different sectors, provided the trustees feel happy about managing direct equity investments. As an alternative, the trustees could consider exempt unit trusts that will provide professional management and diversification. Four or five of the top performing trusts should be chosen. They could also use some investment trusts for the same reasons. There is no specific tax benefit in using exempt unit trusts, and investment trusts are taxed in the same way as exempt unit trusts.

The equity (or equity-based) content of the portfolio will help to achieve the objective of growth of capital and income. Although the initial dividend yield from the equity base will be fairly low, the high income from the fixed-interest element will compensate. The trustees could also consider some overseas equity content to provide capital growth rather than income, and this should be included via exempt unit trusts or by investment trusts investing overseas.

The fund should be reviewed regularly and changes made to take account of market conditions. The managers should also look at any new investment opportunities when the fund is reviewed.

A certain amount of cash should be kept liquid. The amount will depend on the projected expenditure by the trust. The cash should be kept easily accessible in an account giving the highest gross interest, which may be a bank or a building society account.

Suggested portfolio
We shall assume that £5,000 cash is sufficient for immediate needs.

Investment	Amount (£)	% Gross rate	Gross return (£)
Bank/building society	5,000	5.63	282
High-coupon long and			
undated gilts	37,500	7	2,625
Company loan stock	10,000	9	900
15/20 shares	40,000	3	1,200
Unit and investment trusts			
investing overseas	7,500	1	75
	£100,000		£5,082

$$\text{Gross yield on portfolio} = \frac{5,082 \times 100}{100,000}$$

$$= 5.08\%$$

6   Family Trust and Will Settlements

A trust must have a clearly defined beneficiary or beneficiaries. If they are not ascertainable, the trust is void. The two main types of family trust are bare trusts and discretionary trusts.

A bare trust is one where the trustee has no duty other than to transfer the trust property to the beneficiary entitled to it. A discretionary trust allows the trustees to use their discretion as to how the income and/or capital under the trust is to be allocated to the beneficiaries.

The rule against perpetuities

Perpetuity means forever. Where a trust could continue for a long time, e.g. a will trust with successive life tenants, there must still be a time when the trust will cease. Thus there must always be someone who will receive the capital of the trust at a future date on the death of the last life tenant. The trust cannot carry on forever. In fact, the only type of trust that can carry on in perpetuity is a charitable trust.

Will trusts

Most family trusts are created by wills, when the person who has died leaves a life interest in some property (which can be actual bricks and mortar, or cash or stocks and shares or any combination of these) to one or more persons, with the property reverting to another person or persons on the death of the person with a life interest. The person with a life interest is called the life tenant and the person to whom the property passes on death of the life tenant is the remainderman.

Life tenants and remaindermen

The life tenant is entitled to receive any income generated by the trust during his life. The remainderman receives the money in the trust on the death of the life tenant. It is quite common also to see the life tenant being allowed by the will to live in a house for the rest of his or her life, with the house passing to the remainderman on his or her death.

Sometimes there is more than one life tenant. Either there are life tenants who share in the trust, or sometimes succeeding life tenants, i.e. the first life tenant receives all the income during his life, and on his death a second life tenant receives the income. Once all the life tenants have died the remainderman (or remaindermen if there are more than one) receives the capital from the fund.

Trustees have to be very careful when setting up a trust involving life tenants and remaindermen. It is vital to balance the interests of both parties. It is not permissible to opt entirely for high-income stocks and shares or entirely for capital growth investments. The life tenant would prefer high income but this is bound to be detrimental to the remainderman because there will be little scope for capital growth. Likewise, a capital growth policy will favour the remainderman but provide little income for the life tenant. A compromise must be made to give a reasonable income coupled with capital growth. One investment that is suitable for inclusion with such a trust is a convertible preference share or convertible loan stock. This will provide a reasonable fixed-interest of around 7% gross, with the option to convert to equity that should provide capital growth. Such a stock must be purchased bearing in mind the expected span of the life tenant. If the life tenant is 50 there could be at least another 30 years before there was any likelihood of demise.

Trusts for minors

The other type of family trust, again often created by a will, is for a minor. A will often specifies that a person will receive his money only on attaining a certain age, which does not necessarily have to be majority (18 years). With such trusts the fixed-income element should be purchased with a maturity date around the date set in the will. The remainder of the fund should be invested in equities to provide growth of capital unless there is only a fairly short period of, say, two or three years, and a small sum available. In such a case equity investment is not really suitable because the stock market fluctuations in the short term may wipe out any capital gain. Discretionary trusts (i.e. ones where the income and/or capital is paid out at the discretion of the trustees) pay tax at the Schedule F trust rate of 25%, of which the 10% tax credit covers part, leaving an extra 15% to pay.

Powers of retention and postponer

When a trust is set up under a will, the testator, while limiting the trust to the statutory powers of investment, sometimes gives the trustees the right to retain any investments held at the date of death and postpone the sale of them. Other testators can instruct the trustees to sell the investments but give the trustees the power to postpone their sale indefinitely. When this occurs, any investments that are not in the narrower range should be treated as special range property, and it only remains to divide the cash between the two other parts of the fund. When any of the special range investments are sold, the proceeds must be divided equally between the two statutory funds.

An example of a will trust is best understood by studying the following question and answer.

Question

(a) The life tenant of a will trust is a widow aged 55. The remaindermen are her two children aged 27 and 25. The trustees have wide investment powers. The assets consist of £80,000 cash. State with reasons the investment policy you would recommend and suggest suitable types of investment.

(b) The testator's grandson, aged six, has been bequeathed a legacy of £5,000 that cannot be paid to him until he can give a valid receipt at age 18. Income is likely to be applied for his maintenance, education and benefit. Indicate the investment policy you would recommend, and suggest suitable types of investment.

Suggested answer

(a) The trustees must balance the interests of the life tenant and remaindermen and not favour one over the other. They need to provide a reasonable level of income for the life tenant and protection and growth of capital for the remaindermen.

About half the sum, £40,000, should be invested in index-linked gilts that will also provide a real rate of return on both income and capital. (Note, virtually all fixed-interest gilts are over par, thus carrying a capital loss that would not be acceptable to the remaindermen.) Because the life tenant is only 55 there needs to be a spread of medium- and long-dates in the index-linked gilts.

The remaining £40,000 could be invested equally in 15 different shares in different sectors that should provide both growth of income and capital in the long term. The shares should not yield more than the average gross dividend yield on the FT Actuaries Indices in order to balance the interests of life tenant and remaindermen.

Within the equity content, some overseas element could be introduced to provide a greater chance of capital growth, albeit with a lower income. The overseas element should be provided by unit and investment trusts.

The investments should be reviewed regularly to ensure that they keep pace with market and interest rate changes. A liquid element is not needed because the only cash paid out is that generated by the trust itself.

Suggested portfolio

Investment	Amount (£)	% Gross rate	Gross income (£)
Gilts	40,000	4	1,600
Equities	30,000	3	900
Unit and investment trusts			
investing overseas	10,000	1	100
	£80,000		£2,600

$$\text{Gross yield on portfolio} = \frac{2,600 \times 100}{80,000}$$

$$= 3.25\%$$

(b) Half of the £5,000 should be invested in a gilt to mature around his 18th birthday. Because income may be paid out during the life of the trust, a gilt yielding around 7% will provide a reasonable income but may show a capital loss.

The remaining £2,500 should be invested in two general unit trusts that should provide a moderate income to begin with, and growth of both income and capital in the longer term. The unit trust should also counter the effects of inflation in the longer term, although this cannot be guaranteed.

These investments will be easy to manage and fulfil the overall policy of protecting capital in real terms, plus provision of a reasonable income.

7   Probate Valuations

The property to be included as liable to inheritance tax is valued on the general basis of the price it would fetch if sold in the open market on the day of the deceased's death.

Stock exchange securities

These are valued on the basis of the lower of the following two methods. Both methods must be used both in answering examination questions and in practice to arrive at the correct valuation.

Quarter (1/4) up method

The Inland Revenue accepts for quoted stocks and shares the prices ruling on the Stock Exchange (as quoted in SEDOL) at the date of death. Two prices are quoted – the market maker's buying price and the market maker's selling price. The value is obtained in the following way:

(i)   take the difference between the two prices;

(ii)   find one-quarter of this difference;

(iii)   add (ii) (i.e. one-quarter difference) to the lower price quoted.

Example

Stock quoted	=	80-82
Difference	=	2
One-quarter of this	=	½
Add ½ to 80: value	=	80½

Middle market price

This is the middle market price of ordinary bargains recorded. If the prices of bargains were listed '79, 81, 82, 83', the valuation would be $(79 + 83) \div 2 = 81$. Thus the share would be valued at 80½, the lower of the two valuations.

Note: when the Stock Exchange is closed on the date of death, the Stock Exchange Daily Official List (SEDOL), for either the preceding or subsequent business day, is used. The price determined is the lower one shown from these two days' lists.

Quoted shares that have not been dealt with recently are priced at the date when business was last done, as shown in SEDOL.

Foreign securities

The value of the investment in foreign currency is arrived at by adding one-quarter of the difference to the lower quotation.

The price is converted into sterling on the basis of the exchange rate that gives the lowest value in sterling. For example, if the exchange rate is Francs 8.45-8.47, then the price is converted on the basis of FRF8.47 to the £1.

Unit trusts

Holdings in unit trusts are valued at their bid prices.

'Cum div' and 'ex div' quotations

All quotations are presumed cum div unless expressly marked 'xd'.

With cum div quotations, the value of the stock is arrived at in the ordinary way. In the case of ex div quotations, the whole of the impending dividend or interest, less income tax at the basic rate where this is deducted at source, must be added to the value of the holding, because the whole of the next dividend is paid to the seller.

Example

To calculate the market value of a fixed-interest stock quoted xd, the following procedure must be used after the initial valuation on the basis of the lower of the quarter up and middle market price basis:

Date used for valuation purposes: 26 August

Interest payable: 1 March/1 September

Stock: £3,000 MYZ plc 6% Debenture Stock 03-07 probate valuation $54\frac{1}{2}$

Valuation: £1,635 + net interest

$$= 1,635 + \left\{ \frac{3,000}{2} \quad \times \quad \frac{6}{100} \quad \times \quad \frac{80}{100} \right\}$$

$$= 1,635 + £72$$

$$= £1,707$$

Unquoted stocks and shares

Shares not enjoying official quotation must be fairly valued and a certificate from a stockbroker or a letter from the company secretary must support the valuation. Either of these letters must show the basis of valuation, details of previous sales in the open market, or details of the last three years' dividends and of any bonus distributed.

In the case of shares held in a private limited company, which by its articles imposes restrictions on the transfer of its shares, these restrictions are to be ignored, and the value of the shares on the open market must be ascertained. Similar particulars must be furnished, i.e. basis of valuation, dividends paid during last three years, bonus, if any, distributed, and amount of profits carried forward.

The balance sheet may be required, and should be attached to the certificate from the company secretary. Where the deceased holds a controlling interest in a private company, the shares are valued by reference to the total assets of the company, and not by reference to the current open-market value. The shares held by the deceased are calculated pro rata on the net value of the assets.

The valuation of shares in a private limited company presents some difficulty. Unless the shares are dealt in (for example on OFEX), there is no true open market value. Usually, a valuation has to be negotiated between the shares valuation division of the Inland Revenue and the deceased's personal representatives. Normally, the Capital Taxes Office will refer the matter to the Shares Valuation Division. The factors to be considered in such cases are as follows, the:

● Dividend record of the company;

● Asset value of the shares both on the balance sheet values and the actual value at the date of death;

● Proportion that the deceased's shareholding bears to the capital issued.

Where there is a liability for unpaid calls at the date of death, this liability may be deducted from the value of the other assets.

Other assets

The remaining assets are always valued on the basis of their realisable value in the open market at date of death.

● As regards money on mortgage, this is the principal value together with accrued interest.

● As regards freehold and leasehold property, a surveyor's valuation is accepted, subject to agreement with the district valuer. If, however, a property is to be sold within a short time (usually two years) of the death, the proceeds of sale will be taken as the value as at the date of death.

8   Pension Funds

A pension fund aims to pay out the best possible pension to its beneficiaries. The actuary to the fund stipulates the desired level of annual income that the fund managers should achieve to meet their liabilities. Obviously this requirement will affect the investment policy of the fund managers. For example, an income requirement of 6% per annum cannot be met by the managers pursuing an aggressive capital-growth oriented investment policy.

The 'age' of the fund will also determine how much income is needed by the pensioners each year. A relatively new scheme will have few pensioners, thus the manager can look towards capital growth. A well-established, on-going scheme will need to look at both income and growth, whereas a fund that has been closed to new entrants will diminish in value because the capital (and income generated on that capital) will be paid out to an ever-ageing workforce.

Capital growth

Because a pension fund is totally free of all taxes, the distinction between income-producing assets and growth-oriented assets is blurred. A fund can obtain overall growth in value by opting for high income-producing assets and reinvesting the excess income into other assets.

Obviously some funds invest in purely capital growth assets, e.g. paintings, but these are the largest pension funds. Some favour property investment to provide both income and capital growth, others favour overseas investment (which is more growth than income oriented). To a certain extent the split of the money in the fund will depend on whether or not the fund has its own trust deed or comes under the Trustee Investments Act 1961, although it is rare today to see a pension fund governed by the Trustee Investments Act.

To enable the income requirement to be met, the fund managers will generate a large proportion of the income from fixed-interest stocks. It is not uncommon to see up to 25% of even a multi-million pound fund invested in high yielding fixed-interest stocks. One particular type of fixed-interest stock held by pension funds to provide fixed-income in perpetuity (i.e. forever) is an undated gilt.

Although a large portion of the fund is held in fixed-interest stocks, this does not mean that the stocks are never changed. Pension fund managers will use anomaly and policy switching to keep the returns high.

Provided the pension fund complies with the Inland Revenue's rule that assets must not exceed liabilities by more than 5%, the pension fund will be an exempt fund, i.e. it will be free of all UK taxes. If the assets do exceed the 5% figure, the fund could consider a 'contribution holiday', i.e. a period of time when no further contributions are paid into the fund.

The trustees will also invest in equities, both UK and overseas, and in property. If the fund is large enough this investment will be direct investment. Smaller funds may invest directly in UK equities, and indirectly in overseas equities and property.

Overseas equities

These are aimed at capital growth, thus forming part of the pension fund's long-term growth requirement to enable it to maintain and increase the level of pension paid. If the fund is small, it will use indirect investment via unit or investment trusts. Larger funds will invest directly, and thus need to be able to manage, not only the shares, but also the foreign currency exposure.

Property

Mortgages and ground rents are fixed-interest investments with a fixed expiry date, and although higher yields may generally be obtained on them than on gilts of comparable date, their relative unmarketability and the complications of purchase and management are generally considered to make them unsuitable investments for the ordinary pension fund. However, the large funds can, and do, invest in property.

Overseas property

The basic principles applying to UK property investment also apply if investment in overseas property is contemplated. However, apart from foreign currency and tax implications, each country has its own property laws, its own tax laws affecting property, and its own set of relationships between landlord and tenant. The whole structure of the property market in an overseas country can be very different from that in the UK so it is essential to have available expert and local advice on all these aspects. Only the larger funds such as British Telecom are likely to contemplate direct investment in overseas property, but property unit trusts specializing in overseas property investments for pension funds are available as an alternative.

There is an accountancy problem associated with investment in overseas property for a UK-based pension fund with its published accounts denominated in sterling (i.e. the fund's reporting currency is sterling). The overseas property will initially appear as an asset in the published accounts at the sterling equivalent of the original purchase price. However, at future balance sheet dates the sterling value shown in the published accounts will vary because that amount will be based on the currency value of the asset, converted to sterling at the spot rate of exchange ruling on the balance sheet date. This exposure is called translation exposure and it must be managed. Such management has a cost.

Trust deeds and the Trustee Investments Act 1961

Many funds have their own trust deed that allows them to have the widest powers of investment and, providing they comply with their trust deed, there will be no problems.

The Act specifies the initial division of the fund and the way additions to the fund must be made. Initially the fund must be equally divided between narrower range and wider range investments. (Basically, narrower range are fixed-interest and wider range, equities.) Any additions to the fund must also be similarly divided. There are many rules and regulations regarding the division of the fund, and for this reason the Act is rather restrictive for many pension funds. However, it is possible to draw up a trust deed that excludes certain areas of the Act while still being bound by the general principles.

From the fund manager's viewpoint he will require a trust deed that enables him to achieve the objectives of the fund.

'Underweight' and 'overweight'

The terms 'underweight' and 'overweight' are used to describe a position where the fund's exposure to an individual sector is more or less than the percentage that sector represents in the market capitalization of the market.

For example, if the total capitalization of the market was £100 million, and the capitalization of the banking sector of that market was £10 million, then the banking sector would represent 10% of the market. If a pension fund held 5% of its funds in the banking sector it would be 'underweight'. If it held 15% of its funds it would be 'overweight'.

For the UK stock market, weightings are usually measured by the FT Actuaries All Share Indices and if the pension fund weighting is the same as the FT Actuaries Indices, performance will be in line with the market. This approach is a low-risk approach, and is gained by using index funds.

By taking a more active approach, a pension fund will be under- or overweight in certain sectors in order to try to produce a better-than-average performance. This strategy is higher risk but active management should produce better returns.

The problem for a large pension fund in taking the more active approach is the cost involved in employing specialist managers to look after the portfolio. One person cannot be an expert in all market sectors, so the fund has to weigh the cost of employing specialists against the chance of them producing gains in excess of the average and their salaries.

The approach taken by large pension funds is to index, say, 75% of their funds, and this is monitored by computers. They then give their fund managers a free hand with the remainder of the fund to try to outperform the market.

For a large pension fund, weighting is important in order to adequately diversify their funds. However, changing weightings is expensive and is less likely to be done if the fund is taking a long-term view of the market. Weightings may be altered by using the new money that flows into the fund.

An example of the considerations to bear in mind when investing for a pension fund is shown in the following question and answer.

Specimen Question

What points would you consider in forming and implementing an investment plan for a new company pension fund that has a starting capital of £5 million and that is expected to receive in future an estimated £1 million per annum in contributions from the company and its employees? The trust deed contains the widest investment powers. Give reasons in your answer.

Suggested answer

Points to consider in forming the investment plan.

(a)   The actuary's report; specifically the desired level of income specified.

(b)   The pensioners' (beneficiaries') needs:

(i)   Is commutation allowed? If so, how many pensioners are likely to commute part of their pension? What amount of money will be involved because cash will be needed to meet this obligation?

(ii)   How often is the pension to be paid, e.g. weekly or monthly, because again cash must be available to meet the payments?

(c)   Although a certain level of fixed income is required, the need for growth of both capital and income must be borne in mind, along with the need for inflation protection.

(d)   Who are the fund managers, and what are their charges? (With a fund of this size it will not be cost-effective to employ in-house fund managers.)

(e)   Will the fund receive Inland Revenue approval as an exempt fund?

(f)   How frequently should the investments be reviewed, and by whom?

(g)   How will the portfolio be spread? What proportion will be invested in fixed interest, equities, property and overseas?

(h)   In view of the size of the fund, will it be more appropriate to use the special property unit trusts available to pension funds and registered charities rather than direct property investment?

Points to bear in mind in implementing the plan

(a)   Division of the fund:

Approx %

20-25%	Fixed-interest which will include some undated gilts to provide permanent guaranteed interest, and index-linked gilts to give protection against inflation.
10%	Property – with this size of fund property unit trusts will give a better diversification plus professional management.
25-30%	Overseas equities – again it may be wise to consider the use of unit trusts in view of the size of the fund, unless the fund managers have the necessary experience in investing overseas directly themselves.
40%	UK equities.

(b)   Account must be taken of the overall gross yield from the portfolio to ensure that it meets the minimum specified by the actuaries.

(c)   As with all investments, the timing of the purchases is crucial.

(d)   Bearing in mind the cash flow required to pay the pensions and any commuted sums, the amount of liquidity required must be estimated. Because this is a new fund, the initial liquidity requirement will be very low because there will be few, if any, pensions to be paid in the early years. However, account must be taken of future liquidity requirements.

(e) Once the initial £5 million has been invested, the plan must be actively monitored, and consideration of UK and overseas market conditions taken into account when new money is invested.

Summary

Now that you have studied this unit, you should be able to:

- explain the duties of trustees;

- explain the relevant provision of the Trustee Act 1925;

- explain the relevant provisions of the Trustee Investments Act 1961 regarding permitted investments, i.e. narrower range, wider range and special range investments;

- describe the relevance of the Charities Act 1993 for charity investment;

- describe the provision relating to advice under the Trustee Investments Act 1961 and Financial Services Act 1986;

- describe the requirements concerning company securities;

- explain how the fund must be divided and when transfers are allowed between each part of the fund;

- understand the interrelationship between the special, narrower and wider range parts of the fund;

- explain the position regarding investment in land;

- criticise the shortcomings of the Trustee Investments Act 1961;

- explain the rules governing registered charities;

- describe the criteria charities have to consider when investing;

- explain how family trusts are set up;

- differentiate between a bare trust and a discretionary trust;

- explain the meaning of the 'Rule against perpetuities';

- explain what is meant by 'life tenant' and 'remainderman', and the duty of the trustees towards these two parties.

Appendix 1
TAX AND INTEREST RATES

It is not sufficient merely to repeat large chunks of the textbook in this examination. A thorough understanding of the facts and ability to interpret them is essential.

Investment is a rapidly changing subject, and you will need to keep up to date in order to pass the examination. The interest rates, and descriptions of the various cash investments in this book, are not necessarily those ruling at the time of the exam. To aid you, a checklist of rates you should have at your fingertips at the time of the exam is printed below. The tax rates to be used in the exam are given on the exam paper. The rates in this workbook relate to the tax year 1999-00 and will be relevant to the May 2000 and October 2000 examinations.

Interest rates at time of exam

(Obtain Saturday's edition of the **Financial Times** *and* **The Daily Telegraph** *prior to exam.)*

1. Bank D/a - .....% net basic rate tax = ...% gross.

2. Building Soc Instant access account - ..... net basic rate tax = ...% gross.

3. FT Actuaries gross div yield - .....% (obtain from Financial Times).

4. Gilts - high coupon - .....% gross

            low coupon   - .....% gross

            index-linked - .....% gross

5. U/T, I/T, equity yield   –   income   .....% gross (110% Actuaries gross div yield)

                               –   growth   .....% gross (90% Actuaries gross div yield)

                               –   overseas   1% gross

6. Income shares in split level Investment trust - 10% gross.

7. NSB Investment a/c .....% gross.

8. NS *Income bonds* .....*% gross.*

9. NSCs *- current issue* ....., *rate of return over 5 years... .....%, max. holdings* £........., *reinvestment max.* £.....

10. *Index-linked* NSCs *- current issue* ....., *rate of return over* R.P.I. .....%, *max. holding* £ ....., *reinvestment max.* £ .....

11. *General Extension terms for* NSCs .....%.

12. *ISA maximum holding* £ 7,000 *in* 1999/2000 *then* £5,000 *p.a.* 2000/01 *onwards*

13. *Rate of inflation* .....%.

14. *Children's Bonus Bonds min holding* £ ....., *max holding* £ ....., *rate of return* .....% *gross.*

15. *Pensioners Guaranteed Income Bonds min holding* £ ..... , *max holding* £ ....., *rate of return* .....% *gross.*

Appendix 2

USEFUL WEB ADDRESSES

http://www.cib.org.uk/supersite (a useful gateway site)

http://www.reuters.com

http://www.londonstockex.co.uk (London Stock Exchange)

http://www.ftse.com FTSE International

http://www.market-eye.co.uk/

http://www.hemscott.com

http://www.moneyworld.co.uk/stocks (this site offers a power search facility to dig out the best or worst performers from a specified group over a given time period)

http://www.trackdata.co.uk/mytrack.htm

http://www.bmiquotes.com and http://www.bridge.com (both useful for prices and charts)

http://www.icbinc.com (for free annual reports)

http://www.iii.co.uk (information on unit trusts, OIECs and investment trusts)

http://www.esi.co.uk (information on unit trusts, OIECs and investment trusts)

http://www.trustnet.co.uk (information on unit trusts, OIECs and investment trusts)

http://finance.yahoo.com (Yahoo is a search engine – this is a focused part of the engine)

http://www.proshare.org.uk/ Proshare has information about a wide range of investments

http://www.investmentfunds.org.uk Association of Unit Trust and Investment Funds (AUTIF)

http://www.aitc.co.uk The Association of Investment Trust Companies (AITC)

http://www.itsonline.co.uk/ information about Investment Trusts - complements the AITC site

www.listing.co.uk UK Listing Authority

www.dti.gov.uk Department of Trade and Industry

www.fsa.gov.uk Financial Services Authority

www.hm-treasury.gov.uk HM Treasury

www.sfa.org.uk Securities and Futures Authority

http://www.abi.org.uk Association of British Insurers

http://www.napf.co.uk NAPF – National Association of Pension Funds

http://www.imro.co.uk IMRO – Investment Management Regulatory Organisation

www.bankofengland.co.uk Bank of England

www.crestco.co.uk CREST – the settlement system for UK, Irish and a growing range of international securities

www.ir-soc.org.uk/ Investor Relations Society

http://www.infotrade-online.co.uk Infotrade

INDEX

Index

Index

Index

Index

Index

Index